AF352597

SON-JARA

THE MANDE EPIC

Jeli Fa–Digi Sisòkò

SON-JARA

THE MANDE EPIC

Mandekan/English Edition
with Notes and Commentary

Analytical Study
and Translation by
John William Johnson

Text by
Fa-Digi Sisòkò

Transcribed and translated
with the assistance of
Charles S. Bird, Cheick Oumar Mara,
Checkna Mohamed Singaré, Ibrahim Kalilou Tèra,
and Bourama Soumaoro

INDIANA University Press

Bloomington & Indianapolis

African Epic Series
Thomas A. Hale and John W. Johnson, general editors

This book is a publication of

Indiana University Press
601 North Morton Street
Bloomington, Indiana 47404-3797 USA

http://iupress.indiana.edu

Telephone orders 800-842-6796
Fax orders 812-855-7931
Orders by e-mail iuporder@indiana.edu

Originally published as *The Epic of Son-Jara: A West African Tradition*
© 1986, 1992, 2003 by John William Johnson
Third edition 2003
All rights reserved

The paper used in this publication meets the minimum requirements of American
National Standard for Information Sciences—Permanence of Paper for Printed
Library Materials, ANSI Z39.48-1984.

Library of Congress Cataloging-in-Publication Data

Johnson, John William, date
Son-Jara : the Mande epic : Mandekan/English edition with notes and commentary /
analytical study and translation by John William Johnson ; text by Fa-Digi Sisòkò ;
transcribed and translated with the assistance of Charles S. Bird . . . [et al.].— 3rd ed.
p. cm. — (African epic series)
Rev. ed. of: Epic of Son-Jara. c1986.
Includes bibliographical references and index.
ISBN 0-253-34337-2 (cloth : alk. paper)
1. Epic of Son-Jara 2. Keita, Soundiata, d. 1255—In literature. I. Sisòkò, Fa-Digi. II.
Bird, Charles S. (Charles Stephen), date III. Johnson, John William, date
IV. Epic of Son-Jara. English. V. Title. VI. Series.
PL8491.9.E63J613 2003
896'.34—dc21
2003006698

To Nathan and Sam

N'i fòra mògò dòlu kò,
Mògò dòlu de f'i kò!
      As you succeeded some,
      So shall you have successors!

Contents

PART ONE: *THE STUDY*

PART TWO: *THE TEXT*

ILLUSTRATIONS

FIGURES

PREFACE TO THE FIRST EDITION

AMONG THE WORLD'S GREAT GENRES of oral and written literature the epic is unique. Embodying vast chapters of the worldview of the ethnic group which recites it, epic poetry is the social and cultural constitution of a people. From the Babylonian epic of Gilgamesh, through the Greek epics so well known to our Western scholarship, through the European epics of the Middle Ages—Beowulf, Nibelung-enlied, Song of Roland—down to the present day, the epic stands out as one of the oldest and most enduring forms of literature.

Western scholarship has understandably concentrated over the decades on Western epics and on a few others known to exist in other places. Consequently the collective body of scholarship has not been balanced in the survey of this quasi-universal genre. Large land masses and numerous ethnic groups have been neglected, studied by only a few scholars who published in obscure journals. The widespread distribution of the epic still goes unknown to many in the Western world. Such groups as the Ainu of Japan, the Sea Dyaks of North Borneo, and the Altai Tartars in the Soviet Union are themselves almost unknown in the Western world, let alone their oral epic literature.

It had been thought until recent times that the continent of Africa bore no fruit in epic poetry. The debate about epic in Africa begun by Ruth Finnegan has inspired renewed search, both in the field and among neglected publications of the past. Epic has been reported in many places in Africa: The Gambia, Mali, Guinea-Conakry, Nigeria, the Cameroons, Zaire, and Gabon to mention a few.

The great variety of recently uncovered extended narratives has generated a lively theoretical debate concerning the generic definition of epic, especially whether a cross-cultural definition may be applied to extended narratives which have been termed "epic" or "saga" by collectors. While I am actively involved in this debate—and I do think a cross-cultural definition of epic is possible—it is not the purpose of this volume to contribute to that debate. The purpose here is to present one example of the data we are debating, and to present a thorough analysis of it, and I will comment only briefly on this debate in the epilogue to Part One of this book. The debate will continue and theories will change more than once. In the mean time, professional bards in portions of West Africa will continue to recite long poetic, heroic, and legendary, extended narratives about Son-Jara (Sunjata, Soundiata) Keyta.[1]

The epic of Son-Jara celebrates the exploits of the founder of the empire of Old Mali some 750 years ago. It is recited in several languages, among which are Bamana (Bambara), Soninke, Khasonke, Mandinka, Mandenka, and, as in the present volume, Maninka (Malinké). Professional bards *(jelilu,* sing. *jeli),* more well known to readers and viewers of Alex Haley's *Roots* by their French designation *griot,* recite this epic over a widespread area in West Africa: Senegal, The Gambia, Mali, Guinea-Conakry, Ivory Coast, Mauritania, and anywhere else the well-traveled bard can find an audience of Mande language speakers.

Running some 3,084 lines of poetry, this version was recited in 1968 by the renowned bard Fa-Digi Sisòkò in the town of Kita in west-central Mali. The plot begins with a remarkably similar structure to that of the book of Genesis in the Bible. It begins in heaven with the creation of Adam and Eve *(Adama* and *Hawa)* and proceeds through genealogies of Islamic and Mande families down to Son-Jara's father, thus establishing his royal heritage. The plot then shifts to another part of Old Mali to pick up the hero's mother's clan and his heritage of occult power from her, later to become the key to his successes as a ruler. The plot goes on to describe Son-Jara's miraculous birth, his sibling rivalry, his exile and return to power through the defeat of his major adversary, Sumamuru Kantè. Alex Haley might claim Sumamuru as an ancestor, for Kantè is the Maninka pronunciation of the Mandinka *Kinte.* The final episode describes the conquest of The Gambia by Tura Magan Tarawere (Traoré), one of Son-Jara's generals, claimed as an ancestor by Musa Traoré, the president of Mali today.

To date, no one has published a linear English translation of a text of the epic of Son-Jara from its heartland. Several renderings reconstructed by their collectors into French or English prose are available, as are three complete linear poetic translations in English (in one volume) by bards from The Gambia, several hundred miles from the heartland of Old Mali. A pair of complete linear translations in French are also available. This text, then, is a unique rendering of a unique epic.

The present translation has its own claim to uniqueness. The text was collected on 9 March 1968, in an induced natural context on a Nagra-brand tape recorder in Kita by Charles S. Bird, professor of linguistics at Indiana University. The performance lasted roughly four hours, from about 3:00 p.m. to about 7:00 p.m. The tapes became part of the literary and linguistic data in Bird's vast collection and went untranscribed until 1973, Bird being involved in other research projects in Malian studies. As a graduate student in folklore at Indiana University, with a grant from the Social Science Research Council, I set off with my family to conduct field research in Mali on the Son-Jara epic, and Bird turned the tapes over to me to take back to Mali for transcription, translation, and annotation.

Folklorists are interested in multiple variation of the materials they analyze, and Fa-Digi's version served as one of six versions I analyzed, the other five of which I collected during my year and a half in Mali. The text, representing Part Two of the book, has been transcribed and translated twice. It was initially transcribed in Mali by my assistant Cheick Oumar Mara. I executed translation and extensive annotation with the help of two other Malian assistants, Ibrahim Kalilou Tèra and Checkna Mohamed Singaré. Later, Bird had the text again transcribed by Bourama Soumaoro and a second fresh translation was accomplished by Bird, Soumaoro and myself. The final English translation is the result of comparing these two translations.

The analysis (Part One) and the annotations of the text (in Part Two) are based on my field collections and notes and represent the knowledge and opinions of all the bards and other Malians I interviewed in Mali from 1973 to 1975 and subsequently in the United States. Having been so thoroughly pondered by so many individuals for so long, it is perhaps time now to publish the results of these labors.

Many people have given generously of their time and knowledge to make this book a reality, and it would be impossible to mention them all. Foremost on the list is the bard Fa-Digi Sisòkò, who agreed to share his story with us. All those involved in work on the text are to be thanked, and they take their rightful place on the title page. My gratitude is extended especially to Charles S. Bird for his longstanding encouragement of my work on West African epic. Thanks are also due to the Social Science Research Council for providing the major funding for my research project in Mali. The conclusions, opinions, and statements in this book are mine and not necessarily those of the S.S.R.C. or anyone else involved. I appreciate the help of Indiana University, which provided a grant-in-aid for the purchase of equipment, and of M. Mamadou Sarr, the Director of the Institut des Science Humaines du Mali when I was there. I would also like to thank Sandi Clothier for preparing professional versions of my maps and drawings.

My brief encounter with Magan Sisòkò, Fa-Digi's son, has left a lasting impression, as he also sang a version of the epic for me which I have published through the Folklore Students' Association at Indiana University. Magan taught me much about the epic and about his father. The premature death of Magan in an automobile accident shocked and grieved all of us who worked with him and cut short a brilliant career.

Five other people—my parents, Bill Johnson and my late mother, Tina; my parents-in-law, Margaret Land and my late father-in-law, Victor; and my wife, Elizabeth—contributed much to this work and offered continued encouragement and assistance. I would also like to thank Dan Ben-Amos for reading the manuscript and making several helpful comments which led to constructive changes. I am further indebted to George Brooks for reading parts of the manuscript and making corrections and helpful suggestions for improvement. Finally, I should like to express my sincere appreciation to the government and people of the Republic of Mali for permitting me and my family to live and work in their presence. They are among the friendliest and most hospitable people in the world, especially to the foreigner who happens upon the good fortune of paying a visit to their ancient and fascinating culture.

PREFACE TO THE SECOND EDITION

THE FAMOUS EPIC OF SON-JARA (also known in West Africa as Sun-jata, sometimes spelled Soundiata), which celebrates the exploits of the legendary founder of the empire of Old Mali or Manden some 750 years ago, is widely recited today among the Mandekan-speaking peoples of West Africa. As performed by griots, or professional bards, it constitutes a virtual social, political, and cultural charter of society, embodying deep-rooted aspects of Mande cosmology and worldview. Comprising 3,084 lines of poetry, the text presented here is the first full linear translation of a performance of the Son-Jara epic recorded in its heartland, a four-hour recitation by the *griot* Fa-Digi Sisòkò in the town of Kita in west-central Mali. What is unique about this translation is that it is not *reconstructed* or "rewritten" in words chosen by a translator or editor. The linear translation in this text is a word-for-word rendition of the actual words of the *griot*. An introduction precedes the text, which is also followed by a full set of annotations that provide a historical and contextual framework for understanding the recitation of this still-living West African epic.

This translation first appeared as the second section of an analytical volume which included an extensive ethnographic study of the Mande peoples of West Africa, whose bards recite this epic in public.[1] The present edition provides an affordable volume of the epic text available to the public for a variety of uses. Teachers will find the book helpful for classroom use, and it will prove beneficial in various kinds of courses, at both the university and the high school levels, where epic texts are needed. Literary scholars who teach courses on the genre of epic will be pleased to have a readable, authentic, linear translation of one of the world's great epics. Folklore and anthropology scholars who study the social use of text-based traditions and oral literature will also appreciate the volume. Scholars of African written literature who like to begin their course with the flavor of oral performance will find this book inexpensive enough to include on their reading lists. And finally, those among the general public who enjoyed reading *Roots* will recognize Son-Jara's adversary Sumamuru Kantè (pronounced *Kinte* in Gambian Mandinka) as an early kinsman of Alex Haley. This text should be a welcomed contribution to the growing list of famous epics of world history. Becoming more and more publicized, the epic of Son-Jara (Sunjata) is taking its place alongside the great epics *Gilgamesh,* the *Iliad,* the *Odyssey, Beowulf,* the *Nibelungenlied,* the *Song of Roland,* the *Kalevala,* the *Ramayana,* the *Mahabharata,* and *El Cid.*

This text was collected on 9 March 1968, with a Nagra tape recorder, in the city of Kita in western Mali by Charles S. Bird, professor of linguistics at Indiana University. The performance lasted roughly four hours, from about 3:00 P.M. to about 7:00 P.M. The tapes became a part of the literary and linguistic data in Bird's vast collection and were not transcribed until 1973, Bird being involved in other projects in Malian studies. As a graduate student in folklore at Indiana University, with a grant from the Social Science Research Council, I set off with my family to conduct field research in Mali on the Son-Jara epic, and Bird turned the tapes over to me to take back to Mali for transcription, translation, and annotation. I also collected five other texts during this field project, all of which were involved in the overall process of analysis of this form of oral literature in Mali. The present text was transcribed and translated twice. It was initially transcribed in Mali by my assistant Cheick Oumar Mara. I executed the translation and extensive annotation with the help of two other Malian assistants, Ibrahim Kalilou Tèra and Checkna Mohamed Singaré. Later the text was again transcribed, by Bourama Soumaoro and a second translation was accomplished in sessions involving Bird, Soumaoro, and me. The final translation constitutes a synthesis of the two series of work sessions.

Many people have given generously of their time and knowledge to make this book a reality, and it would be impossible to mention them all by name. Foremost on the list is the bard, Fa-Digi Sisòkò, who agreed to share his version of this great epic with us. All those involved in work on the text are to be thanked, and they take their rightful place on the title page. My gratitude is extended especially to Charles S. Bird for his longstanding encouragement of my work on West African epic. Thanks are also due to the Social Science Research Council for providing the major funding for my research project in Mali. All conclusions, statements, and opinions in the book are, however, mine, and not necessarily those of the S.S.R.C. or of anyone else involved. I appreciate the help of Indiana University, which provided a grant-in-aid for the purchase of equipment, and of M. Mamadou Sarr, the director of the Institut des Sciences Humaines du Mali when I was there.

My brief encounter with Magan Sisòkò, Fa-Digi's son, left a lasting impression, as he also sang a version of the epic which I published through the Folklore Students' Association at Indiana University. Magan taught me much about the epic and about his father. The premature death of Magan in an automobile accident shocked and grieved all of us who worked with him.

Five other people—my parents, Bill Johnson and my late mother, Tina; my parents-in-law Margaret Land and my late father-in-law, Victor; and my wife, Elizabeth—gave me much encouragement and assistance. Finally, I would like to express my sincere appreciation to the government and people of the Republic of Mali for permitting me and my family to live and work in their presence. They are among the friendliest and most hospitable people in the world, especially to the foreigner who has the good fortune to experience their ancient and fascinating culture.

PREFACE TO THE THIRD EDITION

THE THIRD EDITION OF THIS BOOK appears in an atmosphere of renewed interest in the occurrence of worldwide epic poetry that has come to preoccupy a large number of scholars over the past thirty years. The lively debate over the occurrence of epic in Africa, begun by Ruth Fennigan in 1971, has all but run its course. The discovery of one epic after another in Sub-Saharan Africa, and the publication of articles and books on this subject, has been matched by an extended interest in epic on the Indian subcontinent and a renewed interest in European and Asian epics. All this scholarship led directly to the establishment of the Fellows of Oral Epics in Finland by the late Lauri Honko, which in turn resulted in two international congresses on the subject, the first in 1996 and the second in 1999.

This volume is preceded by two editions, the first of which appeared in 1986. The second edition in 1992 omitted the extensive exegesis on the social and cultural setting of the epic of Son-Jara, producing an affordable text for use in classroom teaching. Only the text of the epic with its notes, genealogy charts, and bibliography appeared in the second edition, although a short introduction was also published with that volume to give some background to the reader. The third edition restores the full social and cultural study, omits nothing from the text and its annotations, and makes three important changes to the book. First, the original Maninka text of the epic is included with the English translation. In Part Two of the book, the Maninka appears on the even pages facing the English translation on all odd pages. Second, the bibliography at the end of the book has been greatly extended, reflecting the many articles and books published about Son-Jara since the appearance of the first edition, principally due to the work of the prolific Dutch scholar Jan Jansen.

Finally, a CD appears with this edition, which contains the complete text of the epic in Maninka sung by the bard. The work of transferring the epic from tape to CD involved more than merely recording. The sound was clarified and obstructions removed from the original tape by Guy M. Hardy of AuraLabs. The ability to actually hear the performance adds a new dimension to the appreciation of the skill of the poet and brings the epic performance to life. Guy's competence in audio restoration has made this possible, and I wish to express my profound gratitude to him for the hours he spent in preparing the restoration CD.

The additions to the book and the inclusion of the original exegesis now make a rather complete volume for study by the student of this epic. Teachers who use the second edition for classes in epic and in African literature will find the third edition useful as a manual with more extensive information about the ethnic and cultural setting. All those who found the previous editions useful will also find here, a more detailed study, and the CD is particularly useful for classroom demonstration on what the epic actually sounds like when it is performed. The disc is divided into tracts corresponding to the themes listed on pages 95-97. The text can be played without interruption from start to finish, but any theme can be isolated for specific pedagogical use by isolating the track in question. It is hoped that readers will find a number of uses for the third edition of this book, not the least of which is the enjoyment of reading and listening to one of the world's great epic poems still popular and often performed on the continent of Africa.

PART ONE

THE STUDY

INTRODUCTION

The Lion of the Manden

THE SON-JARA OF HISTORY

Western and Western-trained scholars who attempt to reconstruct a chronological history of the great empire period of West Africa have argued that Son-Jara, or as he is more widely known, Sunjata, was a historical person.[1] Unlike their predecessors whose theories were often unacceptable to scholars of oral literature,[2] more recent oral historians have refined their methodologies in searching for the historicity in oral traditions by responding to sound criticism from functional and structural anthropologists.[3] Far from being deterred by the criticism, these historians appear to have been inspired by it. They have not lost their faith in oral tradition as evidence of past history.

However refined the new methodologies of contemporary oral historians may be, the question of *what* Son-Jara represents today remains easier to answer than *who* he may have been in the past. Son-Jara is a culture hero. The epic which celebrates his memory constitutes a social and political charter of Mande culture, reflective of cosmology and worldview. Evidence of its present function is easier to demonstrate than is the possible evidence of historicity.[4] Let me take a case in point.

Historians have often placed faith in genealogies recited in oral tradition.[5] Although the literal historicity of oral genealogies is coming to be questioned by some historians,[6] the lists are often accepted as representing some form of historical survival. Contradictions or rearrangements are seen as disagreements introduced by bards in the past, rather than for what they may represent in the present.[7] Again, there may be some value in the argument that they could represent something of value to the historian, but one is nonetheless left with the question: do these names really represent lost memories about the past, the survivals of old names, or are they only contemporary literary metaphors? As an example, let me cite two instances of names clustered together from separate variants of the epic of Son-Jara. The first is from the variant represented in this volume and sung by Fa-Digi Sisòkò. First appearing on lines 1844ff., Fa-Digi sings the following lines as praise-names for Sumamuru Kantè, Son-Jara's arch enemy:

> Kukuba and Bantanba
> Nyani-Nyani and Kamasiga

The meaning of these names becomes apparent only when they recur as the names of successive battlegrounds (villages?) where Son-Jara defeats Sumamuru.[8] Stylistically, the names of these places appear to parallel or "balance off" Son-Jara's earlier defeats by Sumamuru, which resulted in his founding certain villages after each defeat.[9]

In another variant of the same epic, these same four words, varying slightly in pronunciation and spelled differently by the French-trained collector, appear as four succeeding generations in a genealogy of the Kuyatè bardic family, thus:[10]

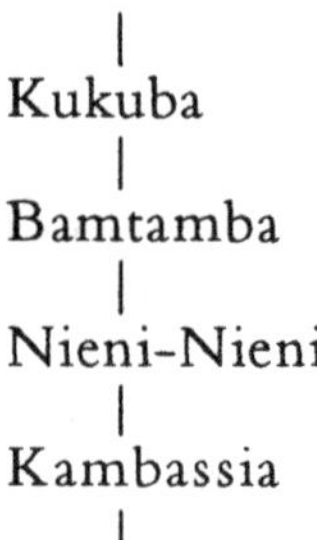

| |
| Kukuba |
| |
| Bamtamba |
| |
| Nieni-Nieni |
| |
| Kambassia |
| |

Genealogy is at least sometimes employed purely as stylistic embellishment by the creative raconteur bent on telling a good story, or needing to sound authoritative by mentioning oft-repeated names from the oral tradition.

Cosmologically, the genealogies are extremely important because they establish the sanctioned authority and power of the culture hero, a power reflective of the Mande worldview concerning heroic behavior. This trait is significant to the present day social scene, whatever historicity may be reflected. The culture hero of Mande societies must be able to harness vast amounts of occult power in order to fulfill his destiny. The genealogies recited in these epics function in part to establish the culture hero's inheritance of occult power. The bard's episode in heaven serves to sanction God's gift of *barakah*, "grace," to the Prophet Muḥammad. However orthodox Moslems view the meaning of *barakah*, Mande audiences see it as one of a variety of different forms of occult power. The genealogical tie between the "Ethiopian" (black man?) Bilāl bin Rabaḥ, black Companion of the

Prophet,[11] and Son-Jara's ancestors, assures that the Islamic power source gained by Bilāl as a Companion will be inherited by the culture hero.

In like fashion, the local Mande version of occult power, called *nyama,* is conferred upon the hero in the traditional Mande method through his mother's ancestry and is accomplished in the epic through genealogy. Thus the long episode with the Buffalo-Woman of Du—in Fa-Digi's variant Son-Jara's great-great aunt—is presented to sanction the gift of *nyama* upon one member of the culture hero's mother's family. Terminating both episodes, the bard turns to the recitation of long genealogies which take the inheritance of power from its source down to Son-Jara himself. Thus he is viewed as the one culture hero of the Mande destined to have more occult power than any other hero before or after his time. Significantly, he is not the founder of the country of the Manden or of the Mande peoples, but he is their greatest culture hero, for he is believed to have harnessed great occult power.

Functionally, the episodes leading up to the birth of Son-Jara establish his heritage, stylistically accomplished through the recitation of genealogy. Variation of the specific ancestors named, with a few exceptions like Bilāl and Magan Konatè (Son-Jara's father), which occurs naturally in the oral tradition from region to region and even from bard to bard in the same region,[12] does not distract from the function of legitimizing the hero's place in destiny.

To return to the original point, the Son-Jara of history is not the subject of the present volume. Our concern is the contemporary conception of Son-Jara in Mande epic poetry. Mali has had a long and colorful history producing many illustrious leaders, several of whom are celebrated in heroic literature, but none are paramount in Mande folklore to Son-Jara Keyta. His memory is recited in several genres wherever Mande languages are spoken (Mandinka, Maninka, Khasonke, Bamana, Jula, Wangara, etc.). The professional bards (griots) who sing of the lion of the Manden do not claim that he founded the state. This distinction is given, at least by Moslem bards, to the sons of Bilāl, the hero of legend mentioned earlier.

Kankan Musa,[13] who ruled Mali from 1312 to 1327, is probably better known than Son-Jara outside of Mali. It might be argued that Musa had a greater impact on the spread of knowledge about the empire to the outside world. His famous and ostentatious pilgrimage to Mecca in 1324-25, resulting in the dramatic inflation of the Egyptian gold standard economy, spread the name of Mali abroad to a greater degree than did Son-Jara. This act went unmatched by any *mansa* before or after him; yet no epic amongst Mandekan speakers celebrates Musa's exploits.

Son-Jara is the *mansa* most celebrated in oral narrative today, and it is to him that the culture has assigned the role of hero. Indeed many exploits of later *mansalu* have been telescoped into Son-Jara's lifetime. Son-Jara is the magnet of great accomplishments, no matter to whom historians accredit these acts. The memory of Son-Jara, like most culture heroes, has been altered to conform with an heroic pattern. In this respect, folk belief holds a much stronger grip over the content of the epic recited about the hero than would any data to which documentation might lend proof.

For these and other reasons, the popularity of Son-Jara has outstripped the other *mansalu* of the empire of Mali. His memory is celebrated in a variety of narratives and other forms of folklore, including praise-poetry and prose legend. But it is in the epic that Son-Jara is fully glorified, for the epic is the most complex and celebrated form of oral literature to be found amongst Mandekan speakers.

SON-JARA AS CULTURE HERO

It has been argued for over a hundred years that the description of a culture hero's life in heroic literature conforms to set patterns of behavior reflective of the culture's worldview. Modern academic treatment of these patterns dates from von Hahn's treatise in 1876, which led to other similar studies by Rank, Raglan, and de Vries.[14] Studying heroic life styles and plot motifs of culturally and historically related areas of Europe, the Middle East, and India,[15] scholars established lists of trait characteristics common to their heroes, some lists more specific than others. Whatever other conclusions these scholars may have drawn from such an exercise,[16] the evidence tended to suggest that heroes' lives conform to narrative stereotyping, again a characteristic which would tend to argue against the searching for historicity in oral traditions.

The aforementioned scholars did not employ narratives about any African hero when they drew up their lists, because next to nothing had been published about African heroic narratives at the time they did their work. A deeper look into the heroic elements of the Mande hero, and other heroes of the African continent like the Zulu warrior king Shaka, reveals significant differences from their Euro-Indian counterparts. Nevertheless, lists of characteristics common to them are possible to compile.

In place of a fifth list of hero traits incorporating the Mande traits, it will perhaps be more productive to describe the Mande hero and then demonstrate how Son-Jara exemplifies these patterns, which in fact is my intention later on in this book. What is important in the studies from von Hahn to the present is not the listing of hero traits, though they are of interest, but the fact that such lists can be made, that in fact the hero's life narrative is molded to conform to an abstract pattern. The evidence argues that whatever actually happened to a hero is not necessarily incorporated into the heroic legend about him/her. Too much similarity occurs in too many narratives about different heroes to lend weight to historicity. Consequently that themes and motifs (Miller's clichés) are chosen for their literary value and for their value in structurally symbolizing worldview, rather than their value in recording history for posterity, is a reasonable conclusion. Aids to memory they are, but functionally they aid the raconteur in remembering the plots and not necessarily the historical events.[17]

The problem the folklorist must face is the necessity of stating "not necessarily." While the oral historian may have not proven that one may isolate historicity in oral tradition, neither has the folklorist nor the anthropologist proven that it cannot be done. While I do not dismiss the possibility of accomplishing this goal in the future, it is not my concern as a folklorist. However historians might choose to view the personage of Son-Jara and his role in the history of West Africa, it can be demonstrated, as mentioned above, that he is the paramount culture hero of most of the Mandekan speaking peoples. His life serves as a contemporary role model, not admired but copied, for any person who might choose to pursue an ambitious life's course. Whatever the narrative may possibly tell about the past, it can tell us a great deal about the present, and it is to that present that we now turn.

CHAPTER **I**

The Social Setting

While a complete ethnology of the Mande peoples is beyond the scope of this study, a minimal amount of social background must be presented in order to render an esoteric text intelligible to the nonindigenous reader. This section outlines a minimal number of topics necessary for the understanding and enjoyment of the literary functions of the plot. Some of these ethnological descriptions may become useful when the social functions of this epic are discussed later. Indeed social and literary constraints always combine with a raconteur's own unique contributions to the creative process which results in the performed text. And it should be understood from the beginning that each version is a unique act, a recreation always encompassing some degree of change.

Tradition is often viewed as static and changeless, but closer to reality is the view that, at any given time in the history of a society, change will be present, change which might conflict with older cultural traits. Mali and the Mande world are no exceptions, for the elements of old and new can be found in its society and, they can be found in layers reflected in the lines of its epic poetry. Because bards consider themselves protectors of cultural heritage, their views concerning older customs and beliefs receive attention in epic performance. Anachronism and telescoping are characteristic of the genre. For these reasons, Mande society must be described. Mention of modern cultural traits is necessary, for however ·much Mande epic speaks of the past, it is a contemporary creation. Some traits are older than others, but the absence of written records in an oral society makes pinpointing these traits in time and space difficult.

Modern Mali is subjected to the pressure of change in many areas of its culture. Economics are affected by many outside influences. Present day urban life may be taking its toll on lineage and other ethnic institutions,[1] although less than ten percent of the population live in towns as large as Kita.[2] Classroom education in Mali and abroad (for higher education) changes the traditional institutions, such as youth organizations *(ton),* and esoteric religious societies *(jo).*[3] This process in turn adds influence for change to many varieties of artistic behavior. Such activities as masking, dancing, and carving evolve newer forms with modern functions. The influence of Islam, which has increased dramatically since the onset of French colonialism, has affected many aspects of society including the artistic.[4] Finally, modern centralized government in Mali influences the patrilineage and village governmental systems. The older institutions are still relevant in the social system, particularly in rural areas, but "no longer form the basis of the political system."[5]

Mande social structure has its beginning in the family organization, a primary institution still intact despite outside influence. The Mande nuclear family (see Figure 1) is the genesis of more than a family; it is the foundation of the larger units of Mande social, cosmological, and political structures. Themes of sanctioned behavior in the family compound find their way into society at large. Moreover, similar themes can be found in the Mande religious legendry (mythology) of both Moslem and non-Moslem peoples. Formerly, the extension of the family beyond the nuclear level, that is to say, into the lineage, formed the basis of spiritual and political leadership. A description of the nuclear family structure, then, is essential to understanding the broader social structures, which will in turn aid in understanding many philosophical themes in epic.

Sanctioned behavior in the polygamous family is reflected by kinship terms.[6] Rivalry *(fa-denya,* "father-child-ness") is expected between half siblings *(fa-denlu,* "father's children"). Indeed, rivalry with one's father is expected, for a male child, it is said, must first make a name for himself in his clan's genealogy by overcoming his father's reputation.[7] Conversely, affection *(ba-denya,* "mother-child-ness") is expected between full siblings *(ba-denlu,* "mother's children"). Thus Son-Jara struggles with his half brother Mansa Dankaran Tuman, but is aided by his full siblings, Sugulun Kulunkan and Manden Bukari.

By the linguistic process of metaphoric extension, these terms are encountered again in Mande worldview concerning the cosmos. Now denoting the forces of social destruction *(fa-denya)* and cohesion *(ba-denya),* they perceive a cosmos polarized by a constant battle between these two forces, first one gaining the upper hand and then losing it to the other. Thus the Buffalo-Woman of Du upsets the balance of the cosmos and *fa-denya* reigns for a time. When she is subdued, the forces of *ba-denya* regain control. It will be noted that her hovel is

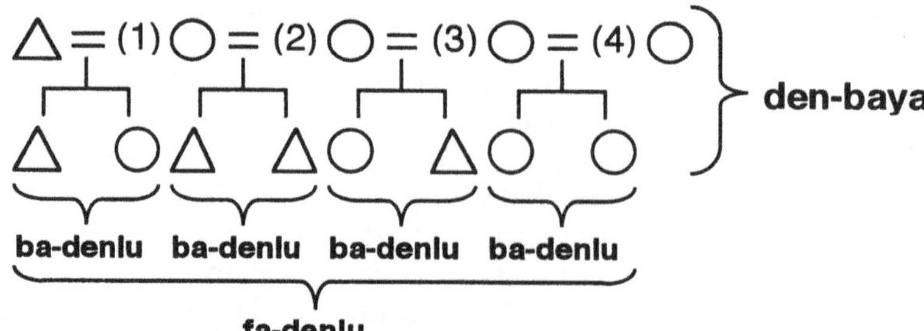

fa	'father'	fa-den	'half sibling' ('father's child')
ba	'mother'	ba-den	'full sibling' ('mother's child')
den	'child'	kòrò-kè	'elder brother'
den-kè	'son'	fa-den-kòrò-kè	'elder half brother'
den-musu	'daughter'	ba-den-kòrò-kè	'elder full brother'
		kòrò-musu	'elder sister'
		fa-den-kòrò-musu	'elder half sister'
		ba-den-kòrò-musu	'elder full sister'
		dògò-kè	'younger brother'
		fa-den-dògò-kè	'younger half brother'
		ba-den-dògò-kè	'younger full brother'
		dògò-musu	'younger brother'
		fa-den-dògò-musu	'younger half sister'
		ba-den-dògò-musu	'younger full sister'

den-baya,	'nuclear family'
fa-denya,	'rivalry/chaos'
ba-denya,	'affection/stability'

FIGURE 1. Mande Nuclear Family Structure

located outside the village. In point of fact, village geography is also integrated into this worldview.

The geography of the cosmos, like the structure of society, begins in the nuclear family's compound (*lu*) and works its way outwards (see Figure 2).[8] The compound is considered the safest locale for a person in terms of the cosmological forces of cohesion.

The farther away from one's own home one goes, the more social dislocation will be encountered and the greater will be the need for assistance from such institutions as the occult arts. Dislocation begins when one leaves one's mother's house and enters the compound shared by one's half siblings. Beyond the borders of the compound, one encounters people not in one's nuclear family. An even more dangerous step is taken when the village border (*dankun*) is crossed, and the ring of women's vegetable gardens (*na-ko*) is entered. A village fetish, a religious object the function of which is to protect the village from social dislocation and imbalance, is often placed here on the border under the village garbage (*nyama*), the word for garbage being a homonym for the word for occult power (*nyama*).

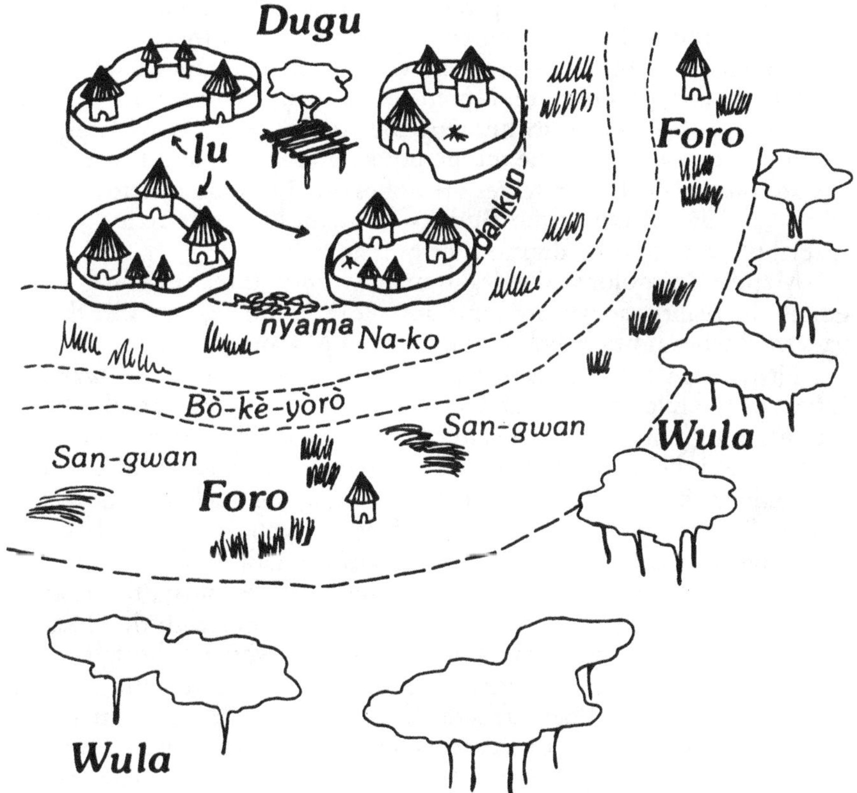

FIGURE 2. Mande Village Geography

The cosmological ring outside the vegetable gardens is that of the toilets (*bò-kè-yòrò*), which is followed by a ring mixed with the men's fields being cultivated (*foro*) and those being left fallow (*san-gwan*). Beyond this ring lies the most dangerous area of all, the wilderness (*wula*), which continues until the fields of the next village are encountered.

Working out from the center of the compound, each new cosmological ring of village geography brings an added degree of danger which reaches its peak in the wilderness. Leaving the compound, one encounters nonfamily members. Leaving the village, more danger is possible, such as encounters with wild beasts. In Mali, I heard farmers complain of the dangers of snakes in the field.[9] The wilderness holds more danger than any other place, and its darkness (because of overgrowth) becomes a symbol in epic poetry of occult power and sorcery.

Townsfolk rarely enjoy going there and take precautions when they do, such as the making of amulets for a journey. But there is one segment of society which thrives in the wilderness. The hunter, who lives outside the lineage structure, is prepared in many ways for his work in the forest. I shall return to hunters' societies in more detail later, for when dislocation crosses the village border and moves into town, hunters are often called upon to restore cohesion. Thus hunters are sought to rid the land of Du of the Buffalo-Woman. Hunters are assigned a special place in Mande divisions of humanity.

Mande cosmology divides humanity into three essential categories. In reality, social divisions are more complex, but this three-patterned tenet is nevertheless employed in Mande worldview.

First, there are the slaves or captives taken in time of warfare. Often only children were abducted so that, by raising them in their captor's compounds, the problem of loyalty would be easier to control. Today many believe that slaves had certain rights and could eventually attain their freedom. Sometimes becoming the nucleus of powerful armies,[10] their social status as slave does not appear to have been as restrictive as that of slaves in other parts of the world.

Although there are no slaves in Mande society today, the institution still plays a role in the social structure. Together with the descendants of adopted orphans, members of a lineage who are thought to be descendants of former slaves have been incorporated into the division of freeman (*hòròn*). They are not, however, considered a part of the core lineage and may not hold office in the authority system. Hopkins even declares that "they are not fully members" of their lineage.[11]

The second division of humanity according to folk belief is the *nyamakala,* or casted members of society. Because of the close association of one of the castes (the bard or griot) with the recitation of the Son-Jara epic, a fuller description of their roles is postponed until the next section of this chapter. Suffice it to say here that, like the descendants of former slaves and orphans, the castes in Mali fall outside the authority structure of the lineages, but unlike the former groups, the castes are endogamous and have their own internal lineage structures and clans.

The third division is called *hòròn* which is translated here for lack of a better term as "freeman." Although a freeman may not be at the center of a specific authority structure in a given village, his social division is sanctioned for political activity.

Some of the clan families in Mande society are designated as royal (*mansalen*); that is, some clans trace their lineage back to the time when their ancestors were considered the rulers of Old Mali. The social structure and government of the Mande world, however, is much more complicated. Indeed, power and authority structures do not always coincide. A look at the authority structure will help to clarify the roles of these two systems.

The authority structure of Mande society may be referred to as a vertical system because of its tendency toward gerontocracy. The actual power structure, together with other segments of society, may be referred to as a horizontal system because of elements which ignore the hierarchy of age and which cut across lineage segments. The addition of a federal government to these systems complicates the political behavior in modern Mali, but social behavior is still largely based on these traditional structures, particularly in rural areas.[12]

The Mande authority structure revolves around the principle of *fa-siya* ("father-lineage-ness"),[13] which means that everyone older than any given member of society is due respect and deference, while one accepts deference from younger members of society. Likewise, one feels great solidarity with one's peers. This system places into office the person considered to be the oldest son of the oldest son, etc., of the core lineage of the ruling lineage in the village. The most immediate representative of this principle is the *lu-tigi*, "household/compound leader," whose duties extend to economic as well as social affairs of those committed to his charge.

The compound leader, as well as other members in the authority strata, must be a freeman and must be from the core lineage, which may be defined as that segment of society whose patrilineage members claim undisputed descent from the common ancestor who founded or conquered the village. The system of rule by core lineage accounts for the exclusion of members thought to be descended from former slaves and orphans. It also excludes nonlineage groups such as strangers, holymen of Islam, hunters, and casted families.

Authority at the village level is shared by two office holders, one with political credentials (now shared with the federal government) and one with a ritual commission still operative in most areas. Both these men are the elders at the sublineage tier[14] of the two dominant families in the village, and their office is held by the authority of the legendary charter of the founding of the village.

The first patrilineage family believed to have settled in the area is usually granted the ritual leadership. The eldest member of the core lineage of this family becomes the ritual leader (*dugu-kolo-tigi*, "earth-surface-master"),[15] whose functions are mostly ritualistic. This man is said to be the spiritual mediator between the earth spirits and the village farmers, and it is his duty to maintain a balanced relationship between them by means of such occult activities as might be needed in any given situation. I was told in Mali that the ritual leader also has some authority in land tenure.

The *dugu-tigi,* "village master,"[16] is usually associated with a power struggle recounted in a legend composing a part of the mythical charter of the village. Sometimes, the sublineage whose member holds this office is thought to be the conqueror of the area. In the case of Kita, the political leadership is held by the Kasuma-si sublineage of the Keyta clan "to whom credit [is] given for Kita's independence from the Traoré [Tarawere]" clan from the neighboring village of Bafing.[17] This event occurred long after the founding of Kita. The other sublineages of a village are ranked according to the legendary account of their arrival in the village. Although modern incursions into Kita and other areas have weakened village legendary charters, social relations symbolically presented in these charters still offer a possible model for sublineage relationships to many people.

Beyond the sublineage level of authority in the village lies the *kafo* or *jamana,*[18] presided over by the titular head of a lineage. According to the principle of *fa-siya,* the *jamana-tigi,* "district leader," is the senior man in the royal lineage of the district. He was considered the steward of the villages in his district and of any property common to the lineage. Effective political unity in Old Mali is said to have ended at this level, though no doubt the social unity then as now extended to the clan and beyond into related ethnic groups such as the Bamana and Jula. The fact that no office of clan leader exists is reflective of the fluidity of the concept of clan, which may be defined vaguely as everyone with the same surname. What is relevant to this study is that "relations between [individuals within the] clans are molded after the relations between their ancestors in the time of Soundiata [Son-Jara],"[19] or at least, what those relations were thought or considered to have been by contemporary bards. It is believed that Son-Jara was able to unite the *jamanalu* and other ethnic areas into a larger political unit and to obtain the Maninka title of *mansa,* the closest English equivalent being "king" or "emperor," although a translation of any kind could be misleading.

Turning to the horizontal structures of the lineage system, the unity of age groups, which is still a powerful force in the Mande world, represents a motivating force larger than any associated with institutionalized authority. Within the village and beyond its borders, a strong bond of unity exists among peers. Voluntary associations exist which are made up of members from several lineages. Because these associations cut across lineage segments, they may be referred to as horizontal structures, but members are freemen who also participate in their respective lineage systems. Many new associations have come about in Mande society since colonial days,[20] but my concern here is for the ones with older histories.

Perhaps the most important cross lineage associations are the age-sets of youth known in different areas as *fulan-ton,* "two/twin association," and *den-misèn-ton,* "youth/young child association."[21] These groups are composed of "all the young men of a village from circumcision to about the age of thirty-five, and of the girls from excision to the time when they are married or at the latest when they start to bear children."[22]

Age-sets serve two main functions at the village level aside from their function in peer solidarity. They provide for much of the entertainment of the village, and they participate in collective work, often of a charitable nature.[23] Their activities in the area of entertainment include one of the traditional forms of theater in Maninka and Bamana communities called *koteba.*[24] In some areas, the production of puppet drama is also the responsibility of the age-set.[25] They organize several forms of dance, including the secularized *ci-wara* dances still found in some areas.[26] Collective work carried out by the age-set of a village may include planting and harvesting the fields of family heads of the village[27] and the repair of such community property as roads and lounging platforms (*bara*) found in the center of most villages.

The cross lineage unity of peers begins before the rites of circumcision and excision. At least two associations involve children of this early age. The *senene-ton,* "cultivation association," is a voluntary group which works the fields of needy families.[28] The other, called the *ndomo,* is an esoteric association considered a religious cult by some scholars. Other religious and esoteric societies which attract members after circumcision also serve to unite Mande peoples in cross lineage manners.

Voluntary associations of a secular nature are smaller than the age-set and often attract members from more than one village. The *sògò* and *gonson* societies have charitable as well as entertainment functions,[29] and are also composed of men of different age-sets. The association of men of different age-sets and different villages serves as a unifying horizontal tie, especially since their work is of a charitable nature.

It is difficult to know if voluntary associations are widespread today. As indicated earlier, new associations have come into being, while others have disappeared. Still other types of groups outside the lineage organizations of freemen exist and serve functions which remain to be described, for an understanding of them is essential in any study of the epic of Son-Jara.

While descendants of orphans and former slaves remain outside the core lineage of Mande organization, they nevertheless remain a part of the overall lineage structure. Several other groups serve well-integrated functions in society, but they operate outside the freeman authority structure. I have already mentioned the casted families, Moslem holymen, strangers, and hunters' societies. In the past, slaves fit into this category.[30]

Mande society provides for and allows nonlineage groups because each plays a role in the unity of the whole. The symbiotic structure of all Mande socioeconomic groups is strongly accentuated in many variants of the Son-Jara epic, which at the same time serves as a model for the sanctioning of the system employed in each region.

The stranger (*dunan*) is welcome in village life for several reasons. Potentially he or she may contribute to the prosperity of the area. Strangers may serve as clients to their host (*ja-tigi*)[31] and thereby increase the host's power in village politics. If the stranger remains for a long time in the village, or even settles there, he or she may come to participate in domestic affairs, and their children may become natives. The relationship between the host and his or her descendants tends to be remembered and might influence their dealings with each other for several generations.

The role of the Moslem holyman (*mori*)[32] is more difficult to access. As prayer leader and Koranic school master, a pedagogical role may be isolated. The holyman also played an early role as a scribe, but the skill becomes less and less important as classroom education spreads in West Africa. Together with the casted families and hunters, the holyman is also involved in occult medicine. The wall around the mosque in Bamako is often the site of the sale of bottled powders and potions as well as amulets of several sorts. A holyman may be consulted for a specific ailment or request, which, as in many Moslem communities, may result in the making of an amulet. The amulet consists of a piece of paper with Koranic verses or magical configurations transcribed on it.[33]

While the stranger and the holyman, as well as the casted families, work in well-integrated ways with lineage members, the hunters' societies are separate.[34] Although they serve a function within Mande society, there are several characteristics about hunters' societies (*dònsòn-ton*) which set them apart from the rest and cause them to be feared.

First, the hunters' society represents a truly egalitarian stratum of society, for they recruit members from all other strata, regardless of the original social status of the initiate. Casted individuals, ruling freeman, or any other male in Mande society may join. In fact, there appears to be a feeling among hunters that lineage association ties should be denounced or at least minimized with respect to hunters' society affiliation.[35]

Second, hunters spend a great deal of their time in the wilderness. They hunt wild game, though the association in modern times is more of a highly complex social organization than an actual society for hunting. Hunting wild animals, which, according to Mande worldview, contains great amounts of occult power, requires ritual preparation. As I have indicated above, the wilderness is considered the most dangerous place on the earth. Hunters' societies educate their members in the knowledge of the wilderness and in the control of the occult, but their knowledge is not shared with outsiders. Such secretive knowledge breeds fear and distrust among nonhunters, but it also breeds a hearty respect, for when the forces of social cohesion are upset the hunter is often called upon for help. Many believe that hunters are capable of rebalancing any upset in the cosmos through their deep knowledge of the occult. The fear people have for them is based upon the belief that they are equally capable of upsetting that balance.

One of the theories of hunters' societies is worth mentioning here. Because of the association of the occult with political and military struggles, and because of the hunters' extensive knowledge of the occult, armies in the past have actively conscripted hunters into their ranks. Like the slaves of the past and the other nonlineage groups, the hunters have contributed to the strength of powerful men. Thus, when Son-Jara becomes a hunter upon standing up, his half brother's mother immediately suspects him of seeking occult knowledge in pursuit of political power, even though he has been eliminated from the authority structure of the village. She fears he will gain power outside this structure.

The institutionalized, traditional authority structure in Mande society, until colonial times and to some extent during and after that period, offered a ready means to power for an ambitious person. Because of the restrictions of age, sex, and lineage superimposed on this system, however, it excluded large numbers of people from its ranks. Moreover, the longevity of a core lineage ruler could mean that his successor was already old and ineffective by the time he took office.[36] As a result, other methods of gaining power have arisen over the years. A man of power (called *mògò-tigi,* "master of men," or *tògò-tigi,* "owner/master of a name/reputation") might rise to his position by circumventing the authority structure altogether. Figure 3 will assist in understanding a potential power structure in relation to the institutionalized authority structure.

The acquisition of power in Mande society is based on two things. Success in influencing public opinion is a necessity, for failure

AUTHORITY STRUCTURE (Symbolic Power)	POWER STRUCTURE (Actual Power)
Hònòn offices: chiefs chosen from core lineage only and on basis of patrilineage (eldest son of eldest son, etc., in genealogy)	*Tògò-tigi* ('Owner of a name/reputation': man of power, who might also be an authority figure, but not necessarily. His power based on:)
Jamana-tigi (District Chief)	1. Wealth
	a. Fields
Dugu-tigi (Political Village Chief)	b. Trade & Commerce
	c. Conquest
Dugu-kolo-tigi (Ritual Village Chief)	(d. Ownership of slaves)
	2. Large household of patrilineage relations (including as many wives as he can support)
Lu-tigi (Compound Chief)	3. Extra-lineage relations
	a. Foreign relations, often solidified by marriages
	b. Domestic extra-lineage relations
	1) With other sublineages
	2) With age-set associations, which cut across lineages
	4. Nonlineage clientage
	a. *Nyamakala* (Castes)
	b. *Mori* (Moslem Holymen)
	c. *Dònsòn-ton* (Hunters)
	d. *Dunan* (Strangers)
	5. Public Opinion

FIGURE 3. Mande Power Structure in Relation to the Institutionalized Authority Structure

to accomplish this goal can cut short any ambition of power. The acquisition of wealth and clients is also necessary, and this process involves both lineage and nonlineage associations, which leads to the growth of a *mògò-tigi's* retinue. A large retinue, in turn, leads to further growth in influence. Moreover, the ability to make others believe in one's personal control over occult power is necessary. It is important to present a picture of invulnerability in the area of the occult.

Wealth may be obtained through agriculture, commerce, conquest, or any combination of the three. The poem said to be Son-Jara's eulogy emphasizes these three means.[37]

Minw bè sènè kè,
I ka sènè kè!

Minw bè jago kè,
I ka jago kè!

Minw bè kèlè kè,
I ka kèlè kè!

Jata ye kèlè kè!

Those who would farm the land,
Let them deal in agriculture!

Those who would trade in wares,
Let them deal in commerce!

Those who would go forth to battle,
Let them deal in warfare!

Jata dealt in warfare!

To attract a large retinue of clients, one may begin at home with good relations with one's own patrilineage and with that of one's spouse. The maximum number of wives one is able to support (only four are allowed under the edicts of Islam) increases the size of one's family. But procreation is a slow process. While waiting for children to grow up, power may be sought through good relations with the other lineages in one's village and district. Horizontal lineage village associations, such as age-sets and work associations, offer possibilities of clientage to a man of power. In the past, a large body of slaves for working in the fields and serving in personal armies increased wealth and clientage and thus increased power.

Finally, groups standing outside the lineage structure are often courted by men seeking power. Casted families and holymen are important because of their neutral position in relation to the authority structure of the lineages. Hunters help one gain knowledge of occult power and also serve in personal armies, thereby potentially intimidating enemies. All three of these groups are involved in the occult sciences, and their skills in this area of religion are essential to the acquisition of power. This process, as well as other aspects of religion, are often alluded to in the epic of Son-Jara.

Mande religion is diverse and complicated, not only in the multifarious practices that any one religion will perform, but also in the diversity of its variation from one region to another.[38] Add the relatively successful proselytizing of Islam and the considerably less

successful spread of Christianity in recent times, and the complexity is
reduplicated. Syncretism of traditional rites and beliefs with Islamic
practices produces a further set of complications. Although to present a
holistic picture of religion in the Mande world is beyond the scope of
this chapter, a minimal amount of data is needed to understand the
text.

With a few exceptions, religious tolerance appears to be common
among most of the peoples of Mali. Widespread mutual acceptance of
religious differences is matched by many examples of borrowings in a
fluid syncretism. Although Islam has made significant progress in con-
verting the populations of Mali since the beginnings of colonialism by
the French, old ways are not always cast off. Most Moslem tenets,
such as belief in jinns, are easily accepted by non-Moslems, for a parallel belief in spirits exists in local faiths. Other tenets require more
adaptation, but the older forms are still recognizable. A pair of etiological legends may be cited to illustrate this point.

Dieterlen's essay, "The Mande Creation Myth,"[39] recounts four
ancestors who, according to her data, are said to be the original human beings on the earth. Folk etymologies of their names are described as follows:[40]

> *Kanisimbo:* from Ka's womb
> *Kani Yogo Simbo:* from the same Ka's womb
> *Simboumba Tangnagati:* the big remaining part
>   of the womb which took command
> *Nounou:* from *nono,* "milk"

In the variant Dieterlen quotes, these four ancestors came to earth in
an ark from heaven. The ark came to rest in a cave called *kaba kɔrɔ* or
ka; thus, the image of Ka's womb.

When Islam enters Mande society, the etiology of humanity is explained in a Moslem variant of the same Adam and Eve legend found
in Christianity and Judaism. The origin of the Mande people must be
explained, as it is by Fa-Digi in our present text, by a different legend which is then related to the Moslem Prophet Muḥammad. According to this legend, Jòn Bilali,[41] a Companion of the Prophet and
said to be the second convert to Islam, sent his three grandsons (sons
in some variants) to found the kingdom of the Manden. These men
were given the following names:

> Kanu Simbon
> Kanu Nyògòn Simbon
> Lawali Simbon, also called Simbon Bata Nyagatè

The son of Kanu Nyògòn (or one of the others in other variants) becomes the ancestor of the ruling freeman clan. The meaning of these

men's names are also assigned through folk etymology. *Simbon* is a hunter's title. *Kanu* is the Mande word for "love," and *nyògòn* means "together." Lawali and Bata are given first names while Nyagatè is a surname. The similarities between Kanisimbo and Kanu Simbon, Kani Yogo Simbo and Kanu Nyògòn Simbon, and Simboumba Tangnagati and Simbon Bata Nyagatè are unmistakable. The transition from traditional religious legend to one oriented toward Islam can be observed here.

Other tenets of Mande non-Moslem cosmology remain in place in spite of Islamic influence. The division of the Universe into the forces of dislocation (*fa-denya*) and cohesion (*ba-denya*) dealt with above will illustrate this point. The traditional religion explains these forces as traits of the personality of God.

Domonique Zahan has described three personalities of the traditional Bamana god Babemba in his monograph *The Bamana*. The first personage of this god to emerge was called Musu-kòròni kun-je, "little old white-haired lady," and was the embodiment of "activity, energy, impetus, secrecy, and desire."[42] She also represented excessive haste, malice, misunderstanding, sorcery, treachery, and disorder. The Buffalo-Woman of Du also exhibits all of these traits.

The second manifestation of Babemba was embodied in the personage of Faro, who represented equilibrium and calmness, the opposite of Musu-kòròni. Musu-kòròni was needed for action, for without her there would have been stagnation and decay. Faro was needed for stability and equilibrium, for uncontrolled action leads to chaos. It was in the third personage of this god, called Ndomajiri, that the proper balance between the other two personages was to be found. The activities of the two extremes were believed to be controlled and directed by the third personage. Although no longer a part of the cosmology in Moslem areas, the underlying tenets of these beliefs are maintained in the concepts of *fa-denya* and *ba-denya*.

Still other non-Moslem tenets survive, such as the Mande religious practice of sacrifice. This rite is often performed in order to attain aid or advice, and often an analogy exists between the method of sacrifice and the need. Put another way, the sacrifice becomes a cosmic metaphor of the problem for which aid is being sought. In general, sacrifice is still accepted by all but the most orthodox of Moslems in Mali today.

In this chapter, I have explained several aspects, by no means exhaustively, of society relevant to the understanding of epic in Mali. Very important to this understanding is the manipulation of occult power. Many believe the bard controls aspects of the occult by his verbal art. Let us now turn to a description of the bard and of his social roles in Mande culture.

CHAPTER 2

The Bard (Griot)

The recitation of the epic of Son-Jara is carried out by professional raconteurs in the Mande world. A description of the social systems surrounding these professionals will help the outsider to understand the context of epic in this culture. The bard must first be placed in perspective in relation to the other castes in Mali. The social roles of the bards must be described, for reciting this important epic is only one of their several roles. The training and various occupations and economic orientation of bards will also be described. Finally, the generic specializations of the bardic caste will be listed.

Throughout the Mande world, there exists a group of clan families which may be described as castes. These families have the right to certain occupational pursuits, although they are not required to participate in their specialties. They also have certain defined social roles, and they practice endogamy. It should be made clear that the Mande endogamous castes are not "despised," as is the case in areas of the world such as India. In Mali, they are more correctly described as socioeconomic family monopolies, and not hierarchical pecking orders. Several characteristics of Mande castes support these conclusions.[1]

Mande terminology would indicate social separation of these groups from the rest of society. The word *nyamakala* encompasses all casted families. Their roles, both economic and social, are hereditary, and their endogamy would seem to serve the functions of preserving their monopoly over these roles, and of avoiding competition to insure that society runs smoothly. Their respective economic pursuits do not overlap. At least four groups exist in Mali and elsewhere in the Mande world:

Numu	blacksmiths, woodcarvers
Garangè	cordwainers (leatherworkers)
Funè (Fina)	mimes, Islamic praise-poets
Jeli (Jali)	bards (griots)

My interest in this book is in the casted families. Noncasted hunters' bards *(dònsòn-jeli)* may also be found in Mande society, but their role is not concerned with political epics like that of Son-Jara. Another aspect, which I do not fully understand, is that some clan families are wholly casted, while others have both casted and freeman branches. Bokor N'Diayé isolates the following bardic families:[2] Kuyatè, Koytè, Jabaatè (Jabagatè), Sumano, Jawara,[3] Makalu, Koyta, Dantè, Sakò, Kònè and Kamisòkò. He points out that the Koyta, Sakò, Kamisòkò, and Kònè have noble freemen branches, and he also fails to list the important bardic family of Sisòkò. In the Gambia, two other families may be added, the Suso and the Kanute. There may be other bardic families, or bardic branches of families, as there appears to be a great deal of regional variation throughout the Mande areas of West Africa.

The economic role of the bard, like those of the other casted groups, may be defined as monopolistic. All his/her roles are concerned with the spoken word, and the power of his or her speech is considered more than merely persuasive. Many believe the power of the occult is conveyed in the bard's words, demonstrated vividly by the formula people often recite when giving gifts to the bard after a performance:

Ka nyama bò!
May the occult power be taken away!

Although it cannot be denied that part of the bard's living is earned by the practice of oral art, Mande worldview considers payment for it to be a function of lessening the power that his or her words convey.

The bard's social roles are varied and complicated. In an oral society, the role of the arbiter of words cannot be overstressed.[4] One of the main roles is that of chronicler, and even more importantly, analyzer and interpreter of the history of the nation, economic group, and patron family (if he or she is so attached). The renowned Malian scholar Amadou Hampâté Bâ expressed this role in his statement that "with the death of each old man, a library is burnt."[5] As I have argued before, this history is legendary and perhaps regionally biased, but written history is also often complicated by social and nationalistic bias contemporary to its writing.[6] Much of the bard's recitation may be described as "official tradition,"[7] and thus considered favorable to his or her patrons. Moreover, the characteristic changes and variation common in any oral tradition are frequent in the bard's materials.

A second role of the bard involves entertainment. The monopoly over musical instruments and certain genres ensures the bard's artistic status.

A third role is that of preserver of social customs and values. In this role, the bard's knowledge of "proper behavior" serves in the arena of social control. Bards often express opinion in public without fear of reprisal, though a bard I interviewed in Mali occasionally refused to answer one of my questions, because, as he said, the information contained too much occult power (*nyama*). This verbal liberty is related to the bard's separation from the freeman lineage structure, as is a fourth role.

The role of mediator is important and has many facets. As a seer, the bard acts as mediator between the temporal and the spiritual. Bards often read divination of various kinds, and they administer curses and blessings.[8] They also serve as mediators between the parties involved in some of the Mande rites of passage, such as Islamic naming ceremonies and marriages.

Bards sometimes act as lineage spokesmen and take part in inter-village affairs as "ambassadors and conciliators."[9] Occasionally they perform valuable duties "in cases of serious rifts between two important families, where the impartiality of even the elders of the town might be questioned...."[10] Even where no rift is involved, a mediator is often needed, especially in cases where there is a difference between the social status of two freemen. It is precisely because bards are outside the lineage structure that they have the license to intervene without being suspected of pursuing personal gain. Moreover, the bard often mediates between two parties, so they do not have to face each other and run the risk of angry confrontation.

Related to the role of mediator, bards are sometimes responsible for initiating action. By praising or insulting a patron, the bard can move him to act. This role is often mentioned in epic poetry, as are several others which are difficult to assess in modern times because social conditions have changed. For instance, bards claim to have been the conscience of kings and to have moved them to action with their praise-poetry. They claim to have followed warriors into battle, singing encouragement to enhance their bravery, and they claim to have been immune from warfare and slavery themselves. If captured, they claim to have been either released by their captors or taken into their service as bards rather than as slaves. Considering their exclusion from lineage affairs in modern times, these claims are not beyond possibility, but the evidence for their former status is now absent.

The roles of the bard, then, are varied and complicated, and his or her integration into society is complete. Many years of training are required for the bard to perform these duties well. Being a bard is a full-time profession, and they are trained within a formal framework for several occupations. Like many Sub-Saharan African institutions, this training is centered in family life. Though other factors contribute to variation of texts, the different "schools" that produce the different variants are based largely on family and regional training.

Training begins at an early age when the child listens to his or her parents and to visiting bards, some of whom may be kinsmen. The first formal step in a male bard's training comes when he reaches early adolescence, when he is taught to play a musical instrument. He may begin with the four-stringed banjo-like *ngòni,* or with the *balan,* a hand-constructed xylophone. When he masters the essentials of the instrument, he may be sent to a kinsman to study as an apprentice.[11]

Apprenticeship is not limited to a specific number of years, but may vary according to the discretion of the master. An important part of the bard's training is itinerant, especially when he is young. He may travel far and wide, earning his keep as an accompanist to his master or to other bards. During this time he hears and assimilates new material. Though his variants may remain fairly true to his master and his region, some change in them results from his travels.[12]

Although there are no formal training centers for bards—they study wherever their masters live—there is one area which attracts many bards because of its prestige. The site of the Mande reroofing ceremony,[13] considered the center of the Mande world, is a village called Kaaba (Kangaba) in southern Mali near the Guinea border. It is often visited by aspiring bards, and boasting about a pilgrimage to Kaaba becomes part of many bardic pedigrees.[14]

Finally, after some years as an apprentice, the bard achieves the status of meistersinger (*nara*). This achievement usually occurs between the ages of forty and fifty. But not all bards become meistersingers. Some pursue other occupations.

In Mali, I observed three main occupations of bards: narrators, singers, and musicians. Only men may be meistersingers whose expertise involves narration. They may, however, specialize only in a musical instrument. Both women and men are involved with praise-poetry and song. Some men may recite and play their own accompaniment, but others will do only the one or the other. A wife will often sing the songs in her husband's epics. Also popular is the musician who accompanies his wife's singing. A full ensemble, such as that of the Kuyatè lineage of the village of Kela near Kaaba, includes a meistersinger who only narrates, a woman who sings praise-poems and songs, a female chorus, a male naamu-sayer,[15] and several male musicians. Their official attachment is to the Keyta clan, Son-Jara's own clan, but they sometimes perform praise-poetry and songs for others, because family patronage is not as economically reliable nowadays as it was in the past.

That bardic families were socially and economically allied to specific freeman lineages in the past is well accepted in Mali today. That this socioeconomic arrangement is no longer so widespread is also well attested. French colonialism changed many aspects of life in Mali, and the older patron/protégé relationships are no exception.

Before colonialism, a bard enjoyed certain privileges and exercised certain duties with regard to the freeman family to which he and his family might be allied. The freeman family often provided his home and food, as well as clothing and other needs and luxuries. I was told by one bard that even bridewealth was sometimes provided by the freeman family when the bard wished to marry.[16]

Some degree of family attachment survives in Mandekan-speaking communities even today. Royal families are often replaced by merchant families to whom many praise-poems are now directed. Not all royal families can afford patronage, but merchants are sometimes wealthy enough to do so. The situation in the Gambia resembles that of Mali, as Seni Darbo points out:[17]

> The situation is quite unfortunate since griot and patron still feel that they need each other. But social and economic circumstances for which neither side is entirely to blame have forced this strained relationship between them.

One solution the bard has found is to "adopt more than one patron."[18] Others take to the roads as "free-lance griots" during the dry seasons.[19] Another solution appears to be the adoption of an entire village as patron. Although I am not certain of this system, it appears to have been the case with the late bard Wa Kamisòkò of Kirina, a village southwest of Bamako. As spokesman for the entire village, Wa supplemented his income with farming, which is another adaptation many bards make. Indeed, some bards are quite successful as farmers, for they often have capital in hand to pay outside workers in their fields.

The state has provided patronage to a limited number of bards, but the competition is fierce. National troupes exist in Mali, Senegal, and Guinea, but they are periodically disbanded. The state offers more stable assistance to some bards, but their number is small.[20] The radio station provides some state assistance, but all these varieties of patronage are irregular, and can provide only partial income for most bards.

Some bards today have adapted even more radically and play in regional dance bands.[21] Others augment their incomes in nonartistic manners. The bard Alkaw Kònè, from whom I also collected a variant of the Son-Jara epic, is associated with the cloth market in Bamako.

Although adaptation has become necessary for the economic survival of the bardic caste, its social status appears to be in no danger of rapid radical change. The roles of the bards are still intact, as are the genres which are their media of expression.

Bards do not specialize in all genres of oral folklore in the Mande world. They do not, for example, recite folktales professionally. Although they sometimes recite fictional romance, their main specialties involve forms concerned with legend and social control.

Because of the belief in the occult power of words by many Mandekan speakers, forms such as curses and blessings are especially respected and feared when recited by bards. Proverbs are often used in the fine art of persuasive public speaking which bards are called upon to perform. Etiological and other legends are a favorite form, and many look to the bard for explanation of the origins of places such as rivers, towns, and villages. Based on the explanation of the names of these places, which are often folk etymologies, etiological legends seem to have a special fascination for Mandekan speakers.[22]

Closely aligned to etiological legends are the long, complicated recitations of genealogies. Like any folkloric form, genealogies exist in multiple variant form, and disagreement often arises between bards who support different patrons.

Heroic literature represents the group of genres for which the bard is perhaps best known. Praise-poetry and its contextual sister the dirge are specialties of the bardic caste. Songs and epic poems are also generic specializations. All the forms mentioned above can be found embedded within the lines of the epic, a point to which I will return later. The epic is indeed the most complex form the bards recite, and over millennia more than one variety have developed in the Mande tradition. A survey of the types of epic in Mali will help to place the epic of Son-Jara in a social and literary context.

Epic in Mali and elsewhere in the Mande world may be differentiated by two sets of criteria (see Figure 4). First, a structural differentiation between cyclic and unified epic can be established. Second, two varieties of epic exist which represent the recitation of two different, though related, bardic traditions: that of the casted families and that of the hunters' societies.[23]

The unified epic may be described as one whose core and augmenting episodes produce a single narrative. The augmenting episodes may vary from performance to performance, from bard to bard, but the core episodes must not be omitted when the epic is recited *in toto*. This is not to say that the unified epic must be recited *in toto* on all occasions. Portions are sometimes excerpted and used for specific purposes, as at Moslem naming ceremonies. The epic of Son-Jara is representative of the unified epic in Mali.

	Political Epic	Hunters' Epic
Unified Epic	Son-Jara	Kambili
Cyclic Epic	Da Mònsòn	?

FIGURE 4. Types of Epic in the Mande World

By contrast, a cyclic epic may be described as several epics, each with its own set of core and augmenting episodes, together making up an extended narrative. The entire cycle may be recited over a given period of time. Biebuyck has suggested as much for the Mwindo epic, stating that the bard "repeatedly asserted that never before had he performed the whole story within a continuous span of days."[24] This variety of epic is represented in Mali by the Bamana cycle surrounding the rise of the eighteenth and nineteenth century state of Segu and its most famous ruler Da Mònsòn.[25]

It should be stressed that this structural differentiation is not an absolute distinction in Mali. This dichotomy may well collapse in some areas where the vagueness of the contrast may have implications concerning the development of epic through time. The structure of the poetic line is basically the same for cyclic and unified epics, and in the case of hunters' and political epics.

Two different varieties of epics exist in Mali which represent differences in bardic tradition, function, and context. Both forms follow the same stylistics and linguistic structure,[26] and both are recited to the accompaniment of a musical instrument, although different ones. The bards who recite both forms are trained in much the same manner and "there are parallels in some of their social roles."[27] Finally, similarities in motif, theme, and general narrative patterns exist between the two varieties, but significant differences can also be isolated.

First, it is important to note that the bard of hunters' epics need not be a member of a casted family. It may be that since hunters recruit their members from all segments of society, the same egalitarian feeling extends to the hunters' bard. Indeed, the bard need not even be a hunter himself.

The social roles played by the casted bard and the hunters' bard differ in several aspects. The *jeli's* art attempts to unite society as a whole by the recitation of epics which deal with the founding of political states. Hunters' bards serve to "cement relations within a particular hunters' group,"[28] but pursue no national identity.

The duties of the hunters' bard further differ from the *jeli* in that ritualistic duties performed by the hunters' bard liken him to a priest. His songs are thought to imbue hunters with occult power before the hunt and to appease that power afterwards. Killing an animal is thought to release its occult power, and this power must be pacified if hunters are to survive its destructive force.

Finally, the context of the verbal arts of these two traditions differs. The *jeli* recites for a city-dwelling population in many circumstances, while the hunters' bard sings almost exclusively for a hunters' society, both in its rituals and for its entertainment. In this respect, the *jeli* can be said to operate from the *ba-denya* axis, while the hunters' bard operates from the *fa-denya* axis.

But whether political or hunter, cyclic or unified, epic is considered the highest art form of the bard. Its structural complexity contributes to its popularity and high status in Mande folklore.

CHAPTER 3

Characteristics of Mande Epic

It shall be the purpose of this chapter to describe the characteristics of African epic as exemplified by the epic of Son-Jara. The first five characteristics are traits which the majority of commentators over the years have isolated as necessary for the definition of oral epic. After extensive field work in Mali and an analysis of the texts I collected, I agree with them. The in-country observation of a living epic tradition has led to the isolation of three further characteristics described in this chapter. Let us begin with a discussion of the poetry.[1]

POETIC TRAITS

In an article published in 1960 which still influences thinking about African poetic scansion systems, Joseph Greenberg concluded that most Sub-Saharan African peoples did not have prosodic poetry.[2] In view of more recent applications of linguistic research on African poetics and of the greater competence of scholars studying in this field, Greenberg's statement appears out of date. The skills employed in linguistics and ethnomusicology are required to aid the literary scholar and folklorist in deciphering the complicated scansion systems in many African traditions. Moreover, an often ethnocentric concept of Western prosodic systems led many scholars down dead end paths of research.

What seems to be called for is a more universal definition of poetry which will admit other metrical bases. Scholars interested in African poetic systems have just begun to explore these possibilities and a full description of epic prosody in the Mande world is thus far incomplete. There are certain characteristics, however, which have been isolated and which I should like to describe.

<table>
<tr><td align="center">STRUCTURAL TRAITS</td><td align="center">CONTEXTUAL TRAITS</td></tr>
</table>

1. Poetic
2. Narrative
3. Heroic
4. Legendary
5. Great Length
6. Multigeneric Qualities

7. Multifunctional
8. Cultural and Traditional Transmission

FIGURE 5. Characteristics of Oral Epic Poetry

Thus far, many scholars have ignored the musical accompaniment of African poetic systems and have attempted to count units in the text alone. These efforts often led to frustration. Mande epic appears to be a variety of poetry that the British ethnomusicologist A.M. Jones called "metrical lyric,"[3] where music and text not only work in harmony, but are inseparable. Generation of the poetry depends upon the rhythm generated by the accompaniment. Bird has described this system of prosody as characterized by *language external constraints*, as opposed to poetry constrained by language grammar.[4]

One of the major differences between the meters found in poems with language internal constraints and those with language external constraints is that while it is easy to count the units of the musical pulse in both systems, it is not always easy to count the units in the textual component in the latter. Indeed, to define meter by counting syllables alone becomes impossible. But it is possible to conclude that Mande epics are poetic, even though we cannot completely describe them yet because of tone pattern differences in colloquial and poetic Mande languages.

Mande languages are tonal languages, and, as in many tonal languages, accentual patterns are subordinated to tonal patterns. Indeed, accent in Maninka is predictable from tone and is therefore not a phonemic element of the language. In poetry, however, nonphonemic accent plays a heavy role, for it is precisely by accent that metrical rhythm is produced, and, in the Maninka case, "accented syllables conform closely to the metrical beats, and in many cases, linguistic accents will be shifted to conform to the musical requirement."[5] The result would involve a change in meaning were context not to maintain the bard's semantic intent. It is this shifting of tones to conform to the prosodic stress pattern, which is nonphonemic in normal speech, that proves the text is poetic.

Having established that the text is poetic, it is also the case that three different scansion patterns are found in the epic. Scholars have termed these systems modes, and each has characteristic properties of form and of literary function. It will help to understand the formal traits of these three modes if we think of the bard's voice as a musical instrument with the same two properties possessed by the mechanical musical instrument: melody and rhythm. In the following discussion, I shall refer to the text as the poetic line and the accompaniment as the measure.

Bird has suggested that an aesthetic tension arises when the rhythm of the poetic lines violates the rhythm in the measure.[6] In fact, the greater the competence of the bard, the greater his ability to alter the rhythm in this way. The process of violating the expected recurrent rhythm is one of the characteristics of the praise-proverb mode in Mande epic.

I should like to suggest that another aesthetic tension is operative in these modes, that of the matching and the violation of the melodies in the poetic line and in the measure. Figure 6 illustrates this aspect of differentiation between the modes, which must be understood as showing a set of continua rather than a set of absolutes. Other differences also exist, such as the literary functions mentioned above. Let us examine each mode separately.

Rhythmically, the narrative mode approaches a zero tension level between poetic line and measure. The bard does not always follow the pulse of the measure, and there are often lines with several rests within a basic 4:4 pattern, but rhythmic tension is not the hallmark of this mode. The melody, almost always maintained in the measure, is seemingly ignored by the bard whose strophe tends to begin on a high pitch and work its way downwards by the end of the strophe. It is this down drift that demarcates strophe boundaries. Melodic parallelism, then, tends toward greater tension. Functionally, the narrative mode is most concerned with the story line, though it may also contain some praise-naming and proverbs.

Aesthetic tension, both rhythmic and melodic, reaches its peak in the praise-proverb mode. Enjambment obscures line boundaries, and melodically the bard's pitch is usually higher. Some bards recite praise-proverb mode very rapidly. Functionally, this mode is often employed as a link between themes in the narrative mode, and the association between specific praise-proverb passages and their placement in the text is usually recognizable. Sometimes the bard seems to use this mode as a way of organizing his forthcoming theme or themes. The occurrence of formulaic passages and expressions is highest in this mode.

The song is unique in that the amount of aesthetic tension between the poetic line and the measure is the lowest for both melody and rhythm. Bard and instrument seem to blend together more than in

	Melody	Rhythm	
Toward Zero Tension		X	
Toward Greater Tension	X		NARRATIVE MODE

	Melody	Rhythm	
Toward Zero Tension			
Toward Greater Tension	X	X	PRAISE-PROVERB MODE

	Melody	Rhythm	
Toward Zero Tension	X	X	
Toward Greater Tension			SONG MODE

FIGURE 6. **Melodic and Rhythmic Tensions in the Modes**

the other two modes. Moreover, each song has its own characteristic melody. In the other two modes, the melody of the accompaniment rarely changes. It is difficult to assess the literary function of the song mode, especially since some bards drop song from their recitation altogether, but one thing is certain. Songs appear at the major points in the narrative and seem to function like arias in grand opera, commemorating the major incidents in the plot.[7]

Mande epic is not memorized verbatim. It is structured around formulas and formulaic expressions and around themes, which shall be described later.[8] In Mande epic, no strict syllable count is involved, which allows the definition of formula to be freer. Formula may be defined here as a group of words which is regularly employed to express a given essential idea and in which substitutions of words with more or fewer syllables may occur. The key to understanding this type of formula is the substitution of words in a general structural framework.

Several formulas may be isolated as examples. Some are simple substitutions, such as the following which occur in the genealogy recitations of Fa-Digi and may be symbolized by Diagram 1.[9]

$$n \left\{ \begin{array}{l} X \ \left(\begin{array}{l} \text{di} \\ \text{ka} \end{array} \right) \ Y \text{ wulu.} \\ \\ (\text{Ka } Z \text{ wulu.}) \end{array} \right\}$$

$$n \ \left\{ \begin{array}{l} X \text{ begat } Y \\ (\text{And begat } Z.) \end{array} \right\}$$

DIAGRAM 1

Another simple substitution formula that Fa-Digi uses may be symbolized by Diagram 2.

$$\left(\begin{array}{l} \text{N' ye} \\ A \end{array} \right) \ X \text{ (le) ma.}$$

$$\left(\begin{array}{l} \text{I sing of} \\ \text{Tis about} \end{array} \right) \ X.$$

DIAGRAM 2

The substitutions Fa-Digi employs here are Hadama "Adam," Subaa, "Wizard," and an untranslatable praise-name for Son-Jara, Biribiriba.

Three examples of the formula in Diagram 3 can be found in Fa-Digi's text.

$$X \text{ ni } Y \ \left\{ \begin{array}{l} \text{tè kilin di.} \\ \text{man kan.} \end{array} \right\}$$

$$X \text{ and } Y \ \left\{ \begin{array}{l} \text{are not one.} \\ \text{are not the same.} \end{array} \right\}$$

DIAGRAM 3

A pair of proverbs structured with this formula are popular with this bard:

Kè kun ni musu kun tè kilin di.
Kumadin kè-nyi ni tonya tè kilin di.

Man's reason and a woman's are not the same.
Pretty words and the truth are not the same.

And this proverb was employed twice:

> Sebaliya ni fa-dinya man kan.

> Powerlessness and rivalry are not the same.

A third example required two lines, thus:

> Fantan kali suu,
> Ni fama keli nya tè kilin di.

> The way the weak swear an oath,
> And the way the mighty swear are not the same.

More complicated formulas require more than one substitution. Two such formulas will be illustrated here. In the formula in Diagram 4, substitution occurs in three slots.

$$\begin{pmatrix} A \\ B \\ C \end{pmatrix} \quad \begin{pmatrix} L \\ M \\ N \end{pmatrix} \quad \begin{pmatrix} X \\ Y \\ Z \end{pmatrix}$$

DIAGRAM 4

This formula structures a praise-name for Son-Jara, and the first substitution slot is filled with a part of the body. The second slot may be filled with any of several verbs, while the third slot may be filled with one of several terms by which Son-Jara is identified. Filling in all possibilities from the text renders Diagram 5.

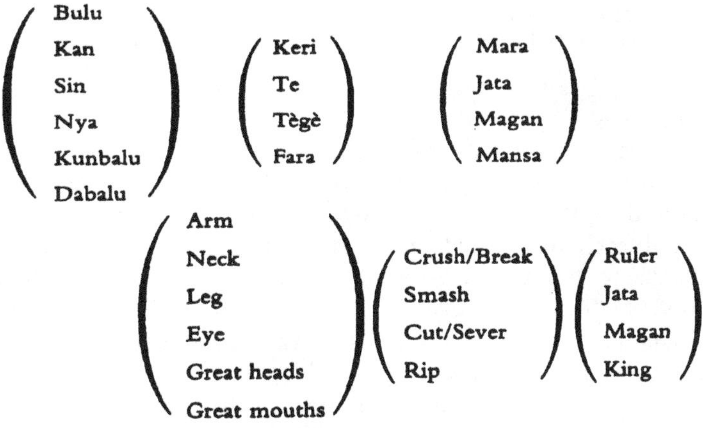

$$\begin{pmatrix} Bulu \\ Kan \\ Sin \\ Nya \\ Kunbalu \\ Dabalu \end{pmatrix} \begin{pmatrix} Keri \\ Te \\ Tègè \\ Fara \end{pmatrix} \begin{pmatrix} Mara \\ Jata \\ Magan \\ Mansa \end{pmatrix}$$

$$\begin{pmatrix} Arm \\ Neck \\ Leg \\ Eye \\ Great\ heads \\ Great\ mouths \end{pmatrix} \begin{pmatrix} Crush/Break \\ Smash \\ Cut/Sever \\ Rip \end{pmatrix} \begin{pmatrix} Ruler \\ Jata \\ Magan \\ King \end{pmatrix}$$

DIAGRAM 5

Another multi-slot substitution formula may be symbolized as follows:

$$\begin{pmatrix} N' \\ I \\ A \end{pmatrix} \begin{pmatrix} \varnothing \\ ye \\ ka \\ t\grave{e} \\ kana \end{pmatrix} \text{X mara (Manden (banku kan)).}$$

n [Ka Y mara (Manden (banku kan)).]

$$\text{(If)} \begin{pmatrix} I \\ you \\ he \end{pmatrix} \begin{pmatrix} will \\ must \\ won't \\ must\ not \end{pmatrix} \text{rule X (in the Manden (country)).}$$

n [And rule Y (in the Manden (country)).]

DIAGRAM 6

In this formula, the following substitutions may occur for X and Y:

numu(lu)	the blacksmith(s)
jeli(lu)	the bard(s)
funè(lu)	the *funè(s)*
garangè(lu)	the cordwainer(s)
tun-tan-mògò (bèè)	(all) the warriors
siya bi kònòntòn	the seventy races
Maraka bunda tan ni luulu	the 15 clans of Marakas
(Mande) mògò bèè	all the people (of the Manden)
siya naani	the four races
Mamuru si kè luulu	the five clans of Mamuru
mori si kanda-kè naani	the four clans of holymen

Fa-Digi employs this formula structure in both narrative and praise-
proverb modes.

Formulaic expressions differ from formulas in Mande epic in that
they are frozen lines or passages which do not involve substitutions.
Although they may have originated as formulas, they usually occur
unchanged each time they are recited. Formulaic expressions occur
most often in the praise-proverb mode. Indeed, praise-names like
Subaa-Minè-Subaa ("Sorcerer-Seizing-Sorcerer"), and Kirikisa,
dunnun-tanba ani sòn-tanba ("Kirikisa, Spear-of-Access, Spear-of-
Service"), are always the same.

Longer formulaic expressions also occur mostly in the praise-
proverb mode. The following expression occurs three times in Fa-
Digi's text with only minor changes.

Jiginè-kòrò-wulu

(Fen min / A) tè lontan sin lòn,

A tè duguren sin lòn.

A mana (mògò / i) sòrò,

K'i kin kè!

(The thing discerning / It discerns) not the footsteps of strangers
Nor the footsteps of the familiar,
Should it come upon anyone,
He will be bitten!

DIAGRAM 7

Another type of formulaic expression uses juxtaposition below the surface structure of wording. Diagram 8 illustrates this form. One such group may be designated formulas and formulaic expressions of juxtaposition. The initial formula may be diagrammed as follows:

X (ka di / diman) (cè / mògò) dò la,

Y man d'i la.

Y (ka di / diman) (cè / mògò) dò la,

X man d'i la.

X (is suitable to / suits) some (men / people),

Y does not suit them.

Y (is suitable to / suits) some (men / people),

X does not suit them.

DIAGRAM 8

Two examples may be cited:

Su ka di cè dò la,
Wula man d'i la,
Wula ka di cè dò [la],
Su man d'i la.

> The village is suitable to some men,
> The outlands do not suit them.
> The outlands are suitable to some men,
> The village does not suit them.

And:

> Sènè diman mògò dò la,
> Jago man di la.
> Jago diman mògò dò la,
> Sènè man di la.

> > Cultivating suits some people,
> > Commerce does not suit them.
> > Commerce suits some people,
> > Cultivating does not suit them.

Many other varieties of formulas and formulaic expressions exist, but the above examples will suffice to illustrate these common structural devices.

In conclusion, the poetry of the bard is comprised of structures and devices which produce three distinct modes of prosody. The structure of the line is determined by the rhythm and sometimes the melody of a musical instrument which accompanies most performances. The presence and absence of aesthetic tension between bard and accompaniment in rhythm and melody produces the modes. Formulas and formulaic expressions help the bard construct his line, but other traits help the bard to construct the narrative.

NARRATIVE TRAITS

Three traits of narrative are found in Mande epic. First there is the episode which groups together smaller units of composition, the themes.[10] The second level of structure is composed of the three modes of poetry discussed above and is in turn made up of a third stratum of smaller units of structure such as narrative lines, motifs, genealogies, and other elements.

Once the bard has begun to recite, there is no clear break in the performance. It is often possible to designate the exact line which will divide themes, but the bard does not stop his performance anywhere, unless he calls for a break unrelated to narrative structure. He may, for instance, sip tea or rest his voice, but he does not pause between themes or episodes.

Structural divisions are difficult to isolate unless the analyst has at least two texts to compare. In fact, I employed the comparative method on five variants to reach conclusions about narrative traits.[11]

The episodes of Mande oral epic are composed of groups of themes held together by their mutual relationship in the advancing of the plot. Lord calls the relationship a "tension of essences,"[12] but he never uses the term or concept of episode. Episodes are easy to divide in the epic of Son-Jara, for their actions are set in specific geographical places which change when the next episode takes over.

There are two types of episodes: core and augmenting. The core episodes are those without which the story of Son-Jara could not be told, and, if my present data is correct, there appear to be only three. Figure 7 lists the episodes employed in the five texts analyzed here. The three core episodes are numbers VI, which tells of Son-Jara's birth and the origin of his rivalry with his half brother King Dankaran Tuman; VII, which relates Son-Jara's exile; and IX, which describes his coming to power in the country of the Manden.

Augmenting episodes are not necessary to the central legend, but they are important to the performance of the epic. All bards have recited more than the core legend, but their choices of augmenting episodes differ.

One final note is needed on the progression of the plot. There is indeed a general order of events, but Fa-Digi and Kèlè Mònsòn

BARDS:	Fa-Digi Sisòkò	Magan Sisòkò	Kèlè Mònsòn Jabaatè	Alkaw Kònè	Ban Sumana Sisòkò
EPISODES: I.	Prologue (Praise-Poem)		Prologue (Pedigree)	Prologue (Pedigree)	Prologue (Pedigree)
II.	Paradise				
III.	Mecca	Mecca			Mecca
IV.			Origin of the Manden		
V.	Sankaran	Sankaran		Sankaran	Sankaran
VI.	The Manden	Daga-Jalan	Kiri	Daga-Jalan	Narena
VII.	Mèma (with Susu)	Mèma	Mèma (with Susu)	Nèma	Nèma
VIII.		Susu			
IX.	Kulu-Kòrò	Kulu-Kòrò	Kulu-Kòrò	Return to the Manden	Return to the Manden
X.	Kanbi		Kanbi		
XI.		Sibi			
XII.			Epilogue (Song)	Epilogue (Conclusion)	Epilogue (Praise-Poem and Song)

FIGURE 7. **Episode Variation in 5 Variants of the Epic of Son-Jara**

combine themes from episodes VII and VIII. The same phenomenon is observable within the internal structure of the themes, which are often collapsed into one passage. Theme boundaries are harder to distinguish because different themes are often bound tightly together. They often combine into one inseparable passage and do not always follow the same order in each variant.

A reason for the occasional nonsequential occurrence of themes is the structural device of the flashback. Flashbacks are sometimes used to repair a hole in the bard's plot. If he has forgotten to include a theme at an earlier point in his narrative but needs to relate it in order to explain some part of the plot at a later time, he may use the flashback. The result is that a theme may appear to be out of its usual order in the variant. To assist the reader in following the plot more easily, I have listed the themes Fa-Digi uses in the introduction to the text in Part Two.

Below the level of theme, there exists a set of structural devices upon which the narrative and descriptive lines are built. A surprising percentage of lines are delivered as monologues or dialogues. Fa-Digi speaks in the first person of his characters in forty-three percent of his lines, a device which has the illusion of bringing his characters to life.

Many themes are built around or augmented by traditional motifs.[13] To cite an example, the theme involving the nine Queens-of-Darkness is essentially built around the motif of the regeneration of the bull by occult means. Although this motif does not appear to be listed in Stith Thompson's *Motif Index of Folk Literature,* it can be found in many variants of the epic of Son-Jara, and it may be found elsewhere in West African folklore.[14] Indeed, variation of plot line and of specific epics follow expectations for any form of oral folklore. Each performance by any bard will differ because of the poetic structure of the line and because performance and composition are simultaneous. Praise-proverb and song modes are less likely to vary, and when they do, it is more likely to be in line transposition than in line recomposition.

One source of variation in the narrative line is in the motivations for action of the characters. Even in the same family tradition, interesting variation occurs. Fa-Digi, for example, has Son-Jara born second and announced first. His son, Magan, on the other hand, has Son-Jara born first and announced second, as does the Gambian variant of Bamba Suso[15] and the variant by the bard from whom Zeltner collected.[16] In the latter case, rivalry arises as Son-Jara attempts to gain his proper birthright. In the former case, Son-Jara's destiny to rule the Manden is stressed in spite of the obvious violation of the principle of *fa-siya,*[17] for heroes are above the normal laws of society.

HEROIC TRAITS

Modern academic treatment of the pattern of the heroic life in epic and other heroic literature dates from von Hahn's treatise in 1876, which has led to similar studies. The similarities and differences between the heroic elements in the epic of Son-Jara and those isolated by a hundred years of Western scholarship will be discussed as a backdrop to a description of the heroic pattern in Mande folklore. Finally the fulfilling of this role by Son-Jara will be described.

At first glance, the heroic elements in the epic of Son-Jara appear typical of other heroic narratives which have been studied over the years. A deeper look into the nature and interpretation of these elements reveals significant differences between the Mande pattern and the patterns of those heroes whose legends have provided the raw data from which Western scholars have generalized. Before examining the characteristics of the Mande hero in particular, a perspective must be established from which this pattern can be viewed.

In his comprehensive essay on epic poetry in the *Encyclopaedia Britannica,* Atsuhiko Yoshida states a case directly applicable to the heroic traits in Mande epic:[18]

> . . . the personages are necessarily transformed into ideal heroes and their acts into ideal deeds that conform to mythological or ideological patterns. Some of these patterns are archetypes found all over the world, while others are peculiar to a specific nation or culture.

Son-Jara's life pattern, like that of other heroes, has been molded to fit the ideal model which is peculiar to Mande society, some elements of which, as Yoshida points out, are found all over the world, and some elements of which are specific to Mande worldview.

Four scholars, von Hahn, Rank, Raglan, and de Vries, established lists of traits characteristic of the heroic life pattern.[19] The heroes whose biographies provided the raw data from which these pattern lists were constructed, however, are almost all "derived from the societies of India, the Middle East, and Europe, whose cultures are historically related."[20] While Son-Jara scores fairly well in all four cases,[21] African heroic patterns played no role in establishing these lists.

In place of a fifth list incorporating Mande traits, it will be simpler to describe the Mande hero and then demonstrate how Son-Jara exemplifies the ideal pattern. What is important in the studies from von Hahn to the present is not so much the listing of specific heroic traits but the obvious conclusion that the culture hero's life is molded to conform to an abstract pattern.

In Mali, I often heard it said of Son-Jara, "he was not like other men." At the same time, it was striking that his chief adversary Sumamuru Kantè was not despised. Indeed the spirit of the latter is revered and worshiped even today in the village of Kulu-Kòrò. The contrast between Son-Jara and Sumamuru is not considered one of good versus evil, of admired hero versus scorned antihero.

A strong folk belief exists among many people in Mali that a hero is destined to fulfill a role. The hero does not represent a role model of morality. He may have to violate social norms in order to fulfill his destiny. Indeed, the praise-names employed for Son-Jara do not paint a picture of virtue, but rather of ruthlessness.[22] He is Arm-Crushing-Jata and Host-Crusher, Village-Crusher and Village-Burner. He is Adversity's-True-Place.

Far from being affectionately revered, the image of the hero presented by these praise-names is one of a "person totally oriented along the *fa-denya* axis."[23] The following Maninka proverb expresses the distance the public places between the hero and themselves:

> Nana ma man di fo ko-jugu-lon.
> The hero is welcome only on troubled days.

In order to fulfill his destiny, the hero must first overcome the reputations of his ancestors, especially that of his father, and establish a name for himself. Son-Jara's accomplishment of this goal is symbolized by his attaining a new surname, Keyta, in place of his father's surname, Kònatè.

Attaining a name for oneself is not easy, for the reputations of many ruthless rivals and ancestors must be surpassed. As Fa-Digi states:[24]

> Sinkula le sòrò man di.
> A man of power is hard to find.

The hero must pursue his task outside the normal limits of acceptable social behavior, which takes him down several paths, all of which call for *fa-denya* behavior. Breaking with his patrimony leads the hero into the camp of the hunter, who, as I have explained earlier, formally breaks ties with his extended family. Pursuit of knowledge of the occult also draws the hero to the hunter.

The role of magic in Mande heroic epic cannot be over stressed. In the epic of Son-Jara, it explains the literary functions of several themes, as well as reflecting Mande worldview. The belief that political power is held not by force alone, but by control of the occult, accounts for the themes which describe the paternal and maternal inheritances of Son-Jara. In this context the Islamic concept of *barakah* may be considered the Moslem equivalent of local Mande occult power (*nyama*). From the father, descendant of immigrants from Mecca, Son-Jara inherits *barakah*; from his mother, descendant of the Buffalo-Woman of Du, he inherits *nyama*. With both of these occult sources, he will seek to gain the political power of his destiny.

Inheritance is not the only way occult power may be obtained. Another method is through violation of the very rules which make society stable (on the *ba-denya* axis). When violation of tabu occurs, *nyama* is believed to be released into the atmosphere. If the hero's preparation is adequate, he may gain control over that power, adding it to his supply of controlled magic. If his preparation is weak, or if it is not his destiny, if he is going too fast with his ambition, the occult may destroy him. The sacrifice of the unborn child of the Moslem holyman,[25] which violates orthodox Islamic beliefs, may be explained in the Mande context of syncretized Islam and local Mande religion. The release of *nyama* by such an abomination is within the control of the hero Son-Jara, but not of the sacrificer. Son-Jara goes to the next village of his exile, strengthened by the sacrifice, while the poor Magasubaa king, not the hero of destiny, must pay the price.

Pursuit of occult knowledge from hunters' societies also accounts for many of Son-Jara's praise-names. He is called Kinsman-Killing-Hunter, a praise-name which also emphasizes the trait of violation of tabu. Another praise-name, Hunter-Imposing-on-the-Hardy, emphasizes this role. A pair of panegyrics stress the favored milieu of the hunter, thus: King-of-the-Wilderness, Kalinka and King-of-the-Wilderness, Kinibi. Finally, the obscure praise-name which has several variants was explained to me in terms of the hunter. Simbon, Lion-Born-of-the-Cat is said to lay stress on the hunters' practice of pursuing occult knowledge by observing wild animals in their natural habitat. Simbon is a hunters' title, and it was explained that man, who is the greatest hunter of them all, learned his skills from observing the lion, who had in turn learned to hunt from his ancestor the cat.[26]

Another group of praise-names stresses the hero's knowledge of the occult without making specific reference to hunters. Son-Jara is called the Wizard and Sorcerer-Seizing-Sorcerer. Three praise-names also emphasize this knowledge: The day I came to know you, Devourer-of-the-Knower; Arrow-of-the-Knower; and Devourers-of-the-Knowing.

To exemplify the Mande heroic stereotype, the life of Son-Jara may be viewed as a series of transformations in the pursuit of power which was his destiny according to Mande worldview. At first he is impotent, the limping hero symbolically castrated (in the sense of that term as used by Hays)[27] by his mother's jealous co-wife.

Even while still crippled, omen after omen indicated his destiny of eventual acquisition of power (the dog fight, the battle of rams). The rank of his birth is even considered irrelevant to his destiny, bards like Fa-Digi's son Magan Sisòkò seeing him as firstborn with his birthright stolen, and bards like Fa-Digi seeing him as the thief of the birthright. As mentioned above, Son-Jara's path to power through the principle of *fa-siya* was cut off. Acquisition of power had to come through the methods Mande society provided outside the authority structure.[28] This necessity was another reason for Son-Jara's link to the hunters' societies, and to other clients and political accessories, especially from casted families, the most important of whom are the bard and the blacksmith. The bard could assist in stamping the hero's name and reputation into history and in helping him to overcome the reputations of his ancestors. The blacksmith could assist in knowledge of the occult as he is often the titular head of *komo* societies.

To illustrate the pursuit of power outside the authority structure, we may again turn to praise-names:[29]

> Hèè Ala!
> Son-Jara k'waa Manden.
> Sini-mògò la di.
> Sini-kènè-mògò la di.
> A jelilu marala,
> Ka numulu mara,
> Ka tun-tan-mògò bi saba ni mògò saba.
> A y'o mògò bè marala.

> Ah God!
> Let Son-Jara go to the Manden.
> He is the man for the morrow.
> He is the man for the day to follow.
> He is to rule o'er the bards.
> He is to rule o'er the smiths.
> And the three and thirty warrior clans.
> He will rule o'er all these people.

The first transformation sees Son-Jara overcome his symbolic castration through acquisition of enough occult power to neutralize the co-wife's hex. Great iron bars, seven-fold forged, are not strong enough to hold up the unbelievably powerful body of the man who was not like other men. But a thin branch of the custard apple tree, a religious object considered plentiful in occult power, accomplishes what force fails to do.

Son-Jara is thus transformed from a crippled youth to a strong hunter and moves from the safety of his mother's compound (on the *ba-denya* axis) to the danger of the wilderness (on the *fa-denya* axis). His chief occupation, which is interpreted as a threat to his enthroned brother, is the pursuit of occult knowledge through becoming a hunter. The threat is concerned with political power, as the following praise line stresses:[30]

> Subaa ni mansaya!
> The sorcerer and sovereignty!

Son-Jara is therefore exiled and what follows are a series of transformations in which his supply of *nyama* is increased. Some of these transformations lead to violations of tabu, such as the sacrifice of the unborn child mentioned above. The acquisition of *nyama* also explains other unorthodox behavior from the Moslem point of view, such as Sugulun's prayer to the God of Islam (on the *barakah* axis) for a miracle which would cause the shea butter tree to bear fruit needed for a sacrifice to a pagan fetish (on the *nyama* axis).[31]

After this series of visits which increases Son-Jara's occult power, he arrives at his destination in Mèma. Meanwhile, other activities, such as the theft of Fa-Koli's wife by his uncle Sumamuru, weaken Son-Jara's adversary's control over the occult and over his clients.

When Son-Jara returns from exile he is a changed person, but he still does not have enough control to defeat Sumamuru. Son-Jara's sister then seduces Sumamuru with the result that Son-Jara learns his enemy's secret over control of the occult and counteracts it. Instead of increasing his own supply of *nyama,* Son-Jara reduces Sumamuru's supply, and thus overcomes him.

Once the major adversary is subdued, the final transformation takes place. Son-Jara takes off the traditional mudcloth robes of the hunter, symbolizing the *fa-denya* axis, and dons the embroidered robes of the village, symbolizing the *ba-denya* axis. After he secures the throne, he delegates the job of expanding the empire to clients, who perform heroic acts for which praise-names are granted. In an interview the bard Ban Sumana Sisòkò stated that a great man is one who attracts other powerful men to his side to do his will and whose clients perform the deeds which further enhance his own place in history. This is the destiny of the hero in the Mande world, and Son-Jara has been given a reputation by Mande bards which no hero since has matched.

LEGENDARY TRAITS

There is no question that the Manden-speaking populations in West Africa consider Son-Jara to be a historical personage. As stated in the last section, however, the narrative elements concerning the life of

Son-Jara have been molded into a heroic pattern similar to the heroic image wherever it is found and partially defined by Mande society. Any narrative concerning Son-Jara may thus be considered a legend.

The narrative structure begins with the entire epic and may be subdivided into episodes and themes. The same is true of the legend structure. The entire epic, for instance, may be designated as one legend. Each episode in the multi-tiered structure may likewise be considered a separate legend. Indeed, the recitation of only certain selected episodes occurs in Mali in such ceremonies as Islamic child naming rites.

On the next tier, themes or combinations of themes relate legend segments which themselves may be considered as narrative wholes. Sometimes, a smaller legend may be found embedded inside a larger legend sequence. The legend of the origin of the Jabaatè clan will serve to illustrate this point. Fa-Digi relates the origin of the family in two themes, the latter being a genealogy of the clan. The sequence is itself a part of the larger legend concerning Son-Jara's maternal family, which comprises the episode I have named Sankaran. The sequence is in turn embedded into the even larger legend sequence leading up to the birth of Son-Jara in which the first core episode is related. In tier after tier the narrative is carried by legend, often supported by a genealogical catalogue.

The etiological legend is undoubtedly the most important variety which occurs in the epic of Son-Jara. The bard Ban Sumana Sisòkò referred to the body of his knowledge as a whole as "origins." A favorite stylistic technique of bards is to introduce or conclude the etiological legend of a clan family with a genealogical catalogue of its members. Fa-Digi relates the origin of the world in this manner and concludes the sequence with genealogies of Adam and Noah. The narrative section concerning Jòn Bilali also concludes with a genealogy.

Fa-Digi, in a burst of etiology in this part of his version, recites a catalogue of the first Mande clan families which he says migrated from the empire of Wagadugu (Gāna). Next he describes the origin of the Jawara ethnic group, the founding of its main villages, and the genealogy of its patriarch. He goes on to describe the origins of the villages of the Tunkara clan and its original genealogy. After a five-line praise-poem, Fa-Digi recites the legend of the origin of the Manden, the founding of its main villages, the genealogies of the three Simbon brothers who founded it, and its social composition. The bard concludes the episode with a discourse on the important Mande family of Tarawere which is to play a crucial role in the next episode, and he recites its genealogy. The next episode, Sankaran, concerns the Tara-were clan and the Kòndè clan, and Fa-Digi begins his recitation with a genealogy of the Kòndès (also called Jaras).

Altogether, Fa-Digi spends some 291 lines on the subject of various etiologies and genealogies leading up to his fourth episode. I cannot overstress the importance of these etiological legends, for they play a major function in the ordering of society in the Mande world today.

Many other etiological legends are embedded in episodes of Mande political epic. One specialized variety is the etiological legend based on a folk etymology, a topic which I have analyzed in detail elsewhere.[32] Tonal patterns in the explanations of various particles of these etymologies do not always match the actual tonal patterns in the language. This fact, together with the occurrence of variant explanations of the same name, leads the student of folklore to conclude that folk etymology is involved in this highly specialized variety of Mande folklore. Many examples of this pairing of genres can be found in the Son-Jara epic[33] and in Mande society as a whole.

LENGTH IN MANDE EPIC

Great length, although a trait of African epic, is a relative concept. While there is no question that this characteristic is typical of African epic, it becomes a question of defining and describing it. With what other form or forms of folklore is epic to be compared if it is to be considered a long genre, and even with that comparison, how long is long?

The fundamental division of pattern in poetry, as Greenberg suggested, is the line.[34] Any discussion of length in poetry, then, may easily be stated in numbers of lines. It is safe to conclude that an epic poem is longer than most lyric poems. Many lyric genres are often constrained by a set number of lines. Not so with epic, which may be described as open-ended. While oral epics are not infinite in length, there is certainly no set number to their definition as a genre. One text I collected from Kèlè Mònsòn Jabaatè was composed of only about 1,332 lines, while the other five texts in my possession are all over twice this length. The text by Fa-Digi Sisòkò numbers 3,084 lines, and that of Magan Sisòkò is 3,631 lines long. Alkaw Kònè's epic is 3,460 lines long, and Ban Sumana Sisòkò's variant numbers some 3,295 lines. The Kèlè Mònsòn version in Moser (1974) is 2,034 lines long.

Another important genre with which epic length can be compared is praise-poetry (*fasa*). Also open-ended, this Mande genre may be fruitfully compared to epic, because they are both from the same Mande tradition. Replacing narrative with allusion, which is one difference between these two forms, has a paramount effect on length.

While most Mande epics number in the thousands of lines, Mande praise-poems usually number in the hundreds. I collected four such poems while on the same field trip in Mali, two celebrating Son-Jara. A variant composed and sung by Sunkala Sakò and his wife Man Kanutè numbered 213 lines. The other Son-Jara *fasa* was composed and sung by Mamadi Jabaatè, Bala Jabaatè, Sira Mori Jabaatè, and a chorus of women from the village of Kela, and it lasted for 343 lines. Two other praise-poems were collected from this latter ensemble, one celebrating Tura Magan Tarawere (174 lines) and the other celebrating Fa-Koli Dumbiya (188 lines). Epic, then, is longer than its closest cousin in Mande folklore, the praise-poem. Furthermore, the epic may be the longest form of oral folklore in Mande society.

Open-endedness, the ability of a professional bard to enlarge or shorten his text, is an important talent in the Mande world, and I propose to call this trait the "accordion effect." Closely resembling de Vries's "theory of swelling,"[35] the former term would also encompass a theory of shrinking. De Vries states at least two methods by which a text may be enlarged, but the reverse process is also possible.

First, a "certain given subject-matter [may] swell as it were from the inside by the addition of ever increasing detail."[36] Likewise, decreasing detail will shrink a given subject matter. Many examples of these processes may be found when different variants of the same epic are compared. Swelling and shrinking is accomplished in several ways. The subject matter of a single theme may be augmented or reduced. A new theme or themes may be added to produce further detail. Stylistic devices such as the genealogy increase length. Finally, the combining of thematic material into a single passage can increase its detail, and therefore its length.[37]

De Vries mentions a second method of expanding a text in the form of "duplication of material."[38] There is a good example of this process in the themes which deal with the *sigi-game* in Fa-Digi's variant. The verbal formulas (*watarawaa,* etc.) are recited four times for a total of fifty-eight lines.

In summary, the main characteristic of length in the epic of Son-Jara is its open-endedness or accordion effect, which permits the bard to add or omit themes and even episodes from his text, and which permits him to swell or shrink the number of lines. In comparison to other forms of oral poetry like the praise-poem, the Mande epic may be described as a long genre of folklore.

MULTI-FUNCTIONAL TRAITS IN MANDE EPIC

Thus far I have presented a great deal of information concerning the structure of this epic, but its multiple functions in society are also part of its impact. Both bard and audience are affected by these functions, and a great deal of the social order of the Mande world is derived from the worldview expressed within the lines of this poem. Let us begin with some social functions.

I have stressed that social change in any society at any point in its history is a phenomenon shared by all the societies of the world. The same is true of Mali and of the other countries of the Mandekan-speaking world. One of the major functions of the epic of Son-Jara is to provide a model for social relations in modern Mali. Textual differences in regional variants reflect bards' opinions of actual differences in regional social behavior. In fact, the epic both reflects and acts upon the social dynamics of group relationships. Let me state a case in point.

An area of social behavior influenced by the epic of Son-Jara is the symbolic relationships between the different segments of society.[39] Through the model provided by the epic, the freeman, the bard, the smith, the cordwainer, the *funè,* the boatman, the holyman, the descendant of former slave and former orphan, the stranger, and many other members of society find their roles defined and sanctioned.

To state one example, bards often stress their own roles in society through the medium of their texts. The role of social mediator between families is exemplified in the theme of the visit of Bala Faseke Kuyatè (Dòka, the Cat) to the court of Sumamuru Kantè.

A closely related function is that of the epic as model for the relationships between clan families. Hopkins states the case like this:[40]

> Relations between clans are modelled after the relations between their ancestors in the time of Soundiata. Thus Coulibaly and Keita are said (in Kita) to be especially close because the Coulibaly are descended from Soundiata's full sister. The relations between Tounkara and Keita are expressed in terms of the Keita having been the guest of the Tounkara because when Soundiata Keita fled from his *faden* he took refuge with some Tounkara who were his hosts and who later supported him in his struggle to regain his land.

The examples of Kulibali (Coulibaly) and Tunkara (Tounkara) given in the above quotation are but two of many in Mande society. Almost every major clan family can be related to the Keita clan through the model of a legend which can be included in the epic of Son-Jara. The content of these legends will differ from region to region, reflecting the differing relations between clans. Indeed, the very presence of certain clans in certain areas is explained by some segment of the epic of Son-Jara. Bards naturally stress the roles of the clans in the area where they find patronage. The practice gives rise multiple variants and even to conflicting interpretations of clan relations. Co-wife rivalry exists between a Berete and a Kònde in the variants by Fa-Digi, Magan, Ban Sumana, and Kèlè Mònsòn, while the struggle is between a Kòndè woman and a Danba woman in Al-kaw's variant. In the Guinean variants collected by D.T. Niane, and Laye Camara,[41] bards include an episode where, at the Council of Kurukan Fugan (or Juru-ke Fua) in Kaaba (Kangaba), Son-Jara formally decrees what social relations in the Malian empire will be. As Niane translates, Son-Jara "pronounced all the prohibitions which still obtain in relations between the tribes."[42]

One of the most important functions of the epic of Son-Jara is its role in the national unity of Mandekan-speaking peoples. Because of its focus on the common origin of widely dispersed clan families and ethnic groups,[43] this epic plays a definite role in building a sense of national identity, even though political boundaries drawn by French and British colonial powers persist in dividing these people politically.

Nowhere is this function of national unity exemplified and stressed more dramatically than in the reroofing celebration of the sacred Mande hut in the village of Kaaba.[44] Here the function of national unification reaches its peak. People from all of the political states containing Mandekan speakers attend the ceremony, which includes recitations of the epic of Son-Jara. It is traditionally recited by bards from the village of Kela, specifically for the Keyta clan family which is formally represented.

Parallel to the unifying function of the epic of Son-Jara in its nation building role exists another role worth mentioning here. The Mande political epic is, on one level of its meaning, "universally recognized as a symbol of the origin, growth, and development of the state."[45] In this role, it exemplifies the charter of society thesis of Bronislav Malinowski. Manipulation of power by men of reputation, which has been discussed above, is augmented by passages which define the roles of people in their society.

Most segments of Mande society are affected by the epic of Son-Jara. Even the signature tunes over Radio Mali have been influenced by this epic.[46] Such varied subjects as land settlement and tenure are affected by legends from the epic.[47] Present day academic research is influenced. In a statement about the *Kalevala,* de Vries points out that even the research devoted to an epic can contribute to its functions in national unity.[48] Such was the case in 1975, when the Société Commerciale de l'Ouest Afrique sponsored a conference on Mande oral traditions in Bamako.[49] The conference attracted many scholars of Mande Society from countries such as Mali, Guinea, the Gambia, Senegal, France, Britain, and the United States. It centered on the study of the epic of Son-Jara, produced massive publications which are a variant of the epic by the late bard Wa Kamisòkò,[50] and included a one-day bus tour of the parts of the Manden located in the modern Republic of Mali.

Another function neglected in studies of oral folklore is that of entertainment. The entertainment value of the epic of Son-Jara and of the other oral epics of Mande bards represents a valuable contribution to society. Many of the bards of West Africa possess talents comparable to the best performers and musicians in any other part of the world.

Finally, several functions of the epic may be described as parallel to those of the bard, for the epic is the property of the bard. As the bard is chronicler of history (legend), so the epic becomes the chronicle of Mande history. As the bard is the initiator of some types of social activity, so the epic becomes one medium by which this goal is accomplished. As the bard is the preserver of social customs and values, so the epic becomes the catalogue of those customs and values. The latter function may even be described as didactic or acculturating in nature, and the deeds of the heroes and the customs and values surrounding them become role models for members of society. As a catalogue of social values and customs, the epic exhibits characteristics of cultural, traditional transmission, a subject to which we now turn.

TRAITS OF CULTURAL TRADITIONAL TRANSMISSION

The characteristics which mirror Mande culture are another set of traits which help to define Mande epic.[51] Biebuyck describes the characteristics of cultural, traditional transmission like this:[52]

> . . . all epics obviously provide rich, unsolicited information on the cultures and societies in which they occur. There are references to customs, institutions, patterns of behavior, techniques, beliefs, and values throughout the epic, particularly at certain stages through catalogues, genealogies, and descriptions.

It does indeed seem obvious that such a long narrative would contain many reflections of the society in which it is composed, but there may also be a social function for this trait as well.

Constant reinforcement of cultural data may well serve as an enculturating force on its audience. Moreover, since the bard often considers himself as the official "protector" of his cultural traditions, the purpose of including so much unsolicited cultural data and description may also be to strengthen his prestige as a bard. Somewhat akin to name dropping, this trait may be used by the bard to enhance his own personal pedigree.

Caution must be exercised while searching the lines of any epic for cultural data. Some of the narrative is undoubtedly employed only for literary purposes. A deliberate distortion or conscious omission of some cultural features may be used only to intensify the drama of a theme.

To cite an example, the bard probably describes the housing of both women in the same recovery hut after each had given birth for the dramatic effect of heightening the tension of the scene. It is hard to conceive of a situation in Mande society which would allow two co-wives to recover in the same room after giving birth.

Observation and analysis of cultural data is thus best performed from the outside inward. Knowledge of the culture gained from first-hand fieldwork is absolutely necessary. Analysis from the inside outward is another way of using internal evidence, and may lead to distorted conclusions, just as the bard may have distorted his recitation for literary reasons. The examples of cultural, traditional traits listed below are based on a year and a half of fieldwork in the Republic of Mali. Let us begin with a straightforward category.

The list of material objects common in Mande society is endless, as different lists could be compiled from different variants..One of the longest lists is that of food stuffs. Mention is made of grains such as rice, fonio, couscous, and millet, and seed foods like groundnuts (peanuts), groundpeas, and beans. Foods used in the preparation of sauces are found in the epic of Son-Jara, including okra, baobab leaf, eggs, and an obscure legume called black *lele*.

A related category is that of household utensils and other family and personal possessions which also find their way into Mande epic. Calabashes often appear, as do swaddling clothes for carrying infants, snuff spoons, charcoal, needles, hammocks, and spindles and distaffs used in weaving. Clothing and bodily decorations such as sandals, hats, coats, pants, and bracelets, are referred to in the epic.

Weapons are naturally a favorite with bards. Mention can be found of objects such as knives, spears, bows, arrows, quivers, guns, swords, and axes. Another favorite with bards are musical instruments. In the lines of poetry, we hear of royal drums, *jinbe* drums, iron rasps, balaphones (a type of xylophone), and the banjo-like, West African stringed instrument called in Mandekan the *ngòni*.

Religious paraphernalia are often mentioned in the epic of Son-Jara, both relating to Islam and to the traditional religion. We find shrouds for corpses, fetishes, amulets, both of Koranic verses and of the variety called *tafu*, and prayer beads and prayer rugs.

One could fill a zoo with the animals referred to in the epic of Son-Jara, and then construct a botanical garden adjacent to it. The text mentions a menagerie of wild animals, including buffaloes, lions, and club rats. Domesticated beasts are not neglected: dogs, cats, rams, bulls, horses, and goats are included. Snakes found in the epic include cobras and mambas. Flying creatures include a contingent of birds (Guinea fowl, chickens, hawks, partridges) and insects (deer flies, termites, mosquitoes, gnats, bees).

Not as abundant as animals, plants are nevertheless included in the epic. Most abundant are trees, for so many are considered sacred amongst Mandekan speakers. One hears of baobab, kapok, custard apple, and flame trees, as well as the shea butter tree. Some tree names are obscure and include the *datu* tree. Other plants mentioned are *fanda* vines, cotton, and the host of plants which produce the food stuffs mentioned above.

Aside from the catalogues of tangible objects found in the lines of the epic are found intangibles such as cultural values. These values serve as the backdrop to the didactic function of the epic. Fa-Digi mentions truthfulness, beauty, morality, and dignity. He refers to the Moslem interdiction against gossip, and the respect for one's elders. The entire episode of Sankaran, which includes the breach of faith between Du Kamisa and her nephew, concerns respect for one's elders, especially kinsmen. The bard praises the cultural value of generosity and stresses the rewards of suffering.

Many beliefs are reflected in Mande epic, the most important set being religious beliefs. One finds reflections of Islamic faith as well as the traditional faith and combinations of both which make up so much of the local syncretized practices. Let us begin with the Islamic tenets of faith.

A variety of Middle Eastern religious legendry is referred to in the epic of Son-Jara. Mention is made of Adam and Eve, of God and Satan, and of jinns, of heaven, hell, and life after death. Sin, damnation, and grace make their way into the epic, and Fa-Digi even mentions the blowing of the trumpet at the end of time. The holy pilgrimage to Mecca (*ḥājj*) is mentioned several times. Many personages from Islamic legendry make their appearances, such as the Prophet Muhammed, Noah, his sons Ham, Shem, and Japheth, and Bilāl bin Rabaḥ, the latter being honored as the ancestor of the founders of the Manden.

References to the occult of Mande traditional religion are almost too numerous to mention. I have already discussed this subject, and only a representative set of examples will be discussed here. Belief in the occult and its power, for example, is reflected in the Buffalo-Woman's magic spindle. The magic obstacle flight, including the transformations of the eggs, is an example of this belief. Belief in the occult power of words is reflected in the Buffalo-Woman's curse, which causes the hunters to fall from the tree. A good example of such a curse is to be found in a variant recited by Fa-Digi's son Magan.[53]

> A ko, "Mògò jujarani,
> "Yirijujarani, a bè ka bin nyògòn ne!"

> Said she, "Let folk of fragile frames,
> "And trees of trembling trunks together tumble!"

Another example of faith in occult power is Dan Mansa Wulandin's magic knife with which he causes Sugulun Kòndè's warts to disappear. An exciting scene of magical conjury occurs later when Sugulun diverts the sexual advances of Dan Mansa Wulanba. In Fa-Digi's variant, her breasts magically sprout spikes from the nipples. In the variant collected by Frantz de Zeltner, Sugulun's pubic hairs stand on end like porcupine quills, wounding the hapless hunter, who fails to have his way with the sorceress.[54]

The reason given for Son-Jara's paralysis is a hex placed on him by his mother's senior co-wife. Much later, after Son-Jara stands up with the aid of the occult power in the custard apple branch, we are witness to a battle of sorcery between his sister Sugulun Kulunkan, who wins, and his brother Manden Bukari, who loses. In this scene, dead meat (or the dead club rat) races back and forth, on and off the cooked rice, at the oral commands of the two practitioners of magic. At one point, Manden Bukari shouts off his sister's dress! This is too much for the sorceress and she finishes the battle by cursing her brother. None of his descendants, we are told, ever become kings in the Manden.

One of the most exciting scenes which reflects belief in the power of the occult is a scene in Magan Sisòkò's variant where the partridge delivers the Boatman's message to Sumamuru. Fa-Digi's variant includes the message but omits the partridge. Magan's version describes how the partridge continues to deliver the message even after it has been killed, and again after it has been cooked. The bard ends the scene with an understatement: "The partridge was hexed!" The above set of examples will serve to illustrate the multifarious occurrences of faith in occult medicine in Mande society reflected in the epic of Son-Jara.

The epic of Son-Jara includes so many references and allusions to Mande customs that a translation of it reads like an uneven ethnology. One may follow the Mande speaker from birth, through social customs and rites of passage that occur during his/her lifetime, and on to death in the descriptions of the bard. The important Moslem child-naming ceremony, for instance, is mentioned twice in the variants sung by Fa-Digi. On the eighth day of a child's life, its head is symbolically shaved and its name is announced to the public. In another place, Magan Sisòkò mentioned the carbon covered straw dust that is found on the thatched ceilings of many Mande kitchens. The custom alluded to is the use of this straw dust by midwives, who rub it on a newly born infant's navel to prevent infection after they have cut its umbilical cord.

An interesting custom which sets the scene for the Sankaran episode is the rearing of children by their paternal aunts. If a man has a barren sister, it is customary for one of his children to be reared in her household. The father retains responsibility for his child, who retains the father's surname, but the social arrangement nonetheless permits the sister to enjoy motherhood as a foster parent. In other situations, I was told, a man may give one of his children to his sister even if she has children of her own. Family ties and affections are strengthened by this custom, which may also account for its reported occurrence among co-wives in the same nuclear family. By "swapping" children, co-wife rivalry can sometimes be diminished.

Marriage customs are not neglected in this epic. The principle of *fa-siya* is reflected in the Mande custom of providing for the marriage bridewealth of the eldest son in a family first. The second oldest son is next to marry, and so on down the line until the youngest son is married at last. An eldest son's reluctance to marry can sometimes cause animosity in his family. Fathers get upset and even younger brothers may become impatient.

Another marriage custom is employed by Fa-Digi to disengage Son-Jara's sister from the household of Sumamuru after she has seduced him and learned the secret of his occult power. There is a tradition which allows a new wife to return to her parent's house about a week after marriage to pay a final visit and to get part of her dowry. When she marries, part of her dowry is composed of her *minèn-kolon,* "useful containers." This collection is made up of calabashes and other containers and stirring devices. A small *minèn-kolon* is considered disgraceful.

There is no description of a funeral ceremony in our text, but one burial custom is used, and I was told that it is still common in Mali today. Son-Jara buries his mother in secrecy and later buries a shrouded kapok log to disguise his actions. Grave robbing of powerful people is avoided by secret burial, for sometimes the deceased's fetishes and amulets are buried with him/her, and such a treasure becomes a great temptation to those who seek reputations.

Since hunters play an important part in the epic of Son-Jara it is not surprising to find customs mentioned which are related to their societies. The traditional gesture for greeting a hunter by embracing his legs provides an appropriate image, for Son-Jara has only just gained use of his paralytic legs. The image might be described as a gestural pun. Another custom among hunters, which is also traditional among many peoples of Africa and the Middle East, is alluded to in this epic. After a kill, hunters may participate in a sort of communion ceremony which takes place over the freshly killed game. Hearts and livers, thought by many to contain occult power, are cooked and shared among the hunters.

Fa-Digi also alludes to the use of dogs as hunting companions by hunters. A different use of dogs in Mali, not related to hunters' societies, is alluded to in one of Son-Jara's praise-names. Farmers and even townsfolk often keep guard dogs for the protection of their compounds, especially the granary.

References to religious customs in the epic of Son-Jara represent one of the most prolific examples of cultural, traditional transmission. Numerous varieties of divination and sacrifice appear throughout the lines of this epic. References to oath swearing also occur.

A detailed description of a religious rite from traditional Mande society will serve to demonstrate this type of reflection of culture in the epic of Son-Jara. When Son-Jara goes to seek refuge with the nine Queens-of-Darkness, who are sorceresses, they are bribed to perform this ritual on him. In the traditional theology of many Mande peoples, the individual is believed to have a spiritual "double" or wraith (*ja*). The wraith may wander outside the body when its master is asleep, and it becomes visible as one's shadow or as one's image in a mirror. The Maninka word for host, *ja-tigi,* "wraith protector," appears to reflect this folk belief.

The form of conjury these sorceresses practice involves the belief that a person's wraith may be unnaturally removed from his/her body by occult means. The wraith is then ritually placed into an animal, which is slaughtered and eaten in a communion service. Once the animal is consumed, there is no turning back. In the epic the sorceresses have no trouble rejuvenating the dead bull. They have the power over life and death in the epic, but a disembodied and digested wraith is believed to be unrecoverable, even by a sorceress. Son-Jara's counter-bribe of nine buffaloes enables him to avoid this fate.

The descriptions, references, and allusions discussed in this section are indeed numerous and fill any variant of the epic of Son-Jara with rich cultural data. A more detailed catalogue has been presented in the notes to the text.

MULTI-GENERIC TRAITS

Portions of the epic of Son-Jara can be isolated as separate genres which occur in Mande society. The epic as a whole may be considered a genre, as its structure, context, and functions are well defined, but the same may be said of the smaller generic forms embedded within it when they occur separately. The multi-generic structure of epic is an important defining characteristic of this form of oral folklore.

The entire epic may be designated as a single legend on its first tier of legend structure. Embedded within the first tier are more tiers of legend structure, which constitute separate narrative passages and which may occur in separate performances elsewhere in Mande society. In short, legends are embedded inside larger legends. The same embedding structure occurs with other generic forms, some complex and some simple.

Considerable discussion has already been devoted to generic forms. Among the more complex forms are at least four varieties found as separate performance genres in Mande society. Legend, of course, occurs elsewhere in poetic and prosaic form, often supported by genealogy recitation. Songs and praise-poems are performed separately and in combination with other genres. Among the simpler generic forms are praise-names, folk etymologies, proverbs, incantations, curses, and oaths.

The blending together of these various forms produces the whole of the epic poem which occurs in the Mandekan-speaking tradition. Biebuyck has noted this characteristic for other African traditions,[55] and Shoolbraid found it in Turkic epic as well.[56] Together with the other characteristics, then, the multi-generic trait may be considered a defining trait for African epic poetry. Every variant collected in Mali contained all of these characteristics.

The African Epic Belt

No epic tradition is ever identical to any other epic tradition. At the same time, the striking similarities of this quasi-universal form argue for a more universal generic description, such as the one proposed by this descriptive analysis. It is not the purpose of this study to debate the issue, but a few words on epic and genre may serve as a fitting conclusion, after which I should like to suggest that an African epic belt appears to be emerging from recent studies of epic on that continent.

A number of debates and panels have been organized over the last ten or so years—indeed the debate continues—as to the correctness of naming the extended heroic narratives in Africa as epics. A number of scholars have participated in this debate, one of the most prominent being Dan Ben-Amos, who has participated in more general studies of genre theory over the years. In an earlier article[1] he argued for an ethno-aesthetic approach to generic definition and description. Later, his view changed on the issue[2] and—if I now understand his position—he argues that the outside analyst may be just as qualified to classify generic forms as are local critics, for boundaries between genres are often fluid.

My own views about defining and delineating genres fall somewhere in between these two extremes. Genres can be defined by listing literary conventions which define the structure, context, function, use, and occurrence of any given form. A listing of specific literary conventions must begin at the ethno-aesthetic level. A complete list of the traits of a genre will be culture-specific and will require that any researcher, foreign or domestic, take into account local occurrence and opinion in order to produce an accurate list.

When comparing lists of similar forms (genres) cross-culturally, certain literary conventions will be the same or very similar, so that two lists of literary conventions can be produced for many genres which have cross-cultural occurrences. One list of traits will appear to be characteristic of the genre in the area where the text under analysis occurs. It will be culture specific. The other list will have more generalized application and will appear to define a cross-cultural form. I find this to be the case with epic, specifically heroic epic. This method of defining genre has been employed for years by folklorists. Folktale and legend, for example, are actually larger categories including many specific forms and shapes of oral narrative, such as Märchen and etiological legend.

The eight traits described in this study are of the second listing. They define epic in general, but also have been observed operating in a living tradition. All reliable variants of the epic of Son-Jara I have reviewed, including those I collected, display these traits, as do several other traditions in other parts of Africa which shall be discussed below. They are not culture-specific traits but rather cross-cultural traits. Such a listing is useful to the folklorist interested in generic theory, for it is and has been one of our primary and sustaining interests to find the characteristics of human literary behavior about which general patterns can be observed. In the actual performance of the text, however, one encounters traits which are almost impossible to generalize about. Let me elucidate.

Below the generic specificity, one encounters the culture-specific traits which represent regional variation where the politics of the area are somewhat different from the neighboring village. Mixed in with the "national" interpretation of events past, the local condition will dictate that the bard support one family over the other, one lineage over the other, one person over the other. *Nyama,* the occult power believed to be contained in the very words the bard performs, is thus manifested on an individual level, and if at that level contradictions occur with the general plot it becomes the bard's task to reconcile them.

At an even more specific level of generic and regional variation, one encounters personalities. The bard adds his own personal views to the text. He is permitted to express personal opinion on matters about which ordinary people are condemned for expressing public views. In the final analysis, the bard lives under the reins of the very *nyama* he sings about, just like everyone else. He is "controlled" by it, just as he "controls" others with it. His patrons must be appeased. But things differ slightly from place to place. Individual A owes deference to individual B, and yet A has a stronger personality and is able to manipulate B. Individual C does not get along with individual D, but the legend dictates that C's lineage was aided by D's family in the narrative which represents the guidelines for contemporary behavior, which I propose to call "law by parable."

At the very bottom of this process, becoming more and more specific from its eight generic rules at the top, one encounters that evening's performance. Which bard is singing (interpreting) the text? Who is in the audience representing his/her lineage/family/self? What are the local alliances between lineages/families/individuals? Who is certain to reward performance more richly than others? How does the bard feel that evening? I once had a performance cut short because the aged bard was becoming fatigued. The text, from its most generalized generic rules down to the evening's performance, becomes a tug-of-war between genre and bard, between cultural guidelines and individual creativity, between legendary content and local social realities, between tradition and the politics of the region and of the day.

Performance manipulates the text within the dictates of the traditional literary conventions of the genre, eight of which I have found to hold true for epic in Africa. It is my hope that the rigid model of Greek epic, a dead tradition that can no longer be observed in action, will not continue to dominate scholarly thinking. The Greek tradition is only one of many. In several places in Africa and elsewhere, living epic traditions can be observed in their natural contexts. Work remains to be done in areas where epic is still recited and nurtured. Some work has already been done and continues in several places on the continent of Africa. Future research in Africa may prove very rewarding.

For a single researcher to pursue the question of the total occurrence of epic on the continent of Africa would be impossible. There are too many languages involved, too many ethnic groups for one scholar to acquaint him- or herself with. Already, however, there are enough publications available to suggest a much broader occurrence of epic beyond West Africa. Indeed, it may be the case that a belt of African epic tradition stretches from the Gambia through western and central Africa to East Africa (see Figure 8). Several points must be made about this possibility.

Initially, it must be stressed and stressed again that the possibility of an African epic belt is a suggestion for future research. It is not a thesis that can be argued on the strength of present research, but a good beginning has been made which enables such a suggestion to be advanced at this time.

One of the weaknesses in this suggestion lies in the definition of the term epic in relation to African traditions, a problem which the eight characteristics put forward in this study may help to solve. Ruth Finnegan correctly points out that praise-poetry has often been confused with epic.[3] The confusion shows up, for example, in an article entitled "The National Epic of the Adangme" by D.A. Puplampu.[4]

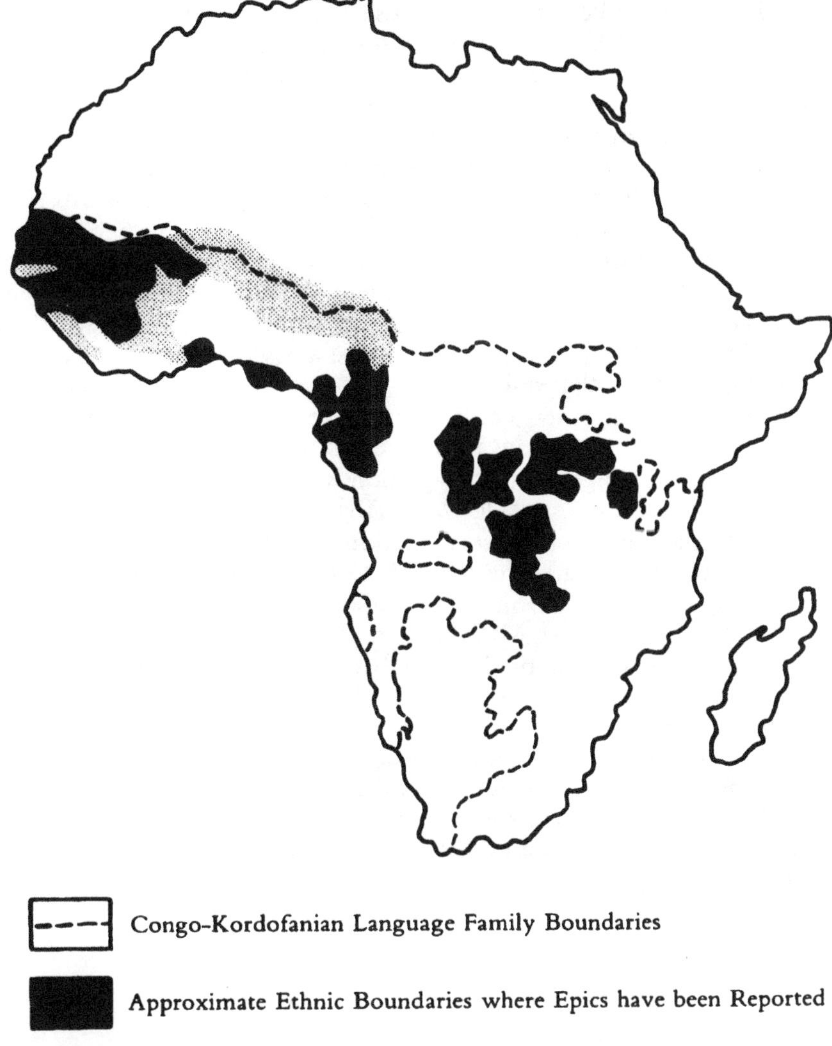

Figure 8. Possible African Epic Belt

The researcher describes allusion in the recitations which are the raw data for his analysis. Narrative is replaced by allusion, for copious notes must accompany each poem. There is little doubt that this researcher is describing praise-poetry.

A related problem is that of field methods. Nowhere can the skills of the folklorist be put to better use than in fieldwork techniques. I suggest text collection by tape recorder in an induced natural context.[6] Transcription should omit nothing, and translation should be linear. Notes should explain every obscurity where possible. Texts collected and published in this manner are much more reliable than condensed, reconstructed texts, and the former may be used in broader generalizations about African epic. The lack of reliable materials of this sort is the second weakness to the suggestion of an African epic belt.

In spite of its drawbacks, there are several strengths to the suggestion. The body of published narratives which has been described as epic all appear to occur in one language family, the Congo-Kordofanian. Though there are gaps between the areas where epic has been reported, it may be that research into this genre has not been carried out in those areas. In other words, occurrence of epic may be much more widespread than we know at the present time.

Another strength of the suggestion is the existence of some reliable scholarship in areas outside West Africa. Biebuyck's descriptions of several epics in Zaire leave little doubt that oral, heroic epic exists throughout the area.[7] The work done on the *mvet* traditions among the Fang in the Camerouns and Gabon is also fairly reliable. Recent work by Mugyabuso Mulokozi in Tanzania reveals that the epic tradition is practiced by Bahaya bards just west of Lake Victoria. There are several other epics reported in many areas which also merit investigation.[8]

A wealth of information remains to be gathered in the pursuit of this knowledge. As defined by the eight characteristics set forth in this analysis, oral epic poetry is definitely present among the Mandekan-speaking peoples of West Africa, and the text which follows is exemplary of the epic tradition there.

NOTES

PREFACE TO THE FIRST EDITION

1. The spelling of Son-Jara in the analysis and text of this book follows the practice of Maninka bard Fa-Digi Sisòkò, whose variant text is here translated. As a folklorist, I feel I should follow the traditions of the bard and not change any of his pronunciations. The hero represented here is more widely known in scholarship as "Sunjata," though his name is spelled in various ways, usually reflecting the spelling conventions of the native language of the collector and not of the Mandekan languages where texts are collected. For a detailed note on Son-Jara's various names and praise-names, see the note for line 1 following the text of the epic.

PREFACE TO THE SECOND EDITION

1. For a more detailed description and analysis of the context and performance of this text, see *The Epic of Son-Jara: A West African Tradition*, Analytical Study and Translation by John William Johnson (Bloomington: Indiana University Press, 1986).

INTRODUCTION

1. A useful and readily available summary of the history of the empire of Old Mali can be found in Trimingham (1970), pp. 60-83. Another useful reference is Monteil (1968), pp. 33-66. Less reliable, but very interesting, is Volume II, *L'Histoire* of Delafosse (1972), pp. 162-220. Levtzion (1963) is especially useful, because he summarizes the writings of several Arab chroniclers who were the first to record the history of Old Mali. His more recent work, Levtzion (1973) puts the writings in even better perspective. These historians, particularly the Arabs, but also Trimingham, often accept oral tradition almost uncritically while not identifying it as such. One is tempted to charge Trimingham with employing oral tradition to "fill in" where documentation fails. Also interesting is the likelihood that the Arab chroniclers obtained their data on Son-Jara, and perhaps other *mansalu,* from oral tradition and not from oral testimony. It appears that everything we know about Son-Jara has come down to us through the memories (first hand or second hand) of the professional bards who maintain these traditions. Compare the comments by Levtzion and Hopkins (1981) concerning Ibn Khaldūn's interest, almost alone among Arab chroniclers, in oral traditions. See their notes 55 and 69 on p. 424.

2. Miller (1980), pp. 19-20, points out the fallacy of employing composite narratives (collapsing variants into one narrative which is, in reality,

not recited by any bard) for arriving at historicity, what he calls a "kind of historical lowest common denominator." Readers interested in observing this method may consult Pageard (1961). Readers interested in an opinion of the strengths and weaknesses of Miller's (and associates') approach to oral history may consult Elizabeth Tonkin's review article (1982).

3. Miller (1980), p. x.

4. The key argument in the essay by Miller (1980), p. 1, would appear to lie in the statement that

> The historian must approach the oral tradition as 'evidence,' whatever scholars in other disciplines choose to do with the same narratives.
>
> Evidence...the historian takes as something that bears witness to a vanished time because it has *survived unchanged* (italics his) from then until the historian examines it.

But is anything in the oral tradition capable of surviving unchanged? Bird and Kendall (1980) have argued that "oral literature is constantly reshaped to its contemporary context—at least in its interpretation." They point out that, although the epic of Son-Jara and other Mandekan heroic literature "date back several millennia . . . , these songs mark ideologies and behaviors that have current relevance" (p. 21). Unlike our disciplinary ancestors in folkloristics who were interested in "survivals," most contemporary folklorists argue that cultural traditions do not survive without contemporary functions. Sometimes these functions are not the original ones, because they have evolved away from their original functions over time. This argument was first communicated to me by Professor Warren Roberts.

5. Levtzion and Trimingham quote genealogies from oral tradition with faith that they represent people from the past. They both place faith in the genealogy quoted by Ibn Khaldūn, which was, as stated above, also taken from oral traditions, and at that secondhandedly. But how much faith these scholars place in genealogy is not always easy to identify. For example, Levtzion (1973), p. 228, note 6, states that "having a grandson of the ancestor as the real founder of a kingdom *may represent the beginning of the historical period freed from the myth*" (italics mine).

6. See Miller (1980), pp. 18–19, for a good treatment of this complexity.

7. See Miller's discussion of variation on pp. 19–20.

8. See the text of the epic in the present volume, lines 2844, 2848, 2852, and 2856.

9. Son-Jara's defeats result in the founding of *Nyani* ("Anguish"), line 2636, *Sòbèya* ("Resolve"), line 2650, and *Nyòòn-sòn* ("Sharing"), line 2661.

10. Laye Camara (1980), p. 72.

11. Bilāl bin Rabaḥ, sometimes called Ibn Hamāma after his mother, is referred to in Mali as Jòn Bilali, "Slave Bilali." One of the bards from whom I collected, Ban Sumana Sisòkò, explained the *jòn*, "slave," by stating a religious connotation in the same sense as the Arabic name 'Abd al-Lāh ('Abdallah), "slave/servant of God." Islamic historical writings do describe Bilāl as a slave, first of Umayya bin Khalaf, an "unbeliever" whom Bilāl later slew in battle, and then of Abū Bakr, the Prophet Muḥammad's father-in-law and the first convert to Islam. For a thorough description of

Bilāl bin Rabaḥ from the Islamic perspective, see the *Encyclopaedia of Islam: New Edition* (1960), vol. 6, p. 1215.

12. Fa-Digi and his late son the Bard Magan Sisòkò did not even agree in their genealogies. Fa-Digi has Son-Jara descending from Kanu Nyògòn Simbon, son of Mamadu Kanu, while Bard Magan has him descending from Kanu Nyògòn's younger brother Lawali Simbon.

13. For a summary of the reign and accomplishments of Kankan Musa, see Trimingham (1970), pp. 67-71. The dates given here are quoted from that source.

14. See citations of these studies in the references under von Hahn (1876), Rank (1959), Ragland (1949), and de Vries (1963).

15. Bascom (1957), p. 111.

16. See the interesting essay listed under Utley (1965).

17. The function of Miller's *clichés* (see Miller, 1980, pp. 6-8) is that by "translating" oral testimony into symbolic literary *clichés*, the historical event is more easily remembered.

1. THE SOCIAL SETTING

1. Hopkins (1972), p. 12, for instance, states: "People think of themselves as Kitans before they think of themselves as belonging to any other group. Much of the first section of this chapter is based on Hopkins' research in Kita. The text for this volume was collected in Kita and may be considered a Kita regional variant. In a larger perspective, Hopkins states (p. 12) that "Kita's distinctive culture . . . is a microvariant of Maninka-Bamana culture which in turn is a variant of a wider regional culture common to the Western Sudan."

2. Ibid., p. 11.

3. Imperato (1970), p. 13.

4. Hopkins (1972), p. 52, points out that at the time of French colonialization, "Islam was a matter for small groups of specialists, the *mori* . . . ." Since that time, he declares, Islam has become the majority religion. Imperato (1970), p. 13, points out that much of the artistic behavior inspired by traditional Mande religion is changing and some of it is disappearing.

5. Hopkins (1972), p. 26.

6. For a discussion of the use of family terminology in Mande cosmology, see Bird (1976), pp. 96-97, Bird and Kendall (1980), pp. 14-17, Griaule (1973), p. 12, Hopkins (1971), p. 100, Jackson (1979), pp. 100-101 and McNaughton (unpublished conference paper). This section is also based on my own field notes and observations.

7. The Maninka terms for name and reputation are the same: tògò. The verb "to praise" *(ka majamu)* is derived from the word for surname *(jamu)*. Overcoming one's father's name/reputation is expressed in the proverb:

> I fa-den fòlò y'i fa de ye.
> It's your father who is your first competitor.

This proverb is quoted from Bird, et al, (1974), p. vii.

8. Information in this section was obtained from Bourama Soumaoro, who is a *komo-tigi,* "master-of-the-komo." The *komo* is an esoteric society

amongst the Mande people, one of the main functions of which is to deal extensively in the occult.

9. A conversation with friends in Mali concerning the danger of encountering snakes while cultivating fields was begun when I showed them a copy of Atkins (1972). The photograph on p. 19 showed a man standing in the wilderness wearing a hunter's tunic made from a piece of mud cloth *(bogolan fini)*. On his left ankle was an amulet which I was told was a prophylactic against snakes.

10. Trimingham (1970), p. 148.

11. Hopkins (1971), p. 103.

12. Hopkins (1972), p. 26.

13. The following description is based on the discussion in Hopkins (1971) and (1972).

14. Hopkins (1971), p. 102, explains that sublineages are known as *ba-bun-da* ("the door of the mother's house"), for sublineages usually trace their lineages from a woman. In the simplest case, the woman from whom the various sublineages of a lineage claim descent are the wives of the men from whom the lineage as a whole claims descent. This method of sublineage division is also operative in Somalia and may be widespread in Africa.

15. Hopkins (1972), p. 27.

16. The semantic sphere of the Maninka word *dugu* includes both "earth" and "village," thus the two translations:

> *dugu-kolo-tigi,* "earth–surface–chief"
> *dugu-tigi,* "village chief"

17. Hopkins (1972), P. 25.

18. The Maninka term *kafo* or *jamana* was translated as *canton* by the French in colonial times. The latter term is often encountered in critical literature, even in English.

19. Hopkins (1971), p. 101.

20. See Meillassoux (1968), especially chapters three and four, for a good description of the newer voluntary associations in the capital city of Bamako, Mali.

21. *Ton,* meaning, "association," may be a metaphoric extension of *ton,* meaning "quiver"; otherwise, the two morphemes may be homonyms.

22. Hopkins (1971), p. 105.

23. Meillassoux (1968), p. 51.

24. Ibid., p. 52. For a good description of *Koteba* theater, see Brink (1977), (1978) and (1982).

25. For a description of Mande puppetry, see Arnoldi (1977), (1981), and (unpublished conference paper).

26. Imperato (1970), p. 13.

27. Meillassoux, (1968), p. 51.

28. Ibid., p. 50.

29. Imperato (1970), p. 11, located these groups in the western Bamana country of Mali and in the Maninka area around Fuladugu. Each group had special masks for its secular entertainment performances. I have a pair of mask crests called *gongon-kun,* but I have not been able to determine if a *gongon* society exists.

30. The following discussion is also based on Hopkins (1971) and Hopkins (1972).

31. *Ja-tigi* means "host/protector of the wraith." The institutionalized relationship between the stranger *(dunan)* and his host *(ja-tigi)* is probably very old. The host may act as a mediator for his guest. He may prevent local people from taking advantage of the newcomer in such matters as market prices. At the same time, the host can keep a close watch on the stranger, and, in this role, protect the local citizens from possible foreign conspiracy. If the stranger is a visitor from another village, as is often the case with itinerant bards and traders, the host may become stranger and the stranger host when the visit is reciprocated.

The host/protector tradition still lives in Mali. As a foreign researcher, I was *dunan* to M. Mamadou Sarr, then Director of the Institut des Sciences Humaines du Mali. He, together with his staff, acted as *ja-tigi* to me and my family. This system opens many opportunities to the foreign scholar and establishes a cooperative relationship, as the foreigner shares his research with his colleagues in this government department. The director, in turn, is responsible to the Minister of Education for the proper behavior of the foreigners committed to his charge.

32. The French colonial referred to the *mori* as *marabout.* The latter term is still common in descriptive literature and scholarly publications, even in English.

33. The paper is most often taken to a cordwainer *(garangè)* and sewn into a leather pouch onto which a leather cord is attached. Amulets of this sort are normally worn around arm, neck, or waist.

34. Information in this section concerning hunters' societies has been drawn from my personal field notes, as well as from Bird, et al. (1974), Cissé (1964), Hopkins (1971), and Meillassoux (1968).

35. See Cissé (1964), pp. 182ff for a variant of the verbal pledge taken by hunters when joining their association. A verbal denunciation of mother, father, and sibling ties is included in this pledge, along with an acceptance of the "cult" and law of the hunter society.

36. Hopkins (1971) and (1972) again were consulted for this section.

37. This poem exists in multivariant form. The text quoted here is in Bamana and was collected directly from Ban Sumana Sisòkò, who is considered the poet laureate of Mali.

38. References useful in studying local Mande religion are Cissé (1974); Dieterlen (1955), (1957), (1960); Dieterlen and Cissé (1972); Griaule and Dieterlen (1951); Henry (1960); Paques (1959); Tauzier (1927); Traoré (1947); Travélé (1929); and Zahan (1960), (1974).

39. Dieterlen (1957). Caution should be taken with this essay. No original text is presented, so the variant described was reconstructed from an unknown genre. Whether the variant is reconstructed from a single text or if it is a composite of several is not clear. The implication is that it was collected in the early 1950's from the Kuyatè bards of Kela, thus making it a Manden heartland variant. Although Dieterlen mentions several shrines along the Niger River as far north as Akka, near the Niger bend, she does not appear to have collected variants in any other place except Kela.

40. Ibid., p. 127.

41. See note 11, p. 64.
42. Zahan (1974), p. 3.

2. The Bard (Griot)

1.   A great deal has been written by western scholars about the social status of the casted families in the Mande world. Earlier writers in colonial times appear to have been convinced that the *nyamakala* were despised. This misunderstanding may have been the result of analogy to casted groups elsewhere in the world. Some of the social sanctions in the Western Sudan may have contributed to this warped viewpoint. Their practice of endogamy is often cited. Burial rites differ between the two groups, but these practices are based on belief systems rather than pecking orders. *Nyamakala* are prevented from membership in certain social organizations, such as the *Kore* society (a Mande esoteric cult), but they appear to have reached the highest position possible in others. Blacksmiths, for instance, are often the leaders of the *Komo* society. A good indicator of the often ambiguous status of the *nyamakala* is described in the following quote from Hopkins (1972), p. 20:

> The government periodically became concerned with the situation of the members of castes . . . , especially the *dieli* [*jeli,* "bards"], alternatively considering the castes to be underprivileged groups whose status should be raised and overprivileged groups whose privileges needed to be reduced.

The castes also deal in the occult and are feared because of their secret knowledge. Conclusions and descriptions in this section are based upon my field notes, plus the observations in Hopkins (1971), (1972), N'Diayé (1970), Bird (1971), Darbo (1976), and Kesteloot (1966).

2.   N'Diayé (1970), pp. 87-88.

3.   Some scholars consider the Jawara a separate ethnic group, rather than a clan family.

4.   N'Diayé (1970), p. 92, states the notion as follows:

> Le rôle du Dieli était donc très important dans un pays qui n'avait pas d'autre moyen d'expression que la parôle transmise de père en fils.

5.   Quoted from Kesteloot (1966), p. 202.

6.   For discussion on the bias of written history, see Bird (1971), pp. 22-23 and Dupree (1967), pp. 50-52 and 69.

7.   The distinction between official and private traditions was first suggested by Vansina (1965). See especially pp. 49-51.

8.   Blessings can be elaborate. I witnessed the administering of a blessing in Mali that lasted about ten minutes. The verbal component was followed by the bard symbolically (not literally) spitting into the hands of the young woman, who then wiped her face with the "blessing" of the bard's spittal. The use of spittal as a tool of healing or a blessing or greeting is a common gesture among many ethnic groups in Africa and the Middle East.

9.   N'Diayé (1970), p. 49.

10.   Darbo (1976), p. 11.

11. Because of sanctioned rivalry between father and son, bards often study with kinsmen, though they cannot help being influenced by their fathers from whom they first hear songs, epics, and other generic forms. Again because of the sanctioned family behavior, maternal uncles who embody family affection and cooperation make favorite masters for aspiring young bards.

12. For a discussion on the general subject of stability and change in bardic narration, see Innes (1973).

13. For a description of this festival, see Dieterlen (1957).

14. Magan Sisòkò commented in this way about his father, Fa-Digi's pilgrimage to Kaaba in an interview conducted with him. In this way Magan was claiming that the variant of the epic in his family was sanctioned as accurate.

15. Often an apprentice, the naamu-sayer *(naamunaamuna)* shouts *naamu* (from Arabic *na/am,* "yes") and other encouraging words after most lines of narration in order to stimulate the meistersinger. The words in parentheses after Fa-Digi's poetic lines in the text are the naamu-sayer's pronouncements.

16. Interview with the bard Ban Sumana Sisòkò.

17. Darbo (1976), p. 15.

18. Ibid., p. 13.

19. Ibid.

20. Ban Sumana Sisòkò gets a state pension and a home from the Malian government. He represents the country and is considered its poet laureate. The famous *kora* musician Baturu Seyku Kuyatè is a favorite of several heads of state, including Sekou Touré of Guinea.

21. Whereas many bards would consider dance bands below their dignity, others, particularly younger bards, move freely between traditional genres and modern Malian adaptations of Western music. Magan Sisòkò, for example, was a member of the Kita regional dance band whose patronage was mainly the youth of the area. Regular performances are staged near the state guest house in Kita.

22. See Johnson (1975a) for a discussion of the use of folk etymology in etiological legendry.

23. Information in this section concerning hunters' epics is described by Bird (1971), (1972) and by Kesteloot et al. (1972).

24. Biebuyck and Kahombo (1971), p. 14.

25. Brief references to Da Mònsòn's career may be found in Trimingham (1970), pp. 147-50, 177. Note that he is called Da Dyara in this reference. A published, albeit reconstructed, set of four cyclic epics can be found in Kesteloot (1972).

26. I am not aware of any cyclic hunters' epics, but further research might uncover their existence.

27. Bird (1972), pp. 290-91.

28. Ibid., p. 290.

3. CHARACTERISTICS OF MANDE EPIC

1. Some of this section and those following dealing with epic traits appeared in more condensed form in my article in *Research in African Literatures,* (1980).

2. Greenberg (1960), P. 928.
3. Jones (1964).
4. Bird (1972) and (1976).
5. Bird (1971a), p. 211.
6. Ibid., p. 208; and (1976), p. 91.
7. Innes (1974), p. 16.
8. While the concept of formula was originated by Parry, the term "formulaic expression" appears to have been Lord's invention. See, for example, Lord (1960), p. 4, where he defines it as "a line or half line constructed on the pattern of the formula."
9. In this and the following diagram, the symbol "n" represents an infinite number of repeats of the basic pattern with different substitutions in each repeat. The "n" is placed before the repeatable pattern which is enclosed in brackets. Parentheses represent optional segments, but if two or more optional segments appear vertically in parentheses, one must be chosen. The letters (A, B, C; L, M, N; X, Y, Z) represent the segments in the formula which may be substituted. In the first formula, note that the bottom optional line occurs only when the ancestor symbolized by X has more than one offspring.
10. The term "theme" is borrowed from A. B. Lord. See his discussion of this narrative unit in Lord (1951) and in Lord (1960), pp. 68-97.
11. Only texts properly collected on tape and transcribed were compared. Three were collected by me personally and are variants composed by Ban Sumana Sisòkò from Segu, Alkaw Kònè from Muruja, and Magan Sisòkò, Fa-Digi's son, from Kita. Two were collected by Charles Bird, including the present text by Fa-Digi from Kita, and one composed by the late Kita bard Kèlè Mònsòn Jabaatè, which appears in Moser (1974).
12. Lord (1960), p. 97.
13. Motif numbers follow those listed in Thompson (1966).
14. See the Jabo narrative entitled "The Cow Tail Switch," found on pp. 85-88 of Courlander (1975). Other motifs are listed in the notes to the text.
15. See Innes (1974), p. 43, lines 59-81.
16. See Zeltner (1913), p. 9.
17. See above, pp. 13ff.
18. *Encyclopaedia Britannica,* vol. 6, p. 911.
19. Publication of these lists of traits are found in the works by these four scholars, listed in the bibliography under von Hahn (1876), Rank (1959), Raglan (1949), and De Vries (1963). For good discussions on the historical development of this scholarship, see Bascom (1957), Taylor (1964), and Dundes' notes to Raglan's article in Dundes (1965).
20. Bascom (1957), p. 111.
21. I have been conservative in estimating Son-Jara's scores on the four lists. Listed below are resumes of the four models and Son-Jara's scores on each. Descriptions followed by a star indicate possible application to Son-Jara. I am grateful to Alan Dundes for supplying me with the first three of these abbreviated lists.

von Hahn (1876)

1. Hero of illegitimate birth.
2. Mother is a princess.*
3. Father is a god.
4. Prophecy of ascendance.*
5. Hero abandoned.
6. Suckled by animals.
7. Hero raised by childless shepherd couple.
8. Hero is high-spirited.*
9. He seeks service abroad.*
10. Triumphant homecoming.*
11. Alays original persecutors and sets mother free.*
12. Founds cities.*
13. Extraordinary death.*
14. Reviled because of incest and dies young
15. Hero dies as an act of revenge by an insulted servant.
16. He murders his younger brother.

Total: 8* of 16 traits 50%.

Rank (1909)

1. Child of distinguished parents.*
2. Father is a king.*
3. Difficulty in conception.*
4. Prophecy warning against birth (e.g. parricide).
5. Hero surrendered to the water in a box.
6. Saved by animals or lowly people.
7. Suckled by female animal or humble woman.
8. Hero grows up.*
9. Hero finds distinguished parents.
10. Hero takes revenge on his father.
11. Acknowledged by people.*
12. Achieves rank and honors.*

Total: 6* of 12 traits

Raglan (1934)

1. Mother is royal virgin.*
2. Father is king.*
3. Father related to mother.
4. Unusual conception.*
5. Hero reputed to be son of god.
6. Attempt (usually by father) to kill hero.*
7. Hero spirited away.*
8. Reared by foster parents in a far country.
9. No details of childhood.
10. Goes to future kingdom.*
11. Is victor over king, giant, dragon, or wild beast.*
12. Marries a princess (often daughter of predecessor).
13. Becomes king.*
14. For a time he reigns uneventfully.*
15. He prescribes laws.*
16. Later he loses favor with gods or his subjects.
17. Driven from throne and city.
18. Meets with a mysterious death. *
19. Often at the top of a hill.
20. His children, if any, do not succeed him.*
21. His body is not buried, but nevertheless,
22. He has one or more holy sepulchres.*

Total: 13* of 22 traits = 50%

De Vries (1963)

I. A. Mother is a virgin.*
I. B. Father is a god.
I. C. Father is an animal, often the disguise of a god.
I. D. Child conceived in incest.
II. A. Birth takes place in unnatural way.*
II. B. "Unborn hero"* (one legend has the reluctant Son-Jara tricked into birth by returning from his nightly play outside his mother's womb and crawling into a mortar disguised as his mother's womb by placement of her dress over top.)

III. A. Child is exposed★ (in Son-Jara's case hexed by mother's co-wife).
III. B. Exposed child fed by animals.
III. C. Child found by shepherds.
III. D. Brought up by mythical figure.
IV. A. Hero reveals strength, courage... At early age.★
IV. B. Child slow in development (in Son-Jara's case, crippled).★
V. Hero often acquires invulnerability.★

VI. Hero fights dragon or monster.
VII. Hero wins a maiden.
VIII. Hero goes to underworld★ (in Son-Jara's case, to 9 Queens-of-Darkness)
IX. Hero is banished but returns in victory.★
X. Hero dies young or miraculously.★

Total: 10★ of 18 traits = 56%.

22. Whatever his views on epic in Africa, or perhaps in spite of them, Bowra (1966) noted the trait of ruthlessness in the (supposed) Zulu epic of Shaka. On p. 12, he states: "the poet then praises Dingan for other qualities, which are not usually regarded as heroic . . . notably for being unapproachable and ruthless." Biebuyck (1976) draws attention to the trait on pp. 25-26 of his essay, and Shoolbraid (1975) found ruthlessness as an heroic trait in Turkic epic (see p. 45).

23. Bird et al. (1974), p. vii. For a discussion on the contrast between *fa-denya* and *ba-denya* , see above, pp. 9ff.

24. Lines 3, 1243, 1276, and 1288.

25. See lines 1725ff.

26. I owe the explanation of this interpretation of this praise-name to the Malian scholar Youssouf Tata Cissé.

27. For a discussion on this concept, see Hays (1971), p. 4.

28. See above, p. 12 and Figure 3, p. 18.

29. Lines 2420ff.

30. Line 2970.

31. Lines 2410ff.

32. Johnson (1977).

33. See, for example, the explanation for the origin of Kisibugu in Guinea on lines 1885ff. Similarly, the origin of the Dabò clan is explained by folk etymology on lines 2556ff. The origin of the Wolof surname Njòp is explained in an onomatopoeic folk etymology, based on the sound of the Njòp's ancestor's head being chopped off. See lines 3070ff.

34. Greenberg (1960), p. 928.

35. De Vries (1963), pp. 260ff.

36. Ibid.

37. Ibid. De Vries notes this process in a comparison of *Der Nibelunge Not* and *Die Nibelungenlied*.

38. Ibid.

39. Hopkins (1971), p. 107.

40. Hopkins (1971), p. 101. Bird (1970), p. 157 and Innes (1974), pp. 32-33 also draw attention to the function of epic as model for clan and family relationships.

41. See bibliography under Niane (1960), (1965), Camara (1978) and (1980).

42. Niane (1965), p. 78.

43. Innes (1974), p. 2.

44. For a description of the ceremony, see Dieterlen (1957).
45. Bird (1972), p. 290.
46. Hopkins (1972) reports that the signature tune for Radio Mali's news broadcasts in 1965 was taken from one of the praise-poems to Son-Jara. When I was in Mali, the signature tune was based on a praise-poem to Tura Magan Tarawere, reflecting the change in administrations between Modibo Keyta and Musa Tarawere.
47. Innes (1974), pp. 32-33.
48. De Vries (1963), p. 152.
49. For a description of the activities and achievements of this conference, see Johnson (1975b).
50. See bibliography under Kamissoko (1975). A follow-up conference the following year resulted in the publication of Kamissoko (1977).
51. Shoolbraid also notes this characteristic for Turkic epic. See his comments on pp. 45-46 of Shoolbraid (1975).
52. Biebuyck (1976), p. 26.
53. Johnson et al. (1979), lines 569-70.
54. Zeltner (1913), pp. 6-7.
55. Biebuyck (1976), p. 29.
56. Shoolbraid (1975), p. 42.

EPILOGUE

1. Ben-Amos (1975).
2. In a paper at the annual conference of the American Folklore Society in 1982 in Minneapolis.
3. Finnegan (1970), p. 109.
4. See bibliography under Puplampo (1951).
5. In collecting epic, two tape recorders are recommended so that the bard need not be interrupted when changes of tape become necessary. Such interruptions may affect the stylistics and narrative flow of the performance.
6. See Goldstein (1967) for a description of this term and the fieldwork method it describes.
7. See Biebuyck (1972).
8. Citations of these epics are found in the references. The following chart outlines those ethnic groups which certainly merit investigation.

Country	Ethnic Group	Example	Reference(s)
Cameroon, Gabon	Fang	Akoma Mba	Awona (1965—66)
		Zwe Nguema	Biebuyck (1976)
			Ekogamve (1969)
			Kesteloot (1971)
			Labatut (n.d.)
			Ndong (1966)
			Ndong (1970)
			Ndong (1975)
			Pepper (1972)

Country	Ethnic Group	Example	Reference(s)
Cameroun Gabon	Fang	Zwe Nguema	Towo-Atangana (1975)
Cameroun	Duala	Djeky la Ndjambe	Kesteloot (1971)
The Gambia	Mandinka	Kaabu	Innes (1976)
		Filadu	Innes (1976)
Mali	Bamana	Da Mònsòn	Bâ (1966)
			Bâ and Kesteloot (1966a)
			Bâ and Kesteloot (1966b)
			Biebuyck (1976)
			Doucouré (1966)
Mali and other West African countries	Fulani	Silamaka	Bâ and Kesteloot (1968a)
		Kaïdara Poullôri	Bâ and Kesteloot (1968b)
			Biebuyck (1976)
			Frobenius (1921)
			Kesteloot (1971)
			Lacroix (1965)
			Seydou (1972)
			Vieillard (1931)
Mali	Maninka (other than Son-Jara)	Kambili	Bird et al. (1974)
			Soumaoro (1976)
		Dispersion of the Mandeka	Cissé and Diabaté (1970)
			Kesteloot et al. (1972)
			Konaté (1966)
Mali and Mauritania	Soninke	Gassier's Lute	Frohenius (1921)
		The Snake of Wagadugu	Frobenius and Fox (1937)
		Dispersion of the Kusa	Frobenius (1968)
			Jablow (1971)
			Meillassoux et al. (1967)
			Monteil (1967)
			Tautain (1895)
Nigeria	Ijaw	Ozidi	Biebuyck (1976)
			Clark (1968)
			Okaro (1957)
Rwanda	?	?	Coupez and Kamanzi (1970)
			Coupez and Kamanzi (1962)
			Papadopoullos (1963)

Country	Ethnic Group	Example	Reference(s)
Senegal	Tukulor	Samba	Labatut (nd.)
Senegal	Wolof	Madior du Cayor	Kesteloot (1971)
Tanzania	Bahaya	Kachwenyanja	Mulokozi (1980)
Zaïre	Basaimba	?	Biebuyck (1972)
Zaïre	Hamba (Kusu)	Kudukese	Biebuyck (1972)
			Biebuyck (1976)
			Jacobs (1963)
Zaïre	Jonga	?	Biebuyck (1972)
Zaïre	Kuba (Bushong)	Nshoong Atoot	Jacobs and Vansina (1956)
			Kesteloot (1971)
Zaïre	Langa	?	Biebuyck (1972)
Zaïre	Lega (Rega)	Mubila	Biebuyck (1953)
		Kiguma	Biebuyck (1972)
			Biebuyck (1976)
			N'Sanda (n.d.)
Zaïre	Luba-Kasai	Kasala	Biebuyck (1972)
			Faïk-Nzuji Madiya (1974)
			Faïk-Nzuji Madiya (1975)
			Mufutu (1965)
Zaïre	Mbole	Lofokefoke	Biebuyck (1972)
			Biebuyck (1976)
			Jacobs (1961)
Zaïre	Mongo (Nkundo)	Lianja	Biebuyck (1972)
			Biebuyck (1976)
			Boelaert (1932)
			Boelaert (1949)
			Boelaert (1957)
			Boelaert (1958)
			Rop (1956)
			Rop (1958)
			Rop (1959a)
			Rop (1959b)
			Rop (1964)
Zaïre	Nkutshu	?	Biebuyck (1972)
Zaïre	Nyanga	Mwindo	Biebuyck (1972)
			Biebuyck (1976)
			Biebuyck and Mateene (1971)
			Biebuyck (1978)
Zaïre	Tetela	?	Biebuyck (1972)

REFERENCES

Arnoldi, Mary Jo, *Bamana and Bozo Puppetry of the Segu Region Youth Societies* (Lafayette: Department of Creative Arts, Purdue University, 1977).

————, "Bamana Puppetry: The Relationship Between Art and Ideology in Theatre," unpublished conference paper from S.S.R.C. Conference on the Verbal and Visual Arts in Africa.

————, "Segou Regional Puppet Theatre," *The Puppetry Journal* 32:4 (Jan.-Feb., 1981): 14-19.

Atkins, Guy (ed.), *Manding Art and Civilisation* (London: Studio International, 1972).

Awona, Stanislas, "La guerre d'Akoma Mba contre Mama (épopée du Mvet)," *Abbia* 9/10 and 12/13 (1965 and 1966): 180-213; 190-209.

Bâ, Amadou Hampâté, "Monzon and the King of Kore," *Présence Africaine* 30:58 (1966): 95-124.

Bâ, Amadou Hampâté, and L. Kesteloot, "Da Monzon et Karta Thiéma," *Abbia* 14/15 (1966a): 179-205.

————, "Une épopée malienne: Da Monzon de Ségou," *Abbia:* 14/15 (1966b): 171-205.

————, "Une épopée peule: Silamaka," *L'Homme* 8:1 (1968a): 5-36.

————, "Les épopées de l'Ouest africaine," *Abbia* 14/15 (1966c): 165-69.

————, *Kaïdara: Réit initiatique peul* (Paris: Julliard, 1968b).

Bascom, William, "The Myth-Ritual Theory," *Journal of American Folklore* 70:2 (1957): 103-14.

Ben-Amos, Dan, "Folklore in African Society," *Research in African Literatures* 6:2 (1975): 165-98.

Biebuyck, Daniel, "The African Heroic Epic," *Journal of the Folklore Institute* 13:1 (1976): 5-36.

————, "The Epic as a Genre in Kongo Oral Literature," in *African Folklore,* ed. Richard Dorson (Garden City: Doubleday, 1972): 257-73.

————, *Hero and Chief Epic Literature from the Banyanga, Zaïre Republic* (Berkeley: University of California Press, 1978).

————, "Mubila, een epos der Balega," *Band* 12 (1953): 68-74.

Biebuyck, Daniel, and Kahombo Mateene, "L'Épopée (Kárisi) de la jeune fille Kahindo Ngarya," in their *Anthologie de la Littérature Orale Nyanga* (Brussels: Académie Royale des Sciences d'Outre Mer, 1970): 24-47.

————, *The Mwindo Epic from the Banyanga (Congo Republic)* (Berkeley: University of California Press, 1971).

Bird, Charles S., "Aspects of Bambara Syntax," (Ph.D. dissertation at the University of California at Los Angeles, 1966).

————, "Aspects of Prosody in West African Poetry," in *Current Trends in Stylistics,* ed. Braj B. Kachru and Herbert F. W. Stahlke (Edmonton: Linguistic Research, Ltd., 1971a): 207-15.

Bird, Charles S., "The Development of Mandekan (Manding): A Study of the Role of Extra-linguistic Factors in Linguistic Change," in *Language and History in Africa,* ed. David Dalby (London: Cass, 1970): 146-59.

______, "Heroic Songs of the Mande Hunters," in *African Folklore,* ed. Richard Dorson (Garden City: Doubleday, 1972): 275-93.

______, "Oral Art in the Mande," in *Papers on the Manding,* ed. Carleton T. Hodge (Bloomington: Indiana University Press and the Research Center for the Language Sciences, 1971b): 15-26.

______, "Poetry in the Mande: Its Form and Meaning," *Poetics* 5 (1976): 89-100.

Bird, Charles S., and Martha Kendall, "The Mande Hero," in *Explorations in African Systems of Thought,* eds. Ivan Karp and Charles S. Bird (Bloomington: Indiana University Press, 1980): 13-26.

Bird, Charles S., Mamadou Koita, and Bourama Soumaoro, *The Songs of Seydou Camara: Vol. 1: Kambili* (Bloomington, Indiana: African Studies Center, 1974).

Boelaert, E., *Lianja-Verhalan 1: Ekofo-versie* (Tervuren: Musée Royale de Congo Beige, 1957).

______, *Lianja-Verhalan, II: de Voorounders van Lianja* (Tervuren: Musée Royale de Congo Belge, 1958).

______, *Nsong'a Lianja: L'épopée nationale des Nkundo* (Antwerp: De Sikkel, 1949). [Note: This work was also published in *Aequatoria* 12:1 (Coquilhatville, Mission Catholique) in 1949.]

______, "Nsong'a Lianja, het groote epos des Nkundo-Mongo," *Congo* 1 (1932): 43-70.

Bowra, C.M., *Heroic Poetry* (London: Macmillan, 1966).

Brink, James T., "Bamana Kore-tlon Theater," *African Arts* 10:4 (July, 1977): 36-37; 61-65; 87.

______, "Communicating Ideology in Bamana Rural Theater Performance," *Research in African Literatures* 9:3 (Winter, 1978): 382-94.

______, "Time Consciousness and Growing Up in Bamana Folk Drama," *Journal of American Folklore* 95:378 (1982): 415-34.

Camera, Laye, *The Guardian of the Word: Kouma Lafôlô Kouma* (Glasgow: Fontana, 1980).

______, *Le Maître de la Parôle: Kouma Lafôlô Kouma* (Paris: Librarie Plon, 1978).

Cissé, Diango, and Massa Diabaté, *La dispersion des Mandeka* (Bamako: Editions Populaires, 1970).

Cissé, Youssouf, "Notes sur les sociétés de chasseurs Malinké," *Journal de Ia Société des Africanistes* 34:1 (1964): 175-226.

______, "Signes graphiques représentations concepts, et tests relatifs à la personne chez les Malinké et les Bambara du Mali," *Colloques Internationaux du Centre Nationale de Ia Recherches Scientifiques* 544 (1974?): 131-79.

Clark, J.P., "The Ozidi Saga," *Black Orpheus* 2:2 (1968): 18-24.

Coupez A., and Th. Kamanzi, *Littérature de cour au Rwanda* (London: Oxford at the Clarendon Press, 1970).

______, *Récis historiques Rwanda* (Tervuren: Musée Royale de l'Afrique Centrale, 1962).

Courlander, Harold (ed.), *A Treasury of African Folklore* (New York: Crown Pubs., 1975).

Darbo, Seni, *A Griot's Self-Portrait: The Origins and Role of the Griot in Mandinka Society as Seen from Stories Told by Gambian Griots* (Banjul: Gambian Cultural Archives, 1976).

Delafosse, Maurice, *Haut-Sénégal-Niger: Tome II. L'Histoire* (Paris: Larose, 1912). Reprinted in *Nouvelle édition* (Paris: G.-P. Maisoneuve et Larose, 1972).

Diabaté, Massa Makan, *Janjon et autres chants populaires du Mali* (Paris: Présence Africaine, 1970a).

______, Kala Jata (Bamako: Éditions Populaires, 1970b).

Dieterlen, Germaine (trans. Katia Wolf), *An Essay on the Religion of the Bambara* (New Haven: Human Relations Area Files, 1960). [This work was first published in French in 1951.]

Dieterlen, Germaine, "The Mande Creation Myth," *Africa* 27:1 (1957): 124-38.

______, "Mythe et organisation sociale au Soudan français, *Journal de la Société des Africanistes* 25:1/2 (1955): 39-76.

Dieterlen, Germaine, and Youssouf Cissé, *Les Fondements de la société d'initiation du Komo,* in *Cahiers de l'Homme, New Series* 10 (1972).

Doucouré, Amadou, "Défi de Déisse-Koro, roi du Kaarta, à Da Monzon, roi de Ségou," *France-Eurafrique* 171 (1966): 43-45.

Dundes, Alan, *The Study of Folklore* (Englewood Cliffs, New Jersey: Prentice-Hall, 1965).

Dupree, Louis, "The Retreat of the British Army from Kabul to Jalalabad in 1842: History and Folklore," *Journal of the Folklore Institute* 4:1 (1967): 50-74.

Ekogamve, Elie, "La Littérature orale des Fang," *African Arts* 2 (1969): 14-19; 77-78.

Encyclopaedia Britannica, The New: 15th Edition (Chicago: Encyclopedia Britannica, 1985).

Encyclopaedia of Islam: New Edition, The (London and Leiden: Luzac and E.J. Brill, 1960).

Études Maliennes 12, (Bamako: Institut des Sciences Humaines du Mali, 1975).

Faïk-Nzuji Madiya, C., *Kasala: Chant Héroïque Luba* (Lumbashi, Zaïre: Presses Universitaires du Zaïre, 1974).

______, "Le Kasala et ses traits essentials dans la littérature orale traditionelle Luba," *Cahiers d'Études Africaines* 15:59 (1975): 457-80.

Finnegan, Ruth, *Oral Literature in Africa* (London: Oxford at the Clarendon Press, 1970).

Frobenius, Leo, "Das Dausi," in his *Atlantis: Volksmärchen und Volksdichtungen Afrikas, Band VI: Spielmannsgeschichten der Sahel* (Jena: Eugen Dieterichs, 1921): 49-90.

______, "The Fight with the Dragon," in his *The Voice of Africa,* vol. 2 (New York: Benjamin Blom, 1968): 467-94. [This work was first published in 1913.]

______, "Sira Maga," in his *Atlantis: Volksmärchen und Volksdichtungen Afrikas, Band VI: Spielmannsgeschichten der Sahel* (Jena: Eugen Dieterichs, 1921): 165-71.

Frobenius, Leo, and Douglas Fox, "Soninke Legends," in their *African Genesis* (New York: Stackpole Sons, 1937): 97-133.

Goldstein, Kenneth S., "The Induced Natural Context: An Ethnographic Folklore Field Technique," in *Essays on the Verbal and Visual Arts,* ed. June Helm (Seattle, Washington: University of Washington Press, 1967): 1–6.

Greenberg, Joseph H., *The Languages of Africa* (Bloomington: Indiana University Press for the Research Center for the Language Sciences, 1970).

__________, "A Survey of African Prosodic Systems," in *Culture in History,* ed. S. Diamond (New York: Columbia University Press for Brandeis University, 1960): 925–50.

Griaule, Marcel, "The Mother's Brother in the Western Sudan," in *French Perspectives in African Studies,* ed. P. Alexandre (London: Oxford University Press, 1973): 11–25.

Griaule, Marcel, and Germaine Dieterlen, "Signes graphiques soudanais," *L'Homme: Cahiers d'Ethnologie, de Géographie et de Linguistique* 3 [published as] *Actualités Scientifiques et Industrielles* 1158 (Paris: Hermann et Cie, 1951).

Hahn, Johann Georg von, *Sagwissenschaftliche Studien* (Jena, Germany: F. Mauke [E. Schenk], 1876).

Hays, Peter L., *The Limping Hero: Grotesque in Literature* (New York: New York University Press, 1971).

Henry, Fr. Joseph (trans. Anne Coleman), *The Soul of an African People: The Bambara: Their Psychic, Ethical, Religious, and Social Life* (New Haven: Human Relations Area Files, 1960). [This work was first published in French in 1910.]

Hopkins, Nicholas S., "Mandinka Social Organization," in *Papers on the Manding,* ed. Carleton T. Hodge (Bloomington: Indiana University Press for the Research Center for the Language Sciences, 1971): 99–128.

__________, *Popular Government in an African Town: Kita, Mali* (Chicago: University of Chicago Press, 1972).

Hopkins, J. F. P., and N. Levtzion, eds., *Corpus of Early Arabic Sources for West African History* (Cambridge: Cambridge University Press, 1981).

Imperato, P. J., "The Dance of the Tyi Wara," *African Arts* 4:1 (1970): 8–13; 71–80.

Innes, Gordon, "Stability and Change in Griots' Narration," *African Language Studies* 14 (1973): 105–18.

Innes, Gordon, *Kaabu and Fuladu: Historical Narratives of the Gambian Mandinka* (London: School of Oriental and African Studies, University of London, 1976).

__________, (ed., trans.), *Sunjata: Three Mandinka Versions* (London: School of Oriental and African Studies, University of London, 1974).

Jablow, Alta, *Gassire's Lute: A West African Epic* (New York: E. P. Dutton & Co., 1971)

Jackson, Michael, "Prevented Successions: A Commentary upon a Kuranko Narrative," in *Fantasy and Symbol,* ed. R. H. Hook (London: Academic Press, 1979): 95–131.

Jacobs, John, "Het epos van Kudukese: de 'Culture Hero' van de Hamba," *Africa-Tervuren* 9:2 (1963): 33–36.

__________, "Le réit épique de Lofokefoke, le héros des Mbole (Bambuli)," *Aequatoria* 24:3 (1961): 81–92.

Jacobs, John, and Jan Vansina, "Nʃɔɔŋ átɔɔt: Het koninklijk epos der Bushong," *Kongo-Oversee* 22 (1956): 1–39.

Johnson, John William, "Etiological Legends Based on Folk Etymologies of Manding Surnames," *Folklore Forum* 9:3/4 (Bloomington: Forum Society, 1975a): 107-14.

———, "On the Heroic Age and Other Primitive Theses," in *Folklorica: Festschrift for Felix J. Oinas,* ed. Egla Žygas and Peter Voorheis (Bloomington: Research Institute for Inner Asian Studies, 1982): 121-38.

———, "SCOA Conference on Oral Traditions," *Research in African Literatures* 6:2 (1975b): 253-54.

———, "Yes, Virginia, There is an Epic in Africa," *Research in African Literatures* 11:3 (1980): 308-26.

Johnson, John William, Cheick Oumar Mara, Ibrabim Kalilou Tèra, Checkna Mohamed Singaré, *The Epic of Sun-Jata According to Magan Sisòkò* (Bloomington, Indiana: Folklore Publications Group, 1979).

Jones, A.M., "African Metrical Lyrics," *African Language Studies* 5 (1964): 52-63.

Kamissoko, Wa (trans. and ed., Youssouf Tata Cissé), *L'Empire du Mali* (Paris: Fondation SCOA pour la Recherche Scientifique en Afrique Noire, 1975).

———, (trans. and ed., Youssouf Tata Cissé), *L'Empire du Mali (Suite)* (Paris: Fondation SCOA pour Ia Recherche Scientifique en Afrique Noire, 1977).

Kesteloot, Lilyan, *L'Épopée traditionelle* (Paris: Fernand Nathan, 1971).

———, "The West African Epics," *Présence Africaine* 30:58 (1966): 197-202.

Kesteloot, Lilyan, et al., trans., ed., *Da Monzon de Ségou: épopée bambara,* 4 vols. (Paris: Fernand Nathan, 1972).

Kisala, Piliwe, "Lubango Nkundungulu: A Kaonde Epic," *Jewel of Africa* 2:3/4 (1969): 9-16.

Konaté, M., "Une épopée malienne: Da Monzon de Ségou," *Abbia* 14/15 (1966): 171-78.

Labatut, S. and R. (eds.), *Épopées Africaines: morceaux choisis* (Youndé, Republic of Cameroon: Ministry of Education, n.d.).

Lacroix, Pierre-Francie, *Poésie peule de l'Adamawa,* 2 vols. (Paris: Julliard, 1965).

Levtzion, Nehemia, *Ancient Ghana and Mali* (London: Methuen, 1973).

———, "The Thirteenth- and Fourteenth-Century Kings of Mali," *Journal of African History* 4:31 (1963): 341-53.

Lord, Albert B., "Composition by Theme in Homer and Southslavic Epos," *Transactions and Proceedings of the American Philological Association* 82 (1951): 71-80.

———, *The Singer of Tales* (Cambridge, Massachusetts: Harvard University Press, 1960).

McNaughton, Patrick, "Nyamakalaw: The Mande Bards and Blacksmiths," unpublished conference paper from S.S.R.C. Conference on the Verbal and Visual Arts in Africa.

Meillassoux, Claude, *Urbanization of an African Community: Voluntary Associations in Bamako* (Seattle: University of Washington Press, 1968).

Meillassoux, Claude, Lassana Doucouré, and Diaowe Simagha, *Légende de la Dispersion des Kusa (Épopée Soninke)* (Dakar: Institut Fondamental d'Afrique Noire, 1967).

Miller, Joseph C., "Introduction: Listening for the African Past," in his *The African Past Speaks* (Folkestone: Dawson, 1980): 1-59.

Miller, Joseph C., "Preface," in his *The African Past Speaks* (Folkestone: Dawson, 1980): ix-xii.

Monteil, Charles, "Les Empires du Mali: étude d'histoire et de sociologie soudanaise," *Bulletin du Comité d'Études Historiques et Scientifiques de l'Afrique Occidentale Française* 12: 3-4 (1929). Republished *in toto* by: (Paris: G.-P. Maisonneuve et Larose, 1968).

Monteil, Vincent, "La légende de Wagadou: Texte Soninke de Malamine Tandyan," *Bulletin de l'Institut Fondamental Afrique Noire* 29, set. B (1967): 134-49.

Moser, Rex, *Foregrounding in the Sunjata, The Mande Epic* (Bloomington, Indiana: Ph.D. dissertation in linguistics, 1974).

Mufuta, Patrice, *Le chant Kasàlà des Luba* (Paris: Julliard, 1965).

Mulokozi, Mugyabuso, *Research in the Nanga Epics of the Bahaya: Final Report* (Dar es Salaam: Institute of Ki-Swahili Research, University of Dar es Salaam, 1980).

N'Diayé, Bokar, *Les Castes au Mali* (Bamako: Éditions Populaires, 1970).

Ndong, Philippe Ndoutoume, "Le Mvett," *Présence Africa me* 59 (1966): 57-76.

Ndong, Tsira Ndoutoume, *Le Mvett* (Paris: Présence Africaine, 1970).

————, *Le Mvett, Livre II* (Paris: Présence Africaine, 1975).

Niane, Djibril Tamsir, *Soundjata, ou l'épopée mandinque* (Paris: Présence Africaine, 1960).

————, (trans. G. D. Pickett), *Sundiata: An Epic of Old Mali* (London: Longman, 1965).

N'Sanda, J. B., "Épopée Kiguma: Essai d'étude d'un genre littéraire Lega," (Kinshasa: PhD. dissertation at Lovanium University, n.d.).

Okaro, Gabriel, "Ogboingba: The Ijaw Creation Myth," *Black Orpheus* I (1957): 9-17.

Pageard, Robert, "Soundiata Keita and the Oral Tradition," Paris, *Présence Africaine* (English Edition), viii/36 (1961): 53-72.

Papadopoullos, T., *Poésie dynastique du Ruanda et épopée acritique* (Paris: Société d'Edition des Belles Lettres, 1963).

Paques, Viviana, (trans. Thomas Turner,) *The Bambara* (New Haven: Human Relations Area Files, 1959). [This work was first published in French in 1954.]

Pepper, H., (réédité par P. et P. De Wolf), *Un Mvet de Zwe Nguéma: Chant épique Fang* (Paris: Librairie Armand Colin, 1972).

Puplampu, D. A., "The National Epic of the Adangme," *African Affairs* 50 (1951): 236-41.

Raglan, Lord Fitz Roy Richard, Baron of Somerset, *The Hero: A Study in Tradition, Myth, and Drama* (London: Watts, 1949). [This work was first published in 1936.]

Rank, Otto, *The Myth of the Birth of the Hero* (New York: Vintage, 1959). [This work was first published by F. Deuticke in Leipzig and Vienna in 1909 as *Der Mythus von der Geburt des Helden.*]

Rop, Albert Josef de, *De Gesproken Woordkunst van de Nkundó* (Tervuren: Musée du Congo Belge, 1956).

————, "L'épopée de Nkundo: l'original et la copie," *Kongo-Oversee* 24 (1958): 170-78.

————, "Het epos van de Nkundo Mongo," *Band* 18 (1959a).

————, *Lianja: l'épopée des Mongo* (Brussels: Academie Royale des SciencesD'Outre-Mer, 1964).

Rop, Albert Josef de, "Lianja-Verhalan," *Band* 18 (1959b): 149-50.

Sankoré 4 (Bamako: Institut des Sciences Humaines du Mali, 1974).

Seydou, Christiane, *Silamâka & Poullôri* (Paris: Librairie Armand Colin, 1972).

Shoolbraid, G. M. H., *The Oral Epic of Siberia and Central Asia* (Bloomington, Indiana: Indiana University Press for the Research Center for Language Sciences, 1975).

Soumaoro, Bourama, et al. (transcr.), *Seyidu Kamara ka Donkiliw: Kambili* (Bloomington: African Studies Center, 1976).

Tautain, D. L., "Légendes et traditions des Soninkes, relatives a l'empire de Ghanata," *Bulletin de la Géographie Historique et Descriptique* (Paris, 1895).

Tauxier, Louis, *La religion bambara* (Paris: Librairie Orientaliste Paul Geuthner, 1927).

Taylor, Archer, "The Biographical Pattern in Traditional Narrative," *Journal of the Folklore Institute* 1:1/2 (1964): 114-29.

Thompson, Stith, *Motif Index of Folk-Literature,* 6 vols. (Bloomington, Indiana: Indiana University Press, 1966).

Tonkin, Elizabeth, "Steps to the Redefinition of Oral History: Examples from Africa," *Social History* 7:3 (October, 1982): 329-35.

Towo-Atangana, G., "Le *Mvet,* genre majeur de la littérature orale des populations pahouines (Bulu, Béti, Fang-Ntumu)," *Abbia* 9/10 (1965): 171-72.

Traoré, D., "Makanta Djigui, fondateur de la magie soudanaise," *Notes Africaines* 35 (1947): 23-25.

Travélé, Moussa, "Le Komo ou Koma," *Outre-Mer: Revue Générale de Colonisation* 1:2 (1929): 127-50.

Trimingham, J. Spencer, *A History of Islam in West Africa* (London: Oxford University Press, 1970).

Utley, Francis Lea, "Lincoln Wasn't There," in *CEA Chap Book* (Washington, D.C.: College English Association, 1965).

Vansina, Jan, Oral *Tradition: A Study in Historical Methodology* (London: Routledge and Kegan Paul, 1965).

Vieillard, G., "Récits peuls du Macina et du Kounari," *Bulletin du Comité d'Études Historiques et Scientiflques de l'Afrique Occidentale Française* 14 (Gorée: Gouvernement Général de l'Afrique Occidentale Française, 1931).

Vries, Jan de, "The Pattern of an Heroic Life," in his *Heroic Song and Heroic Legend* (London: Oxford University Press, 1963).

Yoshida, Atsuhiko, "Epic," *The New Encyclopaedia Britannica: Macropaedia,* vol. 6, 15th ed. (Chicago: Encyclopaedia Britannica, 1974): 906-11.

Zahan, Dominique, *The Bambara* (Leiden: E.J. Brill, 1974).

______, *Sociétés d'initiation bambara: Le N'domo, le Kore* (Paris and The Hague: Mouton, 1960).

Zeltner, Frantz de, "La légende de Soundiata," in his *Contes du Sénégal et du Niger* (Paris: Ernest Leroux, 1913): 1-36.

Jeli Fa-Digi Sisòkò and his Wives

Jeli Fa-Digi Sisòkò with his Wives and his Naamunaamuna

Priest Standing before the Sacred Hut in Kangaba

Kulubali Priest of Sumamuru's Fetish (Nyanan) in Kulu-Kòrò

Nyanan: Fetish and Sacrificial Implements

PART TWO

THE TEXT

Introduction

DATA ON THE BARD, FA-DIGI SISÒKÒ

I gathered information about Fa-Digi Sisòkò primarily from his son Magan whom I interviewed in 1974. Fa-Digi Sisòkò was a formal apprentice to his maternal uncle, a learning relationship which I am told is common among Mandekan-speaking peoples. Both Fa-Digi and his maternal uncle began their careers as agricultural bards. The practice is common among bards, and the tradition is fairly widespread throughout Africa. I have also observed it in the Democratic Republic of Somalia, although bards are not professionals there, the position being filled by an elder skilled in the art of poetry.

Among many African farming groups, work in the fields is done collectively. Sometimes the workers are members of the same age-set. The entire group works on one plot at a time and until all of the fields are either sown or harvested. It is the responsibility of the host of the plot being worked to provide food and drink for the workers. The host often provides for a person specialized in singing or playing a musical instrument. In Mali this position is filled by a professional bard, who is further specialized in folklore relevant to agricultural work. For example, he may know praise-poems concerning respected farmers of the past. The bard's singing in the fields fulfills at least two functions.

First, the singer (or player) may set the tempo and rhythm of the work. And second, he provides inspiring entertainment, which might lighten the work load of the farmers. According to Magan, it is this type of performance in which his father excels.

Magan reported that his father had attended at least one reroofing ceremony of the sacred hut in Kaaba (Kangaba). According to some Mande traditions, Kaaba is considered the mythical center of the world and is certainly the cultural center of the Mandekan-speaking world. This ceremony is performed only once every seven years and attracts Mande speakers, many of them bards, from all over West Africa. One of the ceremony's highlights is the reciting of the epic of

Son-Jara by the Jahaatè bards from neighboring Kela. Fa-Digi's attendance at one of these recitals in Kaaba was offered as a qualification to the authenticity of this text, which can be considered a Kita regional variant because a comparison of his text with one collected in Kela and two collected in Kita has been possible.

DATA ON THE LANGUAGE AND TRANSCRIPTION

Fa-Digi Sisòkò's text is in the Maninka dialect peculiar to the area around Kita. Charles S. Bird[1] considers this dialect significantly different from the Mandekan spoken in extreme southern Mali and Guinea and from the Mandinka of the Gambia. Differences lie mostly in the form of function words (e.g., articles, prepositions) and in some sound and tone shifting, but not in the basic grammatical structures. Joseph Greenberg[2] places Maninka and the other Mande languages such as Bamana (Bambara) and Jula (Dyoula) in the Niger-Congo branch of the Congo-Kordofanian language family.

The transcription used for this text is as close to the original sung epic as possible. The transcriber was instructed to write down exactly what he heard, and the spelling has been edited only to conform to that developed by the Centre d'Alphabétisation (see below). The forms specific to Fa-Digi's dialect, however, have not been changed. I have no objection to the efforts now going on in Mali to standardize the writing system.[3] On the other hand, a transcription of Fa-Digi's own dialect may be of use to linguists and other interested persons. Exact transcription of the bard's words illustrates the interesting process of dialect mixture in oral texts.[4] Although the overwhelming majority of any text will follow the dialect of the bard, forms from other dialects are sometimes mixed into a text. This is particularly common in praise-poems and praise-names, many of which are from Soninke and Khasonke. Bards learning texts, especially when they travel to areas where different dialects are spoken, sometimes maintain the original form of a praise-name they happen to hear. Often they do not hear a praise-name or understand it clearly, especially when chance does not permit a repetition of the form. A bard sometimes learns a praise-name from another bard, who himself does not know its meaning and who may be mispronouncing the original form. Such

---

1. Bird (1966): map, p. 3. Citations quoted in this introduction may be found in the references beginning on page 76.
2. Greenberg (1970), p. 8.
3. See for example, *Sankoré* 4 and *Études Maliennes* 12.
4. See also Charles S. Bird, (1971a), pp. 146-59.

mispronunciation by some bards, and the compounding of the problem by the remispronunciation by other bards, leads to reinterpretation of the praise-name, thus resulting in a new form. Variation of praise-names results, and often a new etiological legend evolves to explain the new form.[5] The process leads to a rich supply of variations, but can be a headache to research and translate. Fa-Digi's actual words were transcribed without any knowledgeable change on our part. The English, then, represents a direct translation of the bard's taped performance.

Concerning the stylistics of the transcription, indentation and italics are important to note, for they separate on printed page what rhythm accomplishes orally: the three modes of poetry. The unindented line is the narrative mode; the indentation denotes praise-proverb mode; and the italicized and indented texts represent the song mode. The responses of the naamu-sayer (see note 15, p. 69) occur in parentheses and to the far right of the bard's poetic lines. The translation is liberal, but footnotes explain any deviation from the original. Errors by the bard, common in an oral text of this length, are corrected in the translation for ease of understanding, and accounted for in the footnotes.

The footnotes are of two types. Linguistic explanations are necessary when problems arise concerning the translation. Notes explaining cultural problems and plotline are also included. Readers not interested in the language and translation problems may ignore the notes dealing with these subjects. It is hoped that all obscurities are accounted for. Footnote numbers, which would number in the hundreds and which might distract from the text, are not used. In their place, line numbers of the poem are given with each note.

DATA ON THE ASSISTANTS

Four assistants contributed most of the transcription, translation, and annotation of this text. I am indebted to these men. Short biographies explaining their qualifications follow.

Assigned to assist me by the Institut des Sciences Humaines du Mali, Cheick Oumar Mara was my chief assistant for collection and transcription. Mara was born in Bamako in 1947 of a Maninka father and a Bamana mother. He has a Maninka wife from Kita, and they have three children.

Mara attended Koranic school for six years as a child, and at the same time began attending l'École Primaire in Burem, which is in the

5. Along this line, see Johnson (1975a): 107-14.

Circle of Gao. He next completed the course at Lycée Askia Mohamed in Bamako and went on to the UNESCO Center in Jos, Nigeria, for a specialized course in museology. Mara returned to work at the Institut des Sciences Humaines du Mali.

Working at the Institut des Sciences Humaines du Mali, Mara assisted in a number of activities for which he is now well qualified. He was the official guide for all visiting scholars, a duty he shared with other Institut members when his work load was especially heavy. He is a competent photographer and does most of the photographic work needed by the Institut. He transcribes oral texts from Maninka, Bamana, Songhoy, French, and Fulani (Peul) as a part of his regular duties. He is fluent in the first four languages mentioned above, and in English. He has also studied German, Latin, and Greek and spoke Wolof as a child. His work with the museum *objets d'art* necessitated his learning about the preservation and care of art objects. Mara has assisted in archaeological excavations in the Dogon region of Mali and in the area around Gao.

Mara was at one time a national football (soccer) player and traveled with his team to Senegal, Upper Volta, Ivory Coast, Algeria, Guinea, Ghana, Sierra Leone, and Niger. He organized the Malian art exhibitions for the Algiers Festival in 1969 and for another similar festival in Tunis in 1973.

His personal interests have led him into private research. He has investigated the Bamana masks of the Segu region, and the Tukolor commerce of the nineteenth century of the same area. The beliefs and practices of Islam in the Kita region also interest him, and he has studied the blacksmith castes of Mali, as well as Fulani epic poetry. Mara has made tape recordings of hunters' bard poetry. Finally, he has studied the Amba and Gende areas of Dogon country.

Born on 24 October 1946, in San, Ibrahim Kalilou Tèra counts several prominent ancestors in his genealogy, including several *q aḍi* (Moslem judges) of the ancient city of Jenne. Although fluent in Bamana, Maninka, and French, and a good speaker of English, Tèra's ethnic affiliation is to the Maraka. Marakas in other parts of Mali call themselves Soninke. He also speaks some Songhoy and writes Arabic.

Beginning his education in a Koranic school taught by his own father, he studied the Koran for ten years, also attending an école primaire from 1954 to 1961. In 1962 he began a *cours normal* at Dire, near Timbuktu and finished his studies in 1965. Next he spent two years in the École Normale Secondaire in Bamako before going to teach French for three years at the École Fondamentale in Mopti. In 1970 Tèra entered the École Normale Supérieure in Bamako, writing his *mémoires* (roughly equivalent to the M.A. thesis in the United States) on an oral epic, which he entitled *Kòrè Duga Kòrò,* about a king of San who unsuccessfully challenged the illustrious king of Segu, Da Mònsòn Jaara. Since 1974 Tèra has taught at the Lycée de Badalabugu in Bamako. At the present time he is teaching French in another *lycée* in Bamako while doing a doctoral course in the linguistics section of the Centre Pédagogique Supérieur in the same city.

Tèra's work on the epic of Duga Kòrò and his weekly broadcasts over Radio Mali on cultural and literary subjects made him invaluable as an assistant in translation and annotation. His own text will be published in Bamako with French translation by the Ministry of Information.

Checkna Mohamed Singaré was born in Kulu-Kòrò (Kulikoro) on 26 December 1946. He attended Koranic school for one year before entering the École Française in Kulu-Kòrò in 1952. In 1953 he went to the École Daniel Brothier in Thies, Senegal, where he finished his primary education in 1959. Returning to Mali, he entered the Lycée Technique in Bamako, studying a year before moving to finish his studies at Lycée Askia Mohamed in 1968. He attended the École Normale Supérieure from 1968 to 1972, writing his *mémoires* on the problem of text translation from Bamana (and other languages in Mali) into French. He went on to study for an advanced degree at Tuskegee Institute in Alabama.

Checkna is fluent in Bamana, Wolof, French, and English, and has studied German, Latin, and Greek. His command of English made him especially valuable for translation work with me. He provided many useful annotations, especially those concerning Sumamuru (Son-Jara's chief adversary) and his fetish cult in Kulu-Kòrò today. Checkna has worked with other American scholars on subjects in anthropology (a study of the blacksmith castes in Mali) and linguistics (a work on Bamana/Maninka to English dictionary). After working as a guide for the Malian tourist bureau, Checkna went to teach French at the Cours Bouyagi Fadiga in Bamako. He directed the language training program for the U.S. Peace Corps and spent the summer of 1976 in a teacher training course at San Francisco State University, which he combined with a U.S. Information Agency tour of the United States.

Bourama Soumaoro was born in 1951 in the town of Kabaya in southern Mali. His education includes both traditional and classroom instruction. His traditional education consisted of training in the *ndomo* and *komo* initiation societies of Maninka and Bamana cultures, and he is now qualified as an initiator (*komo-tigi*) in the latter. The training gave him extensive knowledge of the traditions and history of his own society, and his status as *komo-tigi* testifies to the extent to which he has mastered the data.

Soumaoro's classroom education began at the Catholic mission school in Goualala (region of Yanfolila), which he attended from 1958 to 1965 and again from 1967 to 1970. From 1965 to 1967 he studied at the Centre Professionnel de Niarela in Bamako. Bourama finished his Malian education at the Lycée Prosper Camara, also in Bamako, and served as a research assistant in the Department of Linguistics at Indiana University where be was an undergraduate student.

Bourama's knowledge of French, English, and his own languages of Maninka and Bamana, has assisted him in his travels and professional career. His travels include trips in all major parts of southern Mali, as well as journeys to Senegal, the Ivory Coast, Liberia, Guinea, and the United States. His professional career as a researcher began in 1971 at the Affaires Sociales in Bamako. In 1972, and for some years beginning in 1975, he worked with Charles Bird in a variety of areas, including research into the linguistics and folklore of the Maninka and Bamana cultures. The first, under the direction of André La Plante, was at the Centre de Recherches pour la Développement Internationale. The second was at the Institut de Recherches de la Médicine Traditionnelle et de la Pharmacopie Malienne, under the direction of Dr. Mamadou Koumaré. This work and his present research has led to five publications.

These four men were especially qualified to assist me in the translation of this and other texts, and I am deeply indebted to them for their untiring assistance, both in Mali and later in the United States. Charles S. Bird collaborated on the translation. Bird's career accomplishments are well known and need no elucidation here.

CIRCUMSTANCES OF THE RECORDING

The present text was collected by Charles S. Bird of the Linguistics Department at Indiana University. Assisting him from the Institut des Sciences Humaines du Mali was Massa Makan Diabaté (Jabaatè), who has subsequently published two texts from another well-known Kita bard, Kèlè Mònsòn Jabaatè, and an award-winning collection of praise-poems.[6]

Arriving in Kita, Bird and Massa Makan arranged to bring Fa-Digi to that town the following day by land rover. The performance began at about 3:00 p.m. with Bird and Diabaté recording on a

---

6. These books are listed in the references under Diabaté (1970a) and (1970b), and Cissé and Diabaté (1970).

Nagra tape recorder, and Fa-Digi being accompanied on a guitar by his *naamunaamuna*, a man named Bemba. The *naamunaamuna*, sometimes the bard's apprentice, shouts out *naamu* or other reinforcing words and phrases after most lines of the poem. *Naamu* is the Mandekan pronunciation of the Arabic word *na'am*, "yes." The performance ended at about 7:00 p.m. the same evening.

RÉSUMÉ OF THE PLOT

The complex and detailed plot of the epic requires a résumé of the themes. The following description is designed for use with the accompanying CD and includes disc track, theme, and line numbers, followed by a description of the content of the theme.

CD ONE
EPISODE I: Prologue

Tr.	Th.	Ln.	
1	1	1	Prologue: Praise-poem.
2	2	56	Satan cast out of Paradise.
3	3	126	God places Adam on the earth.
4	4	154	Genealogy of Adam's family.

EPISODE II: Mecca

5	5	160	Genealogy of Noah's family.
6	6	175	Genealogy of Jòn Bilali's family.
7	7	182	Founding of the Manden and populating of its regions; composition of its clan families.
8	8	243	Genealogy of the three Simbon brothers.
9	9	289	Genealogy of the Taraweres.

EPISODE III: Sankaran

10	10	325	Genealogy of the Kòndès.
11	11	356	The breach of faith between Sankaran Naminya Kòndè and Du Kamisa.
12	12	461	Hunters try to kill the buffalo of Du but fail.
13	13	466	Tarawere brothers are prepared by occult means.
14	14	527	Tarawere brothers seek out the Buffalo-Woman and learn her secrets.
15	15	635	Tarawere brothers overcome the Buffalo-Woman.
16	16	749	Origin of the Jabaatè clan.
17	17	752	Genealogy of the Jabaatès.
18	18	916	Tarawere brothers receive Sugulun Kòndè as reward.

EPISODE IV: The Manden

19	19	947	Tarawere brothers try to lie with Sugulun Kòndè, but she turns them away with occult power.
20	20	1027	Fara Magan, the Handsome, King of the Manden, gets Sugulun Kòndè from Tarawere brothers.

<pre>
1   Nare Magan Kònatè!
      Subaa-Minè-Subaa!
      Sin-kula le sòrò man di dè.
      Ani ngara naani. [?]   (Naamu)
5   Kala Jula Sangoyi!
      Subaa-Minè-Subaa!   (Mmm)

      A Hadama le ma.
      Hadama le ma,
      Bani Hadama.   (Cinyè don)
10   N'i fòra mògò dòlu kò,
      Mògò dòlu de f'i kò.
      A Hadama le ma, Hadama.   (Naamu)

      N' ye Biribiriba ma.   (Naamu)
      Nare Magan Kònatè!
15   Subaa-Minè-Subaa!   (Cinyè)
      Ka ta Fatiyataligara,
      Ka taa Sòkòtò,   (Naamu)
      Magan Son-Jara ta le olu di.   (Naamu)
      Fara-finlu y'a f'ole ma, N' fa,
20   Eripibiliki-Mali,   (Naamu)
      Maninka mara: (Mmm, Cinyè don)
      Mali kòrò le nin di.
      Maan Son-Jara,
      A di Bamanan Dankun faga,
25   Fantan na dankun dò-sigi tè bèn,   (Naamu)
      Ka Bamanan Basa faga,
</pre>

The Epic

EPISODE ONE: PROLOGUE IN PARADISE

```
1    Nare Magan Kònatè!
     Sorcerer-Seizing-Sorcerer!
     A man of power is hard to find.
     And four meistersingers. [?]                      (Indeed)
5    Kala Jula Sangoyi!
     Sorcerer-Seizing-Sorcerer!                         (Mmm)

     It is of Adam that I sing.
     Of Adam,
     Ben Adam.                                          ('Tis True)
10   As you succeeded some,
     So shall you have successors!
     It is of Adam that I sing, of Adam.               (Indeed)

     I sing of Biribiriba!                             (Indeed)
     Of Nare Magan Kònatè!
15   Sorcerer-Seizing-Sorcerer!                         (True)
     From Fatiyataligara
     All the way to Sokoto,                            (Indeed)
     Belonged to Magan Son-Jara.                       (Indeed)
     Africans call that, my father,
20   The Republic of Mali,                             (Indeed)
     The Maninka realm:                          (Mmm, 'tis true)
     That's the meaning of Mali.
     Magan Son-Jara,
     He slew Bambara-of-the-Border;
25   Settling on the border does not suit the weak.    (Indeed)
     And slew Bambara-the-Lizard;
```

Fantan kan'i yèrè tògò la basa la,   (Naamu)
Ka Bamanan Kòtu faga,
Fantan na tu-rò-sigi tè bèn.   (Naamu)
30 Nare Magan Kònatè bulu.
Subaa-Minè-Subaa!
Jankuma la wara la sinbon.   (Cinyè don)

N' ye Biribiriba ma.   (Naamu)
Su-rò-gungunrunnin-fin.
35 I man'a madènku,
A y'i madènku.   (Naamu)
Jiginè-kòrò-wulu.   (Naamu)
Fèn mana tè lontan sin lòn,
A tè duguren sin lòn.
40 A mana mògò sòrò,
K'i kin kè.   (Naamu)
Kirikara watita   (Naamu)
Ku jugu kun-yan-fan.   (Naamu)
Kè kun ni musu kun tè kilin di.   (Naamu)
45 Kumadin kè-nyi ni tonya tè kilin di.   (Naamu)
Ala Taala dè Hadama dan,   (Naamu)
Hadama kònòntòn.   (Naamu)
A tanman n'e Bani Hadama di.   (Cinyè)

Bènba le nnn.   (Naamu)
50 Ala Taala dè mama Hadama da,   (Naamu)
K'a lalò dugu-kulu kan,
Ko da-fènnu ka su-juru kè Hadama ye.

Da-fènnu di su-juru kè,   (Naamu)
Fo Hibilisa kilin.
55 Ala m'an takala Sitanè ma.   (Amina, 'Ya Rabi)

Ala Taala ko, "Hibilisa,   (Naamu)
"N'i ma su-juru kè Hadama ye,   (Naamu)
"Ne b'i kunna-guya dè!   (Mmm)
"Hadama laban le nin di."   (Cinyè)
60 Hibilisa ko, "'Ya Ma,   (Naamu)
"Ne tè su-juru Hadama ye.   (Naamu)
"San-ji bi segin,
"N' ye mèlakèlu kalanna.   (Naamu)
"Sibiri kilin ma kè dugu-kulu san fè,   (Naamu)
65 "Ni N' ma su-juru kè yòrò min.   (Naamu)

    No weak one should call himself lizard.   (Indeed)
    And slew Bambara-of-the-Backwoods;
    Settling the backwoods does not suit the weak.   (Indeed)
30   All this by the hand of Nare Magan Kònatè.
    Sorcerer-Seizing-Sorcerer!
    Simbon, Lion-Born-of-the-Cat.   ('Tis true)

    I sing of Biribiriba.   (Indeed)
    Stump-in-the-Dark-of-Night!
35   Should you bump against it,
    It will bump against you.   (Indeed)
    Granary-Guard-Dog.   (Indeed)
    The thing discerning not the stranger,
    Nor the familiar.
40   Should it come upon any person,
    He will be bitten!   (Indeed)
    Kirikara Watita!   (Indeed)
    Adversity's-True-Place!   (Indeed)
    Man's reason and a woman's are not the same.   (Indeed)
45   Pretty words and truth are not the same.   (Indeed)
Almighty God created Adam,   (Indeed)
Nine Adams.   (Indeed)
The tenth one was Ben Adam.   (True)

Ah, Bèmba!   (Indeed)
50 Almighty God created Adam, the forefather,   (Indeed)
And caused him to stand upon the earth,
And said that all creation's beings should submit to
    him.
And all the beings of creation did submit to him,   (Indeed)
Save Iblis alone.
55 May God deliver us from Satan!   (Amen, O my Lord)

Almighty God declared "Iblis!   (Indeed)
"If you do not submit to Adam,   (Indeed)
"I will make you wretched.   (Mmm)
"He is the last of all the Adams."   (True)
60 Iblis replied, "My Lord,   (Indeed)
"I'll not submit to Adam.   (Indeed)
"For eighty years,
"I've taught the angels.   (Indeed)
"Not one hand span, have I traveled o'er the earth, (Indeed)
65 "Where I did not submit to you.   (Indeed)

"Ala, N' sara."   (Naamu)
A ko, "Laa sakafi.   (Naamu)
"Ne b'i sara.   (Naamu)
"Ile tè bana tugun.   (Naamu)
70 "Ile tè nyinè tugun.   (Naamu)
"Sònògò tè s'ile ma,
"Fo buru ka fò mògòlu la lun min.
"I di fèn-fèn nòfili,
"O tè kè mantun di, kiyama."   (Aa, Fa-Digi,
                                                   O ye cinyè ye)

75 Hibilisa ko, "'Ya Ma le!
"N' sara."   (Naamu)
A ko, "N' b'i sara.   (Naamu)
"N' bè fèn dò danla na,
"N' bè fèn dò danla na,   (Naamu)
80 "K'a tògòla nanfulu la.
"Nanfulu tògò tè nanfulu la.
"A tògò le filiman-kan di."   (Naamu)
Filiman-kan!   (Naamu)
A man'a sòrò,   (Naamu)
85 I ye fili mògò bèè ma.   (Naamu)
N'i fòt'a la,
Mògòlu ye fil'i ma.
A tògò filiman-kan di.   (O ye cinyè ye)
A kuma wòòrò le fòla marii-kè ma: (Naamu)
90 "Marigi-kè le,   (Naamu)
"Ni Ne ma ban, k'ile tu,
"Ile ban ka Ne tu, N' marii-kè.
"Ni Ne m'i ni duna jè,   (Naamu)
"Ne b'i ni duna fara.   (Naamu)
95 "Ni N' m'i ladun Arijana,   (Naamu)
"N' b'i ladun Jahanama."   (Naamu)
Ala m'an kisira wo mògòlu ma.   (Amina, 'Ya Rabi)
Ala Taala kan y'o le ma: (Naamu)
"Hadama, N' k'i sòn min na duna?"   (Cinyè)
100 A ko, "'Ya Ma,   (Naamu)
"Kè-nyi di Ne ma, Ala."   (Naamu)
A ko, "Hadama, i fòlò ma N' kòn.   (Naamu)
"N' ye kè-nyi di jinèlu ma, Hadama."   (Naamu)

Ala Taala kan ye, "Hadama, N' k'i sòn mum na?"   (Naamu)

"O God, reward me for all this." (Indeed)
"So be it," the reply. (Indeed)
"I will reward you. (Indeed)
"Ne'er will you catch disease. (Indeed)
70 "Ne'er your memory will fail. (Indeed)
"Ne'er will you need to sleep, (Indeed)
"Until the day the trumpet blows for man.
"Whosoe'er you lead astray,
"Among the next world's chosen will not be." (Ah, Fa-Digi,
That's the truth)

75 And Iblis replied, "My Lord,
"Reward me still!" (Indeed)
"I will reward you," the reply. (Indeed)
"I will create a thing for your reward.
"I will create something just for you,
80 "And call it 'wealth.'
"But the name of wealth should not be 'Wealth.'
"Call it the Voice of Transgression." (Indeed)
The Voice of Transgression: (Indeed)
Should man obtain it, (Indeed)
85 All his kin will he mistake. (Indeed)
And should man want of it,
'Tis he mistaken by his kin.
Its name is thus, the Voice of Transgression. (That's the truth)
These six lines it addresses to its keeper: (Indeed)
90 "O My Keeper! (Indeed)
"Should I not be finished before you,
"You will be finished before me, my Keeper.
"If with this world I do not meld you, (Indeed)
"From this world I will divorce you. (Indeed)
95 "And if I get you not to Heaven, (Indeed)
"Then I'll send you down to Hell." (Indeed)
May God preserve us from these people! (Amen, my Lord)
Almighty God then spoke, (Indeed)
"Adam! what may I offer you in life?" (True)
100 "O Lord," the reply, (Indeed)
"Give me beauty, O God." (Indeed)
"Adam, you are not the first to ask. (Indeed)
"It's to the jinns that I've given beauty, Adam." (Indeed)

Almighty God then asked, "Now what may I offer
to you?" (Indeed)

105 A ko, "'Ye Ma le,   (Mmm)
    "Maluya di Ne ma, Ala."   (Naamu)
    "Hadama, i fòlò ma N' kòn.   (Naamu)
    "N' ye maluya di mèlèkalu ma, Hadama."   (Naamu)

    An mama Hadama kan y'o le rò, N' fa, "Ala,   (Naamu)
110 "Mògòlu mana mògò sòn, a ban.   (Naamu)
    "Ni Ala di mògò min sòn, soli wèrè tè kò.
    "I mana min di Ne ma,
    "N' y'o fè."   (O ye cinyè ye)
    "Hadama,   (Naamu)
115 "N' d'i sòn fusèman-tiiya la.
    "I y'a lòn na min ma
    "N' d'i sòn fusèman-tiiya la?
    "N' tè Kila Mahamadu kè mèlèka di.   (Naamu)
    "N' t'a kè jina di.
120 "N' b'a kè Hadama bònsòn le di."   (Naamu)
    Filardi Samawaati, [?]
    San-kulu ni dugu-kulu dar'o kanu kònsòn.
    . . . ,   (Naamu)
    An tilinda yòrò min na barika dò,
125 Ala m'an sira o rò, amina.   (Amina, 'Ya Rabi)

    Bènba le nnn.   (Naamu)
    Ala Taala d'i t'o rò, N' fa, ka Hadama ta,   (Naamu)

    K'a labò Arjana.   (Naamu)
    A lajiginda banku min kan,   (Naamu)
130 O banku tògò le Hindi.   (Naamu)
    Lònninalu nyininga.
    Hadama jiginta Hindi-banku le kan, nnn,   (Mmm)
    Tili bòtò o banku min kan,
    Sila bòtò a banku kan.   (Naamu)
135 Ala le di da,   (Naamu)
    Sila kèmè saba ni sila bi saba,
    Ni sila saba,   (Naamu)
    Ka karu da,   (Naamu)
    Sila kèmè saba ni sila bi saba ni sila saba.   (Naamu)
140 Tili mana balan sila dò,   (Naamu)
    Ka bila, bila karu la sila dò,   (Naamu)
    A nòrò mana la karu kan,   (Naamu)
    Mògòlu y'i bara, ko,
    Jankuma di karu mina!"

105   "O Lord," the reply,   (Mmm)
      "Give me morality, O God."   (Indeed)
      "Adam, you are not the first to ask.   (Indeed)
      "It's to the angels I've given morality, Adam."

      O father, then Adam, our forefather, said, "O God,   (Indeed)
110   "Whatever man may offer man, such will have an end. (Indeed)
      "Whatever God may offer man, no gift need follow that.
      "Whatever you will give to me,
      "That is what I wish."   ('Tis the truth)
      "Adam," the reply,   (Indeed)
115   "I will grant you dignity.
      "And how will you come to know
      "That I did grant you dignity?
      "Not as angel will Muḥammad the Prophet be,   (Indeed)
      "Nor will I create him as a jinn.
120   "I will make him of Adam's seed."   (Indeed)
      Filardi Samawaati. [?]
      Paradise and Earth were made according to His Love. (Indeed)
      . . . .
      Where we have passed the day in Grace,
125   There may we also pass the night, Amen.   (Amen, O my Lord)

      Ah! Bèmba!   (Indeed)
      Almighty God, after all of this, my father, took Adam, (Indeed)

      And brought him forth from Paradise.   (Indeed)
      He set him down in a land,   (Indeed)
130   The name of which was India.   (Indeed)
      Ask the ones who know of this!
      Adam was placed in the land of India.   (Mmm)
      The land from whence the sun arises.
      The land from whence the moon arises.   (Indeed)
135   'Twas God who created the sun,   (Indeed)
      With its three hundred paths and thirty paths
      And three paths,   (Indeed)
      And created the moon,   (Indeed)
      Three hundred paths and thirty paths and three paths. (Indeed)
140   When the sun leaves its path   (Indeed)
      To sit in the path of the moon,   (Indeed)
      When its light falls behind the moon,   (Indeed)
      The people cry out saying,
      "The cat has seized the moon!"

145 Jankuma tè karu sòrò.   (Naamu)
    Tili nòrò l'a kan, nnn.   (Naamu)
    N' mama Hawa ni N' bènba Hadama,   (Naamu)
    Alu di nyògòn-nyini.   (Naamu)
    Tili bi naani,   (Naamu)
150 Al' ye nyògòn-nyini na.   (Naamu)
    Alu waara nyògòn ye karu min dò,
    Arafan le o di.   (Cinyè)
    Lònninalu nyining'a ma.   (Cinyè. Cinyè don, Fa-Digi)

    N' mama Hawa ni N' bènba Hadama,   (Naamu)
155 Alu di kònò-nya bi naani kè,   (Mmm)
    Din bi segin!
    Bani Hadama,   (Naamu)
    A mama-din fòlò le Nuhun di.   (Naamu)
    Ole di din-kè saba sòrò.

160 Bènba le.   (Naamu)
    Nuhun ne di sin-kè saba sòrò nnn,   (Naamu)
    Haman, Caman, Yafisu.   (Naamu)
    Yafisu, ole taara koko-ji kan nnn.   (Naamu)
    Ole kò kèra Masusu ni Masasa ye.   (Naamu)
165 Haman, fara-finnu bòra ole rò, N' fa.   (Naamu)
    Saman, fara-gèlu bunda tan ni fula,   (Naamu)
    Alu bònin ole dò nnn.   (Naamu)

        N' ye Biribiriba ma.   (Naamu)
        Kirikisa, dunnun-tanba ani sòn-tanba!   (Naamu)
170 Ala Kila Mamadu bangera,   (Naamu)
    Dònba karu tili tan ni fula.   (Naamu)
    O tili tan ni saba,
    Talata, Bilal bangera Samuda.   (Naamu)
    Lònninalu nyininga N' na.   (Mmm)
175 O Bilali dè,   (Naamu)
    Ole den ye Mamadu Kanu di.
    O Mamadu Kanu,   (Mmm)
    Ole di den-kè saba sòrò: (Naamu)
    Kanu Sinbon,   (Naamu)
180 Kanu Nyògòn Sinbon,
    Lawali Sinbon.   (Naamu)

145 The cat has not caught the moon. (Indeed)
    The light of the sun is only behind it. (Indeed)
    Our grandparent Eve and our ancestor Adam, (Indeed)
    They sought each other out, (Indeed)
    For forty days, (Indeed)
150 They were searching for each other. (Indeed)
    The mount whereon they met,
    Its name was Arafan. (True)
    Ask the ones who know of this! (True. That's true, Fa-Digi)

    Our grandparent Eve and our ancestor Adam, (Indeed)
155 Conceived some forty times, (Mmm)
    And begat eighty children!
    Ben Adam, (Indeed)
    His first grandchild was Noah, (Indeed)
    And he had three sons.

EPISODE TWO: MECCA

160 Ah! Bèmba! (Indeed)
    Noah begat three sons: (Indeed)
    Ham, Shem, and Japheth. (Indeed)
    Japheth went forth and crossed the sea. (Indeed)
    His descendants became the Masusu and the Masasa. (Indeed)
165 Ham, black people descended from him, my father. (Indeed)
    Shem, the twelve white clans (Indeed)
    Descended from him. (Indeed)

        I sing of Biribiriba! (Indeed)
        Kirikisa, Spear-of-Access, Spear-of-Service! (Indeed)
170 The Messenger of God, Muḥammad, was born, (Indeed)
    On the twelfth day of the month of Dònba. (Indeed)
    On the thirteenth day,
    Tuesday, Bilāl was born in Samuda. (Indeed)
    Ask the ones who know of this! (Mmm)
175 That Bilāl, (Indeed)
    His child was Mamadu Kanu.
    That Mamadu Kanu, (Mmm)
    He had three sons: (Indeed)
    Kanu Simbon, (Indeed)
180 Kanu Nyògòn Simbon,
    Lawali Simbon. (Indeed)

     Bènba le nnn.   (Naamu)
     Suya-mògò tèrè mògò bi kònòntòn di.   (Mmm)
     Maraka ye bunda tan ni fula di,   (Naamu)
185 Ka bò Wagadugu.   (Naamu)
     Siselu bòra Wagadugu.   (Mmm)
     Janel' bòra Wagadugu.   (Mmm)
     Turelu bòra Wagadugu.   (Naamu)
     Beretelu bòra Wagadugu.   (Naamu)
190 Sakòlu bòra Wagadugu.
     Fulal' bòra Wagadugu.   (Naamu)
     Jawaralu bòra Wagadugu.   (Naamu)
     Nyarèlu bòra Wagadugu.   (Naamu)
     Tunkaralu bòra Wagadugu le nnn.   (Mmm)

195 Wagadugu jènsènda.   (Naamu)
     Bènba!   (Naamu)
     Jawaralu bènba Damangile,   (Naamu)
     Ani Nyarèlu mama, Nyenenba Nyarè,   (Naamu)
     Alu waara dugu sigi Kingi.   (Naamu)
200 A dugu tògò le Banbagile.   (Naamu)
     Damangile kaburu bè Banbagile.   (Naamu)
     A di din fula sòrò,   (Naamu)
     Daman ni Sila Maan.   (Naamu)
     Olu waara Jala.   (Mmm)
205 Siman Kuru ni Wala Kuru bè Jawaralu bulu
        Jala.   (Cinyè don)

     Bènba le, nnn.   (Naamu)
     Tunkaralu bènba Farin Burama,   (Naamu)
     A taara dugu sigi ko Mèma-dugu.   (Naamu)
     Ole di din-kè fula sòrò nò,   (Naamu)
210 Farin Burama ni Jasigi.   (Naamu)
     Farin Burama ni Jasigi dè,   (Naamu)
     Olel' lara Son-Jara kan yan,   (Naamu)
     Ka taa n'a di Manden.   (Naamu)
     Alu bòta Manden,   (Naamu)
215 Ka n'i sigi Kulun.   (Naamu)
     Alu bòra Kulun,   (Naamu)
     Ka i sii Bangasi,   (Naamu)
     Ka yèlèn Genu Kuru san fè,   (Naamu)
     Ka dugu dò sigi dugu-kuru san fè.   (Naamu)
220 O dugu tògò ye ko Kuduguni.   (Mmm, cinyè don)

Ah! Bèmba!   (Indeed)
The races of man were ninety in number.   (Mmm)
There were twelve clans of Marakas   (Indeed)
185 Which came from Wagadugu.   (Indeed)
The Sises came from Wagadugu.   (Mmm)
The Janes came from Wagadugu.   (Mmm)
The Tures came from Wagadugu.   (Indeed)
The Beretes came from Wagadugu.   (Indeed)
190 The Sakòs came from Wagadugu.
The Fulani came from Wagadugu.   (Indeed)
The Jawaras came from Wagadugu.   (Indeed)
The Nyarès came from Wagadugu.   (Indeed)
The Tunkaras came from Wagadugu.   (Mmm)

195 The peoples of Wagadugu thus scattered.   (Indeed)
O Bèmba!   (Indeed)
The ancestor of the Jawaras, Damangile,   (Indeed)
And the forefather of the Nyarès, Nyenemba Nyarè,   (Indeed)
Went forth to found a village in Kingi.   (Indeed)
200 The name of that village was Bambagile.   (Indeed)
Damangile's tomb is there in Bambagile.   (Indeed)
He had two children: (Indeed)
Daman and Sila Ma'an.   (Indeed)
They both went forth to Jala.   (Mmm)
205 Mount Siman and Mount Wala belong to the Jawaras
       in Jala.   (That's true)

Ah, Bèmba!   (Indeed)
The ancestor of the Jawaras, Prince Burama,   (Indeed)
He went forth to found the village called Mèma.   (Indeed)
There he had two sons,   (Indeed)
210 Prince Burama and Jasigi.   (Indeed)
Prince Burama and Jasigi,   (Indeed)
'Twas they who joined Son-Jara here,   (Indeed)
And went with him to the Manden.   (Indeed)
They left the Manden later   (Indeed)
215 And came to settle in Kulun.   (Indeed)
They left Kulun,   (Indeed)
And settled in Bangasi,   (Indeed)
And went up on Genu Mountain,   (Indeed)
And founded a village atop the mountain.   (Indeed)
220 That village's name was Kuduguni.   (Mmm, that's true)

Ko Genu-kòrò-Tunkaralu, (Naamu)
Olu bèè ka din-kè fula sòrò, (Naamu)
Wali ni Gayi, (Naamu)
Sega ni Marama. (Naamu)
225 Tunkara fa naani, (Naamu)
Min bè Kita-banku kan yan, (Naamu)
O mògò lelu wele. (Cinyè)

N' ye Biribiriba ma.
Kirikisa Dunnun-tanba ni Sòn-tanba! (Mmm)
230 Kèlè-mansa n'a dunnun-kasi, fara kinba!
Nare Magan Kònatè, Subaa-Minè-Subaa (Naamu)
Jankuma la wara la Sinbon! (Naamu)

Kanu Sinbon, ni Kanu Nyògòn Sinbon, (Naamu)
Alu sigira Wagadugu. (Naamu)
235 Alu bòra Wagaduu, (Naamu)
Alu waara Jara. (Naamu)
Alu bòra Jara. (Mmm)
Alu waara ki-kè-bugu da sigi, (Mmm)
K'o dugu tògò la ko Ki-bugu. (Naamu)
240 O Ki-bugu la Manden Kiri-kòròni ye. (Naamu)
Manden dugu fòlò-fòlò la Manden
    Kiri-kòròni ye. (Naamu)

Kanu Sinbon, ni Kanu Nyògòn Sinbon,
    ni Lawali Sinbon, (Naamu)
Ole la dugu fòlò-fòlò la Manden Kiri-kòròni ye, (Naamu)
Kiri-kòròni! (Naamu)
245 Kanu Sinbon, (Naamu)
Dankòlu mama l'o di. (Naamu)
Lawali Sinbon, (Naamu)
Ole di Kòròlen Fabu ni Sòkòna Fabu wolo.
Dugunòlu bònin ole dò. (Naamu)
250 Kanu Nyògòn Sinbon, (Naamu)
Ole di Mansa Bèrèmu wulu. (Mmm)
Mansa Bèrèmu ka Mansa Bèrèmu Dana wulu. (Naamu)
Mansa Bèrèmu Dana ka Mansa Juluku Mori wulu. (Naamu)
Mansa Juluku Mori ka Mansa Bèlò Koma'an wulu. (Naamu)
255 Bèlò Komaan ka Juruni Komaan wulu.
Juruni Komaan ka Fata Magan Kè-nyi wulu.
O Fata Magan Kè-nyi, (Naamu)
Ole waara ki-kè-bugu da sigi ko Kakama. (Naamu)

'Tis said the Tunkaras of Genu,   (Indeed)
They each had two sons: (Indeed)
Wali and Gayi,   (Indeed)
Sega and Marama,   (Indeed)
225   The four Tunkara patriarchs   (Indeed)
Who were in Kita country here.   (Indeed)
That is what those people are called.   (True)

I sing of Biribiriba!
Kirikisa, Spear-of-Access and Spear-of-Service! (Mmm)
230   Warlord and wailing at his entry, a pile of stone!
Nare Magan Kònatè, Sorcerer-Seizing-Sorcerer! (Indeed)
Simbon, Lion-Born-of-the-Cat!   (Indeed)

That Kanu Simbon and Kanu Nyògòn Simbon,   (Indeed)
Settled in Wagadugu.   (Indeed)
235   They left Wagadugu,   (Indeed)
And they went to Jara.   (Indeed)
They left Jara.   (Mmm)
And went forth to found a farming hamlet,   (Mmm)
Calling that village Farmtown.   (Indeed)
240   That Farmtown is Manden Kiri-kòròni.   (Indeed)
The very first Manden village was Manden
    Kiri-kòròni.   (Indeed)

Kanu Simbon, Kanu Nyògòn Simbon
    and Lawali Simbon,   (Indeed)
Their first village was Manden Kiri-kòròni,   (Indeed)
Kiri-kòròni!   (Indeed)
245   Kanu Simbon,   (Indeed)
He is the forefather of the Dankòs.   (Indeed)
Lawali Simbon,   (Indeed)
Begat Kòròlen Fabu and Sòkòna Fabu.
The Dugunòs descended from them.   (Indeed)
250   Kanu Nyògòn Simbon   (Indeed)
Begat King Bèrèmu,   (Mmm)
King Bèrèmu begat King Bèrèmu Dana.   (Indeed)
King Bèrèmu Dana begat King Juluku, the Holy.   (Indeed)
King Juluku, the Holy begat King Belo Koma'an.   (Indeed)
255   Belo Koma'an begat Juruni Koma'an.
Juruni Koma'an begat Fata Magan, the Handsome.
That Fata Magan, the Handsome   (Indeed)
Went forth to found a farm hamlet called Kakama,   (Indeed)

Alu kan y'ole ma, N' fa, Bintanya Kamalen.   (Mmm)
260   Nare Magan Kònatè!
           Subaa-Minè-Subaa!   (Naamu)

O Fata Magan-Kè-nyi,
A di Tumun-dò Magan-jan Berete din-musu ta,

Ko Sani Saman Berete.   (Mmm)
265 Alu k'o ma Saman Berete.   (Naamu)
     O man din sòrò.   (Naamu)

Bènba le.   (Naamu)
Manden dè!
Tun-tan-mògò tèrè bi saba ni mògò saba le di
270 Manden-banku kan:
     Tun-tan-jòn tan ni wòòrò,   (Naamu)
     Jabi-fin-jòn naani,   (Naamu)
     Mamuru si luulu,   (Cinyè)
     Mori kanda luulu,   (Naamu)
275 Ani siya mògò naani,   (Naamu)
     Ani mògò-fin-mògò-mògò kilin.   (Cinyè don,
                                                 Èè, Fa-Digi, cinyè)

     Mamuru si luulu: (Naamu)
     Mansa Kuru ni Mansa Kanda,   (Mmm)
     Fa-Banjugu ni Wasa Bukari,   (Naamu)
280 Ani Sinunsi.   (Naamu)
     Mamuru si ye olelu di.
     Mori kanda luulu: (Naamu)
     Tumun-tò Magan-jan Berete,   (Naamu)
     Seri Bukari Janè,   (Mmm)
285 Sira Ma'an Kanda Ture,   (Mmm)
     Ani Jabi Sise,   (Mmm)
     Ani Fodele-jan.
     Olelu tèrè Ala delila Manden.   (Naamu)

     Bènba le.   (Naamu)
290 An nelu la tariku le,   (Mmm)
     A sèbènnin nya min ma, N' fa,   (Mmm)
     Arabulu dò: (Naamu)
     Kuresi ni Hasimi,   (Naamu)
     Hasimi-kalu mama Mutulubi ye.   (Naamu)

And they call that place, my father, Bintanya Kamalen.(Mmm)
260   O Nare Magan Kònatè!
       O Sorcerer-Seizing-Sorcerer! (Indeed)

That Fata Magan, the Handsome,
He married the daughter of Tall Magan
    Berete-of-the-Ruins,
Called Saman Berete, the Pure. (Mmm)
265 They called her Saman Berete. (Indeed)
She had not yet borne a child at first. (Indeed)

O Bèmba! (Indeed)
'Tis of the Manden!
There once were three and thirty noble clans.
270 In the Manden country:
Sixteen of warriors, (Indeed)
Four were agents of Dark Secrets, (Indeed)
Five were descendants of Mamuru, (True)
Five clans of holymen, (Indeed)
275 And four were families-that-came-later, (Indeed)
And one clan was of pariahs. (That's true,
                           Eh, Fa-Digi, true)

And five families of Mamuru: (Indeed)
King-of-the-Mountain, King-of-the-Clan, (Mmm)
Fa-banjugu and Wasa Kubari (Indeed)
280 And Sinunsi. (Indeed)
Those were the families of Mamuru.
Five families of holymen: (Indeed)
Tall Magan Berete-of-the-Ruins, (Indeed)
Seri Bukari Jane, (Mmm)
285 Sira Ma'an of the Ture Clan, (Mmm)
And Jabi Sise, (Mmm)
And Fodele, the Tall.
It was they who prayed to God in the Manden. (Indeed)

Ah! Bèmba! (Indeed)
290 In our chronicles, (Mmm)
It was written in this way, my father, (Mmm)
Amongst the Arabs: (Indeed)
Among the Quraysh and Hāshim, (Indeed)
'Abd al-Muṭṭalib was the forefather of the Hāshim
    Clan. (Indeed)

<table>
<tr><td>295</td><td>Mutubuli di Burulayi wulu.</td><td>(Naamu)</td></tr>
<tr><td></td><td>Burulayi di Mahamadu wulu.</td><td>(Naamu)</td></tr>
<tr><td></td><td>Mahamadu di Fatumata Bintu wulu.</td><td>(Naamu)</td></tr>
<tr><td></td><td>Fatumata Bintu,</td><td>(Naamu)</td></tr>
<tr><td></td><td>A di Lasina ni Fuseni wulu.</td><td>(Naamu)</td></tr>
<tr><td>300</td><td>Lasina,</td><td>(Naamu)</td></tr>
<tr><td></td><td>Sirifilu bònin ole dò.</td><td>(Naamu)</td></tr>
<tr><td></td><td>Fuseni,</td><td>(Naamu)</td></tr>
<tr><td></td><td>Ole di Abulayi sòrò.</td><td>(Mmm)</td></tr>
</table>

<table>
<tr><td></td><td>Abulayi,</td><td></td></tr>
<tr><td>305</td><td>Ole tèrè yeli kèl'a kò fè,</td><td></td></tr>
<tr><td></td><td>Ka yeli k'a nyè ma.</td><td>(Naamu)</td></tr>
<tr><td></td><td>Alu ka y'ole ma, N' fa, ko Tarawara,</td><td></td></tr>
<tr><td></td><td>Nya-fula-tigi.</td><td>(Cinyè)</td></tr>
<tr><td></td><td>Tarawereya kòrò le nin di.</td><td>(Naamu)</td></tr>
</table>

<table>
<tr><td>310</td><td>Abulayi Tarawere dè,</td><td>(Naamu)</td></tr>
<tr><td></td><td>A di din-kè bi saba wulu.</td><td>(Naamu)</td></tr>
<tr><td></td><td>Olu bèè taara Ala Kila la kèlè kè Kayibara.</td><td>(Naamu)</td></tr>
</table>

<table>
<tr><td></td><td>A bèè tura kèlè rò,</td><td>(Naamu)</td></tr>
<tr><td></td><td>Fo Tukuru ni Gasinè.</td><td>(Naamu)</td></tr>
<tr><td>315</td><td>Tukuru ni Gasinè,</td><td>(Naamu)</td></tr>
<tr><td></td><td>Mori kanda luulu di Ala deli kè</td><td></td></tr>
<tr><td></td><td>Tukuru ni Gasinè ye.</td><td>(Naamu)</td></tr>
<tr><td></td><td>Olu fana bèè,</td><td>(Naamu)</td></tr>
<tr><td></td><td>Alu bèè ka din-kè kilin-kilin sòrò.</td><td>(Mmm)</td></tr>
<tr><td>320</td><td>Ole kèla Dan Mansa Wulandin</td><td></td></tr>
<tr><td></td><td>Ni Dan Mansa Wulanba ye.</td><td>(Mmm)</td></tr>
</table>

<table>
<tr><td></td><td>Donbaga!</td><td></td></tr>
<tr><td></td><td>San-jigi Tura Magan!</td><td></td></tr>
<tr><td></td><td>Tura Magan ni Kanke-jan</td><td>(Aa, Fa-Digi,
cinyè don)</td></tr>
</table>

<table>
<tr><td>325</td><td>Bèmba le!</td><td>(Naamu)</td></tr>
<tr><td></td><td>Si kèra Jaralu ma, Sankarandin,</td><td>(Naamu)</td></tr>
<tr><td></td><td>Sankaran Naminya Kòndè.</td><td></td></tr>
<tr><td></td><td>Kòndèlu bènba le Sama Sine di.</td><td>(Naamu)</td></tr>
</table>

<table>
<tr><td>295</td><td>'Abd al-Muṭṭalib begat 'Abdullāh.</td><td>(Indeed)</td></tr>
<tr><td></td><td>'Abdullāh begat Muḥammad.</td><td>(Indeed)</td></tr>
<tr><td></td><td>Muḥammad begat Fāṭimah Bint.</td><td>(Indeed)</td></tr>
<tr><td></td><td>Fāṭimah Bint</td><td>(Indeed)</td></tr>
<tr><td></td><td>Gave birth to al-Ḥasan and al-Ḥusayn.</td><td>(Indeed)</td></tr>
<tr><td>300</td><td>Al-Ḥasan,</td><td>(Indeed)</td></tr>
<tr><td></td><td>The Sharīfs descended from him.</td><td>(Indeed)</td></tr>
<tr><td></td><td>Al-Ḥusayn,</td><td>(Indeed)</td></tr>
<tr><td></td><td>It was he who begat Abdulayi.</td><td>(Mmm)</td></tr>
<tr><td></td><td> </td><td></td></tr>
<tr><td></td><td>Abdulayi,</td><td></td></tr>
<tr><td>305</td><td>Could see in front</td><td></td></tr>
<tr><td></td><td>And see behind.</td><td>(Indeed)</td></tr>
<tr><td></td><td>The name they gave him was Tarawara,</td><td></td></tr>
<tr><td></td><td>"The man of two visions."</td><td>(True)</td></tr>
<tr><td></td><td>That is the meaning of being Tarawere.</td><td>(Indeed)</td></tr>
<tr><td></td><td> </td><td></td></tr>
<tr><td>310</td><td>That Abdulayi Tarawere,</td><td>(Indeed)</td></tr>
<tr><td></td><td>Begat thirty sons.</td><td>(Indeed)</td></tr>
<tr><td></td><td>They all fought the Kayibara battle for
    the Messenger of God</td><td>(Indeed)</td></tr>
<tr><td></td><td>And they all remained on that field of battle,</td><td>(Indeed)</td></tr>
<tr><td></td><td>All save Tukuru and Gasinè</td><td>(Indeed)</td></tr>
<tr><td>315</td><td>Tukuru and Gasinè</td><td>(Indeed)</td></tr>
<tr><td></td><td>The five holy families prayed to God</td><td></td></tr>
<tr><td></td><td>For Tukuru and Gasinè.</td><td>(Indeed)</td></tr>
<tr><td></td><td>Both of them,</td><td>(Indeed)</td></tr>
<tr><td></td><td>They each had one son.</td><td>(Mmm)</td></tr>
<tr><td>320</td><td>It was they who became Dan Mansa Wulandin</td><td></td></tr>
<tr><td></td><td>And Dan Mansa Wulanba.</td><td>(Mmm)</td></tr>
<tr><td></td><td> </td><td></td></tr>
<tr><td></td><td>The One-Who-Enters,</td><td></td></tr>
<tr><td></td><td>The New-Year-Ram, Tura Magan!</td><td></td></tr>
<tr><td></td><td>Tura Magan-and-Kanke-jan!</td><td>(Ah, Fa-Digi,
that's true)</td></tr>
</table>

EPISODE THREE: SANKARAN

<table>
<tr><td>325</td><td>O! Bèmba!</td><td>(Indeed)</td></tr>
<tr><td></td><td>We have come to the Jaras of Sankarandin.</td><td>(Indeed)</td></tr>
<tr><td></td><td>To Naminya Kòndè of Sankaran.</td><td></td></tr>
<tr><td></td><td>The Kòndè's ancestor was Sama Sine.</td><td>(Indeed)</td></tr>
</table>

	Aba Sara din le Sama Sine di.	
330	Ole di Sana Bunuma Sara wulu.	(Mmm)
	Sana Bunuma Sara,	(Naamu)
	Ole din-kè fòlò sòrò.	(Naamu)
	Sana Bunuma Sara,	(Naamu)
	A din-kè fòlò le Dugu-mògòlu-nya-mògò.	(Naamu)
335	O Dugu-mògòlu-nya-mògò,	(Naamu)
	Ole ba-kilinma-musu kèra Du Kamisa di.	(Mmm)
	O Dugu-mògòlu-nya-mògò,	(Naamu)
	Ole di din dò sòrò, ko Du Magan Jata Kòndè.	(Naamu)
	O Du Magan Jata Kòndè dè,	(Naamu)
340	A kun-sii-kunan linin,	(Naamu)
	A binki di kun-sii-kunan ta,	
	K'a bila bata kònò,	
	Ko, "Sini-ku!"	(Naamu)

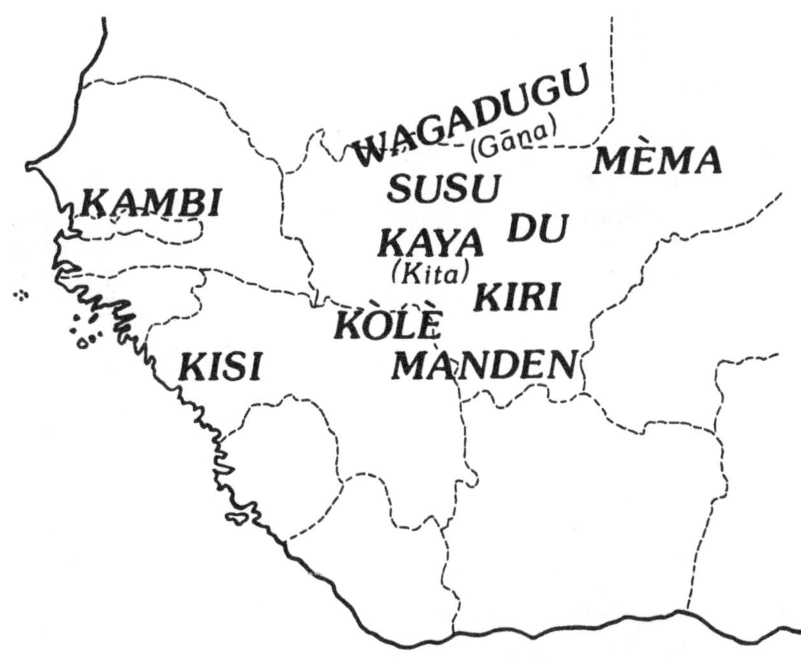

**Figure 9. Map of the Manden (Old Mali) and
Surrounding Kingdoms at the Time
the Epic of Son-Jara Takes Place
(Modern State Boundaries Shown for Reference)**

	Sama Sine was Aba Sara's child,	
330	And it was he who begat Sana Bunuma Sara.	(Mmm)
	Sana Bunuma Sara	(Indeed)
	Bore her first son.	(Indeed)
	Sana Bunuma Sara,	(Indeed)
	Her first son was Leader-of-the-People.	(Indeed)
335	That Leader-of-the-People,	(Indeed)
	His flesh-and-blood sister was Du Kamisa.	(Mmm)
	That Leader-of-the-People	(Indeed)
	Had a son called Magan Jata Kòndè of Du.	(Indeed)
	That Magan Jata Kòndè of Du,	(Indeed)
340	At the shaving of his new-born hair,	(Indeed)
	His father's sister took that birth-hair,	
	And put it in a calabash,	
	Saying, "A thing for tomorrow!"	(Indeed)

A bata-julu min tègèra,
345   A d'o bila bata kònò,
Ko, "Sini-ku!"
A bata-julu tègèra muru min na,
A d'o bila bata kònò,
Ko, "Sini-ku!"   (Cinyè)
350   A banbulan-fini kòrò,   (Mmm)
A d'o bila bata,   (Naamu)
Ko, "Sini-ku!"   (Naamu)
O din-din le bunyada,   (Naamu)
Ka dugu tan ni fula mara.
355   A ta y'o mògò bèè di.
A di lònninalu nyininga.   (Naamu)
Alu di fèlèli kè,   (Naamu)
K'a ka san-kaba tura saraka,   (Mmm)
Kè-kan-mògò kan'o sugu dumu.
360   A dun kèlen jin-kò la binkè-musu ye.
Ma-kè-kòrò-sigi man nyi.   (Naamu)

Biribiriba, a ni wura!
Nare Magan Kònatè!
N' ye Subaa le ma.   (Naamu)
365   Kirikisa, Dunnun-tanba ani Sòn-tanba!   (Mmm)
Kèlè mansa ngana ani lu min mana ta,

Fara kinba!   (Naamu)
Ja-tigi-faga-lòntanba!   (Cinyè)
N' y'i lònna lon min, lònbaga-dumun.

370   An k'an kali,
An k'an kali,   (Naamu)
Fantan kali suu,
Ni fama kali nya tè kilin di.   (O ye cinyè ye)

Dugu labi ni sansan!
375   Ni kèndè-karaba-dunsu!   (Naamu)
Kulu mana nama,   (Mmm)
Bali, wulu kana kè tununnandi.   (Mmm)
Jankuma la wara la Sinbon   (Naamu)
N' ye su-rò-gungurunnin-fin ma.
380   I man'a madènku
A y'i madènku.
Jiginè-kòrò-wulu,   (Mmm)

The umbilical cord that was cut,
345 She put into the calabash,
Saying, "A thing for tomorrow!"
The knife she used to cut the cord,
She put into the calabash,
Saying, "A thing for tomorrow!"   (True)
350 His old swaddling cloth,   (Mmm)
She put into the calabash,   (Indeed)
Saying, "A thing for tomorrow!"   (Indeed)
That small child grew up,
And came to rule over twelve towns.
355 All those people belonged to him.
He sought the counsel of wise men,   (Indeed)
And they performed divination for him,   (Indeed)
Saying that he must sacrifice a white spotted bull, (Mmm)
That an outsider should not eat of the meat.
360 And that was the aunt on the outskirts.
Living with an elder brother is not good.   (Indeed)

Biribiriba, you and the bush!
O Nare Magan Kònatè!
'Tis of the Sorcerer I sing.   (Indeed)
365 Kirikisa, Spear-of-Access and Spear-of-Service! (Mmm)
Warlord Champion, should the compound be
        crushed,
A pile of stones!   (Indeed)
Great-Host-Slaying-Stranger!   (True)
The day I come to know you, devouring of the
        knower.
370 Should we swear an oath,
Should we swear an oath,   (Indeed)
The way the weak swear an oath,
And the manner of the mighty are not
        the same.   (That's the truth)
Village-Crusher and Village-Burier!
375 Hunter-Imposing-on-the-Hardy!   (Indeed)
The league may lose,   (Mmm)
But let them not become lovers of loss.   (Mmm)
Simbon, Lion-Born-of-the-Cat!   (Indeed)
I sing of the Stump-in-the-Dark-of-Night.
380 Should you bump against it,
It will bump against you.
The Granary-Guard-Dog,   (Mmm)

A tè lontan sin lòn,
A tè duguren sin lòn.
385 A man'i sòrò,
A k'i kin kè.   (Mmm)
Kirikara Watita!
Ku Jugu kun-yan-fan!   (Naamu)
Kè kun ni musu kun tè kilin di.
390 Kumadin kè-nyi ni kinyè man kan.
Sila mana janya,
A bòla nògòma-so le kan, nnn.   (Cinyè don)

Bènba le.   (Naamu)
Kafigilu wilila:
395 "Aa, Du Kamisa,   (Mmm)
"Musuya ye bana di.   (Naamu)
"A Ne kònò,   (Naamu)
"Ile min ye Dugu-mògòlu-nya-mògò di,
"Sin-ji kilin di.   (Naamu)
400 ". . . ,   (Naamu)
"Ka nugu kilinma nòn,   (Naamu)
"Ka din min sòrò,   (Naamu)
"O ka duu-kònò-saraka bò,   (Naamu)
"K'ele kò-kan-mògò di,
405 "K'ele kan'o sugu dumu.
"Musuya ye bana di dè!"   (Cinyè)
A diminda ole rò, nnn,   (Naamu)
Ka taga Du Magan Jata Kòndè tèrè: (Mmm)
"I la saga fèlè.   (Mmm)
410 "I la kò-kan-mògò tè N' di.
"Ne n'i fa-dinlu ku-kilinman nòn,
"Ka sin-ji kilin saba,   (Mmm)
". . . . "
Du Magan Jata Kòndè diminda ole rò, N' fa,
415 K'a binki mina,   (Mmm)
K'a kurundu,   (Naamu)
K'w'a bila bunin dò kònò Du tilibe fè,   (Naamu)
K'a sin-furu tègè muru la: magasi!
"I sigi yan!   (Mmm)
420 "I ma din wulu!   (Cinyè)
"I sigi yan!
"I ma din wulu!   (Cinyè)

"Ne fa le Dugu-mògòlu-nya-mògò di.

	It discerns not the stranger,	
	Nor discerns the familiar.	
385	Should he come upon any person,	
	He will be bitten!	(Mmm)
	Kirikara Watita!	
	Adversity's-True-Place!	(Indeed)
	A man's reason and a woman's are not the same.	
390	Pretty little words and truth are not the same.	
	No matter how long the road,	
	It always leads to someone's home.	(That's true)

	Ah! Bèmba!	(Indeed)
	Some old meddlers rose up;	
395	"Ah! Du Kamisa,	(Mmm)
	"Being a woman is a malady!	(Indeed)
	"In my mind,	(Indeed)
	"You who with Leader-of-the-People	
	"Are of the same breast,	(Indeed)
400	. . . ,	(Indeed)
	"And who come from the same belly,	(Indeed)
	"And who had a child,	(Indeed)
	"Who made a family sacrifice,	(Indeed)
	"Saying that you should be the outsider,	
405	"And thus you should not eat of the meat.	
	"Being a woman is a malady!"	(True)
	At that, she became angry.	(Indeed)
	And went to find Magan Jata Kòndè of Du:	(Indeed)
	"Behold your lamb skin!	(Mmm)
410	"I cannot be an outsider to you!	
	"I and your father are of the same cause,	
	"And suckled the same breast."	(Mmm)
	" . . . . "	
	Magan Jata Kòndè of Du became enraged at that,	
415	And seized his aunt,	(Mmm)
	And dragged her off,	(Indeed)
	And cast her in a hovel to the west of Du	(Indeed)
	And slashed off her breasts with a knife, *magasi*!	
	"You remain here!	(Mmm)
420	"You have borne no children!	(True)
	"You remain here!	
	"You have borne no children!	(True)

"My father was Leader-of-the-People.

“I ma din wulu!”   (Naamu)
425   “Iyo! Ne ma din wulu?”   (Mmm)
“I ma din wulu!”
“Na yan!”   (Cinyè)
A nar’a la bata da tan,   (Naamu)
K’i bulu bila bata kònò:
430   “I nyè t’i kun-sii-kunan la?
“Ne ma din wulu?   (Naamu)
“I m’i bata-julu ye?
“N’ ma din wulu?   (Naamu)
“I kisi-ji fòlò-fòlò min kè,
435   “O kèra fini-kuru min na,
“O fini fèlè!
“Iyo, Ne ma din wulu?   (Naamu)
“I m’e bamulan-fini fòlò ye?   (Naamu)
“Ne ma din wulu?”   (Naamu)
440   Sanda dò lara Manden.   (Naamu)
A fòra Kòndèlu ma, Manden ma.   (Naamu)

Su fasan san,   (Naamu)
Su fasan san.   (Naamu)
I mana mògò nègèn,
445   Su fasan san na,
I k’a sòn bin-kala kilin na.   (O ye cinyè ye,
O kun tè)

Kòndèlu mama fiyenyada.   (Naamu)
O musu-kòròni d’i yèlèma,
K’i kè sigi di, Manden.   (Naamu)
450   A gere bèè sanu tanba ni wòri tanba.   (Mmm)
A tulu bèè sanu janba ni wòri janba.   (Mmm)

A ku-kèsè sanu sagilan ni wòri sagilan.   (Cinyè)

A tulu bèè sanu janba ni wòri janba.   (Naamu)
A tòròn bèè sanu sònbè ni wòri sònbè.   (Naamu)
455   Musu d’i yèlèma.
Jinda wòrònwula Du la,
Dugu-sè mana jè,
A mògò faga o jin wo bèè da la,
Ka tògò la ko Du ka Ginda.
460   Kòndèlu yèlèma-sigi tèrè ko Du ka Ginda.

"You have borne no children!"   (Indeed)
425   "What? Did I not bear a child?"   (Mmm)
"You have borne no children!"
"Come here!"   (True)
She ripped off her calabash lid   (Indeed)
And dipped her hand into the calabash:
430   "Do you not see your new-born hair?
"Did I not bear a child?   (Indeed)
"Do you not see your navel cord?
"Did I not bear a child?   (Indeed)
"The water breaking at your birth,
435   "The cloth on which it spilled,
"Behold that cloth before you!
"Alas! Did I not bear a child?   (Indeed)
"Do you not see your swaddling cloth?   (Indeed)
"Did I not bear a child?"   (Indeed)
440   There is a proverb told in the Manden.   (Indeed)
It is said of the Kòndès in the Manden.   (Indeed)

To buy a boney horse.   (Indeed)
To buy a boney horse.   (Indeed)
If you deceive a man
445   To buy a boney horse,
You must deliver a grasscutter, too!   (That's the truth,
                                          There's no doubt)

The Kòndè matriarch grew furious.   (Indeed)
The little old lady transformed herself,
And became a wild buffalo in the Manden.   (Indeed)
450   Each of her horns: a golden spear and a silver spear.   (Mmm)
Each of her ears: a golden snuff spoon, a silver snuff
      spoon.   (Mmm)
The strands of her tail: needles of gold, needles of silver.   (True)
Each of her ears: a golden snuff spoon, a silver snuff
      spoon.   (Indeed)
Each of her hooves: an adze of gold, an adze of silver.   (Indeed)
455   The woman thus transformed herself.
In the seven quarters of Du,
When the dawn would break,
She would slay a man in each quarter,
And thus they called her the Ginda of Du.
460   The Kòndè buffalo witch was called the Ginda of Du!

Aa, Bènba.   (Naamu)
Dunsu fula mana taga sigi kèlè,   (Naamu)
Dò na dò sa–nya fò su.
A kilin faga, ka kilin bila.   (Mmm)
465   O bè taa sa–nya fò su.   (Cinyè don)
Tarawerelu di ole ku mè.   (Mmm)
Tura Magan ni Kanke–jan!
Dan Mansa Wulandin ni Wulanba,   (Naamu)
Al' di kala ta, k'i lò.   (Mmm)
470   Sigi tè ku min nya,
Taama l'o banna.   (Cinyè)
Alu d'i lò.   (Naamu)
Alu sira wulaba rò.   (Mmm)
O tuma, woro man da.   (Naamu)
475   Basi bèè sòntò tiga le la Manden.

Jinè kamaren siginin basi kun na,   (Naamu)
O tògò le Tiningbè Magan di.   (Naamu)
Gemin–jolo gbangbannin a ma.
    "Sanu–kunba bakitò, Tiningbè Magan!   (Naamu)

480   "Wòri–kunba bakitò, Tiningbè Magan!   (Naamu)

    Nyagatè–din!
    "Jula Bani Magan ni Wasobali!   (Naamu)
    "Waso ka di mògò min ye,
    "I tè jula k'i teri ye?   (Naamu)
485   "Sanu ye jula fè,   (Naamu)
    "Sanko, i y'i wuyu N' kun, se–tigiya!   (Naamu)
    "Wòri ye Jula fè,   (Naamu)
    "Sanko, i y'i wuyu N' kun, se–tigiya
    "N' waatò, k'a faga?   (Naamu)
490   "N' natò, k'a faga?"
A mana tiga ròte,
A tiga–kèsè fili.   (Naamu)
Dò ye jan.   (Naamu)
Dò ye biri.   (Cinyè)

495   *Aa, jeli,*
    Min yena sènè kè,
    I ka sènè kè!
    Son–Jara banda!
    Min yena jago–kè,

Ah! Bèmba! (Indeed)
Whenever two hunters went forth to fight the buffalo, (Indeed)
One would come back to tell the way the other died.
She would kill the one and leave the other (Mmm)
465 To go home and tell the way he died. (That's true)
The Taraweres heard about this matter. (Mmm)
O Tura-Magan-and-Kanke-jan! (Indeed)
Dan Mansa Wulundin and Wulanba, (Indeed)
They took their bows and rose up. (Mmm)
470 What sitting will not solve,
Travel will resolve. (True)
They went forth. (Indeed)
They came to the deep forest. (Mmm)
In those days, kolas had not been created. (Indeed)
475 All the Manden fetishes were offered sacrifices of
 groundnuts.
A young jinn lived in one such fetish. (Indeed)
His name was Tinin Magan, the Pale. (Indeed)
Guinea-fowl feathers perforated the fetish.
 "Leprous-head-of-Gold, Tinin Magan, the
 Pale! (Indeed)
480 "Leprous-head-of-Silver, Tinin Magan, the
 Pale! (Indeed)
 "Child of Nyagatè!
 "Merchant Ben Magan without ostentation! (Indeed)
 "The one who loves ostentation,
 "Will he not make a merchant his friend? (Indeed)
485 "Gold is in the merchant's hand, (Indeed)
 "That it may overflow on me, O Power! (Indeed)
 "Silver is in the merchant's hand, (Indeed)
 "That it may overflow on me, O Power!
 "Going will I slay it? (Indeed)
490 "Coming will I slay it?"
As soon as he snapped the groundnut open,
He cast the shells. (Indeed)
One face up. (Indeed)
One face down. (True)

495 *Ah, bards,*
 He who would cultivate,
 Let him cultivate.
 Son-Jara is done!
 He who would deal in commerce,

500 *I ka jago kè!*
  Subaa banin!   (Naamu)
  Nin julu fòla ole rò, N' fa, Manden.   (Mmm)

  Son-Jara kaburu bè Manden.   (Naamu)
  A kaburu ye dugu min nò,   (Naamu)
505 O dugu tògò le Nyani di,   (Cinyè)
  Ba-kungu,   (Naamu)
  Sankarandin ba-kungu dè.
  O dugu tògò le Nyani di.
  Subaa kaburu bè Nyani le.   (Mmm)

510 Bènba le.   (Naamu)
  Dan Mansa Wulandin d'i sigi.   (Mmm)
  A nara jinè mina: (Naamu)
  "N' dògò-kè, na l'an ka jinè faga!"
  "Aa, N' dògò, i kana jinè faga dè!
515 "A bil'a ka aramuru bil'an ye.
  "Jinè ku lòn Hadama-din di."   (Naamu)
  Jinè di aramuru bila: (Naamu)
  "Ilu mana taga,   (Mmm)
  "Ilu b'i karifa garangèlu bènba,

520 "Walali Ibrahima la.   (Naamu)
  "Ilu mana taga,
  "I bara baa sara wòrònwila kè, saraka di, (Mmm)
  "Ani kini donunintò.
  "Musu-kòròni dò ye Du tilibè fè.
525 "Ilu ka kini domunintò di o musu-kòròni ma.
  "Ni Ala sònna, ilu ye sigi fagala la."

  Al' waar'i yèrè karifa garangèlu bènba la, (Naamu)

  Ka baa sara wòrònwula saraka.   (Naamu)
  Alu mana taa wula dò,
530 Sigi ye na su.   (Mmm)
  Alu mana na su,   (Naamu)
  Sigi ye taga wula kònò.
  Kun-nyògòn olu ni sigi ye nyògòn nyinina;
   alu ni sigi ma nyògòn ye.   (Cinyè)

535 Alu di kini dònunitò saraka,
  Ka tag'a di musu-kòròni ma.

<table>
<tr><td>500</td><td>*Let him deal in commerce!*</td><td></td></tr>
<tr><td></td><td>*The Wizard is done!*</td><td>(Indeed)</td></tr>
<tr><td></td><td>These chords were played for him, my Father,</td><td></td></tr>
<tr><td></td><td>   in the Manden.</td><td>(Mmm)</td></tr>
<tr><td></td><td>Son-Jara's tomb is in the Manden.</td><td>(Indeed)</td></tr>
<tr><td></td><td>The village where his tomb is found,</td><td>(Indeed)</td></tr>
<tr><td>505</td><td>The name of that village is Nyani,</td><td>(True)</td></tr>
<tr><td></td><td>By the banks of the river,</td><td>(Indeed)</td></tr>
<tr><td></td><td>On the banks of the Sankaran.</td><td></td></tr>
<tr><td></td><td>The name of the village is Nyani.</td><td></td></tr>
<tr><td></td><td>The Wizard's tomb is in Nyani.</td><td>(Mmm)</td></tr>
</table>

Ah! Bèmba!   (Indeed)

510 Dan Mansa Wulundin sat down. (Mmm)
He came and seized the jinn: (Indeed)
"My elder, come let us kill this jinn!"
"Ah! Little brother, do not kill the jinn.
515 "Leave him be, and he will read the signs for us.
"Jinns know more than the Sons-of-Adam." (Indeed)
And the jinn did conjury for them: (Indeed)
"When both of you go forth, (Mmm)
"You must seek sanctuary with the cordwainer
   patriarch,
520 "With Walali Ibrahima. (Indeed)
"When both of you go forth,
"You should sacrifice seven portions of goat, (Mmm)
"This and yesterday's leftover rice.
"There is an old woman to the west of Du.
525 "Give yesterday's rice to this old woman.
"And if God wills, you'll slay the buffalo." (Indeed)

Thus they sought sanctuary with the cordwainer
   patriarch, (Indeed)
And sacrificed seven portions of goat. (Indeed)
Whenever they would go into the bush,
530 The buffalo would come into the town. (Mmm)
Whenever they would come into the town, (Indeed)
The buffalo would go into the bush.
They tracked each other for a week;
Not once did they and the buffalo meet. (True)

535 They sacrificed the leftover rice,
And offered it to the old woman.

A yèlèla:
"Hè! Ilu ye mògò jòn di?"
"An delu Tarawerel' di."
540 "Tarawerelu, ilu bòra dugu jòn dò, N' fa?" (Naanu)
"An ne bòtò Bintanya Kamalen ne." (Naanu)
"Tarawerelu, Ne le Du-sigi di. (Naamu)
"Ne le di malu ban.
"Ka fini ban,
545 "Ka tiga ban,
"Ka mògòw ban yan, (Mmm)
"K'a tè fò mògò ma tugun, Kòndè. (Mmm)
"Ne le Du-sigi di.
"Tarawerelu, Ala di N' d'ilu ma. (Naamu)

550 "Ilu sisè-kili siyama barabara,
"Ka n'a di musu-kòròni ma." (Cinyè)
Al' di susè-kili siyama barabara, k'a mafara,
Ka ta'a di musu-kòròni ma.
A da'a dumu, k'i min, (Naamu)
555 F'a ju-la-gaari tègèra. (Naamu)

"Tarawerelu,
"Ilu susè-kili fula nyini, (Naamu)
"A ni yirini kèndè, (Naamu)
"A ni finton-kèsè kilin, (Naamu)
560 "A ni genda-kala." (Naamu)
"A d'o bèè madabari. (Cinyè)
"Tarawerelu, an ka sèn. (Naamu)
"Kòndè ni Tarawere k'i sèn dè."
Alu nara ni filen kaban di, k'a dabiri. (Naanu)

565 Alu d'alu bulu-kòni gasu nyògòn na: (Mmm)
    "Tariya duman tè!
    "Si-N'-fèya duman tè: (Naanu)
    "Ba-dinya duman tè!
    "Furu duman tè!
570   "Kanu duman tè!
    "Tarawere bònsòn-bònsòn,
    "N'a di Kòndè janfa,
    "Janfa k'a faga! (Naanu)
    "Kòndè bònsòn-bònsòn, (Naanu)
575   "N'a di Tarawere janfa,
    "Janfa k'a faga!" (Naamu)

She burst out laughing:
"Ha! And whose people are you?"
"We are Taraweres."
540 "Taraweres, what village do you hail from?" (Indeed)
"We hail from Bintanya Kamalen." (Indeed)
"Taraweres, I am the Buffalo of Du. (Indeed)
'Tis I brought an end to rice,
"And brought an end to fonio,
545 "And brought an end to groundnuts,
"And brought an end to people here, (Mmm)
"So none shall hear again the name of Kòndè! (Mmm)
'Tis I who am the Buffalo of Du.
"Taraweres, into your hands God has delivered me! (Indeed)

550 "Many eggs must you boil,
"And give to me, the old woman." (True)
They boiled up many eggs and put them together,
And gave them to the old woman.
She ate them down and drank her fill, (Indeed)
555 Till the folds of fat in her venter vanished. (Indeed)

"O Taraweres,
"Go forth and find two chicken eggs, (Indeed)
"These and a piece of green wood, (Indeed)
"This and a charcoal chunk, (Indeed)
560 "This and a spindle stick." (Indeed)
And she conjured a spell o'er all of that. (True)
"O Taraweres, let us swear an oath. (Indeed)
"Let Kòndè and Tarawere be bound by an oath."
They brought a new calabash bowl and turned it face
  down. (Indeed)
565 They linked their fingers each to the other: (Mmm)
  "No friendship will be good!
  "No lovemaking will be good! (Indeed)
  "No brotherhood will be good!
  "No marriage will be good!
570   "No love will be good,
  "For any Tarawere son,
  "Should a Kòndè he betray,
  "Let that betrayal kill him! (Indeed)
  "For any son of Kòndè, (Indeed)
575   "Should a Tarawere he betray,
  "Let that betrayal kill him!" (Indeed)

Alu d'i kali,   (Naamu)
Tarawerelu, al' d'i kali,   (Naamu)
Karunku-fin na.
580 Tarawerelu, al' d'i kali,   (Naamu)
Kòròsò-nyi na.   (Naamu)
Tarawerelu, al' d'i kali,
Sita-finni na.   (Mmm)
Kòndè-musu, a d'i kali,   (Naamu)
585 Li-mògòba la,
Ani datu kònyò.   (Mmm)
A to kilin, k'a burun, nnn.   (Cinyè don)
     Tura Magan ni Kanke-jan!   (Cinyè)

"Tarawerelu, ilu mana taga sini,   (Mmm)
590 "Ilu mana sigi min ye,   (Naamu)
"A gere bèè sanu tanba ni wòri tanba,   (Naamu)
"A ku-kèsè bèè sanu sagilan ni wòri sagilan.   (Naamu)

"A tulu bèè sanu janba ni wòri janba.   (Naamu)

"A tòròn bèè sanu sònbè ni wòri sònbè.
595 "Ole Du-sigi di,   (Cinyè)

"N'a d'ilu gèn,
"Alu ka sisè-kili dò bila.
"O kèla kòngòba di.   (Mmm)
"San'a ka kòngò tògòma,   (Naamu)
600 "Ilu ye dò kè.   (Mmm)
"A man'ilu gèn,   (Naamu)
"Ilu ka dò wèrè bila.
"I ye kèla dala di.   (Naamu)
"Ilu ka jirini kèndè turu wo dala da la.   (Naamu)
605 "O ye kèla tuba ye.   (Naamu)
"Tun dò ye tuba kò fè,   (Naamu)
"Dan Mansa Wulandin k'i biri tun kò fè.   (Naamu)
"Dan Mansa Wulanba,   (Mmm)
"A ka yèlèn yiri la.   (Naamu)
610 "Dan Mansa Wulandin,   (Naamu)
"A k'i sin lò finton-kèsè kilin kan.   (Naamu)
"O ye kèla dibi di!"   (Naamu)
Hali sini sògòma,
Dunsu y'ò dibi sònla Manden-banku kan.
615 O le dibi di.   (Cinyè)

Thus they swore the oath. (Indeed)
The Taraweres, they swore the oath (Indeed)
Over the black spitting cobra.
580 The Taraweres, they swore the oath (Indeed)
Over the crooked tooth mamba. (Indeed)
The Taraweres, they swore the oath
Over the dark black baobab. (Mmm)
The Kòndè woman, she swore the oath (Indeed)
585 Over the great deer fly
And the deathlike stench of *datu-leaf*. (Mmm)
Whatever may remain, let that too be cast! (That's true)
    O Tura-Magan-and-Kanke-jan! (True)

"Taraweres, when you go forth tomorrow, (Mmm)
590 "The buffalo which you may see, (Indeed)
"Each of her horns: a golden spear and a silver spear. (Indeed)
"The strands of her tail: needles of gold, needles of
    silver. (Indeed)
"Each of her ears: a golden snuff spoon, a silver snuff
    spoon. (Indeed)
"Each of her hooves: an adze of gold, an adze of silver. (Indeed)
595 "That is the Buffalo of Du. (True)

"Should she pursue you,
"You must throw down an egg.
"It will become a great wilderness. (Mmm)
"Before she traverses that wilderness, (Indeed)
600 "You must make some distance. (Mmm)
"When she pursues you again, (Indeed)
"You must throw down the other one.
"It will become a great lake. (Indeed)
"Plant the green stick at the edge of the lake. (Indeed)
605 "It will become a great forest. (Indeed)
"Behind the great forest will rise an anthill, (Indeed)
"Behind which should hide Dan Mansa Wulandin. (Indeed)
"Dan Mansa Wulanba (Mmm)
"Should climb into a tree. (Indeed)
610 "Dan Mansa Wulanba, (Indeed)
"On the charcoal chunk should step. (Indeed)
"Thus will he become a shade!" (Indeed)
Even tomorrow morning,
The Manden hunters will worship that Shadow.
615 That is what Shadow is! (True)

“Ilu mana gènda-kala la kala dò,
“Ilu man’o kè, ka Du sigi bun,
“N’ ye duna tu.
“Tarawerelu, lòn dè, Ne le Du-sigi di.   (Mmm)
620 “Kèsè tè Ne dun.   (Mmm)
“Tanba tè Ne dun, nnn.   (Mmm)
“Muru tè Ne dun.   (Mmm)
“Ne le di mògò ban,
“Ka malu ban,
625 “Ka fini ban.
“Tarawerelu!”   (Mmm)

        Aa, min yena sènè kè,
        I ka sènè kè.   (Mmm)
        Min yena jago kè,
630   *O ka jago kè.*
        O fòra Subaa kaburu le kan, N’ fa,
        Manden Sankarandin,
        Sankarandin ba-kungun.
        O dugu tògò ye Nyani di.

635 Tarawerelu di kala ta.
Alu sira wulaba dò.   (Mmm)
Dan Mansa Wulandin ko, “N’ kòrò-kè,
“Du-sigi fèlè dè!”   (Naamu)
Sigi d’alu gèn.   (Mmm)
640 Alu di sisè-kili dò bila.   (Mmm)
O kèra kòngòba di.
Dugu dò tèr’o kòngò tè ma.
O dugu tògò le Bènbè di.
Tala Mansa Kòngò tèrè Bènbè le.
645   Kiri-la-Kamisòkòlu bènba!
        Tali Mansa Kòngò!

        . . . ,
        Tèrè Kunba ni Kaya!
        Nyani-kò ni Maramu-kò!
650   Jaa, mun sunt’a kòrò marato ni
            kala kò?   (Naamu, è, Fa-Digi,
                                              o ye cinyè ye)

        I mana taa Karata,   (Mmm)
        Alu y’a fòla dòlu ma, ko Magasa.

"Should you arm your bow with the spindle,
"And should you fire on the Buffalo of Du,
"I will leave this world behind.
"Taraweres, know this! I am the Buffalo of Du.   (Mmm)
620   "No shot can pierce me.   (Mmm)
"No spear can pierce me.   (Mmm)
"No knife can pierce me.   (Mmm)
"I brought an end to people,
"And brought an end to rice,
625   "And brought an end to fonio.
"O Taraweres!"   (Mmm)

Ah! He who would cultivate,
Let him cultivate!   (Mmm)
He who would deal in commerce,
630   *Let him deal in commerce!*
That was sung at the Wizard's tomb, my father,
At the Manden Sunkaran River,
On the banks of the Sankarandin.
The name of that village was Nyani.

635   The Taraweres took up the bow.
They reached the high bush country.   (Mmm)
Dan Mansa Wulandin said, "O Elder,
"Behold the Buffalo of Du!"   (Indeed)
The buffalo charged them,   (Mmm)
640   And they threw down the first of the eggs.   (Mmm)
It became a great wilderness.
There was a village in the midst of that wilderness.
The name of that village was Bèmbè.
Rescuer-King-of-the-Wilderness was there in the
      village of Bèmbè.
645   Kamisòkò ancestor from Kiri,
Bee-King-of-the-Wilderness!

. . . ,

Tèrè Kumba and Kaya!
Nyani River and Maramu River!
650   But what grew beneath it apart from
      hammer and bow?   (Indeed, eh, Fa-Digi,
                                             that's the truth)

Should you go north to Kaarta,   (Mmm)
They call some of them there Magasa.

O bèè ye Fa-Koli ye.
Bulu ngana.
655 . . . .   (Cinyè)

Sigi d'alu gèn.
Al' di sisè-kili dò wèrè bila.   (Mmm)
O kèra dala di.   (Naamu)
A di yiridin kèndè bila.
660 O kèra tuba ye.   (Naamu)
Tun dò ye tu kò fè.
Sigi jigira dala kònò, nnn.
A ye nòla.
A ye minna.
665 A ye nòla.
A ye minna.
Jelilu kan ole ma: (Naamu)
    Kòndè-din jara, jiba-min!   (Naamu)
    Dala kunbu kanba!   (Naamu)
670 Dala-jiba-min!   (Naamu)
    Murulu Fa-Kanda!   (Naamu)
    Murumurulu Fa-Kanda!   (Naamu)
    Kun-Jan Fa-Kanda!   (Naamu)
    Kun-Jan Makònòn Fa-Kanda!   (Naamu)
675 Fa-Kanda buran faga!
    A tan ni kònòntòn.
    Tan ni kònòntòn, Fa-Kanda farinyara.
    Bènyè min tèrè cèbalu karada dò,   (Naamu)
    Fa-Kanda la bènyè le.   (Naamu)
680 Bènyè min tèrè cèbalu kènè-tintin kan,   (Naamu)
    Fa-Kanda la bènyè le.   (Naamu)
    Bènyè min tèrè cèbalu salifo le,   (Naamu)
    Fa-Kanda la bènyè la di.
    Garabaya ni Kaya!   (Mmm)

685 Bènba le.   (Naamu, Ne le nara)
    Biribiriba!
    Kirikisa, Dunnun-tanba ni Sòn-tanba!
    Nare Magan Kònatè!
    Subaa-Minè-Subaa!   (Mmm)
690 Jankuma la wara la Sinbon!   (Mmm)

    Kala Jula Sangoyi Mamunaka.   (Naamu)
    Dan Mansa Wulandin siland'a dusu rò dòòni: (Naamu)

They are all of Fa-Koli's line.
Hero-of-Original-Clans.
655   . . . .   (True)

The buffalo charged them again,
And they threw down the other egg.   (Mmm)
It became a great lake.   (Indeed)
Dan Mansa Wulandin planted the green stick,
660 And it became a great forest.   (Indeed)
Behind the forest was the anthill.
The buffalo went down to the lake.
She was swimming,
And she was drinking.
665 She was swimming,
And she was drinking.
Thus the bards sing of that: (Indeed)
     The Kòndè lion child, Great-Water-Drinker!   (Indeed)
     Splasher-in-the-Lake!   (Indeed)
670   Great-Lake-Water-Drinker!   (Indeed)
     Those-who-Turn, Fa-Kanda!   (Indeed)
     Those-who-Turn-About, Fa-Kanda!   (Indeed)
     Those-with-Visions, Fa-Kanda!   (Indeed)
     Those-who-Seek-Visions, Fa-Kanda!   (Indeed)
675 Fa-Kanda, Killer-of-Kin!
Nineteen of them in all!
From these nineteen, Fa-Kanda gains power!
The arrow found in the breast of the brave,   (Indeed)
It was Fa-Kanda's arrow.   (Indeed)
680 The arrow found in the loins of the brave,   (Indeed)
It was Fa-Kanda's arrow.   (Indeed)
The arrow found in the brow of the brave,   (Indeed)
It was Fa-Kanda's arrow.
Garabaya and Kaya!   (Mmm)

685 Ah! Bèmba!   (Indeed, I'm coming)
Biribiriba!
Kirikisa, Spear-of-Access, Spear-of-Service!
Nare Magan Kònatè!
Sorcerer-Seizing-Sorcerer!   (Mmm)
690 Simbon, Lion-Born-of-the-Cat!   (Mmm)

O Kala Jula Sangoyi Mamunaka!   (Indeed)
Dan Mansa Wulandin became deeply frightened: (Indeed)

“Gènda-kala tè nin dun.”   (Cinyè)
A di marafa waraka,
695   Ka kèsèlu k’a kan.
A di mugu bila, kèsè sigi la.   (Naamu)
Nègèlu m’a mina.   (Naamu)
A d’alu gèn: *biri-biri-biri!*
Alu waara yèlèn se-juba la.   (Naamu)
700   Sigi ye nala, a y’i tògòma la.   (Naamu)
A y’a kun-kulu firin-firinna.   (Naamu)
Ani nkoor nara: (Naamu)
“Nyara wo se nyara!”   (Naamu)

Se nyara ni mògòlu bèè bira dugu ma: *biri!*   (Naamu)

705   A d’alu gèn: *biri-biri-biri!*   (Cinyè)
Dan Mansa Wulanba yèlènda yiri la.   (Cinyè)
Dan Mansa Wulandin,
A waar’i biri tunkun o la,   (Naamu)
K’è sin lòn finton-kèsè kilin kan.   (Naamu)
710   A ko marii ma,
Ko, “An ye dò kè!”

Sigi nara tunkun ma.
A y’i nya-lakalanna.   (Naamu)
Ama fèn ye.
715   A y’e nya-lakalanna.
Dibi y’a nya la,
Dunsulu ye dibi min sònla.   (Naamu)
A y’a nya-lakalanna.   (Naamu)
Dan Mansa Wulandin di gènda-kala ta,
720   K’i saba, ka Du-sigi bun: *pan!*
Sigi d’i bara, “O!
      “Du-kalu,
      “Minimini kòlòn!   (Naanu)
      “Lònbaga bènyè!
725   “Sigini wulen mana mògò fa faga,
      “I mana tunni wulen ye,
      “I tè silan ba?
      “Lònbaga bènyè le!”   (O ye cinyè ye)
O kèra sanda ye.   (Mmm, è, Fa-Digi,
                                                      o ye cinyè ye)

730   Sigi bira: *biri!*   (Naamu)

"No spindle stick will ever pierce her hide!"   (True)
He cleared the chamber of his gun,
695 And rammed some shot inside,
And discharged his powder on the buffalo.   (Indeed)
The shot would not strike her.   (Indeed)
She chased them on, *biri-biri-biri!*
They went and climbed a shea-butter tree.   (Indeed)
700 The buffalo came up beneath them.   (Indeed)
She shook her great head from side to side.   (Indeed)
And bellowed out: (Indeed)
"Dense thicket! Shea tree's dense thicket!"   (Indeed)

The shea tree branches with their people came crashing
    down to earth, *biri!*   (Indeed)
705 And she pursued them once again, *biri-biri-biri!*   (True)
Dan Mansa Wulanba climbed into another tree.   (True)
Dan Mansa Wulandin
Went and hid behind the great anthill,   (Indeed)
And stepped upon the charcoal chunk.   (Indeed)
710 He said to his elder brother,
Said, "Let's do something now!"

The buffalo came round the anthill.
She looked both to and fro,   (Indeed)
But nothing did she see.
715 She looked again both to and fro.
It was only Shadow in her sight,
That Shadow worshipped by the hunters.   (Indeed)
She looked again both to and fro.   (Indeed)
Dan Mansa Wulandin took the spindle stick,
720 Drew back and shot the Buffalo of Du, *pan!*
The buffalo bellowed out: "Oh!
    "O People of Du!
    "The Twisted Well!   (Indeed)
    "Arrow-of-the-Knower!
725   "Should your father be slain by the red buffalo,
    "And shall he see a red anthill,
    "Won't he be afraid of it?
    " 'Tis the Arrow-of-the-Knower!"   (That's the truth)
And that has become a proverb.   (Mmm, eh, Fa-Digi,
    That's the truth)

730 The buffalo collapsed, *biri!*   (Indeed)

A d'a ku tègè,
K'a gerelu tègè,   (Naamu)
K'a tululu tègè,   (Naamu)
K'a tòrònlu tègè.   (Naamu)
735 Dan Mansa Wulanba nara: (Naamu)
"N' dògò, a kèra di?"   (Naamu)
A ko, "Ha, N' kòrò, Du-sigi bira dè!"

A ko,
       "Sa-dugu ni basi-dugu!
740   "Siso-suma ani Lènma-suma!   (Naamu)
       "Sòni-kènè-tigo ni binyèni-kènè-tigo!

       "Wula-mansa, Kinibi!   (Mmm)
       "Wula-mansa, Kalinka!
       "Dandan-fè-lò ani Yiriba-fè-lò!

745   "Su ka di cè dò la,
       "Wula man d'i la!
       "Wula ka di cè dò,
       "Su man d'i la!"
A ko, "Aa, N' kòrò,
750 "E mana kè jeli ye,
"Jèbaga tè sor'i la!"   (O ye cinyè ye)
Ole di Kala-jan Sangoyi wulu.   (Naamu)

Kala-jan Sangoyi, a di Tuba Katè wulu,   (Naamu)
Ka Mònsòn Katè wulu,   (Naamu)
755 Ka Fatiyan Katè wulu,   (Naamu)
Ka Sagaburu-jan Katè wulu,   (Naamu)
Ka ... wulu.   (Naamu)
Jebagatè jeli ye bunda wòòrò di.   (Cinyè don)
O bèè di din fula sòrò.
760 O kèra tan ni fula di.
Tala kilin kèra Kòròkolu ye.   (Cinyè)
Kòròkolu ye jeli ye.   (Naamu, naamu)

Bènba le.   (Naamu)
O Mònsòn Katè dè,   (Naamu)
765 Ole di Jeli Bugu wulu.   (Naamu)
Jeli Bugu ka Bura Magasi wulu.   (Naamu)
Bura Magasi ka Jeli Madi wulu.   (Naamu)
Jeli Madi ka Tanba-kèli Mansa Magan wulu.   (Naamu)

He hacked off her tail,
And hacked off her horns,   (Indeed)
And hacked off her ears,   (Indeed)
And hacked off her hooves.   (Indeed)
735   Dan Mansa Wulanba came forward: (Indeed)
"Little brother, what has happened?"   (Indeed)
"Ah, my elder," the reply, "the Buffalo of Du has
        fallen."
At which he cried out:
        "Snake country and fetish country!
740   "Stench-of-Mosquito and Stench-of-Deerfly!   (Indeed)
        "Cutter-of-Fresh-Heart and Cutter-of-Fresh-
              Liver!
        "King-of-the-Wilderness, Kininbi!   (Mmm)
        "King-of-the-Wilderness, Kalinka!
        "He-Who-Stands-within-the-Walls and
              He-Who-Stands-amongst-Great-Trees!
745   "For some the village is suitable,
        "The outlands do not suit them.
        "For some the outlands are suitable,
        "The village does not suit them."
"Ah, my elder," the reply,
750   "Should you become a bard,
"One who could refuse you won't be found!" (That's the truth)
And from him thus descended Sangoyi, the
              Long Bow.   (Indeed)
Sangoyi, the Long Bow, he begat Tuba Kate,   (Indeed)
And begat Mònsòn Katè,   (Indeed)
755   And begat Fatiyan Katè   (Indeed)
And begat Sagaburu Katè the Tall,   (Indeed)
And begat . . .   (Indeed)
These are the six clans of Jebagatè bards.   (That's true)
They each had two sons,
760   And thus became twelve in all.
One branch became the Kòròko.   (True)
The Kòròko are bards.   (Indeed, indeed)

Ah! Bèmba!   (Indeed)
That Mònsòn Katè,   (Indeed)
765   It was he who begat Bugu, the Bard.   (Indeed)
Bugu, the Bard begat Bura Magasi.   (Indeed)
Bura Magasi begat Madi, the Bard.   (Indeed)
Madi, the Bard begat Tamba-keli Mansa Magan.   (Indeed)

<pre>
       Mansa Magan ka Sigiya wulu.   (Naamu)
770   Sigiya din le nin di.   (Mmm, cinyè don)

       Bènba le.   (Naamu)
       Alu waara sigi gere n'a tòrònnu ye,   (Naamu)
       A n'a ku-kèsèlu.   (Naamu)
       Alu waar'a bèè bila bara rò.   (Naamu)
775   Dan Mansa Wulandin di muru b'a la dò,
       K'a den gala la.   (Mmm)
       Dan Mansa Wulanba,   (Naamu)
       A d'i sin bò sanbita dò, nnn,   (Naamu)
       K'a tun gala kòrò,   (Naamu)
780   Ka waa i karifa garangèlu bènba,
       Walahi Ibrahima la.   (Naamu)

       Musu-kòròni ni ku-lakali tè ban.   (Cinyè don)
       Sira min musu-kòròni dò taara:
       "Du Magan Jata Kòndè, sirani du N' ma."   (Naamu)
785   A d'i dira d'a ma.   (Mmm)
       A di sira min, sira nyiginda: (Naamu)
       "N' ye kuma dò fòl'i ye.
       "A ka tò an fula ni nyògòn tè dè!   (Cinyè)
       "I kan'a fò, k'i d'a mè N' da dè!   (Mmm)
790   "Sigi min siginin ye mògòlu da la,
       "Dò di ye sigi faga!
       "N' waara dè!"   (Cinyè)
       Du Magan Jata Kòndè di tantan dòbila.   (Naamu)

       A di tawulen gwèsi,   (Mmm)
795   Faama dundun: (Mmm)
       "Diya-guya,   (Mmm)
       "Bèè ka nyògòn tèrè!   (Naamu)
       "Min nanin sigi faga,   (Cinyè)
       "N' ye Du-dugu tan ni fula talala fula di,
800   "Ka tala kilin di wo mògò ma.
       "Kè-farin bènnin mògò la dugu kònò."
              I kana fèn-fèn faga bagitò ye,
              Fo sin-da-nya kilin kè,   (Naamu)
              Alu ladiyanin le o di.

805   Aa, nin min yena sènè kè,
              I ka sènè kè!
              Aa jeli, min yena jago kè,
</pre>

Mansa Magan begat Sigiya, (Indeed)
770 And Sigiya's son is this one right here. (Mmm, that's true)

O! Bèmba! (Indeed)
They brought the buffalo's horns and her hooves, (Indeed)
These and the strands of her tail. (Indeed)
They went and placed them all in a calabash. (Indeed)
775 Dan Mansa Wulandin drew his knife from its sheath,
And leaned it against the lounging platform. (Mmm)
Dan Mansa Wulanba, (Indeed)
He took his sandals off his feet, (Indeed)
And stacked them near the lounging platform, (Indeed)
780 And went to seek refuge with the cordwainer patriarch,
With Walali Ibrahima. (Indeed)

Old women and gossip are never far apart. (That's the truth)
A snuff-dipping little old woman came forward:
"Magan Jata Kòndè of Du, pass me a pinch of snuff." (Indeed)
785 He passed her a pinch of snuff. (Mmm)
She dipped some snuff and wet it down: (Indeed)
"I have a word to say to you.
"But let it remain between us two! (True)
"Say not you heard it from my lips! (Mmm)
790 "The buffalo that settled near our folk,
"Someone has slain that buffalo.
"And with that I'm off." (True)
Magan Jata Kòndè of Du let loose the great
    village drum. (Indeed)
He beat the royal drum, (Mmm)
795 The drum of power: (Mmm)
"Like it or not, (Mmm)
"Everyone must gather! (Indeed)
"The one who killed the buffalo, (True)
"Into two I have divided the twelve towns of Du,
800 "And to that person will give one half.
"Such a brave man will be an asset to our folk."
        No need to kill for the leper,
        But one footstep forward, (Indeed)
        That is all he wants.

805   *Ah, he who would cultivate,*
        Let him cultivate.
        Ah! Bards, he who would deal in commerce,

I ka jago kè!
Son-Jara banda.
810   Nare Magan Kònatè!

Ka taa Fatiyataligara,
Ka taa Sòkòtò,   (Naamu)
Magan Son-Jara ta le o di.
Fara-finnu y'ole ma, N' fa,
815   Eripibiliki-Mali,   (Naamu)
Maninka mara.   (Mmm)
Mali kòrò le nin di.
A di Bamanan Dankun faga,   (Naamu)
Fantan na dankun-dò-sigi tè bèn.   (Naamu)
820   Ka Bamanan Basa faga,   (Naamu)
Fantan kan'i yèrè tògò la basa la.   (Naamu)
Ka Bamanan Kòtu faga,   (Naamu)
Fantan na tu-rò-sigi tè bèn.   (Cinyè)
N' bi wo le fò Modibo ye,   (Mmm)
825   Daba la Modibo le.   (Naamu)
Modibo bòra Lamuru rò,
Modibo min bòra Daba dò.
Ni Daba bòra Lamuru dò Bakunun
    Jirè.   (Naamu)
Kamara-musu le tèrè nsana Modibo le.
830   Bari Son-Jara ma fiyen kè samara ye,
K'i taam'a kan.   (Naamu)
O kèra Modibo ye.
Nare Magan Kònatè!
Subaa-Minè-Subaa!   (Naamu)

835   Aa Bènba.   (Cinyè dè)
Kamalenba kulun dòlu ye nala,
Ka muru kudun majòsi.   (Naamu)
N'a d'a dun muru le dò,
N'a ma bunya, a ye dògòya.   (Naamu)
840   Dòlu ye nala,   (Naamu)
K'è sin dun samata dò.
N'a bunya ma, a ye dògòya ma.   (Mmm)

Alu di kila lò garangèlu bènba,
Walali Ibrahima ma,   (Mmm)
845   Ibrahima.

Let him deal in commerce!
Son-Jara is done!
810 O Nare Magan Kònatè!

From Fatiyataligara
All the way to Sokoto,   (Indeed)
All that was Magan Son-Jara's,
The Africans call that, my father,
815 The Republic of Mali,   (Indeed)
The Maninka realm,   (Mmm)
That is the meaning of Mali.
He slew Bambara-of-the-Border.   (Indeed)
Settling on the border does not suit the weak.   (Indeed)
820 And killed Bambara-the-Lizard,   (Indeed)
No weak one should call himself Lizard,   (Indeed)
And slew Bambara-of-the-Backwoods,   (Indeed)
Settling the backwoods does not suit the weak.   (True)
I sing this for Modibo,   (Mmm)
825 Daba's Modibo!   (Indeed)
Modibo descended from Lamuru.
Modibo who was fathered by Daba.
That Daba, he was fathered by Lamuru in
     Bukunun Jirè.   (Indeed)
A Kamara woman was Modibo's mother.
830 But Son-Jara did not have the wind as shoes,
To travel far and wide upon.   (Indeed)
But that was done by Modibo.
O Nare Magan Kònatè!
The Sorcerer-Seizing-Sorcerer!   (Indeed)

835 Ah! Bèmba!   (True)
Some strong young braves came forward,
And wiped off the blade of the knife.   (Indeed)
Whoever would put the blade in his sheath,
If it wasn't too big, it was too small.   (Indeed)
840 Others came forward,   (Indeed)
And put their feet into the sandals.
If they weren't too big, they were too small.   (Mmm)

They sent a messenger to the cordwainer patriarch,
To Walali Ibrahima,   (Mmm)
845 To Ibrahima.

Dan Mansa Wulandin ni Wulanba waara
   nyògòn-ye la.   (Naamu)
Tura Magan bòra.
Tarawerelu bòra.   (Naamu)
Alu sira danin-da la,
850 Sununkun da la.   (Naamu)
Wulu-kè kòrò bòra,   (Naamu)
Ani jankuma.   (Cinyè)
Wulu-kè kòrò d'i bara tun: (Cinyè)
"Tarawerelu,   (Naamu)
855 "Abarika ilu la, kini la. (Naamu)
"Abarika kulu kurun la.
"Nya mògò ma,
"I mana nya mògò ma,
"N'a m'a sara,
860 "A k'a lòn i ye.   (Cinyè don)

"Tarawerelu, ilu waatò nyògòn-ye la. (Naamu)
"Du dugu tan ni fula mana tala di,
"Ka tala kilin d'ilu ma,
"K'ilu ka sigi yan,   (Naamu)
865 "Il'i ban!   (Naamu)
"Il'a fò, 'An bòtò Manden. (Naamu)
"'An ye waala Manden ne.'
"Tarawerelu!   (Cinyè)

"Musu sukudun wòòrò ye yan. (Mmm)
870 "N'a fòra, k'elu k'e sako t'a dò, (Naamu)
"N' ye jankumani-fin bilala,
"O ka taga ilu fè.   (Cinyè)
"A mana dun musu min sinda fulan tè, (Naamu)
"Ka bò, k'a laminimini, (Naamu)
875 "Ka dun musu sin fulan tè, (Naamu)
"Ka bò, k'a laminimini, (Naamu)
"Ilu k'o musu ta.   (Naamu)
"A tògò le Sugulun Kòndè di. (Naamu)
"Kuru ni bagi bòn'a ma. (Naamu)
880 "Alu ko a ma Sugulun Kuduma! (Naamu)
"Ilu n'o mana taga,   (Naamu)
"Ole din-kè kilin sòròla, (Naamu)
"Ole ta le Manden di. (Naamu)
"Tarawerelu, abarika!" (Naamu)

Dan Mansa Wulandin and Wulanba went to the
    meeting.   (Indeed)
Tura Magan came forward!
The Taraweres came forward!   (Indeed)
They arrived at the compound door,
850 By the rubbish heap.   (Indeed)
An old male dog sidled up   (Indeed)
With a cat beside him.   (True)
The old dog spoke out: (True)
"Ah! Taraweres!   (Indeed)
855 "I thank you for the rice.   (Indeed)
"I thank you for those bits of bone.
"Be kind to people.
"If one is kind to people,
"Should there be no recompense,
860 "At least it will be known of him.   (That's true)

"Taraweres, you are off to this meeting.   (Indeed)
"When the twelve towns of Du are divided in two,
"And the half offered unto you,
"So that you'll settle here,   (Indeed)
865 "You must refuse!   (Indeed)
"You must say, 'We come from the Manden,   (Indeed)
"'We return to the Manden.'
"O Taraweres!   (True)

"There will be six young maidens there.   (Mmm)
870 "When you are told to choose amongst them,   (Indeed)
"This black cat will I release,
"So that she will approach you.   (True)
"The maiden's legs she goes between,   (Indeed)
"Comes out, goes round and through again,   (Indeed)
875 "And goes again between her legs,   (Indeed)
"Comes out, goes round and through again,   (Indeed)
"That is the maiden you must take.   (Indeed)
"Her name will be Sugulun Kòndè.   (Indeed)
"Warts and pustules cover her.   (Indeed)
880 "They call her Sugulun-of-the-Warts!   (Indeed)
"Should you go forth with her,   (Indeed)
"Her only son once born,   (Indeed)
"The Manden will be his.   (Indeed)
"O Taraweres, I thank you!"   (Indeed)

<pre>
885 Dan Mansa Wulandin waara ole rò, nnn,   (Naamu)
     Ka muru dun a la dò,
     K'è sigi gala la.   (Naamu)
     Dan Mansa Wulanba,   (Naamu)
     A d'i sin dun samata dò,   (Naamu)
890 K'è sigi gala la.   (Naamu)

     Bèè d'i bara, "Nin lelu di sigi faga!   (Naamu)
     "Nin lelu di sigi faga!   (Mmm)
     "Ilelu ye mògò jòn di."
     "An nelu ye Tarawerelu di."   (Cinyè)
895 "Ilelu bòra min?"   (Mmm)
     "An nelu bòtò Bintanya Kamalen ne."   (Naamu)
     "Tarawerelu,   (Mmm)
     "Du-dugu tan ni fula, N' b'a tala fula di,
     "Ka tala kilin d'ilu ma,   (Mmm)
900 "Ilu ka sigi yan.   (Mmm)
     "Kè farin bènnin mògò la dugu kònò."
     "An tè!   (Cinyè)
     "An bòtò Manden.
     "An waatò Manden ne."
905 "Awa, Tarawerelu, ilu nya-lakalan.   (Cinyè)
     "Ilu mana musu min ye,
     "Ilu la kèlè-kòntòn ne, ole le di yen.
     "Ilu mana musu min ye,
     "N' d'o d'ilu ma."   (Cinyè)
910 Alu di sukudunlu labò,   (Cinyè)
     Sukudunlu mògò wòòrò.   (Mmm)
     Kòndè-musudin nan'i bile mògò min kò,   (Naamu)
     O y'i bara, "I bò N' kò dè!   (Naamu)
     "N' kana manguya i fè."   (Cinyè don)
915 Alu d'i mabò, k'i lò fana la.   (Mmm)

     Jankumani-fin ye dugu ma.
     A ye munumununa.
     A ye munumununa.   (Naamu)
     A dunna Kòndè-musu sin fulan tè,
920 Ka bò, k'a laminimini.   (Naamu)
     Tarawerelu ni bori nara,
     Kòndè-musu min'a kilin-bulu ma.
     "An musu fèlè!   (Naamu)
     "An musu fèlè!
925 "An ne y'an musu ye."
</pre>

885 On that, Dan Mansa Wulandin went forth   (Indeed)
And slipped the knife into its sheath,
And sat down on the lounging platform.   (Indeed)
Dan Mansa Wulanba,   (Indeed)
He slipped his feet into the sandals,   (Indeed)
890 And sat down upon the lounging platform.   (Indeed)

All cried out: "'Tis they who killed the buffalo!   (Indeed)
'Tis they who killed the buffalo!   (Mmm)
"Whose people are you?"
"We are the Taraweres."   (True)
895 "And where do you hail from?"   (Mmm)
"We come from Bintanya Kamalen."   (Indeed)
"O Taraweres!   (Mmm)
"The twelve towns of Du, I'll divide in twain,
"And give one half to you,   (Mmm)
900 "So that you'll settle here.   (Mmm)
"Such brave men complement the village folk."   (True)
"That cannot be us!
"We come from the Manden.
"And to the Manden we'll return."
905 "Taraweres, look about you then.   (True)
"Whatever maiden you may see
"Will be your struggle's reward.
"Whichever woman you may see,
"'Tis her that I will give to you."   (True)
910 They brought the maidens forward,   (True)
Six young maidens.   (Mmm)
The one behind whom the Kòndè girl stood,   (Indeed)
She cried out, saying, "Get from behind me!   (Indeed)
"Let me not with you be made so vile!"   (That's true)
915 They all moved away and stood apart.   (Mmm)

The black cat moved upon the ground.
It turned around and round.
It turned around and round.   (Indeed)
It passed between the Kòndè Maiden's legs,
920 Came out, turned round, and through again.   (Indeed)
The Taraweres came running up
And seized the Kòndè Maiden by the right hand.
"Behold our maiden!   (Indeed)
"Behold our maiden!
925 "We have seen our maiden!"

O tuma, sali-muru le,
Tarawerelu bènba,
Tura Magan ni Kanke-jan bulu.
N'a d'a b'a la dò,   (Naamu)
930   A nya mana l'a kèsè kan, nnn,   (Naamu)
A t'a ladun tugun
Ni mògò joli t'a la.   (Naamu)

A d'a la sali-muru bò,   (Naamu)
K'a lamina, k'a lanòn,   (Naamu)
935   N'a d'a la kudu min ma,
O kudu ye tunun.   (Cinyè)

N'a di sali-muru bò,   (Naamu)
K'a lamina, k'a lanòn,   (Naamu)
A man'o la Kòndè-musu la kudu ni bagi min na,
940   O bagi ye tunun.   (Cinyè)

O bagi bèè tunura.   (Naamu)
"Awa, Kòndèlu, an d'an musu ye.
"An ne ye waala le.   (Naamu)
"Sigi tèna ku min nya,
945   "Taama l'o banna.   (Cinyè)
"An ye waala le."   (Cinyè)

Alu wilila,   (Mmm)
K'a ta tili bò tuma,   (Naamu)
Fo tili bira.   (Naamu)
950   Alu ye sila dugu dò rò,   (Naamu)
Dan Mansa Wulandin ko, "N' kòrò-kè,   (Naamu)
"Kòrò ni dògò mana dè,
"Ka fèn nyini,   (Naamu)
"Ilu mana nafulu min sòrò,   (Naamu)
955   "Ilu y'o kè, ka musu furu,
"K'o di kòrò-kè ma.   (Naamu)
"Min mana sòrò sa,   (Naamu)
"O ye di dògò ma.   (Naamu)
"Nin musu la tu ile bulu.
960   "Min mana soro sa,
"O musu ye di Ne ma."   (Mmm)

<table>
<tr><td></td><td>At that time, the sacred knife</td><td></td></tr>
<tr><td></td><td>Of the Tarawere ancestor</td><td></td></tr>
<tr><td></td><td>Was in the hands of Tura-Magan-and-Kanke-jan.</td><td></td></tr>
<tr><td></td><td>When he drew it from its sheath,</td><td>(Indeed)</td></tr>
<tr><td>930</td><td>When his eyes fell upon the blade,</td><td>(Indeed)</td></tr>
<tr><td></td><td>He could not put it back again</td><td></td></tr>
<tr><td></td><td>Were no man's blood upon it.</td><td>(Indeed)</td></tr>
<tr><td></td><td></td><td></td></tr>
<tr><td></td><td>Were he to unsheathe the sacred knife,</td><td>(Indeed)</td></tr>
<tr><td></td><td>And having grasped it, licked it,</td><td>(Indeed)</td></tr>
<tr><td>935</td><td>Were he to lay it on a wart,</td><td></td></tr>
<tr><td></td><td>That wart would fade away.</td><td>(True)</td></tr>
<tr><td></td><td></td><td></td></tr>
<tr><td></td><td>When now he drew the sacred knife,</td><td>(Indeed)</td></tr>
<tr><td></td><td>And having grasped it, licked it,</td><td>(Indeed)</td></tr>
<tr><td></td><td>And when he laid it on the Kòndè maiden's sores,</td><td></td></tr>
<tr><td>940</td><td>Those leprous sores did fade away.</td><td>(True)</td></tr>
<tr><td></td><td></td><td></td></tr>
<tr><td></td><td>All her leprous sores did fade away.</td><td>(Indeed)</td></tr>
<tr><td></td><td>"So, Kòndès, we have found our maiden.</td><td></td></tr>
<tr><td></td><td>"We must be on our way!</td><td>(Indeed)</td></tr>
<tr><td></td><td>"What sitting will not solve,</td><td></td></tr>
<tr><td>945</td><td>"Travel will resolve.</td><td>(True)</td></tr>
<tr><td></td><td>"We must be on our way!"</td><td>(True)</td></tr>
</table>

EPISODE FOUR: THE MANDEN

<table>
<tr><td></td><td>And thus they rose and journeyed forth</td><td>(Mmm)</td></tr>
<tr><td></td><td>From the time the sun rose</td><td>(Indeed)</td></tr>
<tr><td></td><td>Until the sun fell.</td><td>(Indeed)</td></tr>
<tr><td>950</td><td>As they reached a certain village,</td><td>(Indeed)</td></tr>
<tr><td></td><td>Dan Mansa Wulandin said, "My elder,</td><td>(Indeed)</td></tr>
<tr><td></td><td>"Should the elder and the younger venture forth,</td><td></td></tr>
<tr><td></td><td>"To seek their fortune together,</td><td>(Indeed)</td></tr>
<tr><td></td><td>"Should it be wealth they find,</td><td>(Indeed)</td></tr>
<tr><td>955</td><td>"They should use it to marry a wife,</td><td></td></tr>
<tr><td></td><td>"Giving her to the elder.</td><td>(Indeed)</td></tr>
<tr><td></td><td>"Whatever may be found after that,</td><td>(Indeed)</td></tr>
<tr><td></td><td>"Should be given to the younger.</td><td>(Indeed)</td></tr>
<tr><td></td><td>"This woman then should stay with you.</td><td></td></tr>
<tr><td>960</td><td>"Whatever may be found next time,</td><td></td></tr>
<tr><td></td><td>"Let that maiden be mine!"</td><td>(Mmm)</td></tr>
</table>

Alu dunna dugu kònò.   (Naamu)
Dan Mansa Wulanba,   (Naamu)
A ni musu dunna bun na.   (Cinyè)
965   Dugu talala: *lelelele!*   (Mmm)
Dan Mansa Wulandin lanin a kènè ma.   (Naamu)
Dan Mansa Wulanba wilila,   (Cinyè)
K'a ye suna ni farila nyinina.   (Naamu)
A d'i bulu la Kòndè-musu kan,   (Naamu)
970   Musu bèè ka jan Sugulun Kòndè di.
A bèè ka bun Sugulun Kòndè di.
A d'i dòbò: *bililili,*   (Mmm)
K'a sin lò jeju rò,   (Mmm)
K'a kun-gulu la da la,
975   Ka bòrò fula b'a kara la.   (Naamu)

"Tarawerelu, i la!   (Naamu)
"Ne kè ye Manden.
"Ile fana musu ye Manden."   (Cinyè)
Dan Mansa Wulanba bori bòra kènè ma:
980   "Han!"
Dan Mansa Wulandin ko,
"N' kòrò-kè, a kèra di?"
"Aa, N' dògò,
"Musu bèè ka jan Sugulun Kòndè di.
985   "A bèè ka bun Sugulun Kòndè di.
"N' di N' bulu l'a kan,   (Naamu)
"Ko N' bè suna ni farila nyinin'a fè,
"A d'i dòbò: *bililili,*
"K'a sin lò jeju rò,   (Mmm)
990   "K'a kun-gulu la da la,
"Ka bòlò fula b'a kara rò,
"Ko Ne ka N' la,   (Mmm)
"K'ale kè ye Manden.
"Ko Ne fana musu ye Manden."
995   Alu d'i la,   (Naamu)
Fo dugu jèra.   (Mmm)
Alu wilila ole dò.   (Naamu)
Fata Magan Kè-nyi ye bòla dugu dò rò.

A ye waala dògò jò.   (Mmm)
1000 Jinè d'i bulu l'a kan na: (Mmm)
"I sigi yan.   (Naamu)
"Din-din fula nara.   (Mmm)

They entered the town. (Indeed)
Dan Mansa Wulanba (Indeed)
With the maiden entered a hut. (True)
965 The night had passed its prime, *lelelele!* (Mmm)
Dan Mansa Wulandin lay down outside. (Indeed)
Dan Mansa Wulanba rose up, (True)
To seek pleasure and duty with his wife. (Indeed)
He laid his hand on the Kòndè maid. (Indeed)
970 Now, all women were taller than Sugulun Kòndè.
All of them larger than Sugulun Kòndè.
But she stretched out: *bililili,*
Putting her feet against the back wall, (Mmm)
And laying her head at the door,
975 And projected two spikes from her breasts. (Indeed)

"O Tarawere! Lie back down! (Indeed)
"My husband's in the Manden.
"And your wife will be there, too!" (True)
Dan Mansa Wulanba came running outside:
980 "Ha! Hey!"
Dan Mansa Wulandin said:
"My brother, what has happened?"
"Ah, little brother!
"All women are taller than Sugulun Kòndè;
985 "All of them larger than Sugulun Kòndè;
"Yet when I put my hand on her, (Indeed)
"Saying I sought pleasure and duty with my wife,
"She stretched herself: *bililili,*
"Putting her feet against the back wall, (Mmm)
990 "And laying her head at the door,
"And projecting two spikes from her breasts,
"And told me to lie back down, (Mmm)
"Saying that her husband's in the Manden,
"And that my wife would be there, too."
995 They both lay back down (Indeed)
Until the break of day. (Mmm)
At that they rose up. (Indeed)
Now, Fata Magan, the Handsome was about to
    leave that town.
He was leaving to trade in a far market. (Mmm)
1000 But a jinn came and laid a hand on him: (Mmm)
"Stay right here! (Indeed)
"Two youths have come among us, (Mmm)

"Musudin kè-jugu dò y'o din-din fula bulu.   (Mmm)
"I man'o musuni kè-jugu sòrò,   (Mmm)
1005 "O din-kè sòròla.   (Naamu)
"Ole ta ye le Manden di."   (Naamu)

Bènba le.   (Naamu)
    N' ye Subaa kènya le fòla.   (Mmm, cinyè don)
    Son-Jara kènya le nin di!
1010 Foli-kan fula le Manden.   (Mmm)
Kèbalu y'a fòl', "Ilu tuntun."   (Cinyè don)
Alu y'a fòla, "Tuntun bèrè."
Musulu y'a fòla, "Ilu kònkòn."
Alu y'a fòla, "Kònkòn lògòsò."   (Naamu)
1015 Tarawerelu nata: (Cinyè)
"I tuntun."
A d'alu lamita, "Tuntun bèrè.   (Mmm)
"Ilu ye bòla mini?
"Ilu ye waala mini?"
1020 "An bòra Du le.
"An waatò Bintanya Kamalen."
"Ilu ye mògò jòn di?"   (Mmm)
"An ne le Tarawerelu di."   (Mmm)
"Tarawerelu,
1025 "Masaren kamalen mana din-musu nyuman sòrò,   (Mmm)
"Tarawerelu la kèlè-kòntòn ne.   (Cinyè)

"Ne ba-kilinma-musu ye yan,   (Naamu)
"Nakana Tiliba.   (Naamu)
"N' y'a dil'ilu ma.
1030 "Ilu k'e musuni kè-jugu di N' ma.   (Mmm)
"N' bènba Bilali,   (Naamu)
"A ni Ala Kila fara tuma nyògòn na,   (Cinyè)
"A di fèn dò masiri,   (Mmm)
"K'a yèlèma mana kònòntòn bò,   (Naamu)
1035 "N'o d'a musu fòlò furu,   (Cinyè)
"N'a bè fula nyògòn furula,   (Naamu)
"Ko ka fènni la o furu kan.   (Mmm)
"N' y'o fènni lala,
"Nakana Tiliba kan, nnn,   (Mmm)
1040 "K'a d'ilu ma.
"Ilu k'e musuni kè-jugu di N' ma."
O fènni le lara Nakana Tiliba kan,
K'a falin Sugulun Kòndè le.   (Naamu)

    "Two youths with an ugly maid.   (Mmm)
    "Should you come by that ugly maid,   (Mmm)
1005 "She will bear you a son.   (Indeed)
    "The Manden will belong to him."   (Indeed)

    O! Bèmba!   (Indeed)
        I sing of the Sorcerer's future;   (Mmm, that's true)
        Of the life ahead of Son-Jara!
1010 There were two ways to greet in the Manden of old.   (Mmm)
    Brave young men said, "Ilu tuntun!"   (That's true)
    To which the reply, "Tuntun bèrè!"
    The women said, "Ilu kònkòn!"
    To which the reply, "Kònkòn lògòsò!"   (Indeed)
1015 The Taraweres came forward: (True)
    "I tuntun!"
    He answered them, "Tuntun bèrè!   (Mmm)
    "Where do you come from?
    "Where are you going?"
1020 "We have come from the land of Du.
    "We go to Bintanya Kamalen."
    "Whose people are you?"   (Mmm)
    "We are Taraweres."   (Mmm)
    "O Taraweres,
1025 "Were this young prince to find the right wife,   (Mmm)
    "She would be the reward of a Tarawere struggle.   (True)

    "My flesh-and-blood sister is here,   (Indeed)
    "Nakana Tiliba.   (Indeed)
    "I will give her to you.
1030 "You must give me your ugly maid.   (Mmm)
    "My forefather Bilāl,   (Indeed)
    "When he departed from the Messenger of God,   (True)
    "He designed a certain token,   (Mmm)
    "Saying that his ninth descendant,   (Indeed)
1035 "Having taken his first wife,   (True)
    "When he takes his second wife,   (Indeed)
    "Must add that token to that marriage.   (Mmm)
    "I am adding that token
    "Together with Nakana Tiliba,   (Mmm)
1040 "And giving them to you,
    "You must give me your ugly little maid."
    That token was added to Nakana Tiliba,
    Exchanging her for Sugulun Kòndè.   (Indeed)

Ko Fata Magan Kè-nyi,
1045 A di Kòndè-musu bila lalan dò.   (Mmm)
Berete-musu di kònò ta.   (Naamu)
Kòndè-musu di kònò ta.   (Naamu)

Lun dò fajiri ye jèra.   (Naamu)
Berete-musu di din-kè wulu.   (Naamu)
1050 A ko, "He dè! Musu-kòrònilu,   (Naamu)
"Fèn min bè sinaya dò nyògòn ye,
"Sina-musu-dinya.   (Cinyè)
"Ilu wa'a fò N' kè ye,   (Naamu)
"K'a musu fòlò di din-kè wulu."   (Naamu)
1055 Musu-kòròni ni bori nara: (Naamu)
"Alu kònkòn!"   (Mmm)
Alu d'a lamina, "Kònkòn dògòsò!
"Na, an ka domuni kè."   (Mmm)
Olu d'i nya wusu nyògòn dò:
1060 "Aa! Mògò y'i da-ji lakunu dè!"   (Cinyè)
Olu sigira dumuni kun na.   (Naamu)
Kòndè-musu di din-kè wulu.   (Naamu)
Alu di Kuyatèlu mama Tumu Maniya kiya: (Naamu)
"Tumu Maniya, tag'o fò,   (Cinyè)
1065 "Ko Fata Magan Kè-nyi ye,
"Ko Tarawerelu la Du taga diyara.   (Cinyè)
"K'alu ni musuni kè-jugu min nada,
"K'o musu di din-kè wulu."   (Cinyè)

Kuyatèlu mama nada: (Cinyè)
1070 "Alu kònkòn!"   (Mmm)
Alu d'a lamina, "Kònkòn dògòsò!   (Naamu)
"Na, an ka dumuli kè.

	It is said that Fata Magan, the Handsome	
1045	Took the Kòndè maiden to bed.	(Mmm)
	His Berete wife became pregnant.	(Indeed)
	His Kòndè wife became pregnant.	(Indeed)
	One day as dawn was breaking,	(Indeed)
	The Berete woman gave birth to a son.	(Indeed)
1050	She cried out, "Ha! Old Women!	(Indeed)
	"That which causes co-wife conflict	
	"Is nothing but the co-wife's child.	(True)
	"Go forth and tell my husband	(Indeed)
	"His first wife has borne him a son."	(Indeed)
1055	The old women came up running.	(Indeed)
	"Alu kònkòn!"	(Mmm)
	They replied to them, "Kònkòn dògòsò!	
	"Come let us eat."	(Mmm)
	They fixed their eyes on one another:	
1060	"Ah! Man must swallow his saliva!"	(True)
	They sat down around the food.	(Indeed)
	The Kòndè woman then bore a son.	(Indeed)
	They sent the Kuyatè matriarch, Tumu Maniya:	(Indeed)
	"Tumu Maniya, go tell it,	(True)
1065	"Tell Fata Magan, the Handsome,	
	"Say, 'The Tarawere trip to Du was good.'	(True)
	"Say, 'The ugly maid they brought with them,'	
	"Say, 'That woman has just borne a son.'"	(True)
	The Kuyatè matriarch came forward:	(True)
1070	"Alu kònkòn!"	(Mmm)
	They replied to her, "Kònkòn dògòsò!	(Indeed)
	"Come and let us eat."	

[The female bard Tumu Maniya goes to find the king and, like the old women who preceded her, is also invited to eat, but she rejects the food until her message is delivered. The announcing of the birth of Son-Jara first, though he was actually born second, causes the father to designate him as firstborn. The old women then burst out their message of the Berete woman's child, but alas, they are too late. The reversal of announcements is viewed as theft of birthright (see note for line 1 concerning Son-Jara's surname Keyta), and the Berete woman is understandably furious at the old women, who flop their hands about nervously.]

Dòlu b'alu bulu sarin-sarinna:
"N' t'o mèn dò la dè!
1075 "N' silan N' nya la.
"N' nya-gulu jani: *bèrè bèrè bèrè*!   (Cinyè don)
"Nga, N' t'o mèn alu dò la dè!"
Dòlu b'a bulu fula bila nyògòn dò.
Nin kèra ki ye!
1080 Iyo, kasaba-kòrò nyinèra a la kila kò,
K'a kè dumuni di.
Mina-nugumalu!
Kèlè lun dun le nin di Manden.
Makan wilinin: *bòkòlen*!

1085   *N' ye Biribiriba ma!*
             Aa, nin min yena sènè kè,
             I ka sènè kè: (Mmm)
             Hoo, nin min yena jago kè,
             I ka jago kè.   (Cinyè don)

1090   Bènba le, nnn.   (Mmm)
             Kèlè le fèn dila mògò ma, N' fa,
             N'i ta tè.
             Kèlè le fèn mine mògò la,
             N'i ta le.
1095   Ni kèlè ma kè,
             Sebaga tè lòn.   (Naamu)

Wulu-musulu ye bun kilin na.
Makan wilinin: *bòkòlen*!   (Naamu)
Saman Berete,
1100 Tumun-dò Ma'an-Jan Berete din-musu,
Saman Berete,   (Naamu)
A ni juba-jeli bòra kènè ma: (Naamu)
"Mun kèra dun?   (Naamu)
"Ki-dinnu, mun kèra dun?   (Naamu)
1105 "Ki-dinnu, mun bòra ki dò?"   (Naamu)

Kuyatèlu mama ko,
"Fèn ma kè dè!   (Naamu)
"N' fòlò le di N' dan tègè.   (Naamu)
"Ilu kè ko k'ale min fòlò mèn,
1110 "Ko, kòrò l'o di.   (Naamu)
"K'e ta kèra dògò di."   (Naamu)

Some just flopped their hands about:
"I will not hear of this from anyone!
1075 "I spent a sleepless night.
"The lids of my eyes are dried out, *bèrè-bèrè-bèrè*.(That's true)
"But I will not hear of this from anyone!"
Some just clasped their hands together.
What travail it had become!
1080 Ha! The old woman had forgotten her message
And abandoned it for a meal.
Those-Caught-by-their-Craws!
That was the first day of battle in the Manden.
Pandemonium broke loose! *bòkòlen*!

1085　　　I sing of Biribiriba.
　　　　Ah! He who would cultivate,
　　　　Let him cultivate.　　　　　　　　　　(Mmm)
　　　　He who would deal in commerce,
　　　　Let him deal in commerce!　　　　(That's true)

1090　　　Ah! Bèmba!　　　　　　　　　　　　(Mmm)
　　　　War may give to some, my father,
　　　　Although it be not theirs.
　　　　War may take from some,
　　　　Although it be their own.
1095　　　If there be no war,
　　　　Men of power would not be known.　　(Indeed)

Both women were confined in one hut.
Pandemonium broke loose! *bòkòlen*!　　　(Indeed)
Saman Berete,
1100 The daughter of Tall Magan Berete-of-the-Ruins,
Saman Berete,　　　　　　　　　　　　(Indeed)
Still bloodstained, she came out.　　　　　(Indeed)
"What happened then?
"O Messengers, what happened?　　　　　(Indeed)
1105 "O Messengers, what became of the message?"　(Indeed)

The Kuyatè matriarch spoke out:
"Nothing happened at all.　　　　　　　　(Indeed)
"I was the first to pronounce myself.　　　　(Indeed)
"Your husband said the first name heard,　　(Indeed)
1110 "Said, he would be the elder,　　　　　　(Indeed)
"And thus yours became the younger.　　　(Indeed)

A ko, "E musu-kòròninnu,   (Naamu)
"Bari ilu di laban N' ye dè!   (Cinyè dè)
"N' fòlò sigira N' kè kun,
1115   "K'a din-kè fòlò wulu.   (Naamu)
"Ilu d'o kè dògò di.   (Naamu)
"Bari, ilu di laban N' ye dè!"
A kan y'a sina-dògòni ma: (Naamu)
"Kun-nandi Karunga,   (Naamu)
1120   "Kè-lasigi diyanin ile le la.   (Naamu)
"Din-kè-fòlò-wulu, kòrò-ki di,
"K'e ta kèra kòrò di."   (O ye cinyè ye)

Din-dinnu kura.   (Naamu)
A bèè lara fini kòrò.   (Naamu)
1125   Ba waanin lògò-nyini-yòrò.   (Naamu)
Ba-kòròni le tèrè lò..., lògò nyini la.
A bòra lògò-nyini-yòrò dò,
Ka na lògò doni bila.   (Naamu)
A dunda bun na.   (Naamu)
1130   A d'i nya lò Berete-musu ma,   (Naamu)
Kè nya lò Kòndè-musu ma,   (Naamu)
Ka Berete-musu mafèlè,
Ka Kòndè-musu mafèlè.   (Naamu)

A di fini-da-kòrò ta,
1135   Ka Berete-musu din-din mafèlè,
Ka fini da-kòrò ta,
Ka Kòndè-musu din-din mafèlè,   (Naamu)
Ka ta Magan Son-Jara kun-gulu ma,   (Naamu)
Ka wa'a bil'a sin-kònòni na, a bèè shi!   (Naamu)

1140   Ba bòra da la.   (Naamu)
A yèrèra: "Èè! Wululalu Tetare!
"Ne ba di Son-Jara wulu!"   (Cinyè don)
Ba le di Son-Jara tògò da.   (Naamu)
Wululalu, tare!
1145   "Ne na di Son-Jara wulu!
"Tetare! Ne ba di Son-Jara wulu!"   (Cinyè don)
    Biribiriba!   (Naamu)
    Alu kan y'ole ma,
    Son-Jara, Nare Magan Kònatè!   (Naamu)
1150   Jankuma la twara la Sinbon!   (Naamu)
Berete-musu,

She cried out, "Old women,   (Indeed)
"Now you have really reached the limit!   (True)
"I was the first to marry my husband,
1115 "And the first to bear him a son.   (Indeed)
"Now you have made him the younger.   (Indeed)
"You have really reached your limit!"
She spoke then to her younger co-wife,   (Indeed)
"Oh Lucky Karunga,   (Indeed)
1120 "For you marriage has turned sweet.   (Indeed)
"A first son birth is the work of old,
"And yours has become the elder."   (That's the truth)

The infants were bathed.   (Indeed)
Both were laid beneath a cloth.   (Indeed)
1125 The grandmother had gone to fetch firewood.   (Indeed)
The old mother had gone to fe. . . , to fetch firewood.   (Indeed)
She then quit the firewood-fetching place,
And came and left her load of wood.   (Indeed)
She came into the hut.   (Indeed)
1130 She cast her eye on the Berete woman,   (Indeed)
And cast her eye on the Kòndè woman,   (Indeed)
And looked the Berete woman over,
And looked the Kòndè woman over.   (Indeed)

She lifted the edge of the cloth.
1135 And examined the child of the Berete woman,
And lifted again the edge of the cloth,
And examined the child of the Kòndè woman.   (Indeed)
From the very top of Son-Jara's head,   (Indeed)
To the very tip of his toes, all hair!   (Indeed)

1140 The old mother went outside.   (Indeed)
She laughed out: "Ha! Birth-givers! Hurrah!
"The little mother has borne a lion thief."   (That's true)
Thus the old mother gave Son-Jara his name.   (Indeed)
"Givers of birth, Hurrah!
1145 "The little mother has borne a lion thief.   (That's true)
"Hurrah! The mother has given birth to a lion thief."
        Biribiriba!   (Indeed)
        And thus they say of him,
        Son-Jara, Nare Magan Kònatè.   (Indeed)
1150   Simbon, Lion-Born-of-the-Cat.   (Indeed)
The Berete woman,

A di mori wele,
Ko ka Ala deli,   (Naamu)
Son-Jara kana taama.   (Naamu)
1155 Ka kinyè-mansa wele,   (Naamu)
K'o ka kinyè la,   (Naamu)
Son-Jara kana taama.   (Naamu)

San kònòntòn, Son-Jara ye dugu ma.   (Naamu)
Magan Kònatè ma wili.   (Naamu)
1160 Kòndè-musu din magu-nyè-mògò,
Jinè dò le Ma'an Son-Jara.   (Naamu)
A tògò le Tanimunari di.
Tanimunari,   (Naamu)
Ole di Son-Jara nanbara ta,   (Naamu)
1165 Ka ta'a lahiji,   (Naamu)
Alikaba da la.   (Naamu)
I ma lahiji-kan mèn?   (Naamu)
     "Hèè, Ala!   (Naamu)
     "Sini-mògò N' ne di.   (Naamu)
1170   "Sini-kindi-mògò N' ne di.   (Naamu)
     "N' ye jelilu mara,   (Naamu)
     "Ka tun-tan-mògò saba ni mògò bi saba,
     "K'o mògò bèè mara.   (Naamu)
     "Ne le ta ye Manden di!"   (Naamu)
1175 A lahiji-nya le nin di.
A d'a nanbarama ta,
Ka n'a bila Bintanya Kamalen.   (Naamu)

Dònba makònòn,   (Naamu)
A tili mugan ni duuru,
1180 Berete-musu la kinyè-mansa bòra: (Naamu)
"Sakana! Ne bulu-kònòni banda!   (Naamu)
"N' jugidi banda.   (Naamu)
"Jigi-tègè-ku kètò Manden yan.   (Naamu)
"Basi tè la.
1185 "Saraka t'a la.
"A kun tè kè,   (Naamu)
"Fo ni mògò di saga-jigi fula kè saraka di.   (Naamu)

"Son-Jara ta ye saga-jigi-kun-fin di.   (Cinyè)
"Dankaran Tumani ta ye saga-jigi-jè di.   (Naamu)
1190 "K'alu bila kèlè la a lun nin kan ma."   (Naamu)
Salifana sila tuma min na,

<table>
<tr><td></td><td>She summoned to her a holy-man,</td><td></td></tr>
<tr><td></td><td>Charging him to pray to God,</td><td>(Indeed)</td></tr>
<tr><td></td><td>So Son-Jara would not walk.</td><td>(Indeed)</td></tr>
<tr><td>1155</td><td>And summoned to her an Omen Master,</td><td>(Indeed)</td></tr>
<tr><td></td><td>For him to read the signs in sand,</td><td>(Indeed)</td></tr>
<tr><td></td><td>So Son-Jara would not walk.</td><td>(Indeed)</td></tr>
<tr><td></td><td></td><td></td></tr>
<tr><td></td><td>For nine years, Son-Jara crawled upon the ground.</td><td>(Indeed)</td></tr>
<tr><td></td><td>Magan Kònatè could not rise.</td><td>(Indeed)</td></tr>
<tr><td>1160</td><td>The benefactor of the Kòndè woman's child,</td><td></td></tr>
<tr><td></td><td>It was a jinn Magan Son-Jara had.</td><td>(Indeed)</td></tr>
<tr><td></td><td>His name was Tanimunari.</td><td></td></tr>
<tr><td></td><td>Tanimunari,</td><td>(Indeed)</td></tr>
<tr><td></td><td>He took the lame Son-Jara</td><td>(Indeed)</td></tr>
<tr><td>1165</td><td>And made the ḥājj</td><td>(Indeed)</td></tr>
<tr><td></td><td>To the gates of the Ka'bah.</td><td>(Indeed)</td></tr>
<tr><td></td><td>Have you never heard this warrant of his ḥājj?</td><td>(Indeed)</td></tr>
<tr><td></td><td>"Ah! God!</td><td>(Indeed)</td></tr>
<tr><td></td><td>"I am the man for the morrow.</td><td>(Indeed)</td></tr>
<tr><td>1170</td><td>"I am the man for the day to follow.</td><td>(Indeed)</td></tr>
<tr><td></td><td>"I will rule over the bards,</td><td>(Indeed)</td></tr>
<tr><td></td><td>"And the three and thirty warrior clans.</td><td></td></tr>
<tr><td></td><td>"I will rule over all these people.</td><td>(Indeed)</td></tr>
<tr><td></td><td>"The Manden shall be mine!"</td><td>(Indeed)</td></tr>
<tr><td>1175</td><td>That is how he made the ḥājj.</td><td></td></tr>
<tr><td></td><td>He took him up still lame,</td><td></td></tr>
<tr><td></td><td>And brought him back to Bintanya Kamalen.</td><td>(Indeed)</td></tr>
<tr><td></td><td>In the month before Dònba,</td><td>(Indeed)</td></tr>
<tr><td></td><td>On the twenty-fifth day,</td><td></td></tr>
<tr><td>1180</td><td>The Berete woman's Omen Master emerged from
    retreat:</td><td>(Indeed)</td></tr>
<tr><td></td><td>"Damn! My fingers are worn out!</td><td>(Indeed)</td></tr>
<tr><td></td><td>"My buttocks are worn out!</td><td>(Indeed)</td></tr>
<tr><td></td><td>"A tragic thing will come to pass in the Manden.</td><td>(Indeed)</td></tr>
<tr><td></td><td>"There is no remedy to stop it.</td><td></td></tr>
<tr><td>1185</td><td>"There is no sacrifice to halt it.</td><td></td></tr>
<tr><td></td><td>"Its cause cannot be ascertained,</td><td>(Indeed)</td></tr>
<tr><td></td><td>"Until two rams be sacrificed.</td><td>(Indeed)</td></tr>
<tr><td></td><td></td><td></td></tr>
<tr><td></td><td>"The one for Son-Jara, a black-headed ram.</td><td>(True)</td></tr>
<tr><td></td><td>"Dankaran Tuma, an all white ram.</td><td>(Indeed)</td></tr>
<tr><td>1190</td><td>"Have them do battle this very day."</td><td>(Indeed)</td></tr>
<tr><td></td><td>By the time of the midday meal,</td><td></td></tr>
</table>

Son-Jara ta le sira.   (Naamu)
Al' di saga bèè faga,   (Naamu)
K'a bila kòlòn kònò,
1195 K'a kana lòn.   (Naamu)
A lònna le.   (Naamu)
     Ku lòn t'a tuma tula,
     Fo lun sibaliya.   (Cinyè don,
                                             Èè, Fa-Digi,cinyè don)

Dònba makònòn,   (Cinyè don)
1200 A tili mugan wòrònwula,   (Naamu)
Mori bòra: (Naamu)
"Hèè! Jigi-tègè-ku kètò Manden.   (Naamu)
"Basi t'a la.
"Saraka t'a la.   (Naamu)
1205 "A kun tè kè,
"Fo ni mògò di wulu-nyintan kè saraka di."
Jòn dun di wulu-nyintan ye Manden?   (Naamu)
Alu waara Kòn,   (Naamu)
Ka taa wuluni-nun-kudun san,   (Naamu)
1210 Kaba wulu din,
K'a nyinnu bò bando la,
K'a da basi,   (Naamu)
K'a bila Manden Bintanya Kamalen,
Ko wulu-nyintan,   (Naamu)
1215 Ko Magan Kònatè kana taama,   (Naamu)
Son-Jara kana wili dè.
          Aa jeli, min yena sènè kè,
          I ka sènè kè!
          Aa nin min yena jago kè,
1220   *I ka jago kè!*
          K'a ta fo Fatiyataligara,   (Naamu)
          Ka taa Sòkòtò,   (Naamu)
          Magan Son-Jata ta le o di.   (Naamu)
          Fara-finnu kan ye ole ma, N' fa,
1225   Eripibiliki-Mali,   (Naamu)
          Maninka mara.   (Naamu)
          A di Bamanan Dankun faga,   (Naamu)
          Fantan na dankun dò-sigi tè bèn,   (Naamu)
          Ka Bamanan Basa faga,   (Naamu)
1230   Fantan kan'i yèrè tògò la basa la,   (Naamu)
          Ka Bamanan Kòtu faga,   (Naamu)
          Fantan na tu-rò-sigi tè bèn.   (Cinyè)

Son-Jara's ram had won.   (Indeed)
They slaughtered both the rams,   (Indeed)
And cast them down a well,
1195 So the deed would not be known.   (Indeed)
But known it did become.   (Indeed)
        Knowing never fails its time,
        Except its day not come.   (That's the truth, eh,
                                            Fa-Digi, that's true)

In the month before Dònba   (That's true)
1200 On the twenty-seventh day,   (Indeed)
The holy-man emerged from his retreat!   (Indeed)
"Hey! A tragic thing will come to pass in the Manden. (Indeed)
"There is no remedy to stop it.
"There is no sacrifice to halt it.   (Indeed)
1205 "Its cause cannot be ascertained,
"Until a toothless dog be sacrificed."
Now, whoever saw a toothless dog in the Manden?   (Indeed)
They went forth to Kong,   (Indeed)
And bought a snub-nosed dog,   (Indeed)
1210 A little spotted dog,
And pulled its teeth with pliers,
And mixed a potion for its mouth,   (Indeed)
And brought it back to the Manden,
Saying, with this toothless dog,   (Indeed)
1215 Saying, Magan Kònatè should not walk.   (Indeed)
Son-Jara should not rise!
        Ah! Bards, he who would cultivate,
        Let him cultivate!
        Ah, he who would deal in commerce,
1220   *Let him deal in commerce!*
        From Fatiyataligara,   (Indeed)
        All the way to Sokoto,   (Indeed)
        All that was Magan Son-Jara's,   (Indeed)
        The Africans call that, my father,
1225   The Republic of Mali,   (Indeed)
        The Maninka realm.   (Indeed)
        He slew Bambara-of-the-Border;   (Indeed)
        Settling on the border does not suit the weak,   (Indeed)
        And slew Bambara-the-Lizard;   (Indeed)
1230   No weak one should call himself lizard,   (Indeed)
        And slew Bambara-of-the-Backwoods;   (Indeed)
        Settling the backwoods does not suit the weak,   (True)

Bar'a ma abiyòn kè samara,
K'e taama dè!   (Naamu)
1235   O kèra Modibo ye,   (Naamu)
Daba la Modibo,   (Mmm)
Peresidan Deripibiliki.   (Naamu)
Kamara-musu din, lòn-sòn.
Ile le nòn!   (Kamara-musu d'i sangu,
                                              o ye cinyè ye)

1240   Biribiriba! Nare Magan Kònatè!   (Naamu)
Jelilu ye ile le ma, N' fa,
Subaa-Minè-Subaa!
Sin-kula le sòrò man di!   (I ye min kè
                                            Dakar dun?)

Ne le di N' bulu la Daba la Modibo kan na,   (Naamu)
1245   Modibo min bòra Daba dò,   (Naamu)
Ni Daba bòra Lamuru lò Bakunun Jire.   (Naamu)

Fatuma Kamara, musulu sin na!
Modibo le!   (Naamu)
Kamara-musu le wara-yèlèma le.
1250   Modibo!
Nare Magan Kònatè!   (Mmm, cinyè don)

Aa, Bènba.   (Naamu)
Al' di kaba wulu kè saraka di,   (Naamu)
Ko Subaa kana taama.   (Naamu)
1255 Dònba karu,   (Naamu)
A tili fòlò fòlò fòlò fòlò,   (Naamu)
Son-Jara la jinè mori nada: (Naamu)
"Ala di min fò Nde ye,   (Mmm)
"Tanimunari,   (Naamu)
1260 "Ala di min fò Nde ye,   (Naamu)
"A ye kèla ye.   (Naamu)
"Dònba mana tili tan bò,   (Naamu)
"Son-Jara y'i tòòma."   (Naamu)
Dònba karu,   (Naamu)
1265 A tili tan ni fula,   (Naamu)
Ala Kila bangè lun.   (Naamu)
A tili tan ni saba,   (Naamu)
Jòn Bilali bangèra.   (Naamu)
A tili tan,   (Naamu)

But he did not make airplanes his shoes
For to travel far and wide.   (Indeed)
1235   The one to do that was Modibo,   (Indeed)
Daba's Modibo,   (Mmm)
The President of the Republic,   (Indeed)
The Kamara woman's child, beloved one,
It was he!   (The Kamara woman . . . ,
                                        that's the truth)

1240   Biribiriba, Nare Magan Kònatè!
The bards sing of you, my father,
The Sorcerer-Seizing-Sorcerer!
A man of power is hard to find.   (And how about what
                                    you did in Dakar?)

But I have laid my hand on Daba's Modibo,   (Indeed)
1245   Modibo who was fathered by Daba.   (Indeed)
That Daba was fathered by Lamuru in Bakunun
    Jire.   (Indeed)
Fatuma Kamara, Disperser-of-Women!
O Modibo!   (Indeed)
The Kamara woman's lion-man!
1250   Modibo!
O Nare Magan Kònatè!   (Mmm, that's true)

Ah! Bèmba!
They made a sacrifice of the spotted dog   (Indeed)
So that the Wizard would not walk.   (Indeed)
1255   In the month of Dòmba,   (Indeed)
The very, very, very first day,   (Indeed)
Son-Jara's Muslim jinn came forward: (Indeed)
"That which God has said to me,   (Mmm)
"To me Tanimunari,   (Indeed)
1260   "That which God has said to me,   (Indeed)
"So it will be done.   (Indeed)
"When the month of Dòmba is ten days old,   (Indeed)
"Son-Jara will rise and walk."   (Indeed)
In the month of Dòmba,   (Indeed)
1265   On its twelfth day,   (Indeed)
The Messenger of God was born.   (Indeed)
On the thirteenth day,   (Indeed)
Jòn Bilāl was born.   (Indeed)
On its tenth day,   (Indeed)

1270   Son-Jara tòòma lun le nin di.

      Nare Magan Kònatè!   (Cinyè don)
      ...,
      Magan ni Ton-ta-Magan!
      Nare Magan Kònatè!
1275   Subaa-Minè-Subaa!
      Sin-kula le sòrò man di.   (Mmm)
      Mògò o mògò kulan-kulan na,
      O mògò bèè sin-kula-nyinintò.   (Cinyè don)
      Minisiri ni dipitè ani peresidan,   (Naamu)
1280   A bèè si le nò fè sa.
      Sibaya le sòrò man di.   (Cinyè don)

      An na Mali kònò,
      An d'an yèrè sòrò.   (Naamu)
      Ni mògò ma sanu sòrò,
1285   N'i ma wòri sòrò,   (Naamu)
      N'i di k'i yèrè sòrò,
      I kèra hòròn ye dè!   (O ye cinyè ye)
      Sin-kula le sòrò man di.   (Mmm)

      Bènba le.
1290   Dònba karu tili tan,   (Naamu)
      Subaa ba di fidi yèlè,   (Naamu)
      Son-Jara la saraka fidi.
      N'a taara musu min da la,   (Naamu)
      O musu y'i bara: (Naamu)
1295   "Sita na di Ne ma, nnn."   (Naamu)
      Musu y'i bara,
      "Sita na ye Ne kun,
      "Bar'a tè d'i ma.
      "Ta'a f'i la nanbara ye,
1300   "K'a ka dò kari.   (Mmm)
      "Ne din-kè le ka nin kari."   (Cinyè)

      A kasi: *bilika, bilika.*
      A taara musu dò wèrè da la.   (Mmm)
      O fana y'i bara: (Mmm)
1305   "Sita na ye Ne kun,
      "Bar'a tè d'i ma.
      "Ta'a f'i la nanbara,
      "K'a ka dò.

1270 Was the day for Son-Jara to walk.

    O Nare Magan Kònatè!   (That's true)
    . . . ,
    Master and Warrior Master!
    O Nare Magan Kònatè!
1275   O Sorcerer-Seizing-Sorcerer!
    A man of power is hard to find.   (Mmm)
    All people with their empty words,
    They all seek to be men of power.   (That's true)
    Ministers, deputies and presidents,   (Indeed)
1280   All of them seek after power,
    But there is no easy way to power.   (That's true)

    Here in our Mali,
    We have found our freedom.   (Indeed)
    Though a person find no gold,
1285   Though he find no silver,   (Indeed)
    Should he find his freedom,
    Then noble will he be.   (That's the truth)
    A man of power is hard to find.   (Mmm)

    Ah! Bèmba!
1290 On the tenth day of Dòmba,   (Indeed)
    The Wizard's mother cooked some couscous, (Indeed)
    Sacrificial couscous for Son-Jara.
    Whatever woman's door she went to,   (Indeed)
    The Wizard's mother would cry: (Indeed)
1295 "Give me some sauce of baobab leaf."   (Indeed)
    The woman would retort,
    "I have some sauce of baobab leaf,
    "But it is not to give to you.
    "Go tell that cripple child of yours
1300 "That he should harvest some for you.   (Mmm)
    " 'Twas my son harvested these for me." (True)

    And bitterly did she weep: *bilika bilika.*
    She went to another woman's door;   (Mmm)
    That one did also say: (Mmm)
1305 "I have some sauce of baobab leaf,
    "But it is not to give to you.
    "Go tell that cripple child of yours
    "That he should harvest some for you.

"Ne din-kè le ka min kari N' ye dè." (Cinyè)

1310 Kòndè-musu ni kasi nara: *bilika, bilika:*

> *"Nyani-mansa, Nyani-mansa,*
> *"I tè wili ba?* (Mmm)
> *"Nyani-mansa, Nyani-mansa,*
> *"I tè wili ba?* (Mmm)
> 1315 *"Nègè fukula Nyani-mansa kun na,*
> *"K'a tè silan mògò nya.*
> *"I tè wili ba?*
> *"Wili le, Nyani-mansa!* (Cinyè don)
>
> *"Nyani-mansa, Nyani-mansa,*
> 1320 *"I tè wili?*
> *"Nègè dèrèkè ye Nyani-mansa kan na,*
> *"K'a tè silan mògò nya.*
> *"I tè wili ba?*
> *"Wili le, Nyani-mansa!* (Cinyè)

1325 "Subaa, Ne kanyara dè!" (Cinyè)
"Aa, N' na,
"N' ye nògòlan dò ku mèla ko Lele-fin. (Cinyè)
"I t'o kè N' na fidi ladun?
"Bèrètò nògòlan."

1330 A di Lele-fin kè fidi la, nnn.
Subaa di dumuli kè.
Ma'an Kònatè fara: (Cinyè)
"Aa, N' na, (Naamu)
"Taga numulu bènba, (Naamu)
1335 "Dun Fayiri ni Nun Fayiri bara, (Naamu)
"K'alu ka tawun-wòròwula ganya-budu da,
"Ko Magan Kònatè wilila." (Naamu)

Numulu mama di tawun-wòrònwula ganya-budu da. (Naamu)
Subaa nara. (Naamu)
1340 A b'a kini-bulu bil'a numan-bulu nya,
K'i sulumè. (Naamu)
A d'i sulumè.
A sila san ni dugu tèmala dò: (Naamu)
"Ganya-budu lamara."
1345 Ma'an Kònatè ma wili. (Cinyè)

" 'Twas my son harvested these for me."   (True)

1310 With bitter tears, the Kòndè woman came back, *bilika
         bilika.*
         "King of Nyani, King of Nyani,
         "Will you never rise?   (Mmm)
         "King of Nyani, King of Nyani,
         "Will you never rise?   (Mmm)
1315   *"King of Nyani with helm of mail,*
         "He says he fears no man.
         "Will you never rise?
         "Rise up, O King of Nyani!   (That's true)

         "King of Nyani, King of Nyani,
1320   *"Will you never rise?*
         "King of Nyani with shirt of mail,
         "He says he fears no man.
         "Will you never rise?
         "Rise up, O King of Nyani!   (True)

1325 "O Wizard, I have failed!"   (True)
      "Ah, my mother,
      "There is a thickener, I hear, called black *lele*.   (True)
      "Why not put some in my sauce?
      " 'Tis the thickener grown in gravel."

1330 She put black *lele* in the couscous.
      The Wizard ate of it.
      Ma'an Kònatè ate his fill: (True)
      "My mother,   (Indeed)
      "Go to the home of the blacksmith patriarchs,   (Indeed)
1335 "To Dun Fayiri and Nun Fayiri.   (Indeed)
      "Have them shape a staff, seven-fold forged,
      "So that Magan Kònatè may rise up."   (Indeed)
      The blacksmith patriarchs shaped a staff, seven-fold
           forged.   (Indeed)
      The Wizard came forward.   (Indeed)
1340 He put his right hand o'er his left,
      And upwards drew himself,   (Indeed)
      And upwards drew himself.
      He had but reached the halfway point.   (Indeed)
      "Take this staff away from me!"
1345 Magan Kònatè did not rise.   (True)

A ba kisira ka: *bilika, bilika*:   (Naamu)
"Ne bònòda wulu dò!"   (Mmm)
"Aa, N' na,   (Mmm)
"Taga numulu bènba bara,   (Naamu)
1350 "K'a k'o budu da,   (Naamu)
"K'o nyògòn dò wèrè far'a kan, k'a da.   (Mmm)
"Ne la mori ko, ko N' ye wili bi."   (Mmm)

Numulu mama d'o budu da,
K'o nyògòn far'a kan, nnn.   (Cinyè)
1355 A di budu da,
K'a di Ma'an Kònatè ma.   (Naamu)
A di kini-bulu bil'a numan-bulu nya.   (Naamu)
Son-Jara y'i sulumèla.   (Naamu)
Nare Magan Kònatè y'i sulumèla.   (Naamu)

1360 A sira san ni dugu tèmala dò: (Mmm)
"Ganyè-budu lamara!"
Ma'an Kònatè ma wili.
A d'i sigi.   (Naamu)
A ba d'a bulu fula sòò a kun,
1365 Ka kule: "*dèndèlèn*!
"Ne bònòna wulu dò!"   (Cinyè)
"Aa, N' na,   (Mmm)
"Ku min ye e le ni Ala tè,   (Naamu)
"Ta'a fò Ala ye sa!"   (Naamu)

1370 A ba bòra ole dò, nnn,
Ka taa Bintanya kòròn dò,   (Naamu)
Ka waa jònbalu tèrè.   (Naamu)

Bènba le, nnn.   (Naamu)
Ka jònba tèrè,   (Naamu)
1375 Ka kilin tègè,   (Naamu)
K'a kany'a sin fudu ma,   (Naamu)
K'i sali lò: (Naamu)
          "Aa, Ala!
          "Nde ye bele dila Son-Jara ma.   (Naamu)
1380   "Sini-mògò l'a di,   (Naamu)
          "Sini-kini-mògò l'a di,   (Naamu)
          "A ye jeli marala,   (Naamu)
          "A ye numulu marala,   (Naamu)
          "A tun-tan-mògò bi saba ni mògò saba,   (Naamu)

In misery his mother wept: *bilika bilika*:	(Indeed)
"Giving birth has made me suffer!"	(Mmm)
"Ah, my mother,	(Mmm)
"Return to the blacksmith patriarchs.	(Indeed)
1350 "Ask that they forge that staff anew,	(Indeed)
"And shape it twice again in size.	(Mmm)
"Today I arise, my holy-man said."	(Mmm)
The patriarchs of the smiths forged the staff,	
Shaping it twice again in size.	(True)
1355 They forged that staff,	
And gave it to Ma'an Kònatè.	(Indeed)
He put his right hand o'er his left,	(Indeed)
And upwards Son-Jara drew himself.	(Indeed)
Upwards Nare Magan Kònatè drew himself.	(Indeed)
1360 Again he reached the halfway point:	(Mmm)
"Take this staff away from me!"	
Ma'an Kònatè did not rise.	
He sat back down again.	(Indeed)
His mother wrung her hands atop her head,	
1365 And wailed: "*dèndèlen*!	
"Giving birth has made me suffer!"	(True)
"Ah, my mother,	(Mmm)
"Whate'er has come twixt you and God,	(Indeed)
"Go and speak to God about it now!"	(Indeed)
1370 On that, his mother left,	
And went to the east of Bintanya,	(Indeed)
To seek a custard apple tree.	(Indeed)
Ah! Bèmba!	(Indeed)
And found some custard apple trees,	(Indeed)
1375 And cut one down,	(Indeed)
And trimmed it level to her breast,	(Indeed)
And stood as if in prayer:	(Indeed)
"O God!	
"For Son-Jara I have made this staff.	(Indeed)
1380 "If he be the man for the morrow,	(Indeed)
"If he be the man for the day to follow,	(Indeed)
"If he is to rule the bards,	(Indeed)
"If he is to rule the smiths,	(Indeed)
"The three and thirty warrior clans,	(Indeed)

1385   "A y'o mògò bèè mara,   (Naamu)
    "N' mana bele di Nare Magan Kònatè ma,   (Naamu)
    "Ma'an Kònatè ka wili.   (Cinyè)
    "Sini-mògò 'n t'a di,   (Naamu)
    "Sini-kini-mògò 'n t'a di,   (Naamu)
1390   "A tè jeli marala,   (Naamu)
    "A tè numulu marala,   (Naamu)
    "N' mana bele di Nyani-mansa ma,
    "Son-Jara kana wili dè!
    "Ala, kabin'ile di Ne da,   (Naamu)
1395   "Ni Ne ma kè wo kè lòn,   (Naamu)
    "Fo Fata Magan Kè-nyi kilin kò,   (Naamu)
    "N' mana bele di Nyani-mansa ma,
    "Son-Jara ka wili.   (Naamu)
    "Kabin'i ka N' da,   (Cinyè)
1400   "Ni Ne di kè fula lòn,
    "N'a ma kè fo Fata Magan Kè-nyi di,   (Naamu)
    "Ma'an Kònatè kana wili!"   (Cinyè)

A di bele tègè,
Ka n'a di Nare Magan Kònatè ma,
1405 Kòndè-musu din, magu-nyama.   (Cinyè)
Subaa di bele ta,   (Mmm)
K'a kini-bulu bil'a numan-bulu nya.   (Naamu)
A ye surumèla,   (Naamu)
A ye surumèla.
1410 Ma'an Kònatè wilila!   (Mmm)
A bani bori nara,
K'a sin fula minè,
K'a ròdigi,   (Naamu)
K'a ròdigi: (Cinyè)
1415   *"An nelu la bulun nin,*
    "Hèrè bulun!   (Naamu)
    "Hèrè ma tamin yan na habada!
    "Magan Kònatè bara wili.   (Naamu)
    "Bi wo!   (Naamu)
1420   *"Bi ka di le!*   (Naamu)
    "Mansa Ala ma bi nyògòn da!   (Naamu)
    "Ma'an Kònatè bara wili.   (Naamu)
    "Lò-nya man dògòn!
    "Lò-nya fèlè: danka!
1425   *"Bunkun ni bantanba!"*   (Fa-Digi,
    cinyè don)

1385   "If he is to rule all those,   (Indeed)
         "When this staff I give to Nare Magan Kònatè,   (Indeed)
         "Let Magan Kònatè arise.   (True)
         "If he be not the man for the morrow,   (Indeed)
         "If he be not the man for the day to follow,   (Indeed)
1390   "If he is not to rule the bards,   (Indeed)
         "If he is not to rule the smiths,   (Indeed)
         "When this staff I give to the King of Nyani,
         "Let Son-Jara not arise.
         "O God, from the day of my creation,   (Indeed)
1395   "If I have known another man,
         "Save Fata Magan, the Handsome alone,
         "When this staff I give to the King of Nyani,
         "Let Son-Jara arise.   (Indeed)
         "From the day of my creation,   (True)
1400   "If I have known a second man,
         "And not just Fata Magan, the Handsome,   (Indeed)
         "Let Ma'an Kònatè not arise!"   (True)

         She cut down that staff,
         Going to give it to Nare Magan Kònatè,
1405   To the Kòndè woman's child, the Answerer-of-Needs!   (True)
         The Wizard took the staff,   (Mmm)
         And put his right hand o'er his left,   (Indeed)
         And upwards drew himself,   (Indeed)
         And upwards drew himself.
1410   Magan Kònatè rose up!   (Mmm)
         Running, his mother came forward,
         And clasped his legs
         And squeezed them,   (Indeed)
         And squeezed them: (True)
1415   *"This home of ours,*
             "The home of happiness.   (Indeed)
             "Happiness did not pass us by.
             "Magan Kònatè has risen!"   (Indeed)
             "O Today!   (Indeed)
1420   *"Today is sweet!*   (Indeed)
             "God the King ne'er made today's equal!   (Indeed)
             "Ma'an Kènatè has risen!"   (Indeed)
             "There is no way of standing without worth.
             "Behold his way of standing: danka!
1425   *"O Kapok Tree and Flame Tree!"*   (Fa-Digi,
                                                                           that's true)

"N' na,   (Mmm)
"Sita min ye Manden dugu,
"Sita min nyugu diman Manden sita bèè di,   (Naamu)
"O sita ye min tun, N' ba?"   (Naamu)
1430 "N' nanbara,   (Naamu)
"I dun m'i tògòma fòlò."   (Naamu)

Subaa d'a kini-sin ta,
K'a bil'a numan-sin na.   (Naamu)
A ba d'i bil'a kò,
1435 Ka dònkili l'a ma: (Naamu)
     "Tunyu tanya!   (Naamu)
     "Cè farin bènda tun-tun rò!   (Naamu)
     "Tunyu tanya!   (Naamu)
     "Farin ... bènda tun-tun rò!   (Naamu)
1440 *"Ma'an Kònatè, jaa i bare wili!*   (Naamu)

     "Tutatò ji,   (Naamu)
     "Kan'i sanka bèrè-rò-ji ma.   (Naamu)

     "Bèrè gènin wasili!   (Naamu)
     "...,   (Naamu)
1445 *"...,*   (Naamu)
     "Ni tògò diman.   (Naamu)
     "Kalifaya Magan Kònatè wilila!   (Cinyè)

     "Sa ba, sa ba,   (Naamu)
     "N' y'i dòndò.   (Naamu)
1450 *"I mana baga N' ma, k'i dòndò.*   (Naamu)
     "Sula-kan-na-sa-ba,   (Naamu)
     "Min mana baga N' ma, N' y'i dòndò.   (Naamu)

     "Bènyè-kala hèrè!   (Naamu)
     "Kèmè kò yan.   (Naamu)
1455 *"Kèmè lò su,*
     "Fo Son-Jara.   (Cinyè dè)

     "Sanna bèrèni titò le!   (Naamu)
     "Jòn di fili ju-tègèbaa ma?
     "Nare Magan Kònatè bulu!"

1460 Hè! Biribiriba nada.   (Naamu)
A di sita giji-giji.   (Naamu)

"My mother,   (Mmm)
"That baobab there in Manden country,
"That baobab from which the best sauce comes,   (Indeed)
"Where is that baobab, my mother?"   (Indeed)
1430 "Ah, my lame one,   (Indeed)
"You have yet to walk."   (Indeed)

The Wizard took his right foot,
And put it before his left.   (Indeed)
His mother followed behind him,
1435 And sang these songs for him: (Indeed)
    "Tunyu Tanya!   (Indeed)
    "Brave men fit well among warriors! (Indeed)
    "Tunyu tanya!   (Indeed)
    "Brave men fit well among warriors! (Indeed)
1440   *"Ma'an Kònatè, you have risen!"*   (Indeed)

    "Muddy water,   (Indeed)
    "Do not compare yourself to water among the
        stones.   (Indeed)
    "That among the stones is pure, wasili! (Indeed)
    ". . . ,   (Indeed)
1445   *". . . ,*   (Indeed)
    "And a good reputation.   (Indeed)
    "Khalif Magan Kònatè has risen.   (True)

    "Great snake, O great snake,   (Indeed)
    "I will tolerate you.   (Indeed)
1450   *"Should you confront me, toleration.* (Indeed)
    "O great snake upon the path,   (Indeed)
    "Whatever confronts me, I will tolerate. (Indeed)

    "Arrow-shaft of happiness.   (Indeed)
    "It is in one hundred.   (Indeed)
1455   *"The one hundred dead,*
    "All but Son-Jara.   (True)

    "The higher stones get crushed!   (Indeed)
    "Who can mistake the Destroyer-of-Origins!
    "And this by the hand of Nare Magan Kònatè!"

1460 Hey! Biribiriba came forward.   (Indeed)
He shook the baobab tree.   (Indeed)

Bilakoroni dò bira.
O sin karila.
Jelilu ko, "Sin-kari-mara!
1465 "Magan Kònatè wilila!"   (Naamu)
A di sita giji-giji.   (Naamu)
Bilakoroni dò bira.
O bulu karila.   (Naamu)
Jelilu ko, "Bulu-kari-mara!
1470 "Magan Kònatè wilila!"   (Naamu)
A di sita giji-giji.   (Naamu)
Bilakoroni dò bira.   (Naamu)
O kan karila.   (Naamu)
Jelilu ko, "Kan-kari-mara!
1475 "Magan Kònatè wilila!"   (Naamu)
Subaa di sita bò,
K'a l'a kan na.   (Mmm)
Nare Magan Kònatè wilila.   (Naamu)

Musulu nara: *yirrrrrr!*   (Naamu)
1480   *"Al' nanin mun na bi?*   (Naamu)
          "Ku-dò-gè!   (Naamu)
          "Kòri, ku ma n'a bulu?   (Naamu)
          "Ku-dò-gè!   (Naamu)

          "Kosalu!   (Naamu)
1485   *"Manden Kosalu!*
          "K'o dòtèrèmè!   (Naamu)
          "Bi ta tè sòrò k'a ròwoloma.   (Naamu)

          "Mògò-tigi, si, si, si.   (Naamu)
          "Mògòntan wo hoyo.
1490   *"Musuni ka din o bila tòntò dò, [?]*
          "Suya tòntò." [?]   (Mmm)

Ilu nya lò Magan Son-Jara lònin na:
"N'an ka taa, nnn.
"Nare Magan Kònatè wilila.

1495   *"Kèlènna-sii wo, N' y'a lòn.*   (Naamu)
          "An nelu si kò, ka nin nya lòn,   (Naamu)
          "Din-nyuman wulubaga, mal'o t'i la.   (Naamu)
          "Jama mana sigi, malo t'i la.

A young boy fell out.
His leg was broken.
The bards thus sing, "Leg-Crushing-Ruler!
1465 "Magan Kònatè has risen!"   (Indeed)
He shook the baobab again.   (Indeed)
Another young boy fell out.
His arm was broken.   (Indeed)
The bards thus sing, "Arm-Breaking-Ruler!
1470 "Magan Kònatè has risen!"   (Indeed)
He shook the baobab again.   (Indeed)
Another young boy fell out.   (Indeed)
His neck was broken.   (Indeed)
And thus the bards sing, "Neck-Breaking-Ruler!
1475 "Magan Kònatè has risen!"   (Indeed)
The Wizard uprooted the baobab tree,
And laid it across his shoulder.   (Mmm)
Nare Magan Kònatè rose up.   (Indeed)

A crowd of women surged out: *yrrrrrrr.*   (Indeed)
1480   *"Why have you come today?*   (Indeed)
          "What a spectacle!   (Indeed)
          "Have they no reason to be here?   (Indeed)
          "What a spectacle!"   (Indeed)

          "O witch-wives!   (Indeed)
1485   *"O witch-wives of the Manden!*
          "You go find the answer.   (Indeed)
          "Today's cannot be found by searching."   (Indeed)

          "The Master of men, O power, power, power.   (Indeed)
          "One without people, the wind, the wind.
1490   *"The woman put the child in a web,* [?]
          "A web of sorcery!" [?]   (Mmm)

They fixed their eyes on Magan Son-Jara standing there:
"Come, let us go!
"Nare Magan Kònatè has risen!

1495   *"Living alone, I know it.*   (Indeed)
          "After coming to understand that,   (Indeed)
          "Bearer of good children, have no shame.   (Indeed)
          "Whenever there's a crowd, have no shame.

<table>
<tr><td></td><td>"Faan-tigiya,</td><td>(Naamu)</td></tr>
<tr><td>1500</td><td>"N'i d'i ròbèn faan-tigi nyè,</td><td></td></tr>
<tr><td></td><td>"A nya ye malu i ma.</td><td>(Naamu)</td></tr>
</table>

"Jufa nya ye bi la,
"O nya tè sini na.   (Naamu)
"Jufa nya ye bi le la.   (Naamu)
1505   "O nya tè sini na.
"Jòn-kunandi ta ye, k'a nya la le. [?]   (Naamu)

"Katatòlu ta ye, k'a kò. [?]

"Nyani le!   (Naamu)
"Jòn tè i yèrè faga nyani ye.
1510   "I ma nyani laban lòn.   (Cinyè)
"Kalifaya Magan Kònatè!

"Dòlu ta ye tumu di.
"Tunyu tanya!   (Naamu)
"An dè ta ye bandan di,
1515   "Sanu-bandan dè!   (Mmm)
"Kalifaya Magan Kònatè wilila!"

Biribiriba nara.   (Mmm)
A di sita bil'a ba la bun kò fè:
"Manden ni Manden lamini,   (Mmm)
1520   "Bèè ka nyugu-nyini N' ba la."   (Mmm)
A ba d'i bara-ko, "N' m'a mè."   (Mmm)
"N' na le,   (Naamu)
"I ta le Manden sita bèè di sa dè!"
"N' m'a mè."
1525   "N' na le,   (Naamu)
"Musulu minw d'i jè nyugu la,
"O bèè ye nyugu-nyin'i la sa."   (Naamu)
A ba d'i nyòngiri: gèjèbu!
A sin fula kun dò,
1530   K'a tanban la sita kan: (Naamu)

"San wo san wo,
"N' tulu geden le.   (Naamu)
"Fo nyinan wo,
"N' tulu di ku mèn.
1535   "Kalifaya Magan Kònatè wilila!"   (Cinyè don)

<table>
<tr><td>1500</td><td>*"Having power,*
"If you prepare yourself for the powerful,
"They will respect you.</td><td>(Indeed)

(Indeed)</td></tr>
<tr><td></td><td>*"The pocket sees only today,*
"Its eye is not on tomorrow.
"The pocket sees only today,</td><td>
(Indeed)
(Indeed)</td></tr>
<tr><td>1505</td><td>*"Its eye is not on tomorrow.*
"A fortunate man's happiness occurs while he
    lives. [?]
"The unfortunate man's happiness occurs after
    he dies. [?]
"O misery!
"But one should not kill himself for misery.</td><td>

(Indeed)

(Indeed)</td></tr>
<tr><td>1510</td><td>*"No one knows where misery leads.*
"Khalif Magan Kònatè!</td><td>(True)</td></tr>
<tr><td></td><td>*"The one for those behind is Kapok.*
"Tunyu tanya!
"Ours is the Flame Tree,</td><td>
(Indeed)</td></tr>
<tr><td>1515</td><td>*"The golden Flame Tree!*
"Khalif Magan Kònatè has risen!"</td><td>(Mmm)</td></tr>
</table>

Biribiriba came forward. (Mmm)
He planted the baobab behind his mother's house:
"In and about the Manden, (Mmm)
1520 "From my mother they must seek these leaves!" (Mmm)
To which his mother said, "I do not think I heard." (Mmm)
"Ah, my mother, (Indeed)
"Now all the Manden baobabs are yours."
"I do not think I heard."
1525 "Ah, my mother, (Indeed)
"All those women who refused you leaves,
"They all must seek those leaves from you." (Indeed)
His mother fell upon her knees, *gejebu!*
On both her knees,
1530 And laid her head aside the baobab. (Indeed)

<table>
<tr><td></td><td>*"For years and years,*
"My ear was deaf.
"Only this year
"Has my ear heard news.</td><td>
(Indeed)</td></tr>
<tr><td>1535</td><td>*"Khalif Magan Kònatè has risen!"*</td><td>(That's true)</td></tr>
</table>

Biribiriba,   (Naamu)
Kamin'a taamara,   (Mmm)
N'a taara wula dò,   (Naamu)
A mana subu faa,   (Naamu)
1540 A ye n'a ku d'a kòrò-kè ma.
A t'i miiri ku ma tugun,

. . . .   (Naamu)

Bara kala ta le!
Wula-tigi Sinbon ne!
1545 *Bara kala ta le!*
Bara kale ta!   (Naamu)
Jelilu ni numulu mara-mògò,
Bara kala ta!
Bara kala ta le!
1550 *Kòndè-musu din,*
Magu-nyè-mògò,
Bara kala ta le!
Sugulun Ma'an bara kala ta le!

Subaa bara wili!
1555 *Nyani-mansa, Nare Magan Kònatè!*
Subaa wili!   (Naamu)
Aa, Bènba.   (Naamu)
N'a taara wula dò, nnn,   (Naamu)
A ye subu faa,   (Naamu)
1560 A ye ku d'a kòrò-kè ma.
A t'i miiri ku ma tugun.
. . . .   (Naamu)
Lun dò, Biribiriba y'i yaalala,   (Cinyè don)
Jinè nara,
1565 K'è bulu le Son-Jara kan na:
"Son-Jara le!   (Mmm)
"Janfa dunnin ile ma Manden dè.   (Mmm)
"I nya ye kaba-wulu min na,
"Ole kèn'i la saraka di,   (Naamu)
1570 "K'e kana jelilu mara,   (Naamu)
"N'i kana numulu mara,   (Naamu)
"K'i kana tun-tan-mògò bi saba ni mògò saba,
"I kan'o mògò si mara.   (Mmm)
"I mana waa bi,   (Mmm)
1575 "I ka safo-wulu-kè saraka di.   (Naamu)
"Ni Ala sònda,

Biribiriba!   (Indeed)
Since he began to walk,   (Indeed)
Whenever he went into the bush,   (Mmm)
Were he to kill some game,   (Indeed)
1540   He would give his elder the tail,
And think no more of it.

. . . .   (Indeed)

Took up the bow!
Simbon, Master-of-the-Bush!
1545   *Took up the bow!*
Took up the bow!   (Indeed)
Ruler of bards and smiths
Took up the bow!
Took up the bow!
1550   *The Kòndè woman's child,*
Answerer-of-Needs,
He took up the bow.
Sugulun's Ma'an took up the bow!

The Wizard has risen!
1555   *King of Nyani, Nare Magan Kònatè!*
The Wizard has risen!   (Indeed)
Ah! Bèmba!   (Indeed)
Whenever he went to the bush,   (Indeed)
Were he to kill some game,   (Indeed)
1560   He would give to his elder the tail,
And think no more of it.

. . . .   (Indeed)
As Biribiriba walked forth one day,   (That's true)
A jinn came upon him,
1565   And laid his hand on Son-Jara's shoulder:
"O Son-Jara!   (Mmm)
"In the Manden, there's a plot against you.   (Mmm)
"That spotted dog you see before you,   (Indeed)
"Is an offering made against you,   (Indeed)
1570   "So that you not rule the bards,   (Indeed)
"So that you not rule the smiths,
"So, the three and thirty warrior clans,
"That you rule over none of them.   (Mmm)
"When you go forth today,   (Mmm)
1575   "Make an offering of a safo-dog,   (Indeed)
"Should God will it,

"Ile ta le Manden di."   (Naamu)

Aa, Bènba.
Biribiriba waata ole rò, N' fa,
1580 Ka tafo-wulu-kè saraka di,
Ka kulunbalan kè wulu kan na,
Ka nègè-jòlòkò kè wulu kan na.   (Naamu)
Hali sini sògòma,
Tubabulu ye ole ladegenna.
1585 Tubabu mana wulu bila,   (Mmm)
A kulunbalan,
A nègè-jòlòkò kè wulu kan na, Manden.   (Naamu)

Bènba le, nnn.
A di kulunbalan wulu la,
1590 Ka nègè-jòlòkò kè wulu la.   (Mmm)
A man'a kè, tèmènna bulun min da la,   (Naamu)
O mògò bèè ye yèl'a ma:
"Hèn-nabònòn!   (Naamu)
"Misi ni kulunbanda,
1595 "Wulu ni kulunbanda?"   (Naamu)
Subaa y'i bara,
"Ilu fara N' na   (Cinyè)
"Ilu nya faama-wulu la.
"Nyin tè o wulu da.
1600 "Nyin dun ye Ne wulu da,
"Ne faanntan wulu. Ilu fara N' na dè!   (Naamu)
"Ne wulu tògò le, ko Sinin Ku."

Son-Jara la saraka-wulu,
O wulu tògò le ko Sinin Ku.

1605 O wulu le di kulunbalan tègè,
Ka nègè-jòlòkò tègè, nnn,   (Naamu)
Ka taa Dankaran Tumani la wulu kan na,   (Naamu)
K'a ròfasa: *fèsè fèsè fèsè*!   (Naamu)
K'a bèè kè nyògòn kan.   (Naamu)
1610 Dankaran Tumani ba d'a bulu fula sòò a kun,

Ka kule: *dèndèlen*!   (Naamu)
"Wulu ka wulu kin, nnn,   (Naamu)
"Manden ku kòrò.   (Naamu)
"Wulu ka wulu faga,

"The Manden will be yours!"   (Indeed)

Ah! Bèmba!
On that, Biribiriba went forth, my father,
1580   And made an offering of a safo-dog,
And hung a weight around its neck,
And fastened an iron chain about it.   (Indeed)
Even tomorrow morning,
The Europeans will imitate him.
1585   Whenever the Europeans leave a dog,   (Mmm)
Its neck weight,
They fasten that dog with an iron chain, Manden!   (Indeed)

O! Bèmba!
He hung a weight around the dog's neck,
1590   And fastened it with a chain.   (Mmm)
That done, whatever home he passed before,   (Indeed)
The people stood gaping at him:
"Causer-of-Loss!   (Indeed)
"A cow with its neckweight,
1595   "But a dog with a neckweight?"   (Indeed)
To which the Wizard did retort:
"Leave me be!   (True)
"Cast your eyes on the dog of the prince.
"There's not a tooth in that dog's mouth!
1600   "But there are teeth in my dog's mouth,
"My commoner's dog. Leave me be!   (Indeed)
"My dog's name is Tomorrow's Affair."

Son-Jara's sacrificial dog,
That dog was called Tomorrow's Affair.

1605   From his neckweight he broke loose,
And also from his chain,   (Indeed)
And charged the dog of Dankaran Tuman,   (Indeed)
And ripped him into shreds, *fèsè fèsè fèsè!*   (Indeed)
And stacked one piece atop the other.   (Indeed)
1610   The mother of Dankaran Tuman, she wrung her hands
atop her head,
And gave a piercing cry: "*dèndèlen!*   (Indeed)
"That a dog would bite a dog,   (Indeed)
"A natural thing in the Manden.   (Indeed)
"That a dog would kill a dog,

1615 "Manden ku kòrò.   (Naamu)
     "Wulu ka wulu finin-kòròn-ròfara ten,
     "N' ba, fèn ne wulu-tigi rò."
     Dankaran Tumani ko, "Aa, N' na,   (Mmm)
     "Ne l'a fòla wulu ma, Bò-N'-kò-N'-Dògò.   (Mmm)
1620 "Aa, N' ba, i kana sin-ji tègè dè!   (Cinyè)
     "N' na le,   (Naamu)
     "Wulu le taatò wula rò,
     "K'a taa subu faa,
     "K'a n'a di Ne ma, N' ba.   (Cinyè)
1625 "Kana sin-ji tègè dè, N' ba."   (Cinyè)

     Dankaran Tumani ba ma kuma tugun: (Naamu)
     "Son-Jara bò-tuma sira wula dò.   (Mmm)

     "Jaa, lònnilalu di min fò,   (Mmm)
     "Ole tuma sinin di.   (Mmm)
1630 "Ne la wulu,   (Mmm)
     "O tutò kò. O tè nya ye.   (Mmm)
     "Son-Jara,   (Mmm)
     "Kòndè-musu la wulu,   (Mmm)
     "Ole ye Manden tòntòn n'a saan bèè tala,   (Mmm)
1635 "Ka jelilu mara,
     "Ka numulu mara,   (Naamu)
     "Ka funè ni garangèlu mara,   (Naamu)
     "K'o le ta ye Manden di.
     "O le tuma sira,   (Naamu)
1640 "Nare Magan Kònatè bulu.
     "Ku le t'a tuma tula."
          Biribiriba!
          Kirikisa, Dunnun-tanba, Sòn-tanba!
          Kaya-kalu wo, Son-Jara dunna Kaya!
1645   Nare Magan Kònatè bulu!
          Sebaaya le sòrò man di.   (Naamu)
     Aa, Bènba le, nnn .   (Naamu)
     Mansa Dankaran Tumani ba,   (Naamu)
     Subaa bòra wula dò,   (Naamu)
1650 Ka na ku bil'a ba-kilin-kòrò-kè kòrò,   (Naamu)
     A ko, "E la ku ta!"
     "I ba, Sugulun Kòndè, k'è ku ta!   (Naamu)

     "An'i dògòni Sugulun Kulunkan,   (Naamu)
     "An'i dògòni Manden Bukari.   (Naamu)

1615   "A natural thing in the Manden.
       "That a dog shred another like an old cloth,
       "My mother, there must be something with his master!"
       Dankaran Tuman replied, "Ah! my mother,   (Mmm)
       "I called my dog Younger-Leave-Me-Be.   (Mmm)
1620   "Ah! My mother, do not sever the bonds of family.   (True)
       "My mother!   (Indeed)
       "That is the dog that stalked the bush
       "To go and kill some game,
       "Bringing it back to me, my mother.   (True)
1625   "Do not sever the bonds of family, my mother!"   (True)

       The mother of Dankaran Tuman had no answer: (Indeed)
       "One afternoon, the time will come for Son-Jara to
            depart.   (Mmm)
       "Indeed what the wise men have said,   (Mmm)
       "His time is for the morrow.   (Mmm)
1630   "The one that I have borne,   (Mmm)
       "He is being left behind without explanation.   (Mmm)
       "Son-Jara,   (Mmm)
       "The Kòndè woman's offspring,   (Mmm)
       "He will take the Manden tribute,   (Mmm)
1635   "And he will rule the bards,   (Mmm)
       "And he will rule the smiths,   (Indeed)
       "And rule the funès and the cordwainers.   (Indeed)
       "The Manden will be his.
       "That time will yet arrive,   (Indeed)
1640   "And that by the hand of Nare Magan Kònatè.
       "Nothing leaves its time behind."
               O Biribiriba!
               Kirikisa, Spear-of-Access, Spear-of-Service!
               People of Kaya, Son-Jara entered Kaya.
1645   All this by the hand of Nare Magan Kònatè.
               Gaining power is not easy!   (Indeed)
       Ah! Bèmba, nnn!   (Indeed)
       The mother of King Dankaran Tuman,   (Indeed)
       When the Wizard had left the bush,   (Indeed)
1650   And offered his flesh-and-blood-brother the tail,   (Indeed)
       And when he said, "Here take the tail!"
       She retorted: "Your mother, Sugulun Kòndè, will
            take the tail!   (Indeed)
       "And your younger sister, Sugulun Kulukan,   (Indeed)
       "And your younger brother, Manden Bukari.   (Indeed)

1655 "Ilu k'waa sa-yòrò nyini. (Naamu)
"N'o tè, N' y'i kan tègè,
"Fo ka sibiri tègè dugu rò.
"N'o tè, i tè dun Manden yan." (Naamu)
Son-Jara kasira: *bilika, bilika,* (Naamu)
1660 Ka ta'a f'a ba ye. (Naamu)
A ba ko, (Naamu)
"Aa, N' din, (Naamu)
"La, k'i kòrò-kè fo. (Naamu)
"A dun min 'i nanmarama gèn,
1665 "I ye waala min?
"An k'an sòn.
"An ka taa.
"Sigi tèna ko min ban,
"Taama le o banna." (Cinyè don)

1670 Alu wilira. (Mmm)
Kuyatèlu mama di karinyan ta. (Mmm)
A di dunsu-dònkili la, Nare Magan Kònatè:
    " *Bara kala ta le!* (Naamu)
    " *Wula-tigi Sinbon ne!*
1675   " *Bara kala ta le!*
    " *Bara kale ta le!* (Naamu)
    " *Subu-tigi Sinbon ne!*
    " *Bara kala ta le!* (Naamu)
    " *Bara kala ta!* (Naamu)
1680   " *Tun-tigi, jòn-tigi!*
    " *Bara kala ta!* (Naamu)
    " *Kòndè-musu din,*
    " *Magu-nyè-mògò,* (Naamu)
    " *Bare kala ta!* (Naamu)
1685   " *Sugulun Ma'an bara kala ta!* (Naamu)
    " *I y'a muta le, jara!* (Naamu)
    " *Subaa y'a faga!*
    " *Sinbon, o juru dè kan ye!"* (Cinyè)

A di nyani mabori. (Mmm)
1690 A waar'i karifa nun-mogòlu bènba la. (Naamu)
Fa-dinya la gèlèya ma. (Mmm)
Alu di duu-mòò nya kilin sanu suman, (Mmm)

1655	"Go and seek a place to die,	(Indeed)
	"If not, I will chop through your necks,	
	"Cutting a handspan down into the ground.	
	"Be it so; you'll never return to the Manden again."	(Indeed)
	Son-Jara bitterly wept, *bilika bilika!*	(Indeed)
1660	And went to tell his mother.	(Indeed)
	His mother said,	(Indeed)
	"Ah! My child,	(Indeed)
	"Be calm. Salute your brother.	(Indeed)
	"Had he banished you as a cripple,	
1665	"Where would you have gone?	
	"Let us at least agree on that.	
	"Let us depart.	
	"What sitting will not solve,	
	"Travel will resolve."	(That's true)

EPISODE FIVE: MÈMA

1670	They rose up.	(Mmm)
	The Kuyatè matriarch took up the iron rasp.	(Mmm)
	She sang a hunter's song for Nare Magan Kònatè:	
	"Took up the bow!	(Indeed)
	"Simbon, Master-of-the-Bush!	
1675	*"Took up the bow!*	
	"Took up the bow!	(Indeed)
	"Simbon, Master-of-Wild-Beasts!	
	"Took up the bow!	(Indeed)
	"Took up the bow!	(Indeed)
1680	*"Warrior and Master-of Slaves!*	
	"Took up the bow!	(Indeed)
	"The Kòndè woman's child,	
	"Answerer-of-Needs,	(Indeed)
	"Took up the bow.	(Indeed)
1685	*"Sugulun's Ma'an took up the bow.*	(Indeed)
	You seized him, O Lion!	(Indeed)
	"And the Wizard killed him!	
	"O Simbon, that, the sound of your chords."	(True)
	He fled from suffering	(Mmm)
1690	To seek refuge with the blacksmith patriarch,	(Indeed)
	Because of the hardships of rivalry.	(Mmm)
	But they counted out one measure of gold,	(Mmm)

Ka wa'a di nun-mògòlu bènba ma,   (Naamu)
Ko n'a ma Subaa gèn,   (Naamu)
1695 K'ale ye dugu kanda la,   (Naamu)
Ko Subaa ta le Manden di,   (Naamu)
Fa-dinya la gèlèya ma.   (Naamu)
Subaa di nyani mabori kè.   (Mmm)
A waar'i karifa Karangalu bènba.   (Naamu)
1700 I m'o mògò tòò lòn?   (Mmm)
Soma Jobi.   (Naamu)
Karangalu mama le Soma Jobi di.   (N'm'o lòn dè,
bari fon'i k'a fò N' ye)

O Soma Jobi dè,   (Naamu)
Ole di Sika Danba ta,
1705 Ka Sika Jata wulu.   (Naamu)
O Sika Jata le di Dabakala Kònatè wulu.
Karangalu mama l'o di.   (Naamu)
... jinè-kè ta, Genu Kuru san fè, [?]   (Naamu)
Ka taa tili-bi tuma ma,
1710 Fo tili dò wèrè bòra,   (Naamu)
Jinè-kamalen b'i kònkòn ni kalaman la, [?]
Binbiri-kèsè sagi kilin ta, [?]   (Naamu)
K'a di Karangalu bènba ma,
K'a ka waa i sigi Bisan-dugu,
1715 Ko ka sènè kè.

Fa-dinya le gèlèya ma,   (Naamu)
Al' di Subaa gèn.   (Naamu)
A waar'i karifa Kòlè Mansa Tulunbèn ma.   (Naamu)

Fa-dinya le gèlèya ma,
1720 Al' di duu-mòò nya kilin sanu suman,   (Mmm)
Ko k'a di Kòlè Mansa Tulunbèn ma.
N'a ma Subaa gèn,   (Mmm)
K'a ye Manden-banku kandala dè,   (Mmm)
Ko mògòlu sigan'a ma.   (Cinyè don)

1725 A waar'i karifa,
Sigiri Magasubaalu bènba la.   (Cinyè don)
Janelu bènba Seri Bukari Jane waala hiji.   (Naamu)

Ole d'a musu kònòma karifa,

    And gave it to the blacksmith patriarch,   (Indeed)
    Saying, were he not to cast the Wizard out,   (Indeed)
1695 Saying, he would jeopardize the land,   (Indeed)
    Saying, the Manden would be the Wizard's,   (Indeed)
    Because of the hardships of rivalry.   (Indeed)
    The Wizard fled anew from suffering.   (Mmm)
    He went to seek refuge with the Karanga patriarch. (Indeed)
1700 Do you not know that person's name?   (Mmm)
    Jobi, the Seer.   (Indeed)
    The Karanga patriarch was Jobi, the Seer. (I did not know that
                               until you told me)

    That Jobi, the Seer,   (Indeed)
    Married Sika Danba,
1705 And fathered Sika Jata.   (Indeed)
    Sika Jata begat the Kònatè of Dabakala.
    He was the Karanga ancestor.   (Indeed)
    A group of jinns was at the top of Genu mountain. [?] (Indeed)
    From the time the sun set,
1710 Until the next sun rose,   (Indeed)
    The brave jinns readied themselves.
    They took a basket of millet seed,   (Indeed)
    And gave it to the Karanga patriarch,
    Saying, he should settle in Bisan-dugu,
1715 Saying, he should cultivate the land.

    Because of the hardships of rivalry,   (Indeed)
    He cast the Wizard out.   (Indeed)
    He went then to seek refuge with Tulumbèn, King
       of Kòlè.   (Indeed)

    Because of hardships of rivalry,
1720 They counted out one measure of gold,   (Mmm)
    To give to King Tulumbèn of Kòlè.
    Were he not to cast the Wizard out,   (Mmm)
    He would jeopardize Manden country,
    Since the folk had lost their faith in him. (That's true)

1725 He went to seek refuge
    With the patriarch of the Magasubaas in Sigiri. (That's true)
    The Jane patriarch, Bukari Jane, the Pure, made
       his ḥājj.   (Indeed)
    He entrusted his pregnant wife

Magasubaalu bènba Kòlè Mansa Tulunbèn na,

1730 Ka taa hiji.   (Naamu)
A waara hiji kè.   (Mmm)
Basi dò le tèrè Magan Son-Jara bulu,   (Mmm)
A basi tè sòn fèn wo fèn na,
Fo musu mana kònò ta,   (Naamu)
1735 O din ne kètò ka basi sòn.   (Èè, Fa-Digi)
Seri Bukari Jane waara hiji.   (Cinyè don)
A d'a musu kònòma karifa, nnn,   (Cinyè don)
Sigiri Magasubaalu bènbe Kòlè Mansa
        Tulunbèn na.
Seri Bukari Jane,   (Naamu)
1740 Al' d'o musu faa,   (Mmm)
K'a din kè, ka basi son,
K'a di Son-Jara ma,
K'a ka w'i karifa,
Dibi-rò-mansa mògò kònòntòn la,
1745 K'a ta le Manden di.   (Cinyè don)

O tili saba,
Mori bòra hiji.
Fo dugu talada tuma min na,   (Naamu)
A di arakan fula lò:
1750 "Aa, Ala!
"Ne di mun kè Ala la?   (Naamu)
"Iyo, kafiri ka N' musu faa,
"K'a din kè, ka basi sòn,
"Ka' di mògòlu ma,
1755 "Ko sebaaya nyini,
"Ne le di mun kè Ala la?"

Ala d'i tu ole dò,   (Naamu)
Ka jòlòkò dò bile,   (Naamu)
Kòlè Mansa Tulunbèn kan na,   (Naamu)
1760 Ka jòlòkò dò bil'a kinin-bulu la,   (Naamu)
Ka dò bil'a numan-bulu la,   (Naamu)
Ka Kòlè Mansa Tulunben ta,   (Naamu)
San ni dugu tè la.   (Mmm)
A lajigira dala min dò,
1765 Firiki!   (Mmm)
Jòlòkò-fè-jigin kòrò le nin di.

To the patriarch of the Magasubaas, Tulunbèn,
   King of Kòlè.
1730 And went forth upon his ḥājj.   (Indeed)
He went forth to make the ḥājj.   (Mmm)
Now, Magan Son-Jara had this fetish,   (Mmm)
A fetish accepting no offering,
Unless, if a woman grow great with child,   (Indeed)
1735 The unborn babe be that offering.   (Eh, Fa-Digi)
And Bukari Jane, the Pure, was making his ḥājj. (That's true)
He had entrusted his pregnant wife,   (That's true)
To the patriarch of the Sigiri Magasubaa,
   Tulunbèn, King of Kòlè.
Bukari Jane, the Pure,   (Indeed)
1740 They slew his wife,   (Mmm)
And offered the babe to the fetish,
And then gave it to Son-Jara,
So he could go seek refuge
With the nine Queens-of-Darkness,
1745 Saying, the Manden would thus be his.   (That's true)

Three days after this,
The holy-man returned from his ḥājj.
When night had reached its midpoint,   (Indeed)
Having said his pair of litanies:
1750 "Ah! God!
"What have I done to Thee?   (Indeed)
"Alas, for pagans to slay my wife,
"And to make an offering of her babe,
"And to give it to some person,
1755 "In his search for power,
"What have I done to Thee?"

And God carried on from there,   (Indeed)
And cast a chain round the neck   (Indeed)
Of that Tulunbèn, King of Kòlè,   (Indeed)
1760 And cast a chain round his right arm, (Indeed)
And cast one round his left,   (Indeed)
And raised Tulunbèn, King of Kòlè,   (Indeed)
Up between heaven and earth.   (Mmm)
The lake in which he was sent splashing down,
1765 *Fikiri!*   (Mmm)
This is what is meant by Lowering-by-Chain.

Ole ko kèra Sigiri Magasubaalu bènba.   (Mmm)

Biribiriba war'i karifa,
Dibi-rò-mansa mògò kònòntòn la.
1770 Olu ko, "Mun d'i si yan?   (Mmm)
"Ile m'a mè, ko mògò tè si yan?   (Naamu)
"Mun d'i si yan?"   (Naamu)
Subaa d'i bara,
"Aa, bèè silannin mògò min nye,
1775 "N'i sira o ma, i ye kisi.
"Ole di N' si yan."
A d'i sigi.   (Naamu)
A ba-kilin-kòrò-kè Mansa Dankaran Tumani,   (Naamu)
A d'a din-musu fòlò ta,   (Naamu)
1780 Ta-Suma Gani-Latè,   (Naamu)
K'a di Kuyatèlu bènba Jankuma Dòka ma,   (Naamu)
Ko ka wa'a di Susu Kulu Sumamuru ma,   (Naamu)
Ko n'a ma waa Nyani Mansa faga,
K'a waar'i karifa Dibi-rò-mansa mògò kònòntòn la,

1785 Ko mògòlu sigan'a ma.   (Cinyè dè)

O tuma, balan tè jeli bulu.   (Cinyè)
Balan tè numu bulu.
Balan tè funè bulu.
A dun tè garangè bulu.   (Naamu)
1790 Fo Susu Kulu Sumamuru.   (Naamu)
     Sori-Jan Kantè,   (Naamu)
     Min di Susu Bala Kantè wulu,   (Naamu)
     Ka Kabani Kantè wulu,   (Cinyè dè)
     Ka Kankuba Kantè wulu,
1795 Ka Susu Kulu Sumamuru Kantè wulu.

Sumamuru tèrè dugu min do,
O dugu le Tu-fin ye.   (Cinyè dè)

A nara ole dò, N' fa, nnn,   (Naamu)
Bènba le.   (Naamu)
1800 A fòtò Sumamuru kò.   (Naamu)
Jankuma Dòka,   (Naamu)
A di Sumamuru nyininga.   (Naamu)
Alu ko, "N'i bè Sumamuru nyiningala,
"Sègè nyininga!"   (Mmm)

That is what happened to the Sigiri Magasubaa
    patriarch. (Mmm)
Biribiriba went on to seek refuge
With the nine Queens-of-Darkness.
1770 "What brought you here?" they asked of him. (Mmm)
"Have you not heard that none come here? (Indeed)
"What brought you here?" (Indeed)
The Sorcerer spoke out,
"Ah! Those who are feared by all,
1775 "If you join them, you are spared.
"It is that which made me come here."
He sat down. (Indeed)
His flesh-and-blood-elder, King Dankaran Tuman, (Indeed)
He took his first-born daughter, (Indeed)
1780 Caress-of-Hot-Fire, (Indeed)
And gave her to the Kuyatè patriarch, Dòka the Cat, (Indeed)
Saying, "Give her to Susu Mountain Sumamuru," (Indeed)
Saying, "Should he not slay the King of Nyani,"
Saying, "He's gone to seek refuge with the nine
    Queens-of-Darkness,"
1785 Saying, "The folk have lost their faith in him." (True)

At that time, the bards did not have balaphones, (True)
Nor had the smiths a balaphone,
Nor had the funès a balaphone,
Nor did the cordwainers have one, (Indeed)
1790 None but Susu Mountain Sumamuru. (Indeed)
    Sori Kantè the Tall, (Indeed)
    Who begat Bala Kantè of Susu, (Indeed)
    And who begat Kabani Kantè, (True)
    And who begat Kankuba Kantè,
1795   And who begat Susu Mountain Sumamuru
    Kantè.
The village where Sumamuru was,
That village was called Dark Forest. (True)

It was there he came forth, my father, (Indeed)
Ah! Bèmba! (Indeed)
1800 He came in Sumamuru's absence, (Indeed)
Dòka the Cat, (Indeed)
He asked for Sumamuru. (Indeed)
They said, "If you seek Sumamuru,
"Ask of the hawk!" (Mmm)

1805 Bala-kèsè wòrònwula,   (Mmm)
     Sumamuru man'a la bala fò, nnn,   (Naamu)
     A bala-kalama ta,
     K'a d'i sègè ma.   (Naamu)
     A yèlèn banda la,
1810 K'i sigi Susu tu wo kun dò.   (Naamu)
     A pèrènda sègè la.   (Naamu)
     A di bala d'a ma.   (Naamu)
          "Dun Fayiri, Nun Fayiri!   (Naamu)
          "Manda Kantè ni Soma Kantè!   (Naamu)
1815   "Sori-Jan Kantè!   (Mmm)
          "Susu Kulu Sumamuru Kantè!   (Naamu)
          "Sumamuru fo.   (Naamu)
          "Sumamuru duntò,
          "Mògò-gulu-kurushi.   (Naamu)
1820   "Sumamuru duntò,
          "Ni mògò-gulu-jèrèkè.   (Naamu)
          "Sumamuru duntò,
          "Ni mògò-gulu-fukula.   (Naamu)
          "Mansa fòlò fòlò,
1825   "Mansa duuren.   (Naamu)
          "Awa, tulun tè sòbè sa.
          "Sumamuru, N' fòr'i kò.
          "Janjonba wo!"

     Sumamuru ni kèlè bè nyògòn na,
1830 A ni mògò-gulu-kurushi,
     Ni mògò-gulu-jèrèkè.
     A mana kulu dò yèlèn,
     A dò jigin.
     A dò yèlèn, a dò jigin.
1835 Ala ba mògò?
     A nara Kuyatèlu bènba, Jankuma Dòka: (Mmm)
     "Ala ba mògò?"   (Naamu)
     A ko, "Nde mògò le di!"
     "Ile bòra min?"   (Mmm)
1840 Ko, "Ne bòta Manden ne.   (Naamu)
     "Ne bòta Nyani."   (Naamu)

     A ko, "Fèn fò N' k'a mè."   (Naamu)
     A di bala ta: (Naamu)
          "Kukuba ni Bantanba!
1845   "Nyani-nyani, Kamasiga!

1805 The balaphone of seven keys, (Mmm)
After Sumamuru had played that balaphone, (Indeed)
The mallets of the balaphone he would take,
And give them to the hawk. (Indeed)
It would fly up high in a Flame Tree,
1810 And there in the depths of Susu Forest sit. (Indeed)
Dòka the Cat called to the hawk. (Indeed)
The balaphone mallets it delivered to him. (Indeed)
    "Dun Fayiri, Nun Fayiri! (Indeed)
    "Manda Kantè and Sama Kantè! (Indeed)
1815   *"Sori Kantè, the Tall!* (Mmm)
    "Susu Mountain Sumamuru Kantè! (Indeed)
    "Salute Sumamuru! (Indeed)
    "Sumamuru came amongst us,
    "His pants of human skin. (Indeed)
1820   *"Sumamuru came amongst us,*
    "His coat of human skin. (Indeed)
    "Sumamuru came amongst us,
    "His helm of human skin. (Indeed)
    "The first and ancient king,
1825   *"The King of yesteryear.* (Indeed)
    "So, respite does not end resolve.
    "Sumamuru, I found you gone.
    "O Glorious Janjon!"

Sumamuru was off doing battle,
1830 With pants of human skin,
And coat of human skin.
Whenever he would mount a hill,
Down another he would go.
Up one and down another.
1835 Was he God or man?
He approached the Kuyatè patriarch, Dòka the Cat: (Mmm)
"God or man?" (Indeed)
"I am a man," the reply.
"Where do you hail from?" (Mmm)
1840 "I come," he said, "from the Manden. (Indeed)
"I am from Nyani." (Indeed)

"Play something for me to hear," he said. (Indeed)
He took up the balaphone: (Indeed)
    "Kukuba and Bantanba!
1845   *"Nyani-nyani and Kamasiga!*

             " Farima din-kisè!
             " Ni kè duman talabaga!
             " Sumamuru duntò,
             " Ni mògò-gulu-kurushi.
1850   *" Sumamuru duntò,*
             " Ni mògò-gulu-jèrèkè.
             " Sumamuru duntò,
             " Ni mògò-gulu-fukula.
             " Mansa fòlò fòlò,
1855   *" Mansa duuren.*
             " Awa, tulun tè sòbè sa!
             " Sumamuru, N' fòr'i kò.
             "Janjonba wo!"

A ko, "Aa! Ile tògò di?"
1860 "Ne tògò le Jankuma Dòka."   (Mmm)
"I tè sigi N' fè ba?"
"N' tè! N' tè mansa fula badu.
"Son-Jara la jeli le Ne di.
"Ne bòta Manden.
1865 "N' ye waala Manden ne."   (Cinyè)

A di Kuyatèlu bènba mina,
K'a sin fasa fula tègè,
K'a lasigi Susu bala kun na.   (Naamu)
"I tògò di?"   (Naamu)
1870 "N tògò le Jankuma Dòka."   (Naamu)
"Jankuma Dòka man di."   (Naamu)
A di ji ta, k'a l'a kun-kulu la,   (Naamu)
K'a li,   (Naamu)
K'a tògò la Bala Faseke Kuyatè.
1875 O Bala Faseke Kuyatè,   (Naamu)
Ole di din-kè saba wulu,   (Naamu)
Musa ni Mansa Magan,   (Naamu)
Ka Baturu Mori kè sin-naban di Manden. (Naamu)

Kuyatè ye olelu di.

1880 Sumamuru bulu.
A di kila lò,
Ko k'w'a fò Mansa Dankanan Tumani ye,   (Naamu)
K' "I man'i la wulu jugu faga,"

> *"Brave child of the warrior!*
> *"And Deliverer-of-the-Benign.*
> *"Sumamuru came amongst us,*
> *"With pants of human skin.*
1850 > *"Sumamuru came amongst us,*
> *"With coat of human skin.*
> *"Sumamuru came amongst us,*
> *"With helm of human skin.*
> *"The first and ancient king,*
1855 > *"The king of yesteryear.*
> *"So, respite does not end resolve!*
> *"Sumamuru, I found you gone.*
> *" O Glorious Janjon!"*

He said, "Ah! What is your name?"
1860 "My name is Dòka, the Cat."   (Mmm)
"Will you not remain with me?"
"Not I! Two kings I cannot praise.
"I am Son-Jara's bard.
"From the Manden I have come,
1865 "And to the Manden I must return."   (True)

He laid hold of the Kuyatè patriarch,
And severed both Achilles tendons,
And by the Susu balaphone set him.   (Indeed)
"Now what is your name?"   (Indeed)
1870 "Dòka, the Cat is still my name."   (Indeed)
"Dòka, the Cat will no longer do."   (Indeed)
He drew water and poured it over his head,   (Indeed)
And shaved it clean,   (Indeed)
And gave him the name Bala Faseke Kuyatè.
1875 That Bala Faseke Kuyatè,   (Indeed)
He fathered three children,   (Indeed)
Musa and Mansa Magan,   (Indeed)
Making Baturu, the Holy his last-born son in the
    Manden.   (Indeed)
Those were the Kuyatès.

1880 And this by the hand of Sumamuru.
He sent forth a messenger,
Saying, "Go tell King Dankaran Tuman,"   (Indeed)
Saying, "If you kill your own vicious dog,"

Ko, "Dò ta y'i kin dè."   (Naamu,
                                                  o ye cinyè ye)

1885   A di kèlè wili ole dò, N' fa,
       Ka bò Susu,
       Ka taa bin Mansa Dankaran Tumani kan,   (Naamu)
       Ka Manden daga-kunun-te,   (Naamu)
       Ka Manden filen-kurun-te,   (Naamu)
1890   Ka tan-kònòntòn dibi-rò-mansa mògò kònòntòn faga,
       Ka tan-kònòntòn masaren-kè kònòntòn faga,
       Ka Mansa Dankaran Tumani gèn.
       O taara Nsèrè-kòrò,
       Ko, Ne kisira!   (Naamu)
1895   "N' kisir'i tòrò ma.   (Cinyè)
       "Ne kisira sa dè!"   (Naamu)
       Ole sigira nòn.
       A di din minw sòrò nòn, N' fa,   (Naamu)
       Olu kèra Kisinnu di.
1900   Alu bèè ye Masanta.
       Alu bòta Manden yan.
       Olu jamu le ko Gindo.   (Naamu)

       Bènba le, nnn.   (Naamu)
       Biribiriba!
1905   A di bata dun faantan ni faama bèè da ma.   (Naamu)

       Susu Kulu Sumamuru bulu,   (Naamu)
       Ko bèè ka kuma bata kònò.
       Ko faantanya man di,
       K'ale ta le Manden di.

1910   Ka Kankira Wòròni wele,   (Naamu)
       Ani Kankira Sanuni,   (Naamu)
       Saginugulu mama l'o di,   (Naamu)
       Ka tura-wulenni kilin di olu ma,   (Naamu)
       Ko k'w'a di,
1915   Dibi-rò-mansa mògò kònòntòn ma,   (Naamu)
       K'alu ka Son-Jara faga,   (Mmm)
       K'a kana na Manden tugun dè,
       K'ale ta le Manden di,
       K'alu di tan-kònòntòn dibi-rò-mansa kònòntòn faga,

1920   Ka tan-kònòntòn masaren-kè kònòntòn faga,

Saying, "Another man's will surely bite you."   (Indeed,
                                                       that's the truth)

1885 With this he declared war, my father,
      And went forth from Susu.
      Going to fall on King Dankaran Tuman,   (Indeed)
      Breaking the Manden like an old pot,   (Indeed)
      Breaking the Manden like an old gourd,   (Indeed)
1890 Slaying the nine and ninety Masters-of-Shadow,
      Slaying the nine and ninety royal princes,
      And ousting King Dankaran Tuman.
      He fled to Nsèrè-kòrò,
      Saying, "I was spared.   (Indeed)
1895 "From your torment, I was spared.   (True)
      "From death, I have been spared."   (Indeed)
      And thus he settled there.
      The sons he there begat, my father,   (Indeed)
      They became the Kisi people.
1900 They are all in Masanta.
      They had come from the Manden.
      Their family name, it is Gindo.   (Indeed)

      Ah! Bèmba!   (Indeed)
      O Biribiriba!
1905 He put gourds in the mouths of the poor and the
          powerful.
      This by the hand of Susu Mountain Sumamuru,   (Indeed)
      Saying each must speak into his gourd,
      Saying there is no pleasure in weakness,
      Saying the Manden was now his.

1910 He summoned Kankira-of-Silver,   (Indeed)
      And Kankira-of-Gold,   (Indeed)
      The latter, the Saginugu patriarch,   (Indeed)
      And one red bull did give to them,   (Indeed)
      Saying they should offer it
1915 To the nine Queens-of-Darkness,   (Indeed)
      Asking them to slay Son-Jara,   (Mmm)
      That he not enter the Manden again,
      To say that the Manden be his,
      Saying they have slain the nine and ninety Masters-
          of-Shadow,
1920 Saying they have slain the nine and ninety royal princes,

Ka bata dun faantan ni faama bèè da la,   (Naamu)

K'alu k'a faga,   (Naamu)
Ka kana na Manden,   (Mmm)
K'ale ta le Manden di.   (Naamu)

1925 O ki-dinnu nara.   (Naamu)
Alu nara nyagalu tèrè: (Naamu)
"Ilu tuntun."   (Naamu)
Nyagalu ma kuma.   (Mmm)
"Ilu salamalekun."   (Mmm)
1930 Nyagalu ma kuma.   (Mmm)
"Alu tuntun."
Nyagalu ma kuma.
"Alu salamaleku."
Nyagalu ma kuma.   (Cinyè don)

1935 "Misi faganin,   (Naamu)
"Ka la sara kònòntòn di."   (Naamu)
Nakana Tiliba ko nyagalu ma,
"Bèè k'i ta ta.   (Naamu)
"Nyinigali dabilabali, a ka lanyini na.   (Cinyè don)
1940 "Ilu subu ta, an ka taa su."   (Naamu)
Nakana Tiliba ko,
"Ilu kana subu ta dè!
"Son-Jara le,   (Naamu)
"Ki le bònin Manden,   (Naamu)
1945 "Susu Kulu Sumamuru fè,   (Naamu)
"Ko ka n'a f'ande ye,   (Naamu)
"Ko l'an k'i faga,   (Naamu)
"K'i kana waa Manden tugun dè,
"Ko mògòlu sikan'i ma,   (Naamu)
1950 "K'ale di tan-kònòntòn dibi-rò-mansa kònòntòn
        faga,   (Naamu)
"K'a di tan-kònòntòn masaren-kè kònòntòn faa,   (Naamu)

"K'a di Manden te ku kònòntòn,
"Ka Manden lò ku kònòntòn,   (Naamu)
"Ka bata dun faantan ni faama bèè da ma,   (Naamu)

1955 "Bèè ka kuma bata kònò,
"Ko faantanya man di,
"K'a di Mansa Dankaran Tumani gèn,

And put gourds o'er the mouths of the poor and the
    powerful,   (Indeed)
Saying that they should slay him,   (Indeed)
So he not enter the Manden again,   (Mmm)
To say that the Manden be his.   (Indeed)

1925   Those messengers arrived.   (Indeed)
They came upon the witches there: (Indeed)
"Ilu tuntun!"   (Indeed)
The witches did not speak.   (Mmm)
"Peace be unto you."   (Mmm)
1930   The witches did not speak.
"Alu tuntun!"
The witches did not speak.
"Peace be with you!"
The witches did not speak.   (That's true)

1935   "The slaughtered bull,   (Indeed)
"Lay it out in nine piles."   (Indeed)
Nakana Tiliba then said to the witches,
"Each must either take her own,   (Indeed)
"Questions without end looking for trouble, (That's true)
1940   "Then take the meat and be off,   (Indeed)
"Or," Nakana Tiliba continued,
"You must not take the meat.
"O Son-Jara,   (Indeed)
"A message has come from the Manden,   (Indeed)
1945   "From Susu Mountain Sumamuru,   (Indeed)
"Saying to come and tell us,   (Indeed)
"Saying we should slay you,   (Indeed)
"So that you not enter the Manden again,
"Saying, the folk have lost their faith in you. (Indeed)
1950   "Saying, he has slain the nine and ninety Masters-
    of-Shadow,   (Indeed)
"Saying, he has slain the nine and ninety royal
    princes.   (Indeed)
"Nine were the times he razed the Manden,
"And nine were the times he rebuilt it,   (Indeed)
"Saying, he put gourds on the mouths of the poor
    and the powerful,   (Indeed)
1955   "Saying, all must speak into their gourds,
"Saying, there is no pleasure in weakness,
"Saying, he has ousted King Dankaran Tuman,

"Ko waara Nsèrè-kòrò,
"K'o l'an k'i faga,
1960 "K'i kana waa Manden tugun dè!
"O subu le nin di."
A k', "Elu N' faga.
"Mògò ye borila le, k'è ka kisi,
"N'i tèna kisi, ilu N' faga!" (Cinyè)

1965 Biribiriba, (Mmm)
A bòra so kò la,
K'i yèlèma k'i kè wara di, (Mmm)
Jara min tè mògò mina,
N'a ma wurunnu. (Mmm)
1970 A waara sigi dò mina,
Ka n'o la,
Ka taga dò wèrè mina,
Ka n'o la,
Ka waa dò wèrè mina,
1975 Ka n'o la.
Sigi-dan kònòntòn, nyagan kònòntòn. (Mmm)
"Bèè k'i ta ta!" (Cinyè)
Nyagalu ko ole ma,
"An ka taa nyòòn-ye.
1980 "Nyògòn-ye tè dugu min dò,
"O dugu sigi man di."
Alu waara nyògòn-ye:
"Manden ni Manden lamini, (Naamu)
"A bèè ladèlin, tura wulen kilin! (Naamu)
1985 "Son-Jara, ile kilin ye sigi-dan kònòntòn!
"Ale le ta ye Manden di.
"An k'a bila." (Cinyè)
Alu di jònba-bele tègè. (Naamu)
"I mana bò Dibi-rò-mansa mògò kònòntòn bara, (Naamu)

1990 "I tè dugu ye tugun, (Mmm)
"Fo Jula Fundu, (Mmm)
"Mòsilu bènba la dugu fòlò fòlò, (Naamu)
"Jula Fundu ani Wagadugu, (Naamu)
"Mèma Farin Tunkara la Mèma-dugu kònò."
1995 Alu nada, ka subu bèè fara nyògòn kan, (Mmm)
K'a gulu l'a kan,
K'a kun-gulu l'a kan. (Mmm)
"Nyagalu bèè k'a la Haya tara!" (Naamu)

      "Saying, who has fled to Nsèrè-kòrò,
      "Saying, we should slay you,
1960 "So that you not enter the Manden again,
      "And that is the reason for this meat."
      "Then kill me," his reply.
      "A person flees to be spared,
      "But should one not be spared, then kill me!"   (True)

1965 Biribiriba!   (Mmm)
      He went to the back of the house.
      Into a lion he transformed himself,   (Mmm)
      A lion seizing no one,
      Before he had sounded a roar.   (Mmm)
1970 He went and seized a buffalo,
      And came back and laid it down,
      And went and seized another,
      And came and laid it down,
      And went and seized another,
1975 And came and laid it down.
      "Nine water buffalos, nine witches!   (Mmm)
      "Each take your own!"   (True)
      The witches then replied to him,
      "Let us hold a council.
1980 "The town where people hold no council,
      "There will living not be good."
      They went to hold their council.
      "From the Manden and its neighbors,   (Indeed)
      "All of it together, and only one red bull! (Indeed)
1985 "Son-Jara, you alone, nine buffalos!
      "It is to him the Manden must belong!
      "Let us then release him!"   (True)
      They trimmed a branch of the custard apple tree: (Indeed)
      "When you leave the land of the nine Queens-of-
          Darkness,   (Indeed)
1990 "You will see no village,   (Mmm)
      "Until you see Jula Fundu,   (Mmm)
      "The original town of the Mossi patriarch, (Indeed)
      "Jula Fundu and Wagadugu,   (Indeed)
      "In Mèma Farin Tunkara's land of Mèma."
1995 They stacked the bull meat in one pile,   (Mmm)
      And upon it laid its skin,
      And upon this placed its head.   (Mmm)
      "All of you witches, say your verses!   (Indeed)

	"Nyagalu bèè k'a la Haya karan, nnn!"	(Naamu)
2000	Nakana Tiliba,	
	A d'a kun-na-jala bò,	
	Ka kudu saba k'a dò, nnn,	
	K'a bila subu kan,	
	Ko, "Wili!	
2005	"Kitibili Kintin!	(Naamu)
	"Mògò f'an nelu bila nyòòn na.	
	"Tunya ku tè mògò silanna."	
	O misi wilila, ka muruli-marali.	(Mmm)
	A ye Mamadu welela.	(Mmm)
2010	Ala Kila Mamadu welela.	(Cinyè don)

	O misi wilila, muruli-marali, nnn.	(Naamu)
	Bènba le.	(Naamu)
	Son-Jara nara:	(Naamu)
	"Kankira Wòrini ni Kankira Sanuni,	(Naamu)
2015	"Ki tè gosi.	(Naamu)
	"Ki-din tè nòni.	(Naamu)
	"Ilu mana taa,	
	"Ilu k'w'a fò Susu Kulu Sumamuru ye,	(Naamu)
	"Ilu mana taa,	(Naamu)
2020	"Ilu w'a fò Susu Kulu Sumamuru ye,	(Naamu)
	"'Misi-gènla tè tura saraka bò,	
	"'Fo Juma nònò.'	
	"'Din-marala mana kònò-diya nya wo nya,	
	"'A tè din-sèrè dè.'	
2025	"Ko, 'Din dò fòlò wulu, kòrò t'o di.'	

	"Ko, 'Dò ta le bi ye,
	"'Sini ye dò ta ye.'
	"Ko, 'N'i fòra mògò dò kò,
	"'Mògò dò di f'i kò.'
2030	"Ko, 'N' waatò N' karifa Mèma Farin Tunkara la,
	"'Mèma-dugu dò.'"

	Sègè le dibi y'a ta. [?]
	I y'a ta, Nare Magan Kònatè.
	Biribiriba ni wura la kala…,
2035	… nyani mabori.
	Sibaaya le sòrò man di.

Bènba le, nnn.

"All of you witches, read your signs!"   (Indeed)
2000 Nakana Tiliba,
From her head she took her scarf,
And tied three knots into it,
And laid it o'er the meat,
Saying, "Rise up!
2005 "Kitibili Kintin!   (Indeed)
" 'Twas a man that puts us in conflict.
"A matter of truth is not to be feared."
The bull rose up and stretched.   (Mmm)
It bellowed to Muḥammad.   (Mmm)
2010 The Messenger of God was thus evoked.   (That's true)

That bull rose up and stretched.   (Indeed)
Ah! Bèmba!   (Indeed)
Son-Jara came forth: (Indeed)
"O Kankira-of-Silver and Kankira-of-Gold,   (Indeed)
2015 "A messenger is not to be whipped.   (Indeed)
"A messenger is not to be defiled.   (Indeed)
"When you go forth from here,
"You should go tell Susu Mountain Sumamuru,   (Indeed)
"When you go forth from here,   (Indeed)
2020 "You should go tell Susu Mountain Sumamuru: (Indeed)
"'The cowherd offers naught of the cow,
"'But the milk of Friday past.
"'No matter how loving the wet nurse,
"'The child will never be hers.'
2025 "Say, 'A child may be first-born, but that does not
      always make him the elder.'
"Say, 'Today may belong to some,
"'Tomorrow will belong to another.'
"Say, 'As you succeeded some,
"'So shall you have successors.'
2030 "Say, 'I am off to seek refuge with Mèma's Prince Tunkara,
"'In the land of Mèma.'"

He took the shape of a hawk.
You took it, Nare Magan Kònatè.
      Biribiriba and Bow-of-the-Bush. . . ,
2035   . . . fled because of suffering.
      Gaining power is not easy.

Ah! Bèmba!

Son-Jara waar'i karifa Mèma.
Tunkaralu la dugu dò, N' fa, Mèma.   (Naamu)
2040   Alu di Dugunò jelilu bènba Kabala Sinbon wele,   (Naamu)

Ka sanu furuku d'a ma, nnn,
Ka sigi l'a kan.

Bènba le.   (Naamu)
O sigi,   (Naamu)
2045   Wori bònin ole rò.   (Naamu)
Pari bòra ole rò.   (Naamu)
Damuye ni marisi bòra pari dò.   (Naamu)

Ka sigi l'a kan, nnn: (Naamu)
"N'alu waada Mèma,   (Naamu)
2050   "Ni Son-Jara d'i bara,   (Naamu)
"'Kòtò Sinbon nata,   (Naamu)
"'Kòtò Sinbon nata,'
"K'a k'a fò,
"'Aa, N' dògò,   (Naamu)
2055   "'Ala d'i kè gan-munun di.   (Naamu)
"'Jugu nya le le.   (Naamu)
"'Jugu bulu tè s'i ma.   (Naamu)
"'Aa, N' dògò,   (Mmm)
"'Ala bara jelilu ni numulu d'ile ma.   (Naamu)
2060   "'N' dògò, ile ta le Manden di.'"

Kabala Sinbon wilila.
Alu ye dunna Mèma,
Son-Jara ni Manden Bukari ye waala wula dò.   (Naamu)
A ko, "Aa, N' dògò, Manden Bukari,   (Naamu)
2065   "Kòtò Sinbon nata!   (Naamu)
"Kòtò Sinbon nata!"   (Naamu)
"Aa, N' dògò,   (Naamu)
"Ala d'i kè gan-munun di.   (Naamu)
"Jugu nya le le.
2070   "Jugu bulu tè s'i ma.
"Aa, N' dògò,
"Ala di jelilu ni numulu d'ile ma.   (Naamu)
"Son-Jara, ile ta le Manden di!"   (Cinyè)

A waara sanu furuku di,
2075   Tunkaralu bènba Mèma Farin Tunkara ma,   (Naamu)

    Son-Jara went to seek refuge in Mèma,
    In a town of the Tunkaras, my father, in Mèma.   (Indeed)
2040 Kabala Simbon, the Dugunò bard patriarch was
        summoned,   (Indeed)
    And given a pouch of gold,
    And given a game called sigi.

    Ah! Bèmba!   (Indeed)
    That sigi-game,   (Indeed)
2045 From that comes the wori-game.   (Indeed)
    From that comes the mperi-game.   (Indeed)
    From the mperi-game come checkers and cards.   (Indeed)

    And thus they gave him a sigi-game: (Indeed)
    "When you arrive in Mèma,   (Indeed)
2050 "If Son-Jara calls out,   (Indeed)
    "'Simbon the Elder has come!   (Indeed)
    "'Simbon the Elder has come!'
    "You should say,
    "'Ah! My little brother,   (Indeed)
2055 "'God has made you like the beehive.   (Indeed)
    "'The eye of the enemy is on you.   (Indeed)
    "'The hand of the enemy cannot touch you.   (Indeed)
    "'Ah! My little brother,'   (Mmm)
    "'God has given you the bards and the smiths.   (Indeed)
2060 "'My little brother, the Manden belongs to you.'"

    Kabala Simbon rose up.
    As they were entering Mèma,
    Son-Jara and Manden Bukari were going to the bush.   (Indeed)
    He exclaimed, "O my brother, Manden Bukari!   (Indeed)
2065 "Simbon the Elder has come!   (Indeed)
    "Simbon the Elder has come!"   (Indeed)
    "Ah! My little brother,   (Indeed)
    "God has made you like the beehive.   (Indeed)
    "The eye of the enemy is on you.
2070 "The hand of the enemy cannot touch you.
    "Ah, my little brother,
    "God has given you the bards and the smiths.   (Indeed)
    "Son-Jara, the Manden belongs to you!"   (True)

    He went then and gave the pouch of gold
2075 To the Tunkara Patriarch, Prince Tunkara of Mèma,   (Indeed)

K'alu ka sigi fayi.   (Naamu)
Son-Jara mana bò wula dò...,   (Naamu)
Kamini Son-Jara dun waata Mèma,   (Naamu)
A ni Tunkaralu din-musu fòlò fòlò kanuda.   (Naamu)
2080 Ile m'o mògò tògò lòn?   (Naamu)
A tògò le Mèma Sira di.

Mèma Sira,   (Naamu)
Dan-tègèli kèra ole nya la.
"Sini dugu mana gè,
2085 "Son-Jara dè,
"Ani Farin Birama ka sigi fayi.   (Naamu)
"N'a ma sigi jabi,"
Ko, "Ka Subaa faga,
"K'a kana waa Manden tugun dè."
2090 Ko, "Mògòlu sigan'a ma."   (Naamu)

I ma sigi makili-kan mè?   (Naamu)
"Farin Birama mana sigi ta, nnn:
      "'Watarawaa!   (Naamu)
      " 'I mana k'i fa fagala,   (Naamu)
2095 " 'I fa faga.   (Naamu)
      "'Watarawaa!   (Naamu)
      " 'I mana ki na fagala,   (Naamu)
      " 'I na faga.   (Naamu)
      "'Watarawaa!
2100 " 'Mògò mana ki ki min na,
      " 'I k'a kè.
      " 'Sigi, k'i lò: nderen!'
      "O mana kè,
      "Sigi y'i lò.

2105 "Ni Son-Jara ma sigi jabi:
      "'Watarawaa!   (Naamu)
      "'Faringa!   (Naamu)
      "'Nkuramè!
      " 'Mògò ye k'i fa fagala,   (Naamu)
2110 " 'I y'a bila.   (Naamu)
      "'Watarawaa!   (Naamu)
      "'Faringa!   (Naamu)
      "'Nkuramè!
      " 'Mògò ye k 'i ba fagala,
2115 " 'I ba bila.

Saying they should cast the sigi.   (Indeed)
When Son-Jara returned from the bush . . . , (Indeed)
Since Son-Jara entered Mèma,   (Indeed)
The eldest Tunkara daughter had loved him. (Indeed)
2080 Don't you know that person's name?   (Indeed)
Her name was Mèma Sira.

Mèma Sira,   (Indeed)
She saw these instructions take place:
"When dawn would break on the morrow,
2085 "Son-Jara,
"He must cast the sigi with Prince Birama. (Indeed)
"If he cannot answer the sigi,"
Said, "Then you should slay the Sorcerer,
"So that he not enter the Manden again."
2090 Said, "The folk have lost their faith in him." (Indeed)

Haven't you heard the sigi formula?   (Indeed)
"Should Farin Birama take the sigi:
  " '*Watarawaa!*   (Indeed)
  " 'Should you be sent to slay your father, (Indeed)
2095   " 'Then you must slay your father. (Indeed)
  " '*Watarawaa!*   (Indeed)
  " 'Should you be sent to slay your mother, (Indeed)
  " 'Then you must slay your mother. (Indeed)
  " '*Watarawaa!*
2100   " 'The commission you were sent for,
  " 'You must see it through.
  " 'O sigi, you must stand: *nderen!* '
"That being done,
"The sigi will stand.

2105 "Should Son-Jara not answer the sigi like this:
  " '*Watarawaa!*   (Indeed)
  " '*Faringa!*   (Indeed)
  " '*Nkuramè!*
  " 'Should you be sent to slay your father, (Indeed)
2110   " 'You must let him go!   (Indeed)
  " '*Watarawaa!*   (Indeed)
  " '*Faringa!*   (Indeed)
  " '*Nkuramè!*
  " 'Should you be sent to slay your mother,
2115   " 'You must let her go!

  "'Watarawaa!
  "'Faringa!
  " 'Nkurame!
  " 'Ni mògòlu ye ban N' dò,
2120 " 'Ni ka nònò i ye sara dò.
  " 'Sigi, k'i lò: jòn jòn jòn!'
  "O mana kè,
  "Sigi y'i lò."
Ko, "N'a t'o fò,"
2125 Ko, "K'a faga,"
K', "A kana faga Manden-banku kan."

Biribiriba!
Dugu talala: lelelele!
Mèma Sira wilira ole dò, N' fa,
2130 K'w'è bulu la Nyani Mansa kan:
  "Wili le, Nyani Mansa!   (Naamu)
  "Nègè fukula Nyani Manse kun na,
  "K'a tè silan mògò nya.
  "I tè wili ba?
2135 *"Wili le Nyani Mansa!*
  "Wili le Nyani Mansa!   (Naamu)
  "Bènyè lò i kini-bulu rò.
  "Mògò mana tèmèn i kini-bulu rò,
  "Bènyè l'o faga.
2140 *"Bènyè lò Nyani Mansa numan-bulu rò.* (Naamu)
  "N'i tamir'a numan-bulu rò,
  "Bènyè l'i faga.
  "Bènyè lò Nyani Mansa kun dò.
  "I mana tèmèn a kun dò,
2145 *"Bènyè l'i faga.*
  "Bènyè lò Nyani Mansa nya ma.
  "I mana tèmèn nya ma,
  "Bènyè l'i faga.
  "Wili le Nyani Mansa.   (Naamu)
2150 *"Bènyè lò Nyani Mansa kò fè.* (Naamu)
  "Mògò mana tanb'a kò fè,
  "Bènyè l'i faga.
  "Wili le Nyani Mansa!
  "Subaa, i tè wili ba?   (Naamu)
2155 "Ki bònin Manden,   (Naamu)
  "Ko ka na sanu-furuku di N' fa ma, (Naamu)
  "Ani sigi.   (Naamu)

        " '*Watarawaa!*
        " '*Faringa!*
        " '*Nkuramè!*
        " 'If the people are to reject me,
2120   " 'You must refuse your reward.
        " 'O sigi, you must stand: *jòn jòn jòn!* '
        "Should that be done,
        "The sigi will stand."
Said, "If he does not say that,"
2125 Said, "Then he should be slain,"
Said, "So in the Manden he will not be killed."

O Biribiriba!
When the night had reached its midpoint: *lelelele!*
On that, Mèma Sira rose up, my father,
2130 And laid her hand on the King of Nyani:
        "Rise up, O King of Nyani.   (Indeed)
        "King of Nyani with helm of mail,
        "He says he fears no man.
        "Will you not rise up?
2135   *"Rise up, O King of Nyani!*
        "Rise up, O King of Nyani!   (Indeed)
        "An arrow at your right hand.
        "Should someone pass you on the right,
        "That is the arrow to slay him.
2140   *"An arrow at the Nyani King's left,*   (Indeed)
        "Should you pass him on the left,
        "That is the arrow to slay you.
        "An arrow o'er the Nyani King's head,
        "Should you pass o'er his head,
2145   *"That is the arrow to slay you.*
        "An arrow to the Nyani King's front,
        "Should you pass before him,
        "That is the arrow to slay you.
        "Rise then, O King of Nyani!   (Indeed)
2150   *"An arrow to the Nyani King's back,*   (Indeed)
        "Should a person pass behind him,
        "That is the arrow to slay him.
        "Rise then, King of Nyani!
"O Wizard, won't you rise?   (Indeed)
2155 "A message has come from the Manden,   (Indeed)
"That a pouch of gold be given my father,   (Indeed)
"And a game called sigi.   (Indeed)

"Sini,
"I ni N' fa ka sigi fayi.   (Naamu)
2160 "N'i ma sigi jabi,
"N' fa y'i faga,
"I tè taga Manden tugun dè.
        "Nare Magan Kònatè!
        "Subaa-Minè-Subaa!

2165 "N' fa mana sigi ta: (Naamu)
        "'Watarawaa!
        " 'I mana k'i fa fagala,
        " 'I fa faga.   (Naamu)
        "'Watarawaa!   (Naamu)
2170   " 'I mana k'i na fagala,
        " 'I na faga.   (Naamu)
        "'Watarawaa!   (Naamu)
        " 'Mògò mana ki ki min na,
        " 'O kè.
2175   " 'Sigi, i lò!
        "'Nkura...,
        "'Nkuramè!'
"Ni N' fa di o fò,   (Naamu)
"N'ile ma sigi ta:
2180   "'Watarawaa!   (Naamu)
        "'Faringa!   (Naamu)
        "'Nkuramè!   (Naamu)
        " 'Mògò k'i fa fagala,
        " 'I y'a bila.   (Naamu)
2185   "'Watarawaa!
        "'Faringa!
        "'Nkuramè!
        " 'Mògò ye k'i ba fagala,
        " 'I ba bila.
2190   "'Watarawaa!
        "'Faringa!
        "'Nkuramè!
        " 'Ni mògò le ban N' dò,
        " 'K'i dè bòn'a sara dò,
2195   " 'Sigi y'i lò: jòn jòn jòn!'
"N' m'o fò,
"N' fa y'e faga,
"I tè taa Manden-bankun kan tugun."

"Tomorrow,
"You and my father must cast the sigi,   (Indeed)
2160 "Should you not answer the sigi,
"My father will then slay you,
"That you not enter the Manden again.
         "O Nare Magan Kònatè
         "O Sorcerer–Seizing–Sorcerer!

2165· "When my father takes the sigi: (Indeed)
         " '*Watarawaa!*
         " 'Should you be sent to slay your father.
         " 'You must slay your father,   (Indeed)
         " '*Watarawaa!*
2170   " 'Should you be sent to slay your mother,
         " 'You must slay your mother.   (Indeed)
         " '*Watarawaa!*   (Indeed)
         " 'The commission you were sent for,
         " 'You must see it through!
2175   " 'O sigi you must stand!
         " '*Nkura...,*
         " '*Nkuramè!*'
"When my father has said that,   (Indeed)
"Should you not take the sigi:
2180   " '*Watarawaa!*
         " '*Faringa!*
         " '*Nkuramè!*
         " 'Should you be sent to slay your father,
         " 'You must let him go!   (Indeed)
2185   " '*Watarawaa!*
         " '*Faringa!*
         " '*Nkuramè!*
         " 'Should you be sent to slay your mother,
         " 'You must let her go!
2190   " '*Watarawaa!*
         " '*Faringa!*
         " '*Nkuramè!*
         " 'If the people are to reject me,
         " 'You must refuse your reward.
2195   " 'O sigi, you must stand: *jòn jòn jòn!*'
"Should you not say that,
"My father will then slay you,
"That you not enter the Manden again.

Biribiriba!
2200 Dugu gèra tuma min na,   (Mmm)
Farin Birima di tantan dòbila,   (Naamu)
Faama dundun: (Naamu)
"Diya-guya!"
Tabule fò-kan le o di.   (Naamu)
2205 Bèè di nyògòn tèrè.   (Naamu)
A di sigi fayi, nnn.   (Naamu)
Subaa di sigi jabi.   (Naamu)
Dugunò jelilu bènba, Kabala Sinbon ko,   (Naamu)
"Ki min dunna Ne da,
2210 "O ki le nin di: (Naamu)
"'Subaa bila.
"'A ta le Manden di.'"   (Naamu)

    . . . .

Bènba.
2215   Biribiriba!
         Nare Magan Konatè!   (Naamu)
         Jelilu kan ye Subaa ma,
         Nare Magan Konatè!
         Subaa-Minè-Subaa!   (Naamu)
2220   Kala Jula Sangoyi Mamunaka!   (Naamu)

Son-Jara di sigi fayi, nnn.   (Naamu)
Dugunò jelilu bènba, Kabala Sinbon,   (Naamu)
Farin Birima b'i nya lò Kabala Sinbon na.   (Naamu)
A ko, "Subaa bila.   (Naamu)
2225 "Ale le ta ye Manden di!"   (Naamu)

Dugunò jelilu bènba, Kabala Sinbon, nnn,   (Naamu)
A taara Manden,   (Naamu)
Ka tag'a fò Susu Kulu Sumamuru ye,
Ko, Son-Jara ye Mèma.   (Naamu)
2230 Fèn ma kè Nare Magan Kònatè la dè,   (Naamu)
Jankuma la wara la Sinbon.   (O ye cinyè ye)
Son-Jara ba-kilinma-musu, Kankuba Kantè,   (Naamu)
A ba-kilinma-musu, Sugulun Kòndè,   (Naamu)
Sugulun Kòndè,   (Naamu)
2235 A di bata bò Fa-Koli da ma,   (Naamu)
Ka bata bò Tura Magan da ma,   (Naamu)
Ka bata bò Jarawa bènba Sira da ma.   (Naamu)

    O Biribiriba!
2200 When the day had dawned,   (Mmm)
    Prince Birama let loose the royal drum,   (Indeed)
    The drum of power: (Indeed)
    "Like-It-Or-Not."
    That is the tabule's sound.   (Indeed)
2205 All thus found themselves together.   (Indeed)
    He cast the sigi.   (Indeed)
    The Sorcerer answered the sigi.   (Indeed)
    Kabala Simbon, the Dugunò bard patriarch said,   (Indeed)
    "The message entrusted to me,
2210 "That message is this: (Indeed)
    " 'Let the Wizard go,
    " 'The Manden belongs to him.' "

    . . . .

    Bèmba!
2215   Biribiriba!
    Nare Magan Kònatè!   (Indeed)
    The bards sing thus of the Sorcerer,
    Nare Magan Kònatè!
    Sorcerer-Seizing-Sorcerer!   (Indeed)
2220   Kala Jula Sangoyi Mamunaka!

    Son-Jara cast the sigi.   (Indeed)
    Kabala Simbon, the Dugunò bard patriarch,   (Indeed)
    Prince Birama beheld Kabala Simbon,   (Indeed)
    "Let the Wizard go," he said.   (Indeed)
2225 "The Manden belongs to him."   (Indeed)

    Kabala Simbon, the Dugunò bard patriarch,   (Indeed)
    He went back to the Manden,   (Indeed)
    And told Susu Mountain Sumamuru,
    Saying that Son-Jara was in Mèma,   (Indeed)
2230 No harm had come to Nare Magan Kònatè,   (Indeed)
    To Simbon, Lion-Born-of-the-Cat.   (That's the truth)
    Son-Jara's flesh-and-blood-sister, Kankuba Kantè,   (Indeed)
    His flesh-and-blood-sister, Sugulun Kòndè,   (Indeed)
    That Sugulun Kòndè,   (Indeed)
2235 She stripped off that gourd from Fa-Koli's mouth,   (Indeed)
    Stripped off that gourd from Tura Magan's mouth,   (Indeed)
    Stripped off that gourd from Sira's mouth, the Jawara
        patriarch.   (Indeed)

O mòglu wilila ole dò, N' fa. (Naamu)
Alu ni kòtò-dinnu, (Naamu)
2240 Ani gan kèndè, (Naamu)
Ani jagaro nyugun, (Naamu)
Alu waata Mèma, (O ye cinyè ye)
Ko ka waa Nare Magan Kònatè sègèda. (Naamu,
naamu, naamu)

O tuma lògò-lòn Mèma. (Naamu)
2245 Alu waara lògò-lòn, nnn, (Naamu)
Musu dò le di ngan kèndè san, nnn, (Nàamu)
Ani jagatu nyugun, (Naamu)
Ka taa dun Sugulun Kòndè kan. (Naamu)
Kòndè-musu-kòròniba ye bun kònò. (O ye cinyè ye)
2250 "An di fèn dò ye bi. (Naamu)
"An ma dalilu lòn dè." (Naamu)
Kòndè-musu d'a sunbu: (Naamu)
"Nin min ye 'in di, (Naamu)
"Nin ye bòla Manden ne.
2255 "Nin bònin mana kè mògò min bulu,
"Il'o mògòlu wele. (Naamu)
"Nin bòtò Manden ne." (Naamu)
Alu di Tura Magan wele, (Naamu)
Ani Tani Mansa Kònkòn, (Naamu)
2260 Ani Fa-Kanda Tunandi, (Naamu)
Ani Jawara bènba Sura. (Naamu)
Alu di Tura Magan ni Kanke-jan wele. (Naamu)
Al' nata. (Naamu)
Kòndè-musu d'i bara, (Naamu)
2265 "Tun-ta-jònlu nara!
"Kala-ta-jònlu nara!
"Alu ni sènè! (Mmm, naamu)
"Aa, Terawelelu! (Naamu)
"Manden mògòlu ka kèndè? (Naamu)
2270 "Alu ni sènè! (Naamu)
"Manden mògòlu ka kèndè?" (Naamu)

Biribiriba, Subaa ye wula rò, nnn. (Naamu)
A ba-kilinma-musu Sugulun Kòndè..., (Naamu)
Son-Jara nanin sigi kònòntòn faga, (Naamu)
2275 Ani kò-nyina kilin. (Naamu)
A ba-kilinma-musu, Sugulun Kòndè, (Naamu)
A di sigi sònnu ta, (Naamu)

On that, those people rose up, my father, (Indeed)
With cotton seeds, (Indeed)
2240 With fresh okra, (Indeed)
And flour of eggplant leaf. (Indeed)
They set forth to Mèma, (That's the truth)
In search of Nare Magan Kònatè. (Indeed,
 indeed, indeed)

It was market day in Mèma. (Indeed)
2245 They went there to market their goods. (Indeed)
A woman bought the fresh okra (Indeed)
And the flour of eggplant leaf, (Indeed)
And brought it back to Sugulun Kòndè. (Indeed)
The old Kòndè woman was in her hut. (That's the truth)
2250 "We have seen some things today. (Indeed)
"We know not of their essence." (Indeed)
The Kòndè woman sniffed of it. (Indeed)
"Whatever this may be, (Indeed)
"From the Manden it has come.
2255 "From whosoever's hand this came,
"Summon those people here! (Indeed)
"This has come from the Manden!" (Indeed)
They summoned Tura-Magan,
And Bee-King-of-the-Wilderness, (Indeed)
2260 And Fa-Kanda Tunandi, (Indeed)
And Sura, the Jawara patriarch. (Indeed)
They summoned Tura-Magan-and-Kanke-jan. (Indeed)
They came forward. (Indeed)
The Kòndè woman spoke out: (Indeed)
2265 "The quiver-bearers have come!
"The bow-bearers have come!
"Greetings on your arrival! (Mmm, indeed)
"Ah! Taraweres! (Indeed)
"How do the folk of the Manden fare? (Indeed)
2270 "Greetings on your arrival! (Indeed)
"How do the folk of the Manden fare?" (Indeed)

Biribiriba, the Wizard was in the bush. (Indeed)
His flesh-and-blood-sister Sugulun Kòndè, . . . (Indeed)
Son-Jara had killed nine buffaloes, (Indeed)
2275 And one club rat. (Indeed)
His flesh-and-blood-sister, Sugulun Kòndè, (Indeed)
She took the buffalo hearts, (Indeed)

<table>
<tr><td></td><td>K'a binyèlu ta,</td><td>(Naamu)</td></tr>
<tr><td></td><td>Hali subu ma busu fòlò,</td><td>(Naamu)</td></tr>
<tr><td>2280</td><td>Ka kò-nyina ta,</td><td>(Naamu)</td></tr>
<tr><td></td><td>Ka kini tobi.</td><td>(Naamu)</td></tr>
<tr><td></td><td>Subu busura tuma min na,</td><td>(Naamu)</td></tr>
<tr><td></td><td>Manden Bukari ma sòn ye.</td><td></td></tr>
<tr><td></td><td>A ma binya ye.</td><td>(Naamu)</td></tr>
<tr><td>2285</td><td>A ko, "Èè, N' kòrò,</td><td>(Naamu)</td></tr>
<tr><td></td><td>"Sòn tè sigi la,</td><td></td></tr>
<tr><td></td><td>"Binya t'a la!"</td><td>(Naamu)</td></tr>
<tr><td></td><td>A ko, "N' dògò,</td><td>(Naamu)</td></tr>
<tr><td></td><td>"An ka taa so.</td><td>(Naamu)</td></tr>
<tr><td>2290</td><td>"I b'a sòrò, luntan ne fònin N' kò."</td><td>(O ye cinyè ye)</td></tr>
<tr><td></td><td>Aa, jeli! Min yena sènè kè,</td><td></td></tr>
<tr><td></td><td>I ye sènè kè!</td><td>(Naamu)</td></tr>
<tr><td></td><td>Son-Jara banda!</td><td>(Iyo, Fa-Digi)</td></tr>
<tr><td></td><td>Nin min yena jago kè,</td><td></td></tr>
<tr><td>2295</td><td>I ka jago kè!</td><td>(Naamu)</td></tr>
<tr><td></td><td>Sènè diman mògò dò la,</td><td></td></tr>
<tr><td></td><td>Jago man d'i la.</td><td>(O ye cinyè ye)</td></tr>
<tr><td></td><td>Jago diman mògò dò la,</td><td></td></tr>
<tr><td></td><td>Sènè man d'i la.</td><td>(Naamu)</td></tr>
<tr><td>2300</td><td>A fòra Son-Jara kaburu le kan,</td><td></td></tr>
<tr><td></td><td>Manden Sankarandin.</td><td>(O ye cinyè ye)</td></tr>
<tr><td></td><td>A dugu tògò le Nyani di,</td><td>(Naamu)</td></tr>
<tr><td></td><td>Sankarandin ba-kungu.</td><td>(Naamu)</td></tr>
<tr><td></td><td>Joma-nugu ni Joma-nganya,</td><td>(Naamu)</td></tr>
<tr><td></td><td>Ba kò n'a nyè,</td><td></td></tr>
<tr><td>2305</td><td>A bèè ye masaren ye.</td><td>(Naamu)</td></tr>
<tr><td></td><td>Sebaaya masòrò man di!</td><td>(O ye cinyè ye)</td></tr>
<tr><td></td><td></td><td></td></tr>
<tr><td></td><td>Garan ne, nnn.</td><td>(Naamu)</td></tr>
<tr><td></td><td>Ngaralu bè Biribiriba ma!</td><td></td></tr>
<tr><td>2310</td><td>Nare Magan Kònatè</td><td>(Naamu)</td></tr>
<tr><td></td><td>Nyani-Mansa, Nyani-Mansa!</td><td>(Naamu)</td></tr>
<tr><td></td><td>Nègè-fugula Nyani-Mansa kun na.</td><td></td></tr>
<tr><td></td><td>A tè silan mògò nya.</td><td></td></tr>
<tr><td></td><td>Kana silan!</td><td></td></tr>
<tr><td>2315</td><td>Sebaliya ni fa-dinya man kan.</td><td>(O ye cinyè ye)</td></tr>
<tr><td></td><td></td><td></td></tr>
<tr><td></td><td>Nyani-Mansa, Nyani-Mansa!</td><td>(Naamu)</td></tr>
<tr><td></td><td>Nègè-jèrèkè ye Nyani-Mansa kan na,</td><td></td></tr>
<tr><td></td><td>K'a tè silan mògò nya.</td><td></td></tr>
</table>

And also took their livers.	(Indeed)
And that meat had yet to be butchered,	(Indeed)
2280 And took the club rat,	(Indeed)
And cooked it up with the rice.	(Indeed)
When the meat was being butchered,	(Indeed)
Manden Bukari saw no hearts,	
Nor did he see any livers.	(Indeed)
2285 He said: "Ah, my elder brother,	(Indeed)
"This buffalo has no heart,	
"Nor does it have a liver!"	(Indeed)
"My little brother," the reply,	(Indeed)
"Let us be off for home.	(Indeed)
2290 You will find strangers came in our absence."	(That's the truth)

2290 You will find strangers came in our absence." (That's the truth)

Ah, Bards! He who would cultivate,
Let him cultivate! (Indeed)
Son-Jara is done! (Yes, Fa-Digi)
He who would deal in commerce,
2295 *Let him deal in commerce!* (Indeed)
Cultivating is suitable to some,
Commerce does not suit them. (That's the truth)
Commerce is suitable to some, (Indeed)
Cultivation does not suit them.
2300 This was sung at Son-Jara's tomb,
By the Manden Sankarandin, (That's the truth)
The name of the village was Nyani, (Indeed)
On the banks of the Sankarandin. (Indeed)
Joma, the Smooth and Joma, the Rough. (Indeed)
2305 On each bank of the river there,
They were all of royal clan. (Indeed)
Gaining power is not easy! (That's the truth)

O Garan! (Indeed)
The mastersingers sing of Biribiriba,
2310 Of Nare Magan Kònatè! (Indeed)
O King of Nyani! King of Nyani! (Indeed)
King of Nyani with helm of mail,
He says he fears no man.
Have no fear!
2315 *Powerlessness and rivalry are not the*
same. (That's the truth)
King of Nyani! King of Nyani! (Indeed)
King of Nyani with shirt of mail,
He says he fears no man.

Kana silan!   (Naamu)
Sebaliya ni fa-dinya man kan.   (O ye cinyè ye)

Biribiriba, ngaralu kan y'i welela.   (Naamu)
Nare Magan Kònatè!
Subaa-Minè-Subaa!   (Naamu, iyo,
                                                 iyo, iyo, iyo)

Aa, Garan.   (Naamu)
Alu bòta wula rò, nnn.   (Naamu)
Alu nara.   (Naamu)
Sugulun Kulunkan di kini bò,   (Naamu)
Ka na kini sigi.   (Naamu)
Subu b'a kan.   (Naamu)

A ba-kilinma-kè Manden Bukari diminda.   (Naamu)
Ale le di kòngòn munyun,   (Naamu)
Ka min-nògò munyun,   (Naamu)
Ka tòrò,   (Naamu)
Ka taa wula rò, nnn,   (Naamu)
Ka nyani kè,   (Naamu)
Ka wòlòwòlò munyun,   (Naamu)
Ani lèn.   (Naamu)
"N'o bèè tonya di,"
Ko, "Subu ka wili kini kan!"   (Naamu)
Kò-nyina wilira kini kan,   (Naamu)
Ka bun da bèn,   (Naamu)
K'i nya lò Nyani Mansa ma: (Naamu)
Kòndè-musu din, magu-nya-mògò!"   (Naamu)

A d'i nya lò alu ma tan: (Naamu)
     "Jankuma le wara la Sinbon!   (Naamu)
     "Nare Magan Kònatè!"   (Iyo, iyo, iyo,
                                                 iyo, iyo, iyo, iyo)

A d'i nyè lò Nyani-Mansa ma:
"Subaa-Minè-Subaa!"   (Naamu)
A ma-musu-din d'i bara,
"Aa, N' kòrò,   (Naamu)
"Ne di sigi sòn ta, k'a binyè ta.   (Naamu)
"N' m'a kè kenu ladiyalan di.   (Naamu)
"N' m'a kè N' diya-nyè-ku di.   (Naamu)
"Son-Jara ka sin-ji susu,   (Naamu)

Have no fear! (Indeed)
2320 *Powerlessness and rivalry are not the*
 same. (That's the truth)
 O Biribiriba, the mastersingers call upon you. (Indeed)
 O Nare Magan Kònatè,
 O Sorcerer-Seizing-Sorcerer. (Indeed, yes,
 yes, yes, yes)

 Ah! Garan! (Indeed)
2325 They left the bush. (Indeed)
 They came back home. (Indeed)
 Sugulun Kulunkan brought out the rice, (Indeed)
 And came to set it down. (Indeed)
 The meat lay upon it. (Indeed)

2330 Her flesh-and-blood-brother Manden Bukari raged. (Indeed)
 It was he after all had suffered the hunger. (Indeed)
 It was he after all had suffered the thirst, (Indeed)
 And undergone those hardships, (Indeed)
 Having gone into the bush, (Indeed)
2335 And having suffered the misery, (Indeed)
 And having endured the gnats, (Indeed)
 And the dreadful deer flies! (Indeed)
 "If all of that be true,"
 Said, "Let the meat rise from the rice!"
2340 The club rat rose up off the rice, (Indeed)
 And ran toward the door of the hut, (Indeed)
 Fixing its eyes on the King of Nyani: (Indeed)
 "O Kòndè woman's child, Answerer-of-Needs!" (Indeed)

 It fixed its eyes upon them thus: (Indeed)
2345 "Simbon, Lion-Born-of-the-Cat! (Indeed)
 "Nare Magan Kònatè!" (Yes, yes, yes,
 yes, yes, yes, yes)

 It fixed its eyes upon the King of Nyani:
 "O Sorcerer-Seizing-Sorcerer!" (Indeed)
 His little sister then spoke up:
2350 "Ah, my elder brother, (Indeed)
 "I took the buffalo hearts and livers. (Indeed)
 "I did not take them to please a lover. (Indeed)
 "I did not take them to please myself. (Indeed)
 "The breast that Son-Jara once did suckle, (Indeed)

2355 "Subaa di o bila, nnn,   (Naamu)
     "Ile di ole ta.   (Naamu)
     "Ile di sin-ji bila,   (Naamu)
     "Ne di ole ta, N' fa.   (Naamu)
     "Malu min nanin Magan Son-Jara ma,   (Naamu)
2360 "N' t'o malu le jara.   (Naamu)
     "N'o ye tonya di,"   (Naamu)
     Ko, "Subu k'è la kini kan!"   (Naamu)
     Subu d'i la kini kan.   (Naamu)
     A ko, "Ilu ye dumuni kè!"   (Naamu)
2365   Nare Megan Kònatè!
          Subaa-Minè-Subaa!   (Naamu,
                                                   è, Fa-Digi)

     Manden Bukari pèrènda Sugulun Kulunkan la.   (Naamu)
     Fini wòrònwula sirinin,
     Fini bèè bira, f'a la pèndelu.   (Naamu)
2370 A ko, "Aa N' kòrò,   (Naamu)
     "Danga man nyi.   (Naamu)
     "Ma-kè-danga man nyi.
     "N'o tè, N' tèr'i danga,   (Naamu)
     "Bar'ile bònsòn, bònsòn,   (Naamu)
2375 "O si tè mugu-ti yan tugun!   (Naamu)
     "O si tè kèlè-marifa ti yan tugun!"   (Naamu)
     Ole kò Hamina-kalu di.   (Naamu)
          Nare Magan Kònatè!
          Subaa-Minè-Subaa!   (Naamu)

2380 Manden Bukari kò le olu di.
     Olu bè Hamina.   (Naamu)
          Aa, Ala le faama di.
          Se b'Ala ye,   (Naamu)
          Ka dòlu kè banda di,
2385   O mògò ma fèn kè Ala ye,   (Naamu)
          Ka dòlu kè faantan ye,   (Naamu)
          O mògòlu me, ma fèn kè Ala la.   (Naamu)
          Ala le faama di!   (Naamu)
          ...,   (Naamu)
2390   Nare Magan Kònatè!
          Subaa-Minè-Subaa!   (Naamu)

          Garan ne.   (Naamu)
          Sangoyi yoo!   (Naamu)

2355 "When the Wizard gave it up,   (Indeed)
      "It was you who then did take it.   (Indeed)
      "When you did give it up,   (Indeed)
      "It was I who then did take it, my father.   (Indeed)
      "The dishonor bound for Son-Jara,   (Indeed)
2360 "That dishonor did I avert.   (Indeed)
      "If all of that be true,   (Indeed)
      "Then let the meat lie on the rice!"   (Indeed)
      The meat lay back upon the rice.   (Indeed)
      She invited, "Come and eat!"   (Indeed)
2365   O Nare Magan Kònatè!
            Sorcerer-Seizing-Sorcerer!   (Indeed,
                                                        eh, Fa–Digi)

      Manden Bukari cursed Sugulun Kulunkan.   (Indeed)
      The seven skirts about her waist,
      All those skirts fell off save her slip.   (Indeed)
2370 She said, "Ah, my elder brother,   (Indeed)
      "No good can come from a curse.   (Indeed)
      "Cursing an elder can bring no good.
      "Were that not so, I would curse you,   (Indeed)
      "But, each of your descendants,   (Indeed)
2375 "No powder will they here discharge,   (Indeed)
      "No rifle of war will they fire again!"   (Indeed)
      And his descendants became the people of Hamina.   (Indeed)
            O Nare Magan Kònatè!
            O Sorcerer-Seizing-Sorcerer!   (Indeed)

2380 Those were the descendants of Manden Bukari.
      They can be found in Hamina.   (Indeed)
            Ah! God is the King.
            God has the power   (Indeed)
            To render some folk wealthy,
2385   Yet they do naught for Him,   (Indeed)
            And some to render destitute,   (Indeed)
            And yet they did naught to Him.   (Indeed)
            God is the King!   (Indeed)
            . . .   (Indeed)
2390   O Nare Magan Kònatè!
            O Sorcerer-Seizing-Sorcerer!   (Indeed)

            O Garan!   (Indeed)
            O Sangoyi!   (Indeed)

Ala le faama di!
2395 Sin-kula....   (O ye cinyè ye)
Mansa Magan nanin Ne le ye, nnn.   (Naamu)
Lètèrè dira Ne le ma,
Ko, k'waa N' da lò Arajo Mali la,
Fa-Koli makuma dè.   (Naamu, o kèra!
                                                      o kèra pati!)

2400 Ne bè N' na ki-kè-bugu da la,   (Naamu)
Ba-dinya ni sin-jiya.   (Naamu)
Mansa Magan nanin Ne le ta, N' fa,
Ko Ne ni tubabu ka kuma.   (Naamu)
Ala le faama di!   (O ye cinyè ye)

2405   Garan ne.   (Naamu)
Ja-tigi-faga-lòntanba ni mini-kòlòn.   (Naamu)

            Ni lònnibaga-domu.   (Naamu)
Dan-tègèli kèra Subaa ye,   (Naamu)
Nare Magan Kònatè nya na.   (Naamu)
2410 Basi dò le ye Magan Son-Jara bulu.   (Naamu)
A basi te sòn fèn fèn na, fo se-tulu.   (Naamu)
Se dun tè Mèma.   (Naamu)
Mansa Magan, nnn,   (Naamu)
I mana sòn ni se ye yòrò yòrò,   (Naamu)
2415 Manden-banku l'o dugu le di.   (Naamu)

O bèè le Manden di.   (Naamu)
Se tè Mèma.   (Naamu)
Se jaran kòrò dò tèrè Mèma.   (Naamu)
Son-Jara ba bòda: (Naamu)
2420   "Hèè Ala!   (Naamu)
         "Son-Jara k'waa Manden.   (Naamu)
         "Sini-mògò l'a di.   (Naamu)
         "Sini-kènè-mògò l'a di.   (Naamu)
         "A jelilu marala,   (Naamu)
2425   "Ka numulu mara,   (Naamu)
         "Ka tun-tan-mògò bi saba ni mògò saba.   (Naamu)
         "A y'o mògò bèè marala,   (Naamu)
         "Hèè, Ala!   (Naamu)
         "Sani dugu ka gè,   (Naamu)
2430   "Se jalan kòrò min ye yan,   (Naamu)
         "O ka naron kè din.   (Naamu)

<pre>
                God is the King!
2395   A man of power. . . .   (That's the truth)
          Mansa Magan came for me,   (Indeed)
          A letter was given to me,
          Saying I should speak on Radio Mali,
          To sing the praise of Fa-Koli.   (Indeed, that happened!
                                               That really happened!)

2400   I was there at my farming village,   (Indeed)
          In brotherhood and affection.   (Indeed)
          Mansa Magan came to get me, my father,
          Saying I should sing for the whiteman.   (Indeed)
          God is the King!   (That's the truth)

2405   O Garan!   (Indeed)
                O Great-Host-Slaying-Stranger and the
                     Twisted Well.   (Indeed)
                And the Devourers-of-the-Knowing! (Indeed)
          The explanations were made to the Wizard, (Indeed)
          To Nare Magan Kònatè   (Indeed)
2410   Son-Jara had a certain fetish,   (Indeed)
          Accepting no sacrifice save shea butter. (Indeed)
          There were no shea trees there in Mèma.   (Indeed)
          O Mansa Magan!   (Indeed)
          Wherever you sacrifice to the shea tree, (Indeed)
2415   That town must be in Mandenland.   (Indeed)

          All of them are in the Manden.   (Indeed)
          No shea trees were there in Mèma,   (Indeed)
          Save one old dry Shea tree in Mèma.   (Indeed)
          Son-Jara's mother came forward: (Indeed)
2420   "Ah! God!   (Indeed)
                "Let Son-Jara go to the Manden.   (Indeed)
                "He is the man for the morrow.   (Indeed)
                "He is the man for the day to follow. (Indeed)
                "He is to rule o'er the bards,   (Indeed)
2425   "He is to rule o'er the smiths,   (Indeed)
                "And the three and thirty warrior clans. (Indeed)
                "He will rule o'er all those people. (Indeed)
                "Ah, God!   (Indeed)
                "Before the break of day,   (Indeed)
2430   "That dried up shea tree here,   (Indeed)
                "Let it bear leaf and fruit.   (Indeed)
</pre>

"A dinnu ka bòn.   (Naamu)
"Son-Jara k'a dinnu tòmòn,
"K'a kè se-tulu di,   (Naamu)
2435   "K'a basi sòn a la.   (Naamu, iyo, Fa-Digi)

"Aa, Ala!   (Naamu)
"Son-Jara k'waa Manden.   (Naamu)
"Sini-mògò l'a di.
"Sini-kènè-mògò l'a di.   (Naamu)
2440   "A jeli ni numulu mara.   (Naamu)
"Subaa ta le Manden di.   (Naamu)
"Sani dugu ka gè,   (Naamu)
"Ne ka su mayèlèma.   (Naamu)
"Ne kòrònin ne. N' tè se tòòma la.   (Naamu)
2445   "Nare Magan Kònatè ka waa."   (Naamu)
Dugu ye gèla tuma min na,   (Naamu)
Se jalan kòrò narunnin.   (Naamu)
A dinnu bònin.   (Naamu)
Ko, Son-Jara duntò Kòndè-musu kan, nnn.   (Naamu)
2450 Kòndè-musu di duniya tu.   (Naamu)
A d'a ba ku,   (Naamu)
K'a kaburu sen,   (Naamu)
K'a kasanke,   (Naamu)
K'a ba dun dugu-kulu rò,   (Naamu)
2455 Ka bunbun natègè,   (Naamu)
K'o kasanke,   (Naamu)
K'o la bun kònò,   (Naamu)
Ka biri-fini bir'a ma,   (Naamu)
Ka kila lò Farin Birima ma,   (Naamu)
2460 K'a k'a sòn dugu-kulu la,   (Naamu)
K'a ba dunna Mèma-dugu dò,
K'a ye waala Manden ne.   (Naamu)
Olu kan ye ole ma,
K'a tè dugu-kulu sòrò,
2465 Fo n'a di dugu sòngò bò.   (Naamu)

Farin Birima kan,   (Naamu)
K'a tè dugu-kulu sòrò,   (Naamu)
Fo n'a di dugu sòngò bò.   (Naamu)
A di kami-si ni wòlò-si ta,   (Naamu)
2470 Ka bènyè kala fira ta,   (Naamu)
Ka waga fira ta,   (Naamu)
Ka fanda-kuna-wulen ta,   (Naamu)

"Let the fruit fall down to earth,   (Indeed)
"So that Son-Jara may gather the fruit,
"From it to make shea butter,   (Indeed)
2435   "To offer his fetish.   (Indeed, yes, Fa-Digi)

"Ah, God!   (Indeed)
"Let Son-Jara go to the Manden.   (Indeed)
"He is the man for the morrow.
"He is the man for the day to follow.   (Indeed)
2440   "He will rule the bards and smiths.   (Indeed)
"The Manden belongs to the Wizard.
"Before the break of day,   (Indeed)
"Let me change my dwelling,   (Indeed)
"Old am I and cannot travel.   (Indeed)
2445   "Let Nare Magan Kònatè go home."   (Indeed)
When the day was dawning,   (Indeed)
The dried up shea tree did bear leaf.   (Indeed)
Its fruit did fall to earth.   (Indeed)
Son-Jara looked in on the Kòndè woman,   (Indeed)
2450   But the Kòndè woman had abandoned the world.   (Indeed)
He washed his mother's body,   (Indeed)
And then he dug her grave,   (Indeed)
And wrapped her in a shroud,   (Indeed)
And laid his mother in the earth,   (Indeed)
2455   And then chopped down a kapok tree,   (Indeed)
And wrapped it in a shroud,   (Indeed)
And laid it in the house,   (Indeed)
And laid a blanket over it,   (Indeed)
And sent a.messenger to Prince Birama,
2460   Asking of him a grant of land,   (Indeed)
In order to bury his mother in Mèma,
So that he could return to the Manden.   (Indeed)
This answer they did give to him
That no land could he have,
2465   Unless he were to pay its price.   (Indeed)

Prince Birama decreed,   (Indeed)
Saying he could have no land,   (Indeed)
Unless he were to pay its price.   (Indeed)
He took feathers of Guinea fowl and partridge,   (Indeed)
2470   And took some leaves of arrow-shaft plant,   (Indeed)
And took some leaves of wild grass reed,   (Indeed)
And took some red fanda-vines,   (Indeed)

Ka buna-gbesi kilin ta,   (Naamu)
Ka muru-gwanan kilin ta,   (Naamu)
2475 Ka sigi-nègè l'a kan,   (Naamu)
K'a kè furuku kònò,   (Naamu)
Ko k'w'a a di Farin Birama ma,   (Naamu)
K'a le dugu sòngò l'o di.   (Naamu, haa, Fa-Digi)

O waara di Farin Birama ma.   (Naamu)
2480 Farin Birima kan ye kè-mògò saba ma,   (Naamu)
Kè-Mògò-Ku-Bèè-Lòn,   (Naamu)
Kè-Mògò-Ku-Bèè-Fò,   (Naamu)
Kè-Mògò-Ku-Bèè-Ye.   (Naamu)
O kè-mògò saba tèrè Farin Birama lajè.   (Naamu)
2485 A ko, "Kè-mògòlu,   (Naamu)
"Ba-tula dòkòlun tè. [?]   (Naamu)
"Ilelu fana ka nin ta,   (Naamu)
"Min fòlò nada,   (Naamu)
"Ne t'o la.   (Naamu)
2490 "Ilelu ta le nin di."   (Naamu)

Garan ne.   (Naamu)
Kè-Mògò-Ku-Bèè -Ye,
Kè-Mògò-Ku-Bèè-Fò,
Kè-Mògò-Ku-Bèè-Lòn,   (Naamu)
2495 Alu di furuku da foni,
K'a jugu-jugu.   (Naamu)
Kè-Mògò-Ku-Bèè-Ye d'i bara,   (Naamu)
"Bèè nya ye nin na.   (Naamu)
"Nde waata su!"   (Naamu)
2500 Kè-Mògò-Ku-Bèè-Lòn d'i bara,   (Naamu)
"Bèè ye nin lòn.   (Naamu)
"Nde waata su!"   (Naamu)
Kè-Mògò-Ku-Bèè-Fò a d'i bara,   (Naamu)
"Bèè ye nin lòn?   (Naamu)
2505 "O ye kalun di!   (Naamu)
"Bèè nya ye nin na?   (Naamu)
"O ye kalun di.   (Naamu)
"Mògò ye fèn dò ye,
"N'a ma f'i ye,
2510 "I t'a lòn.   (Naamu)

"Farin Birama,   (Naamu)
"I ma kamin-si ni wòlò-si ye?

And took one measure of shot,   (Indeed)
And took a haftless knife,   (Indeed)
2475 And added a cornerstone fetish to that,   (Indeed)
And put it all in a leather pouch,   (Indeed)
Saying go give it to Prince Birama,   (Indeed)
Saying it was the price of his land.   (Indeed, ha, Fa–Digi)

That person gave it to Prince Birama.   (Indeed)
2480 Prince Birama summoned his three sages,   (Indeed)
All-Knowing-Sage,   (Indeed)
All-Seeing-Sage,   (Indeed)
All-Saying-Sage.   (Indeed)
The three sages counseled Prince Birama.   (Indeed)
2485 He said, "O Sages!   (Indeed)
"The forest by the river is never empty. [?]   (Indeed)
"You also should take this.   (Indeed)
"That which came first,   (Indeed)
"I will not take it.   (Indeed)
2490 "Tis yours."   (Indeed)

O Garan!
All-Seeing-Sage,
All-Saying-Sage,
All-Knowing-Sage,   (Indeed)
2495 They untied the mouth of the pouch,
And shook its contents out.   (Indeed)
The All-Seeing-Sage exclaimed,   (Indeed)
"Anyone can see that!   (Indeed)
"I am going home!"   (Indeed)
2500 The All-Knowing-Sage exclaimed,   (Indeed)
"Everybody knows that!   (Indeed)
"I am going home."   (Indeed)
All-Saying-Sage exclaimed,   (Indeed)
"Everyone knows that?   (Indeed)
2505 "That is a lie!   (Indeed)
"Everyone sees that?   (Indeed)
"That is a lie!
"There may be something one may see,
"Be it ne'er explained to him,
2510 "He will never know it.   (Indeed)

"Prince Birama,   (Indeed)
"Did you not see feathers of Guinea fowl and partridge?

"Tumun dè fèn ne! (Naamu)
"I ma bènyè kala fira ye?
2515 "Tumun dò fèn ne! (Naamu)
"I nya tè waga fira da? (Naamu)
"Tumun dè fèn ne! (Naamu)
"I ma tègèni gwangwada ye? (Naamu)
"Tumun dè fèn ne! (Naamu)
2520 "I ma buna-gbesi kilin ye? (Naamu)
"Mèma telan ne! (Naamu)
"I ma muru-ganan kilin ye? (Naamu)
"Kèbalu-kan-tèrè-muru! (Naamu)
"I nya tè fanda-kunan wulen na? (Naamu)
2525 "Kèbalu-kan-tègè-jeli! (Naamu)
"N'ilu ma dugu-kulu di, (Naamu)
"I nya ye sigi-nègè kilin min na,
"Kèbalu la san-kalima-nègè le! (Naamu)
"N'ilu ma dugu-kulu di,
2530 "Nare Magan Kònatè,
"Subaa ye dugu tumun. (Naamu)
"Son-Jara ye waala Manden!" (O ye cinyè ye)

Alu di dugu-kulu di Subaa ma. (Naamu)
A d'a na dun Mèma-dugu dò.
2535 A wilira.
Sigi banna ku min nya,
Taama l'o banna. (Naamu)

Kuyatèlu mama di karanya ta,
Ka dunsu-dònkili da Ma'an Kònatè kò: (Naamu)
2540 *"Bara kala ta le!* (Naamu)
"Wula-tigi Sinbon ne,
"Bara kala ta le!
"Bara kala ta le! (Naamu)
"Sugu-tigi Sinbon ne, (Naamu)
2545 *"Bara kala ta le!* (Naamu)
"Bara kala ta! (Naamu)
"Jeli ni numulu mara-mògò,
"Bara kala ta!
"Kòndè-musu din,
2550 *"Magu-nya-mògò,* (Naamu)

"They are the things of ruins.   (Indeed)
"Did you not see the leaf of arrow-shaft plant?
2515 "That is a thing of ruins.   (Indeed)
"Was not your eye on the wild grass reed?   (Indeed)
"That is a thing of ruins.   (Indeed)
"Did you not see those broken shards?   (Indeed)
"They are the things of ruins.   (Indeed)
2520 "Did you not see that measure of shot?   (Indeed)
"The annihilator of Mèma!   (Indeed)
"Did you not see that haftless knife?   (Indeed)
"The warrior-head-severing blade!   (Indeed)
"Was not your eye on the red fanda-vine?   (Indeed)
2525 "The warrior-head-severing blood!   (Indeed)
"If you do not give the land to him,   (Indeed)
"That cornerstone fetish your eye beheld,
"It is the warrior's thunder shot!   (Indeed)
"If you do not give the land to him,
2530 "To Nare Magan Kònatè,
"The Wizard will reduce the town to ruins.   (Indeed)
"Son-Jara is to return to the Manden!"   (That's the truth)

They gave the land to the Sorcerer,   (Indeed)
He buried his mother in Mèma's earth.
2535 He rose up.
That which sitting will not solve,
Travel will resolve.   (Indeed)

EPISODE SIX: KULU-KÒRÒ

The Kuyatè matriarch took up the iron rasp,
And sang a hunter's song behind him: (Indeed)
2540   *"Took up the bow!*   (Indeed)
          "Simbon, Master-of-the-Bush
          "Took up the bow!
          "Took up the bow!   (Indeed)
          "Simbon, Master-of-the-Beasts   (Indeed)
2545   *"Took up the bow!*   (Indeed)
          "Took up the bow!   (Indeed)
          "Ruler of bards and smiths,
          "Took up the bow!
          "The Kòndè woman's child,
2550   *"Answerer-of-Needs,*   (Indeed)

   "Bara kala ta!   (Naamu)
   "Sugulun Ma'an bara kala ta le! (Naamu)
   "I y'a minè le, Jara!   (Naamu)
   "Subaa y'a faga!
2555 *"Sinbon, o julu dè kan nin!"* (Naamu)

Biribiriba wilila,
Ka taa Dabò numulu mama tèrè. (Naamu)
A ye sila-barun do basi barabarala. (Naamu)
Dabò mama kan: (Naamu)
2560 "Subaa le, an ka kèba-tulun dòòni kè!" (Naamu)
A di Subaa nyòòn-girin a kini-bulu kan. (Naamu)
Tarawerelu bènba Tura Magan ni Kanke-jan ko:

  "An ka bò Son-Jara kò.   (Naamu)
  "Dabò ye mògò min bila,   (Naamu)
2565 "Ni la an ma b'a kò,   (Naamu)
  "An mana taga Manden,
  "Sumamuru ye mògò ban dè!" (Naamu)
Son-Jara diminda ole rò,   (Naamu)
K'è sin lò Dab'olu mama sin fasa kan,
2570 K'a ròsaman,   (Naamu)
K'a kun-gulu bò!   (Naamu)
Alu ko, "A d'a bò!"   (Naamu)
Ole kèra Dabòlu la ... di.   (Naamu,
            o ye cinyè ye)
  A ni nyani-ma-bori nada!   (Naamu)
2575 Biribiriba!   (Naamu)
A n'a ba waala Mèma lun min,   (Naamu)
A d'a bulu-kan-na-wòri bò,
K'a di Sòmònòlu bènba,
Sasagalò-jan ma.   (Naamu)
2580 Sòmònò mama le Sasagalò-jan di.
A d'a bulu-kan-na-wòri bò, nnn: (Naamu)
"I mana lun-jan-kòlòn sen,
"Lun-jan-minògò mana s'i min!" (Naamu)

Wòlò le kira ka kila fò, nnn,   (Naamu)
2585 Susu-Kulu Sumamuru ye.   (Naamu)
  "Mande ni Sama Kantè!   (Naamu)
  "Susu Bala Kantè!
  "Kukuba ni Bantanba!
  "Nyani-nyani, Kamasiga!   (Naamu)

"Took up the bow!   (Indeed)
"Sugulun's Ma'an took up the bow!   (Indeed)
"You seized him, O Lion!   (Indeed)
"The sorcerer slew him.
2555   *"Simbon, 'tis the sound of your chords!"*   (Indeed)

Biribiriba rose up,
And went to find the Dabò patriarch.   (Indeed)
He was sitting at the crossroads boiling a potion.   (Indeed)
It was the voice of the Dabò patriarch: (Indeed)
2560 "Sorcerer, let us play awhile the warrior game!"   (Indeed)
He made Son-Jara fall to his right.   (Indeed)
Said the Tarawere patriarch, Tura-Magan-and-
    Kankè-jan:
"Let us abandon Son-Jara.   (Indeed)
"This person that Dabò has thrown,   (Indeed)
2565 "Given that, if we not abandon him,   (Indeed)
"Were we to go to the Manden,
"Sumamuru would destroy our folk!"   (Indeed)
Son-Jara was enraged at that,   (Indeed)
And jamming his foot on Dabò's instep,
2570 He stretched him out by the neck,   (Indeed)
Ripping off his head.   (Indeed)
The clamor, *"A d'a bò!* He ripped it off!"   (Indeed)
Thus, that became the Dabò surname.   (Indeed,
                                   that's the truth)

    He fled because of suffering!   (Indeed)
2575   O Biribiriba!   (Indeed)
When he and his mother were going to Mèma,   (Indeed)
She took her silver bracelet off,
And gave it to the Boatman patriarch,
To Sasagalò, the Tall.   (Indeed)
2580 The ancestor of the boatman was Sasagalò, the Tall.
She took her silver bracelet off: (Indeed)
"When one digs a distant-day well,
"Should a distant-day thirst descend, then drink!"   (Indeed)

A partridge was sent to deliver the message   (Indeed)
2585 To Susu Mountain Sumamuru: (Indeed)
    "Manda and Sama Kantè!   (Indeed)
    "Susu Bala Kantè!
    "Kukuba and Bantanba!
    "Nyani-nyani and Kamasiga!   (Indeed)

2590   *"Farima din-kise!*
    "Ni kè duman talabaga!
    "Sumamuru duntò,
    "Ni mògò-gulu-kurusi!   (Naamu)
    "Sumamuru duntò,
2595   *"Ni mògò-gulu-jèrèkè!*   (Naamu)
    "Tègèrè!   (Naamu)
    "Susu-Kulu Sumamuru!
    "Subaa ni kèlè bòta Mè..., Mèma.   (Naamu)
    "A ye nala Manden dè!"   (Naamu)

2600 Susu-Kulu Sumamuru,   (Naamu)
    A di sanu mutukali naani ta,   (Naamu)
    Ka tag'a di Sòmònòlu bènba,
    Sasagalò-jan ma,   (Naamu)
    Ko kèlè min ye bòla Mèma,   (Naamu)
2605 Ko kèlè kana tanbi dè!   (Naamu)

    Karu kilin,   (Naamu)
    Magan Son-Jara ni kèlè lanin dan-kan na.   (Naamu)
    Ko munumununa.   (Naamu)
    Lun dò, Subaa wilila,
2610 Ka ba julu mina: (Naamu)
    "Nya galu.   (Naamu)
    "Nyabaliya galu.   (Naamu)
    "Ne ni N' ba waala Mèma,   (Naamu)
    "A d'a bulu-kan-na-wòri bò,   (Naamu)
2615 "K'a di mògò dò ma yan,   (Naamu)
    "K'e mana lun-jan-kòlòn sen,
    "Ko lun-jan-min-nògò mana si, k'e y'i min.   (Naamu)
    "Ne dun ni N' na kèlè nanin.   (Naamu)
    "An korinin ka tanbi."   (Naamu)
2620 Sòmònòlu bènba ko,   (Naamu)
    "Aa, ile le Son-Jara di ba?"   (Naamu)
    Ko, "Ne le Son-Jara di."   (Naamu)
    "Son-Jara l'ile di?"   (Naamu)
    "Nde le Son-Jara di!"   (Naamu)
2625 "Ile le Nare Magan Kònatè?   (Naamu)
    "Ni Ala sònna,
    "Ni dugu gèra,
    "Kèlè ye tanbi sini."   (Naamu)

    Dugu gèra, nnn,   (Naamu)

2590   *"Brave child of the warrior!*
   "And Deliverer-of-the-Benign!
   "Sumamuru came among us
   "With pants of human skin!   (Indeed)
   "Sumamuru came among us
2595   *"With coat of human skin.*   (Indeed)
   "Applaud him!   (Indeed)
   "Susu Mountain Sumamuru!
   "The Sorcerer with his army has left Mèma. (Indeed)
   "He has entered the Manden!"   (Indeed)

2600 Susu Mountain Sumamuru,   (Indeed)
He took four measures of gold,   (Indeed)
To the Boatman patriarch,
Sasagalò, the Tall, did give them,   (Indeed)
Saying, "That army coming from Mèma, (Indeed)
2605 "That army must not cross!"   (Indeed)

For one entire month,   (Indeed)
Son-Jara and his army by the riverbank sat. (Indeed)
He wandered up and down.   (Indeed)
One day Son-Jara rose up
2610 And followed up the river: (Indeed)
"Being good, a bane.   (Indeed)
"Not being good, a bane.   (Indeed)
"When my mother and I were going to Mèma, (Indeed)
"She took her silver bracelet off,   (Indeed)
2615 "And gave it to a person here,   (Indeed)
"Saying when you dig a distant-day well,
"When a distant-day thirst descends, then drink. (Indeed)
"Thus have I come with my army,   (Indeed)
"And we have not yet made a crossing." (Indeed)
2620 The Boatman patriarch responded: (Indeed)
"Ah! Is it you who are Son-Jara?"   (Indeed)
The reply, "It is I who am Son-Jara." (Indeed)
"You are Son-Jara?"   (Indeed)
"Indeed I am Son-Jara!"   (Indeed)
2625 "It is you who are Nare Magan Kònatè? (Indeed)
"If God wills,
"With the break of day,
"Tomorrow will the army cross."   (Indeed)

At the break of day,   (Indeed)

2630 Sòmònòlu banba, Sasagalò-jan,   (Naamu)
     A di Son-Jara latanbi.   (Naamu)
     Subaa ni kèlè nara.   (Naamu)
     A bira Sumamuru kan Tu-fin.   (Naamu)
     A d'a gèn.   (Naamu)
2635 Susu Kulu Sumamuru di Son-Jara gèn.   (Naamu)
     A nara dugu sigi Nyani.   (Naamu)
     Jelilu ko,
           "An te waa Nyani.   (Naamu)
           "Mògò mana waa Nyani,
2640   "N'i ma nyani,   (Naamu)
           "I tè fèn sòrò.   (Naamu)
           "An tè waala Nyani."   (Naamu)

     O Nyani dè,   (Naamu)
     Maninkalu kan ye ole ma, N' fa,
2645 Nyagaru t'e la.   (Naamu)
     A tògò le Nyani di.   (Naamu)

     Subaa ni kèlè wilila.   (Naamu)
     Alu waara bin Susu Kulu Sumamuru kan.   (Naamu)
     A di Son..., Son-Jara gèn.   (Naamu)
2650 A waara dugu sigi Sòbèya.   (Naamu)
     Jelilu ko,
           "An nelu tè waa Sòbèya.   (Naamu)
           "Mògò mana waa Sòbèya,
           "Ni ma sòbè kè,
2655   "I tè fèn sòrò.   (Naamu)
           "An nelu tè waa Sòbèya."   (Naamu)
     Subaa wilila.   (Naamu)
     A ni jelilu wilila.   (Naamu)
     Alu waara bin Susu Kulu Sumamuru kan.   (Naamu)
2660 Sumamuru d'a n'a ka ngaralu gèn.   (Naamu)
     Alu waara dugu sigi ko Nyò'òn-sòn.   (Naamu)
     Alu ko,
           "An k'waa Subaa la dugu dò, N' fa,
           "Nyò'òn-sòn.   (Naamu)
2665   "Nyògòn sòn tè dugu min dò,
           "O dugu sigi man di."   (Naamu)
     Alu waara Nyò'òn-sòn sigi.   (Naamu)

     Son-Jara ba-kilinma-musu le Sugulun Kulunkan,   (Naamu)
     Ole ko, "Magan Son-Jara,   (Naamu)

2630 The Boatman patriarch, Sasagalò, the Tall,   (Indeed)
     He brought Son-Jara across.   (Indeed)
     The Wizard advanced with his army.   (Indeed)
     They fell upon Sumamuru at Dark Forest.   (Indeed)
     But he drove them off.   (Indeed)
2635 Susu Mountain Sumamuru drove Son-Jara off.   (Indeed)
     He went and founded a town called Anguish,   (Indeed)
     Of which the bards did sing:
          "We will not move to Anguish.   (Indeed)
          "Should one go to Anguish,
2640   "Should not anguish he endure,   (Indeed)
          "Then nothing would he reap.   (Indeed)
          "We will not move to Anguish."   (Indeed)

     That Anguish,   (Indeed)
     The Maninka sing this of it, my father:
2645 "There is no joy in you.   (Indeed)
     "Our name for that town is Anguish (Nyani)."   (Indeed)

     The Wizard advanced with his army.   (Indeed)
     They went to fall on Susu Mountain Sumamuru.   (Indeed)
     He drove Son-Jara off again.   (Indeed)
2650 He went to found the town called Resolve.   (Indeed)
     The bards thus sing of it:
          "We will not move to Resolve.
          "Should one move to Resolve,
          "Should not resolve he entertain,
2655   "Then nothing would he reap.   (Indeed)
          "We will not move to Resolve."   (Indeed)
     The Wizard advanced again.   (Indeed)
     He with his bards advanced.   (Indeed)
     They went to fall on Susu Mountain Sumamuru.   (Indeed)
2660 Sumamuru drove him off with his bards.   (Indeed)
     They went to found the town called Sharing.   (Indeed)
     And they sang:
          "Let us move to the Wizard's town, my father.
          "To Sharing,   (Indeed)
2665   "The town where sharing is not done,
          "Founding that town is not easy."   (Indeed)
     They went to found the town called Sharing.   (Indeed)

     Son-Jara's flesh-and-blood-sister, Sugulun Kulunkan, (Indeed)
     She said, "O Magan Son-Jara,   (Indeed)

2670 "Mògò kilin tè si kèlèla dè.   (Naamu)
"A tu N' ka taa bò Sumamuru ma.   (Naamu)
"N' man'a sòrò,
"N' n'a d'i ma,   (Naamu)
"I ta ka kè Manden-mògòlu di.   (Naamu)
2675 "I kè Manden bèè dugu kanda."   (Naamu)
Sugulun Kulunkan wilila,   (Naamu)
Ka tag'i lò Sumamuru la jin da la: (Naamu)
  "Manda ni Sama Kantè!   (Naamu)
  "Kukuba ni Bantanba!
2680 *"Nyani-nyani, Kamasiga!*   (Naamu)
  "Farima din-kisè!
  "Ni kè duman talabaga!   (Naamu)
  "Sumamuru duntò,
  "Ni mògò-gulu-kurusi!   (Naamu)
2685 *"Sumamuru duntò,*
  "Ni mògò-gulu-jèrèkè!   (Naamu)
  "Sumamuru duntò,
  "Ni mògò-gulu-fukula.   (Naamu)
"Na da yèlè le Susu Kulu Sumamuru!   (Naamu)
2690 "I ka N' kè i nyòòn-musu di!"   (Naamu)

Sumamuru nara da ma: (Naamu)
"Ile mògò jòn di?"   (Naamu)
"Nde le Sugulun Kulunkan di."   (Naamu)
"Awa, Sugulun Kulunkan,   (Naamu)
2695 "N'i nanin N' mira,   (Naamu)
"K'e waatò N' di mògò ma,   (Naamu)
"Mògò tè si N' na dè!   (Naamu)
"Ne le di Manden kun-nyini,   (Naamu)
"Ka Manden saraka,   (Naamu)
2700 "K'a dun kenike-kala kèmè dò,   (Naamu)
"K'a dun dugu dò yan.   (Naamu)
"Ne le di Manden kun-nyini,   (Naamu)
"Ka Manden saraka,   (Naamu)
"K'a dun ntura-wulen kabatò dò.   (Naamu)
2705 "K'o dun dugu dò yan.   (Naamu)
"Mògò tè si N' na dè!   (Naamu)
"Ne le di Manden kun-nyini,   (Naamu)
"K'a saraka,   (Naamu)
"K'a dun dundun-gè-lew-lew dò.   (Naamu)
2710 "N'i d'o faga,   (Naamu)
"Ka tiga-banan bò,   (Naamu)

2670 "One person cannot fight this war.   (Indeed)
"Let me go seek Sumamuru.   (Indeed)
"Were I then to reach him,
"To you I will deliver him,   (Indeed)
"So that the folk of the Manden be yours,   (Indeed)
2675 "And all the Mandenland you shield."   (Indeed)
Sugulun Kulunkan arose,   (Indeed)
And went up to the gates of Sumamuru's fortress: (Indeed)
         "Manda and Sama Kantè!   (Indeed)
         "Kukuba and Bantamba!
2680   *"Nyani-nyani and Kamasiga!*   (Indeed)
         "Brave child of the Warrior,
         "And Deliverer-of-the-Benign.   (Indeed)
         "Sumamuru came amongst us
         "With pants of human skin.   (Indeed)
2685   *"Sumamuru came amongst us*
         "With shirt of human skin.   (Indeed)
         "Sumamuru came amongst us
         "With helm of human skin.   (Indeed)
"Come open the gates, Susu Mountain Sumamuru!   (Indeed)
2690 "Come make me your bed companion!"   (Indeed)

Sumamuru came to the gates: (Indeed)
"What manner of person are you?"   (Indeed)
"It is I Sugulun Kulunkan!"   (Indeed)
"Well, now, Sugulun Kulunkan,   (Indeed)
2695 "If you have come to trap me,   (Indeed)
"To turn me over to some person,   (Indeed)
"Know that none can ever vanquish me.   (Indeed)
"I have found the Manden secret,   (Indeed)
"And made the Manden sacrifice,   (Indeed)
2700 "And in five score millet stalks placed it,   (Indeed)
"And buried them here in the earth.   (Indeed)
"'Tis I who found the Manden secret,   (Indeed)
"And made the Manden sacrifice,   (Indeed)
"And in a red piebald bull did place it,   (Indeed)
2705 "And buried it here in the earth.   (Indeed)
"Know that none can vanquish me.   (Indeed)
"'Tis I who found the Manden secret   (Indeed)
"And made a sacrifice to it,   (Indeed)
"And in a pure white cock did place it.   (Indeed)
2710 "Were you to kill it,   (Indeed)
"And uproot some barren groundnut plants,   (Indeed)

"K'o mabò,
"Ka jin wo da-bèn,   (Naamu)
"Ka tiga-banan bò,   (Naamu)
2715 "K'o fili jin wo kònò,   (Naamu)
"I ye si Ne la."   (Naamu)
A ba gilinna ole dò: (Naamu)
"Èhèè, Susu Kulu Sumamuru,   (Naamu)
"Kan'i bèè fò musu ye dè,
2720 "Su-kilin-si-musu.   (Naamu)
"Musu man nyi, Sumamuru."   (Naamu)
Sumamuru gilinn'a ba kò,   (Naamu)
Ka n'a ba mita,   (Naamu)
K'a sin-fudu tègè muru la; *magasi*!   (Naamu)
2725 A taara jaliba-kòrò tègè,   (Naamu)
A ko, "Èhèè, Sumamuru,   (Naamu)
"Wulu mana kè tònya ye,
"I jaliba-kòrò tègèra."

Kala Jula Sangoyi Mamunaka!   (Naamu)
2730 A di Sugulun Kulunkan lalan dò.   (Naamu)
Kun-nyògòn sera tuma min na,
Sugulun Kulunkan d'i bara,   (Naamu)
"Aa, N' kè,   (Naamu)
"I t'a tu N' ka taa Manden,   (Naamu)
2735 "N' ka filen-kurun-din ni galama-kurunni ta,
"N' ka na kèla-sigi kan ma?"   (Naamu)
A lun ni bi tè,
I mana musu furu Manden-banku kan,   (Naamu)
A kun-nyògòn mana si,
2740 A y'i kò-fèlè le.   (Naamu)
A kòrò le nin di.   (Iyo, Fa-Digi,
                                                            o ye cinyè ye)

Sugulun Kulunkan waara saraka bèè fò,
A ba-kilinma-kè Magan Son-Jara ye.   (Naamu)
Son-Jara di saraka bèè bò.   (Naamu)
2745 A di saraka bèè bò.   (Naamu)
Musu kèmè tèrè Susu Kulu Sumamuru,   (Naamu)
Musu kèmè tèrè Sumamuru kun.   (Naamu)
Musuni kilin ne tèrè a ba-kilin-barin-din Fa-Koli
    kun.   (Naamu)

Fa-Koli...,   (Mmm)

"And strip them of their leaves,
"And spread them round the fortress,   (Indeed)
"And uproot more barren peanut plants,   (Indeed)
2715 "And fling them into the fortress,   (Indeed)
"Only then can I be vanquished."   (Indeed)
His mother sprang forward at that: (Indeed)
"Heh! Susu Mountain Sumamuru!   (Indeed)
"Never tell all to a woman,
2720 "To a one-night woman!   (Indeed)
"The woman is not safe, Sumamuru."   (Indeed)
Sumamuru sprang towards his mother,   (Indeed)
And came and seized his mother,   (Indeed)
And slashed off her breast with a knife, *magasi*! (Indeed)
2725 She went and got the old menstrual cloth.   (Indeed)
"Ah! Sumamuru!" she swore.   (Indeed)
"If your birth was ever a fact,
"I have cut your old menstrual cloth!"

O Kala Jula Sangoyi Mamunaka!   (Indeed)
2730 He lay Sugulun Kulunkan down on the bed.   (Indeed)
After one week had gone by,
Sugulun Kulunkan spoke up: (Indeed)
"Ah, my husband,   (Indeed)
"Will you not let me go to the Manden,   (Indeed)
2735 "That I may get my bowls and spoons,
"For me to build my household here?"   (Indeed)
From that day to this,
Should you marry a woman in Mandenland,   (Indeed)
When the first week has passed,
2740 She will take a backward glance,   (Indeed)
And this is what that custom means.   (Yes, Fa-Digi,
                                               that's the truth)

Sugulun returned to reveal those secrets
To her flesh-and-blood-brother, Son-Jara.   (Indeed)
The sacrifices did Son-Jara thus discover.   (Indeed)
2745 The sacrifices did he thus discover.   (Indeed)
Now five score wives had Susu Mountain Sumamuru,   (Indeed)
One hundred wives had he.   (Indeed)
His nephew, Fa-Koli, had but one,   (Indeed)

Fa-Koli. . . ,   (Mmm)

2750 Sumamuru musu kèmè!   (Naamu)
     Alu mana filen kèmè tobi,
     K'a kè kèlè-fanda di,   (Naamu)
     Fa-Koli fènè musu di filen kèmè tobi,
     K'a kè kèlè-fanda di.   (O ye cinyè ye, è,
                                              Fa-Digi, naamu, naamu)
2755   "Fini tòmòn bèrè!   (Naamu)
          "Malu tòmòn bèrè!   (Naamu)
          "Tiga tòmòn bèrè!   (Naamu)
          "Tiganin-kurun tòmòn bèrè!   (Naamu)
          "Sòsò tòmòn bèrè!"   (Naamu)
2760 A b'a bèè kilin kilin ta,   (Naamu)
     K'a bèè kè daga kilin dò.   (Naamu)
     A bèè ye tobi daga kilin kònò,   (Naamu)
     K'o bèè kè, a ta filen di,   (Naamu)
     Fa-Koli bulu.   (Naamu)
2765 . . . .

     . . . .   (O ye cinyè ye)
     Garan ne.   (Naamu)

2770 Bula ngana ni Magan Sukudana!   (Naamu)
     Son-Jara d'i bara,   (Naamu)
     "Jòn waatò saraka bò Manden?"   (Naamu)
     Fa-Koli ko, "Nde!   (Naamu)
     "Fèn min di Nde gèn,   (Naamu)
2775 "Ka N' musuni kilin ne mita N' na,"
     Ko, "faantan musu tèn N' bulu.   (Naamu)
     "Ne dè ye saraka bèè bò!"   (Naamu)
     Fa-Koli d'i saraka bèè bò.   (Naamu)
     A nad'a fò Subaa ye.
2780 Son-Jara d'i bara,   (Naamu)
     "Jòn dun ye an lasela nyògòn ma,
     "An ka kèlè sa?"   (Naamu)
     Fa-Koli ko, "Nde!"   (Naamu)
     Fa-Koli wilira ole dò, nnn.   (Naamu)
2785 O sela Tu-fin.   (Naamu)
     A di Sumamuru la dugu kun ye Tu-fin,   (Naamu)

2750 And Sumamuru, five score!   (Indeed)
     When a hundred bowls they would cook
     To make the warriors' meal,   (Indeed)
     Fa-Koli's wife alone would one hundred cook
     To make the warriors' meal.   (That's the truth, eh,
                                                        Fa-Digi, indeed, indeed)
2755   "Let the fonio increase!   (Indeed)
             "Let the rice increase!   (Indeed)
             "Let the groundnuts increase!   (Indeed)
             "Let the groundpeas increase!   (Indeed)
             "Let the beans increase!"   (Indeed)
2760 She took them all one by one,   (Indeed)
     And put them all in one pot,   (Indeed)
     And in that pot they all were cooked,   (Indeed)
     And served it all in her calabash,   (Indeed)
     And all of this for Fa-Koli.   (Indeed)
2765 . . . .

[Sumamuru takes Fa-Koli wife from him.]

. . . .   (That's the truth)
Ah! Garan!   (Indeed)

[Fa-Koli leaves Sumamuru and comes to Son-Jara's camp.]

2770 Hero-of-the-Original-Clans and Magan Sukudana!   (Indeed)
     Son-Jara called out,   (Indeed)
     "Who in the Manden will make this sacrifice?"   (Indeed)
     "I shall!" Fa-Koli's reply.   (Indeed)
     "The thing that drove me away,   (Indeed)
2775 "And took my only wife from me,
     "So that not even a weak wife have I now,   (Indeed)
     "I shall make the whole sacrifice!"   (Indeed)
     Fa-Koli thus made the whole sacrifice.   (Indeed)
     He came and reported to the Wizard.
2780 Son-Jara then called out: (Indeed)
     "Who will bring us face to face,
     "That we may join in battle?"   (Indeed)
     "I shall," Fa-Koli's reply.   (Indeed)
     On that Fa-Koli rose up.   (Indeed)
2785 He arrived in Dark Forest.   (Indeed)
     As he espied the rooftops of Sumamuru's city,
         Dark Forest,   (Indeed)

A mana sin-danya kilin kè,   (Naamu)
A bènyè dò sòròn dugu kònò,   (Naamu)
Ka dò ha yiri-barun rò.   (Naamu, iyo, Fa-Digi)
2790 A mana sin-danya kilin kè,   (Naamu)
A bènyè dò sòròn dugu kònò,   (Naamu)
Ka dò la yiri-barun rò,   (O ye cinyè ye)
F'a dunda jin wo kònò,
F'a dunda dugu kònò.   (Naamu)
2795 Garan.   (Naamu)
Mansa Dankaran Tumani d'a din-musu min di,   (Naamu)
Ko k'w'a di Susu Kulu Sumamuru ma,   (Naamu)
K'a k'waa Son-Jara faga,   (Naamu)
Fa-Koli nada k'o din-musu mita,   (Naamu)
2800 "Na! I fa bòda Mèma.   (Naamu)
"I fa y'i welela.   (Naamu)
"I fa nara. A bòda Mèma."   (Naamu)
Susu-kalu d'a gèn: *biri biri biri!*   (Naamu)
Alu ni kèlè y'a kò: *yirrrrrrr!*   (Naamu)
2805 A mana sin-danya kilin kè,   (Naamu)
A bènyè dò saman dugu kòrò,
K'a fili Susu-kalu ma.   (Naamu)
A dò ta yiri-barun dò,   (Naamu)
K'o fili Susu-kalu ma.   (Naamu)
2810 "Hèè, ilu N' dèma!   (Naamu)
"San-kulu ni dugu-kulu ka N' dèma!
"Susu Kulu Sumamuru ye N' kò!"   (Naamu, iyo, baba)

A mèna i bori.   (Naamu)
A bènyè dò bò dugu kòrò,
2815 K'o fili Susu-kalu ma,   (Naamu)
Ka dò ta yiri-barun dò,   (Naamu)
Ka Susu-kalu bun: (Naamu)
"Hèè! Ilu N' dèma!   (Naamu)
"San-kulu ni dugu-kulu ka N' dèma!
2820 "Susu Kulu Sumamuru ye N' kò!"   (O ye cinyè ye)

Susu-kalu kan ye ole ma, N' fa,   (Naamu)
"N'i l'an ma bò Fa-Koli kò,   (Naamu)
"Fa-Koli ye mògò banna dè!   (Naamu)
"An ka bò Fa-Koli kò!"   (Naamu)
2825   Bula Ngana ni Magan Sukudana!

      . . . .   (O ye cinyè ye)

       With every single step he took,   (Indeed)
       He thrust a dart into the earth,   (Indeed)
       And in a tree fork laid another.   (Indeed, yes, Fa-Digi)
2790 With every single step he took,   (Indeed)
       He thrust a dart into the earth,   (Indeed)
       And in a tree fork laid another,   (That's the truth)
       Until he entered the very gates,
       Until he entered the city.   (Indeed)
2795 O, Garan!   (Indeed)
       The daughter given by King Dankaran Tuman, (Indeed)
       Given to Susu Mountain Sumamuru,   (Indeed)
       That he should go and kill Son-Jara,   (Indeed)
       Fa-Koli went and seized that maiden,   (Indeed)
2800 "Come! Your uncle has left Mèma!   (Indeed)
       "Your uncle has summoned you.   (Indeed)
       "Your uncle has now come. He has left Mèma!" (Indeed)
       The people of Susu pursued them: *biri biri biri.* (Indeed)
       They came attacking after them: *yrrrrrrr!*   (Indeed)
2805 With every single step he took,   (Indeed)
       He drew a war dart from the earth,
       And hurled it at the Susu,   (Indeed)
       And from a tree fork grabbed another,   (Indeed)
       And hurled it at the Susu,   (Indeed)
2810 "Heh! Come to my aid!   (Indeed)
       "Heaven and Earth, come aid me!
       "Susu Mountain Sumamuru is after me!"   (Indeed,
                                    yes, father)

       He retreated on and on.
       He drew a war dart from the earth,
2815 And hurled it at the Susu,   (Indeed)
       And from a tree fork grabbed another,   (Indeed)
       And fired it at the Susu.   (Indeed)
       "Heh! Come to my aid!   (Indeed)
       "Heaven and Earth, come to my aid!
2820 "Susu Mountain Sumamuru is after me!" (That's the truth)

       At that, the Susu said, my father,   (Indeed)
       "If we do not fall back from Fa-Koli,   (Indeed)
       "Fa-Koli will bring all our folk to an end! (Indeed)
       "Let us fall back from Fa-Koli!   (Indeed)
2825   Hero-of-the-Original-Clans and Magan
           Sukudana.
         . . . .   (That's the truth)

Alu bòra Fa-Koli kò. (Naamu)
Alu d'i dòbèn. (Naamu)
Su…, Susu Kulu Sumamuru nara, (Naamu)
2830 K'a baara-musu ta,
K'a sigi kirikè-tulu la, (Naamu)
Ani sanu-galama ni wòri-galama. (Naamu)
Son-Jara di kèlè kè, ka jin wo da bèn. (Naamu)
A di kèlè tala, (Naamu)
2835 Ka dugu da mina. (Naamu)
Susu Kulu Sumamuru ni su-bori bòra. (Naamu)
Fa-Koli, (Naamu)
Ani Tura Ma'an ni Kanke-jan, (Naamu)
Ani Talu Mansa Kònkòn, (Naamu)
2840 Ani Fa-Kanda Tunandi, (Naamu)
Ani Jawara bènba Sura, (Naamu)
Ani Son-Jara, (Naamu)
Alu tanbira Sumamuru kò. (Cinyè)
Alu sira Kukuba. (Naamu)
2845 A ko, "N' ma N' dòbèn." (Naamu)
Alu d'a bila: (Naamu)
"I dòbèn!" (Naamu)
Alu sira Kamasiga: (Naamu)
"N' ma N' dòbèn." (Naamu)
2850 Al' d'a bila: (Naamu)
"I dòbèn!" (Naamu)
Alu sira Nyani-nyani. (Naamu)
Ko, "N' ma N' dòbèn." (Naamu)
Al' d'a bila:
2855 "I dòbèn!" (Naamu)
Alu sira Bantanba: (Naamu)
"N' ma N' dòbèn." (Naamu)
Alu d'a bila:
"I dòbèn!" (Naamu)
2860 Alu ni kèlè b'a kò,
Susu Kulu Sumamuru kò. (O cinyè ye,
iyo, Fa-Digi)

Sumamuru d'i ba tègè Kulu-kòrò, (Naamu)
K'a la bara-musu lajigin, (Naamu)
K'a ka sanu-galama d'a ma,
2865 K'a k'i min, (Naamu)
Ko n'o tè, min-dògò y'a fagala. (O ye cinyè ye)
Bara-musu di sanu-galama ta, (Naamu)

And thus they fell back from Fa-Koli.   (Indeed)
They readied themselves for battle.   (Indeed)
Susu Mountain Sumamuru came forward,   (Indeed)
2830 And taking his favorite wife,
On the saddle's cantle sat her,   (Indeed)
With golden ladle and silver ladle.   (Indeed)
Son-Jara attacked and encircled the walls.   (Indeed)
He had split the enemy army,   (Indeed)
2835 And taken the fortress gates.   (Indeed)
Susu Mountain Sumamuru charged out at a gallop.   (Indeed)
Fa-Koli,   (Indeed)
With Tura-Magan-and-Kanke-jan,   (Indeed)
And Bee-King-of-the-Wilderness,   (Indeed)
2840 And Fa-Kanda Tunandi,   (Indeed)
And Sura, the Jawara patriarch,   (Indeed)
And Son-Jara,   (Indeed)
They all chased after Sumamuru.   (True)
They arrived at Kukuba.   (Indeed)
2845 He told them, "I am not ready!"   (Indeed)
They let him go: (Indeed)
"Prepare yourself!"   (Indeed)
They arrived at Kamasiga,   (Indeed)
"I am not ready."   (Indeed)
2850 They let him go: (Indeed)
"Prepare yourself!"   (Indeed)
They arrived at Nyani-Nyani.   (Indeed)
Said, "I am not ready."   (Indeed)
They let him go again: (Indeed)
2855 "Prepare yourself!"   (Indeed)
They arrived at Bantanba,   (Indeed)
"I am not ready."   (Indeed)
And again they let him go:
"Prepare yourself!"   (Indeed)
2860 And still they attacked him from behind,
Behind Susu Mountain Sumamuru.   (That's the truth,
                                                         yes, Fa-Digi)

Sumamuru crossed the river at Kulu-Kòrò,   (Indeed)
And had his favored wife dismount,   (Indeed)
And gave her the ladle of gold,
2865 Saying that he would drink,   (Indeed)
Saying else the thirst would kill him.   (That's the truth)
The favored wife took the ladle of gold,   (Indeed)

<pre>
        K'a fa ji la,   (Naamu)
        K'i bulu dòsaman Susu Kulu Sumamuru ma,
2870   Ka ji dil'a ma.   (Naamu)
        Fa-Koli ni bènyè nara:
            "Sama wo,   (Naamu)
            "An bar'i mina, wo!   (O ye cinyè ye)
            "An bar'i mina, sama wo!
2875   "An bar'i mina, sama wo!
            "An bar'i mina, wo!"   (Naamu)
        Tura Ma'an di bènyè l'a kan.   (Naamu)
        Jawara bènba Sura di bènyè l'a kan.   (Naamu)
        Fa-Koli nara bènyè l'a kan.
2880   Son-Jara di bènyè l'a kan na.   (Naamu)
            "An bar'i mina, sama wo!   (O ye cinyè ye)
            "An bar'i mina, wo!"   (Naamu)
        Sumamuru jara: nyònyòwu!   (Naamu)
            Ole kèra nyanan ye Kulu-kòrò.   (Naamu)
2885   Bamanal' lagènin ole ma, N' fa.
        Susu Kulu Sumamuru,
        A kèra nyanan di.   (O ye cinyè ye, naamu,
                                                    baba, iyo, iyo, iyo, iyo)

        Biribiriba d'i kò-sagin Son-Jara!   (Naamu)
            Saguma lònntan, wurè la dugu-tigi!   (Naamu)

2890   Ja-tigi-faga-lònntan!
            Su-rò-gunguruni fin!   (Naamu)
            I man'a madènku,
            A y'i madènku!   (O ye cinyè ye)
            Jiginè kòrò wulu.   (Naamu)
2895   Fèn min tè lònntan silòn,
            A tè duguren silòn.
            A mana mògò soro,
            A y'i kinna le.   (O ye cinyè ye)
            Kirikara Watita!   (Naamu)
2900   Ku Jugu kun-yan-fan!
            Kè kun ni musu kun tè kilin di.
            Kumadin kè-nyi ni kènya tè kilin di. (O ye cinyè ye)

        Sila mana janya,
</pre>

<table>
<tr><td>2870</td><td>And filled it up with water,</td><td>(Indeed)</td></tr>
</table>

And filled it up with water,   (Indeed)
And to Sumamuru stretched her hand,
2870 And passed the water to him.   (Indeed)
Fa-Koli with his darts charged up:
    "O Colossus,   (Indeed)
    "We have taken you!   (That's the truth)
    "We have taken you, Colossus!
2875   "We have taken you, Colossus!
    "We have taken you!"   (Indeed)
Tura Magan held him at bladepoint.   (Indeed)
Sura, the Jawara patriarch held him at bladepoint.   (Indeed)
Fa-Koli came up and held him at bladepoint.
2880 Son-Jara held him at bladepoint: (Indeed)
    "We have taken you, Colossus!   (That's the truth)
    "We have taken you!"   (Indeed)
Sumamuru dried up on the spot: *nyònyòwu!*   (Indeed)
He has become the sacred fetish of Kulu-Kòrò.   (Indeed)
2885 The Bambara worship that now, my father.
Susu Mountain Sumamuru,
He became that sacred fetish.   (That's the truth, indeed,
                                          Father, yes, yes, yes, yes)

EPISODE SEVEN: KANBI

Biribiriba turned back, Son-Jara!   (Indeed)
    Stranger-in-the-Morning, Chief-in-the-
      Afternoon!   (Indeed)
2890   Great-Host-Slaying-Stranger!
    Stump-in-the-Dark-of-Night!   (Indeed)
    Should you bump against it,
    It will bump against you!   (That's the truth)
    The Granary Guard Dog.   (Indeed)
2895   The thing discerning not the stranger,
    Nor the familiar.
    Should it come upon any person,
    He will be bitten.   (That's the truth)
    Kirikara Watita!   (Indeed)
2900   Adversity's true place!
    Man's reason and woman's are not the same.
    Pretty words and truth are not the
      same.   (That's the truth)
    No matter how long the road,

       A bòla mògòma su le kan dè.   (Naamu)
2905 Nyani-mansa ni kèlè nara,   (Naamu)
       K'a ta le Manden ye sa,   (O ye cinyè ye)
       K'ale ni mògò tè fa-din ye tugun dè,   (O ye cinyè ye)
       K'a ta le Manden di.   (O ye cinyè ye)

       A nara Kuyatèlu bènba sin-fasa fula tègènin tèrè,   (Naamu)
2910 K'a ka wil', "An ka taa!   (Naamu)
       "Bala Faseke Kuyatè, wil'an ka taa."   (Naamu)
       A girida,   (Naamu)
       K'a bè wili.
       A bin dugu ma yen,   (Naamu)
2915 A sin-fasa fula tègènin.   (Naamu)
       Nare Magan Kònatè!   (Naamu)
       "Wil'an ka taa sa!   (Naamu)
       "Ne ni mògò tè Manden-banku kan tugun.   (Naamu)
       "N' kilin ta le Manden di."   (Naamu)
2920 A girida,   (Naamu)
       K'a be wili.   (Naamu)
       A bira dugu ma.   (O ye cinyè ye)
       Alu ko, "Din tè Sumamuru bulu ba?"   (Naamu)
       K', "A din-kè fòlò yan."   (Naamu)
2925 "O tògò di?"   (Naamu)
       "O tògò le Mansa Saman."   (Naamu)
       Al' di Mansa Saman wele,   (Naamu)
       Ka Jankuma Dòka ta,
       K'a sigi Mansa Saman kan na,   (Naamu)
2930 Ka bala l'a kun cè: *serew*!   (Naamu)
       A bilanin Subaa kò: (Naamu)
          "Biribiriba!   (Naamu)
          "Nare Magan Kònatè!   (Naamu)
          "Dunda Kaya,
2935   *"Son-Jara dunda Kaya.*   (O ye cinyè ye)
          "Dunda Kaya,
          "Sugulun Ma'an dunda Kaya.   (Iyo, Fa-Digi)
          "N'alu ma sanu ta yan,   (Naamu)

          "N'alu ma Subaa sègè-sanu ta,   (Naamu)
2940   "Son-Jara nanin Manden te-kan ne ma,

          "Ka Manden lakanya,
          "Ka mògò bèè latilen: *jon jon*!   (O ye cinyè ye)

	It always comes out at someone's home.	(Indeed)
2905	The Nyani king with his army came forward,	(Indeed)
	Saying the Manden belonged to him,	(That's the truth)
	Saying no more was he rival to any,	(That's the truth)
	Saying the Manden belonged to him.	(That's the truth)

He found the Kuyatè patriarch with tendons cut,   (Indeed)
2910 And beckoned him to rise, "Let us go!   (Indeed)
"Bala Faseke Kuyatè, arise. Let us go!"   (Indeed)
He lurched forward,   (Indeed)
Saying he would rise.
He fell back to the ground again,   (Indeed)
2915 His two Achilles tendons cut: (Indeed)
"O Nare Magan Kònatè!"   (Indeed)
"Arise and let us go!   (Indeed)
"I have no rival in Mandenland now!   (That's the truth)
"The Manden is mine alone."   (Indeed)
2920 He lurched forward,   (Indeed)
Saying that he would rise.   (Indeed)
He fell back to the ground again.   (Indeed)
"Had Sumamuru no child?" they queried.   (Indeed)
"Here is his first born son," the reply.   (Indeed)
2925 "What is his name?"   (Indeed)
"His name is Mansa Saman."   (Indeed)
They summoned Mansa Saman   (Indeed)
And brought forth Dòka the Cat,
And placed him on Mansa Saman's shoulders,   (Indeed)
2930 Laying the balaphone on his head, *serew*!   (Indeed)
He followed after the Wizard: (Indeed)
    "Biribiriba!   (Indeed)
    "O Nare Magan Kònatè!   (Indeed)
    "Entered Kaya,
2935   *"Son-Jara entered Kaya.*   (That's the truth)
    "Entered Kaya,
    "Sugulun's Ma'an entered Kaya.   (Yes, Fa-Digi)
    "If they took no gold,   (Indeed)
    "If they took no measure of gold for the
        Wizard,   (Indeed)
2940   "The reason for Son-Jara's coming to the
        Manden,
    "To stabilize the Manden,
    "To improve the people's lot: *jon jon*! (That's the truth)

"Subaa, i na-kun kèra Manden-kalu kama.   (Naamu)

"Nare Magan Kònatè!   (Naamu)
2945 "Kalifaya Magan Kònatè!"   (O ye cinyè ye)
Alu sida Manden.   (Naamu)
Subaa di bèè mara.   (Naamu)
A d'i tu ole rò, nnn,   (Naamu)
Bulanbulan Sulemani,   (Naamu)
2950 Ani Yari Sise,   (Naamu)
K'olu bila,   (Naamu)
K'alu k'waa sulu nò fè,   (Naamu)
K'a ta le Manden di.   (Naamu)
Bulanbulan Sulemani,   (Naamu)
2955 Ani Yari Sise,   (Naamu)
Alu waada sulu nò fè,   (Naamu)
Jòlò-fin.   (Naamu)
Jòlò-fin Mansa bira ki-dinnu kan, nnn,   (Naamu)
Ka tan kònòntòn su-kè kònòntòn mina,   (Naamu)
2960 Ka tango-wulu bi-saba tègè,   (Naamu)
Ko ka n'a di Nyani-mansa ma,   (Naamu)
Ka ma Son-Jara kòn fèn gèrè di,   (Naamu)
Ko wulu lagènna le Nyani-mansa di,
K'a ma sig'ale ma fòlò.   (O ye cinyè ye)

2965 Garan ne.   (Naamu)
Biribiriba bun dò n'a furu-musu,   (Naamu)
Jelilu nara dònkili la,
      "Kalifaya Megan Kònatè!   (Iyo, Fa-Digi)
      "Sera faama sera!   (Naamu)
2970 "Subaa ni mansaya!   (Naamu)
      "Jòn di be ye wulu kinna?
      "Nare Megan Kònatè!
      "I tè wili ba?"   (Naamu)
Son-Jara d'i yèlèma,
2975 K'i kè wara di,   (Naamu)
K'a bòtò jelilu kan ma N' ma.   (Naamu)
A furu-musu d'a mina, k'a sanba,   (Naamu)
K'a lala,   (Naamu)
. . . ,   (O ye cinyè ye)
2980 . . . .   (Naamu)
Aa! Kala Jula Sangoyi!   (Naamu)
Nin kuma ye jelilu da bi.   (Cinyè)
"Subaa le,   (Naamu)

        "O Sorcerer, you have come for the Manden
              people!   (Indeed)
        "O Nare Magan Kònatè,   (Indeed)
2945   "O Khalif Magan Kònatè!"   (That's the truth)
They arrived back in the Manden.   (Indeed)
The Sorcerer ruled over everyone.   (Indeed)
He continued on at that.   (Indeed)
Bulanbulan Sulemani,   (Indeed)
2950   Along with Yari Sise,   (Indeed)
He sent them forth,   (Indeed)
That they should go after horses,   (Indeed)
Saying the Manden belonged to him.   (Indeed)
Bulanbulan Sulemani,   (Indeed)
2955   Along with Yari Sise,   (Indeed)
They went on after the horses,   (Indeed)
In the land of Dark Jòlòf.   (Indeed)
The Dark Jòlòf king fell on the messengers, (Indeed)
And seizing the nine and ninety stallions, (Indeed)
2960   Selected hound dogs one score and ten, (Indeed)
Saying give them to the Nyani King,   (Indeed)
Saying he knew Son-Jara for naught   (Indeed)
Save a runner of dogs,
Saying he had no reason to doubt that.   (That's the truth)

2965   O Garan!   (Indeed)
Biribiriba [went ?] in his hut with his wife, (Indeed)
The bards came up to him singing:
        "Khalif Magan Kònatè!   (Yes, Fa-Digi)
        "Succeeded, the King succeeded! (Indeed)
2970   *"The Sorcerer and Sovereignty!* (Indeed)
        "Who has seen the goat bite the dog?
        " O Nare Magan Kònatè!
        "Will you not arise?"   (Indeed)
Son-Jara transformed himself on the spot,
2975   And turned into a lion,   (Indeed)
Saying he was going out after those bards. (Indeed)
His wife grabbed hold and soothed him,   (Indeed)
And had him lay back down,   (Indeed)
    . . . . ,   (That's the truth)
2980   . . . .   (Indeed)
Ah! Kala Jula Sangoyi!   (Indeed)
Those are the words the bards said that day: (True)
"O Wizard,   (Indeed)

"Ile le di Bulanbulan Sulemani,
2985 "Ni Yari Sise bila,   (Naamu)
"K'alu k'waa tan-saba...,   (Naamu)
"Tan kònòntòn su-kè kònòntòn nò kan,   (Naamu)
"Ka tan saba, nnn.   (Naamu)
"Ole binlin sulu kan, nnn,   (Naamu)
2990 "Ka tan saba...,   (Naamu)
"Tango wulu saba bila,   (Naamu)
"Ko ka n'a d'ile ma,   (Naamu)
"K'ile le wulu lagènna di,
"K'ele ma si kèlè ma fòlò.   (O ye cinyè ye)
2995 "Subaa, ba tè wulu kindè!"   (O ye cinyè ye)

Tun-tan-mògòlu d'i kali, nnn: (Naamu)
"Ne le kètò kèlè-tigi di!"   (Naamu)
Fa-Koli ni Tura Ma'an d'i kali.   (Naamu)
Fa-Koli ko, "Ne le kèlè tala!"   (O ye cinyè ye)

3000 Tura Ma'an ko, "Ne le kèlè tala!"   (Naamu)
Son-Jara k'a diban,   (Naamu)
"Ne le kèlè tala,
"Ka taa Jòlòf-fin."   (Naamu)
Nare Magan Kònatè!   (Naamu)
3005 Tura Ma'an diminda,   (Naamu)
Ka taa kaburu sen sarelo dò,   (Naamu)
K'è la sare-dinga kònò.   (Naamu)
Jelilu waara: "Nare Magan Kònatè!   (Naamu)
"N'i ma waa Tura Ma'an ni Kanke-jan lajè,   (Naamu)
3010 "I la kèlè ti sin dè!"   (Naamu)
A di jelilu bila,
K'alu k'waa Tura Ma'an wele.
Jelilu waara,   (Naamu)
Alu ma Tura Ma'an ni Kanke-jan ye.   (O ye: cinyè ye)
3015 Son-Jara nata e lò, sarelo dò: (Naamu)
      "Bugu Turu ni Bugu Bò!   (Naamu)
      "Muke Muse ni Muke Dantuman!   (Naamu)
      "Juru Kèta ni Juru Moriba!   (Naamu)
      "Tunbila Manden jòn!   (Naamu)
3020   *"Kalabila Manden jòn!*   (Naamu)
      "Sanan Fa Buren, Danka Fa Buren!   (Naamu)
      "Makan-taa Finman ni Makan-taa Gèman!   (Naamu)
"Jelilu le,   (Naamu)
"L'an ka kèlè-kè-bun di Tura Magan ma,   (Naamu)

	"'Twas you who sent Bulanbulan Sulemani	
2985	"Along with Yari Sise,	(Indeed)
	"That they should go	(Indeed)
	"After nine and ninety stallions.	(Indeed)
	"To thirty.	(Indeed)
	"It was he who plundered the horses,	(Indeed)
2990	"And thirty. . . ,	(Indeed)
	"And gave the hound dogs, score and ten,	(Indeed)
	"Saying we should give you them,	(Indeed)
	"Since you are but a runner of dogs,	
	"Saying you have not yet mastered war.	(That's the truth)
2995	"O Wizard, the goat bites not the dog!"	(That's the truth)

In turn, the warriors swore their fealty:　　　　　　(Indeed)
"Let me the battle-master be!"　　　　　　　　　　(Indeed)
Fa-Koli and Tura Magan swore their fealty.　　　　(Indeed)
"Let me lead the army!" Fa-Koli adjured.　　(That's the truth)

3000	"Let me lead the army!" Tura Magan adjured.	(Indeed)
	Son-Jara finally spoke,	(Indeed)
	" 'Tis I who will lead the army,	(Indeed)
	"And go to Dark Jòlòf land."	(Indeed)
	O Nare Magan Kònatè!	(Indeed)
3005	Tura Magan plunged into grief,	(Indeed)
	And went to the graveyard to dig his grave,	(Indeed)
	And laid himself down in his grave.	(Indeed)
	The bards came forth: "O Nare Magan Kònatè	(Indeed)
	"If you don't go see Tura Magan,	(Indeed)
3010	"Your army will not succeed!"	(Indeed)
	He sent the bards forth,	
	That they should summon Tura Magan.	
	And so the bards went forth,	(Indeed)
	But Tura Magan they could not find.	(That's the truth)
3015	Son-Jara came and stood in the graveyard:	(Indeed)
	"Bugu Turu and Bugu Bò!	(Indeed)
	"Muke Musa and Muke Dantuman!	(Indeed)
	"Juru Kèta and Juru Moriba!	(Indeed)
	"Tunbila, the Manden Slave!	(Indeed)
3020	*"Kalabila, the Manden Slave!*	(Indeed)
	"Sana Fa-Buren, Danka Fa-Buren!	(Indeed)
	"Dark-Pilgrim and Light-Pilgrim!	(Indeed)
	"Ah! Bards,	(Indeed)
	"Let us give the army to Tura Magan,	(Indeed)

<pre>
3025   "Su-sare-jòn wo, Tura Magan.   (Naamu)
       "Tura Magan ni Kanke-jan!"   (O ye cinyè ye)

       Tura Magan d'i bara,   (Naamu)
       "N' tulu fòlò fòlò fòlò fòlò!"   (Naamu)
       Alu di tun ni kala di Tura Ma'an ma.   (Naamu)
3030   Tura Ma'an nada ba tègè yan,   (Naamu)
       Tura Ma'an Tègèn-danna.   (Naamu)
       Ki-din dò d'i bara,   (Naamu)
       "Hèè! An waatò kèlè min ken ma, han,   (Naamu)
       "Kèlè ti diya!   (Naamu)
3035   "Nègè dunun tan kònòntòn ye Jòlòf-fin Mansa kun. (Naamu)
       "Dunun tè Manden,   (Naamu)
       "Balan tè Manden.   (Naamu)
       "Ku si tè Manden,   (Naamu)
       "Fo Jawaralu bènba, Sita Fata,   (Naamu)
3040   "F'o mana da kutukutu,   (Naamu)
       "K'a kè dunun ni bala di,
       "Ka taa Nyani-mansa lakunun.   (Naamu)
       "Nin kèlè tè diya dè!"   (Naamu)
       Alu di ku-dò-kabala gèn.   (Naamu)
3045   Ko wula dò kè-ba-jitò,
       Ka wusa ku-dò-kabala di.   (O ye cinyè ye)
       O waada ba tègè.   (Naamu)
       Alu kan ye, ole ma, ko Salakan,   (Naamu)
       Ko Jitòlu-Tègèn-Dan.   (Naamu)
3050   Kèba-Jitòlu-Tègèn-Dan,   (Naamu)
       Tura Magan ni kèlè nyògòn na.   (Naamu)
       A di wulu-di-mansa faga,   (Naamu)
       K'ale le wululu lagènda.   (O ye cinyè ye)
       Tura Magan ni kèlè taara.   (Naamu)
3055   A waata Nyani-mansa faga,
       K'ale le wululu lagènda.   (O ye cinyè ye)
       Tura Magan ni kèlè taara.   (Naamu)
       A di Sanumu Mansa faga,
       K'a le wululu lagènda,   (Naamu)
3060   Ka ba-dugu Mansa faga,
       K'ale le wululu lagènda,   (Naamu)
       Ka taa Jòlòf.   (Naamu)
       Bèrè le tògò ye Jòlòf.   (Naamu)
       Mansa-kè le tèrè...,   (Naamu)
3065   Bèrè min wulennin dè,   (Naamu)
       Wòlòflu kan ole ma, ko Jòlòf.   (Naamu)
</pre>

3025 "To the Slave-of-the-Tomb, Tura Magan,   (Indeed)
     "O Tura Magan-and-Kanke-jan!"   (That's the truth)

     Tura Magan spoke out,   (Indeed)
     "That is the best of all things to my ear!"   (Indeed)
     To Tura Magan they gave quiver and bow.   (Indeed)
3030 Tura Magan advanced to cross the river here,   (Indeed)
     At the Passage-of-Tura-Magan.   (Indeed)
     A member of the troop cried out,   (Indeed)
     "Hey! The war to which we go,   (Indeed)
     "That war will not be easy!   (Indeed)
3035 "Ninety iron drums has the Dark Jòlòf King.   (Indeed)
     "No drum like this has the Manden,   (Indeed)
     "Nor balaphone has the Manden.   (Indeed)
     "There is no such thing in the Manden,   (Indeed)
     "Save the Jawara patriarch, Sita Fata,   (Indeed)
3040 "Save when he puffs out his cheeks,   (Indeed)
     "Making with them like drum and balaphone,
     "To go awaken the Nyani King.   (Indeed)
     "This battle will not be easy!"   (Indeed)
     But they drove this agitator off,   (Indeed)
3045 Saying better in the bush a frightened brave
     Than a loudmouthed agitator.   (That's the truth)
     He went back across the river,   (Indeed)
     At the place they call Salakan,   (Indeed)
     And Ford-of-the-Frightened.   (Indeed)
3050 The Ford-of-the-Frightened-Braves.   (Indeed)
     Tura Magan with battle met.   (Indeed)
     He slayed that dog-giving king,   (Indeed)
     Saying he was but running the dogs.   (That's the truth)
     Tura Magan with army marched on,   (Indeed)
3055 He went to slay Nyani Mansa,
     Saying he was but running the dogs.   (That's the truth)
     Tura Magan with the army marched on,   (Indeed)
     He slayed the Sanumu King,
     Saying that he was but running the dogs,   (Indeed)
3060 He slayed Ba-dugu King,   (Indeed)
     Saying he was but running the dogs,   (Indeed)
     And marched on thus through Jòlòf land.   (Indeed)
     Their name for stone is Jòlòf.   (Indeed)
     Once there was this king. . . ,   (Indeed)
3065 The stone there that is red,   (Indeed)
     The Wòlòf call it: Jòlòf.   (Indeed)

Mansa-kè le tèrè o dugu kònò, N' fa,

Ko Jòlòf-fin Mansa.   (Naamu)
A kòrò le nin di.   (O ye cinyè ye)
3070 A di Jòlòf-fin Mansa faga,   (Naamu)
K'a kunba tèg'a kanba da dò,   (Naamu)
Fo ka Wòlòfòlu jamu kè, ko Njòpò.   (Naamu)
Ole Tarawere di.   (Naamu)

Sane ni Mane,   (Naamu)
3075 Ole Tarawere di.   (Naamu)
Mayga, ole Tarawere di.   (Naamu)
Magaraga, ole Tarawere di.   (Naamu)
Tura Magan ni Kanke-jan,   (Naamu)
Ani kèlè taara,
3080 Ka t..., taa sanu-muru, lakuru-jan kuru.   (O ye cinyè ye)

Tura Magan ni Kanke-jan bulu.   (Naamu)

Kirikisa, dunun-tanba ni sòn-tanba!   (Naamu)

Garan ne.   (Naamu)
An ka kuma bila yan.   (O ye cinyè ye,
                                                 naamu, k'a sera sa!)

There once was a king in that country, my
    father,
Called King of Dark Jòlòfland.   (Indeed)
And that is the meaning of this.   (That's the truth)
3070 He slew that Dark Jòlòf King,   (Indeed)
Severing his great head at his shoulders,   (Indeed)
From whence comes the Wòlòf name, Njòp!   (Indeed)
They are Taraweres.   (Indeed)

Sane and Mane,   (Indeed)
3075 They are Taraweres.   (Indeed)
Mayga, they are Taraweres.   (Indeed)
Magaraga, they are Taraweres.   (Indeed)
Tura Magan-and-Kanke-jan,   (Indeed)
He with the army marched on,
3080 To destroy the golden sword and the tall
    throne.   (That's the truth)
This by the hand of Tura Magan-and-
    Kanke-jan.
    Kirikisa, Spear-of-Access, Spear-of-Service!   (Indeed)
Ah! Garan!   (Indeed)
Let us leave the words right here.   (That's the truth,
indeed, it's over now!)

Annotations to the Text

(1) *Nare Magan Kònatè*. Aside from the many and varied praise-
names and dialectical pronunciations applied to Son-Jara (Sun-
Jata), there are several names by which he is known in Mali.
Nare Magan Kònatè is explained as follows. Narena (literally,
'at Nare') is the name of a modern town in Mali, which many
people believe was one of the capitals of Son-Jara's empire. There
are other towns which claim this prominence—notably Nyani in
Guinea—but such variation is to be expected in an oral society.
Prefixing the name of one's village of birth or residence (in this
case without the suffix -*na*) is a common practice in Mali. Magan
is Son-Jara's given name (some say it means 'master'), and
Kònatè is the clan name of his father's family.

Another common name follows the Moslem practice in Mali
of giving one's first-born son the name of the prophet Muḥammad. Thus, Son-Jara is called Mamadu Kònatè, Mamadu being
the Mande pronunciation for the Arabic name. Note here also
that the father's surname is added.

Etiological legends based on folk etymologies (see my article
on this subject in *Folklore Forum* 9:3/4, 1977) is a favorite combination of genres in Mali and accounts for the name Son-Jara
Keyta. Being considered the founder of a clan as well as the empire of Mali entitles this patriarch to a surname of his own. Keyta
is explained as being a combination of two Maninka morphemes:
kè, 'inheritance,' and ta, 'to take,' thus, 'He-who-took-(stole)-
the-Inheritance,' (implying, 'from his elder brother'). The given
name is more complicated, and several variants for its explanation
exist. Some lengthen the vowel of Son (Sun), thus Soon (Suun),
and claim that it is a contraction of Son-Jara's mother's name

Sogolon (Sugulun). Here again we observe a common naming custom in Mali, that of prefixing one's own name with one's mother's name. Others prefer to define Son as 'thief' (*nson*). Jara (Jata) is almost always considered to mean 'lion.' Thus the full meaning could be 'So'on's (shortened form of Sogolon) Lion' or 'Lion Thief-Who-Took-the-Inheritance.' This folk etymology is generally followed by an etiological legend stating that, because Son-Jara was the second-born son, and yet gained the throne, he usurped Mali from his elder brother; he 'took the inheritance' of his brother. For another legend explaining the thief etymology in the Gambia, see Gordon Innes, *Sun-jata Three Mandinka Versions* (London: School of Oriental and African Studies, 1974): pp. 47–48, lines 136–80.

(2) *Subaa-Minè-Subaa,* 'Sorcerer-Seizing-Sorcerer.' Praise-name for Son-Jara, sometimes heard in conjunction with two clan names (Magasubaa and Jarasubaa), which form a rhyming three-pattern. It is an important praise-name for Son-Jara, because it emphasizes his occult power. Many consider the skillful use of magic a necessity for kings to maintain their power.

(4) *Four Mastersingers.* Slightly obscure, this line may be an invocation to the bard's inherited social status as a casted mastersinger. All four casted groups in Mali deal in the occult and thus in secretive and skillful use of language: therefore, four mastersingers. Each caste specializes in the unique economic activity reserved for its profession. The *jeli* (bard) passes along certain types of verbal information, notably narrative and epic poetry, for remuneration. The *numun* (blacksmith) may specialize in a number of skills associated with metal work and woodcarving. Leather work is sanctioned for the *garangè* (cordwainer), while religious (Islamic) praise-poetry is reserved for the *funè*. Other economic pursuits such as weaving are not casted among Mande peoples, but are casted among neighboring groups such as the Fulani (Peul).

A note must be given on the social status of casted peoples in Mali. Castes are not vertical, as in India, but horizontal. By this image, I mean that Mande castes function more like trade monopolies than pecking-order social classes.

(5) *Kala Jula Sangoyi Mamunaka Jabaatè.* An invocation to a legendary bard of Old Mali. Fa-Digi considers this bard to be the son of the Tarawere hunter Dan Mansa Wulanba (see lines 468ff and the genealogy charts in the appendix). Some people in the Kita area believe that this bard originated the epic of Son-Jara. Some bards describe Kala Jula as a hunting companion to Son-Jara (see, for example, Massa Makan Diabaté, *Kalajata,* Bamako, Mali: Éditions Populaires, 1970).

(9) *Ben Adam*. First man on earth by Moslem, Jewish, and Christian traditions. Ben, *bani,* is borrowed from Arabic here as a name. In Arabic, it is actually the plural form of *ibn* (*bin* medially). *Bani Adama,* 'sons of Adam,' is a common epithet for humanity in the Koran.

(10-11) These lines set the scene for the beginning of the narrative. Epic poetry amongst Mande peoples often begins with an etiological, sometimes allegorical, scene-setting legend.

(13) *Biribiriba*. Praise-name for Son-Jara, the meaning of which is obscure.

(16-17) *Fatiyataligara* and *Sokoto*. Description of the land mass of the ancient empire of Mali. Sokoto is a city in modern northern Nigeria and was an important settlement in the nineteenth-century Fulani theocratic empire in that region. Fatiyataligara is obscure, but one assistant considered it the homeland of the Soninke in present-day Mauritania.

(19) *My father*. A term of respect directed to the bard's audience. This stylistic device is employed often by Fa-Digi.

(20) *Republic of Mali*. Note how the bard employs the modern name of the country for the old empire. The word Mali, according to M. Delafosse, *La Langue Mandingue et ses Dialects* (Paris: Paul Geuthner, 1929): Vol. I, p. 9, is derived from the West African ethnic group called Fulani, and is not actually a Mande word. The Manden (Mandin, Manding) is the indigenous term for the original kingdom, now a small portion of Mali and Guinea. (Note that I am using the term Manden for the kingdom and, following I. H. Greenberg, *The Languages of Africa,* Bloomington, Indiana: Indiana University Press, 1966, I use the term Mande to denote the language group.) The first chroniclers of this region were north African Arabs, and they probably acquired the name of the region from Fulani merchants involved in the trans-Saharan trade. Another, perhaps more realistic, explanation for the modern word Mali involves natural sound shifts in the language. The alveolar "nd" shifts to "l" and the terminal vowel denasalizes and raises; thus "Manden" shifts to "Mali."

(21) *Maninka*. Name of Son-Jara's ethnic group, and a Kita regional variant of Manden-ka, 'citizen of/person from the Manden.'

(23-30) Praise-poem symbolizing the conquests of Son-Jara. Note that the names of the three fictitious men slain in the poem form word plays with the stated motivation for the slayings. This type of formulaic expression is common in praise-poetry and can be found in many such poems.

(24-25) *Dankun,* 'border,' literally 'village border.' Description of a normal Mande farming community is necessary to understand this symbol. The cosmologically safest place in Mande worldview is the village (*dugu*), composed of several family compounds (*lulu,* sg. *lu*) around a village square (*bara*). The farther outward one goes from the core, the more dangerous life becomes, thus increasing the need for occult preparation to face the outside. Passing over the village border (*dankun*), where many sacrifices are performed, one enters the ring of women's vegetable gardens (*na-ko*). Farther out is the toilet ring (*bɔ-kɛ-yɔrɔ*), bordered by the men's main cultivation fields (*foro*). This latter ring may be mixed with fields laying fallow (*san-gwan*), and on the other side of these outreaches of civilization lies the wilderness (*wula*), the most dangerous of regions, literally and cosmologically. The wilderness continues to the fields of the next village.

These lines imply that only strong men with sufficient knowledge of the occult should settle anywhere outside the village border. For the weak, it could spell disaster.

(26-27) *Basa,* 'lizard.' The lizard is considered the property of youth, that is, uncircumcised boys, who are said to practice their first task as a hunter by stalking lizards. The boys cook and eat their catch in a form of communion similar to that of their elders in a communion of heart and liver meat cooked immediately after the kill. These lines imply that if a man takes lizard as his name (or totem?), he takes on the attributes of a weak animal. Note the contrast with the praise-name of the conqueror, *Jara,* 'lion.'

(28-29) These lines carry the same cosmological significance as lines 24-25. See the note above.

(32) *Simbon, Lion-Born-of-the-Cat.* Praise-name for Son-Jara emphasizing his knowledge of hunting and the occult. The latter praise-name is translated here according to one variant folk etymology reported to me by Youssouf Tata Cissé. According to Youssouf, hunters in Mali are said to gain their knowledge of hunting, as well as herbal and occult medicine, by observing the animals of the wilderness (a dangerous business) and passing on their secret knowledge only to apprentices. The valiant hunter (*simbon*) is thus said to have learned his profession from the lion, who himself learned to hunt from his ancestor, the master-hunter cat. *Simbon* is an honorific title for a hunter, which D. T. Niane reports was derived from the Maninka word for hunter's whistle in his, *Soundiata: An Epic of Old Mali* (London: Longman, 1965): note 5, p. 86. For other variant explanations, see Gordon Innes, *Sunjata: Three Mandinka Versions* (London: School of Oriental and African Studies): note 154, p. 106. The variant cited there is

Nyankumolu Khaba la Simbong, 'Cats on the shoulder Simbong.' Another variant explanation I collected is *Dan- kun-ba la wara la Simbon,* 'At-the-Great-Border, Simbon-of-the-Bush.'

(34-36) *Stump-in-the-Dark-of-Night.* Praise-name for Son-Jara, emphasizing his ruthlessness, which can strike before the enemy knows it.

(37-41) *Granary-Guard-Dog.* Praise-name for Son-Jara, emphasizing his ruthlessness. Farmers often keep guard dogs to protect their compounds, especially the granary. This guard dog is so ruthless he will bite even members of the compound who are familiar to him.

(42) *Kirikara Watita.* Idiophone representing the rising and falling of the hero's shoulders, symbolizing the arrogance of power. Another assistant reported this praise-line as an epithet used in the Komo Society for a berserk, a ruthless and fearless warrior. The Komo Society is an esoteric cult among the Mande peoples concerned with occult medicine.

(43) *Adversity's-True-Place.* Praise-name for Son-Jara, emphasizing his ruthlessness.

(44) The Maninka line is vague and could mean that the reason for a man's and a woman's existence, or their ability to reason and think, are not the same.

(46-48) *Nine and ten Adams.* The reference is obscure. Possibly a metaphor for the races of humanity, the nine Adams might symbolize the creation of other heavenly creatures, such as jinns and angels (e.g., "the company of heaven").

(49) *Bènba.* Name of the Bard's naamu-sayer. The naamu-sayer, often the bard's apprentice, is the representative of the audience in a performance. It is his job to show attentiveness and encouragement to the bard. His responses can even direct the course of the narrative to some degree. An excited response can cause the bard to develop an idea, while a weak response can discourage him. I witnessed a naamu-sayer go to sleep on his bard one night and begin to snore, but he never missed a response!

(54) *Iblis.* Arabic name of God's most beloved Angel. According to the Islamic faith, he refused to bow down before Adam and was transformed into the *shaydan,* 'satan,' and cast out of heaven.

(64) *Sibiri,* 'hand span.' A traditional measurement which is the length of the distance between the middle finger and the outstretched thumb, used in Mali for measuring such items as cloth and rope. Its counterpart is the *nogon,* 'cubit,' measuring the distance between elbow and middle finger. Variation of length occurs since not all people have the same measurements.

(66) Etiological explanation of how the power of satan came to be established. Because of his greed, he demands repayment for his years of service. God creates wealth (line 80) and gives it to satan, thereby unleashing its misuse upon humanity through the power of the devil.

(72) *Trumpet blows.* In Moslem (as in Christian) theology, the angel Jilbril (Gabriel) will blow the horn announcing the end of time. This traditional motif will be recognized as Motif A 1093: end of world announced by trumpet, in Stith Thompson's, *Motif Index of Folk-Literature* (Bloomington, Indiana: Indiana University Press, 1966). All motifs cited in the text are from Thompson's index.

(75-97) Parts of a poem sometimes get "lost in translation." This passage serves as a good example of that problem. Here the bard plays on the verb root *fili,* 'to throw/be mistaken/fail to recognize.' His skillful use of this verb with prefixes and suffixes yields several words and phrases such as *nòfili,* 'to lead astray' in line 73 and *filiman-kan,* 'the voice of sin/transgression' in line 82.

The obscurity of this passage also requires explanation. From lines 56 to 82, the characters of the narrative speak. Then the bard comments on the nature of the Voice of Transgression from lines 83 to 88, explaining that if one has wealth, one will ignore one's kinsmen. If one has no wealth, one's kinsmen will ignore him. Lines 90 through 96 are the Voice of Transgression itself metaphorically speaking to its disciples, the sinners. In three couplets, the Voice of Transgression explains that if a person does not use his wealth for others, his downfall is secured. In line 97 the bard again comments, invoking God's protection for the weak from the wealthy.

(103) *Jinn.* A spirit in Moslem theology that is invisible to human beings, though some live in communities on the earth. Some jinns are beneficial to humanity—the English words genie and genius derive from this Arabic word—and others are hostile. Many people in Mali believe that some cohabit with humans to produce superheroes like Fa-Koli, one of Son-Jara's generals. In Mande folklore, jinns are often thought to live in fetishes and are consulted for advice and guidance.

(106) *Morality.* Other possible translations for *maluya* are 'conscience,' 'decency,' and 'shame.'

(115-17) *Dignity.* According to Moslem theology, human beings were the most important of God's creatures, so all of heaven's company was told to bow down before Adam (see note for line 54). Satan's refusal caused him to be cast from heaven. Whereas the Christian concept of original sin tends to place humanity at the bottom of the cosmological pecking order, Islam puts them at the top. A confirmation of this belief may be observed in the tenet that God forgave Adam for the first sin. The Moslem messiah, *mahdi,* does not function as the reconciler of the sin of Adam. Another confirmation of this belief may be observed in lines 116-20, where God creates the most important of his creations, Muhammad the Prophet, as a human, not as a jinn or angel.

(121) *Filardi Samawaati.* Obscure passage. Could be the Maninka pronunciation for the Arabic *fi 'l-ardi wa samāwāti,* 'on earth and in heaven.' Line 122 below would seem to confirm this possibility.

(123) Line unclear on tape. Ellipses will be used throughout the text to indicate unintelligible words or lines.

(130) *India.* The term in Maninka, *Hindi,* may simply mean 'the East.' See lines 133-34 below.

(140-44) The bard metaphorically describes an eclipse of the moon by the sun. The phrase concerning the cat is commonly recited by youths during such an eclipse.

(147-52) Reference to Islamic theology. Omitting the episode of Adam and Eve in the Garden, the bard resumes his narrative when the pair have been cast out of paradise. In Moslem belief, God cast them out separately and caused them to seek after each other for forty days and forty nights. Eventually Adam sees Eve before she sees him, thus ordaining masculine initiative in seeking a spouse. Since this narrative still exists in the oral tradition, variants exist. Some say Adam found Eve in Lebanon, while others, including Fa-Digi, claim that Eve was found atop Mount Arfa (Arafan). The mountain is in Mecca and plays a role in Moslem pilgrimage (ḥajj) ceremonies.

(155-56) In other words, they had forty sets of twins, a boy and a girl each time. Twins could not marry each other, but were permitted to intermarry with their siblings, thus beginning the world's population.

(164) *Masusu* and *Masasa.* Obscure place names. The Bible calls the descendants of Japheth 'the Coastal Peoples' (Gen. 10:5), which would agree with line 163. Masusu and Masasa may be the same as the Bible's Mesha, (Gen. 10:30), but this was the home of Shem, not Japheth. Kalilou Tèra recounted a legend that credits Alexander the Great (Julu Kara Nayini) for building a great range of mountains (the Himalayas?) to keep out these people, who were considered barbaric. The suggestion is that these are the yellow races, which is confirmed by Moslem tradition. They complete the three-patterned descendants of Noah (See notes for lines 165-67).

(165) *Ham.* Note that Fa-Digi credits Ham as the ancestor of the black race, although not for the pejorative reasons suggested by Motif

A 1614.1, Negroes as curse on Ham for laughing at Noah's nakedness. (Thompson, *op. cit.*, 1966).

(169) *Kirikisa.* Term obscure to all the assistants. *Spear-of-Access, Spear-of-Service.* Praise-name for Son-Jara implying a force for the good of humanity.

(171) *Dònba month.* This word does not appear to be Arabic in origin. The Prophet's birthday (*Mawlīd*) is celebrated on the twelfth day of the month of <u>Sh</u>awwal.

(173) *Bilāl bin Rabaḥ,* sometimes called Ibn Ḥamāma after his mother, is referred to in Mande as Jòn Bilali, 'Servant/Slave Bilali.' One of the bards from whom I collected, Ban Sumana Sisòkò, explained the name *jòn* as a religious one, with the same connotation as the Arabic 'Abd al-Lāh ('Abdallāh), 'slave/servant of God.' Islamic historical writings do describe Bilāl as a slave, first of Umayya bin <u>Kh</u>alaf (an unbeliever whom Bilāl later slew in battle) and then of Abū Bakr (the Prophet Muḥammad's father-in-law and the first convert of Islam). Whether genealogical claims of kinship between the Mande peoples and Bilāl are historical or merely legendary is of little consequence to folk belief. Many African Moslems claim kinship to the Prophet or to those close to him, because of the Islamic belief that *barakah,* 'grace/power,' can be inherited from Muḥammad's descendants or intimates. The Mande peoples probably claim kinship to Bilāl, because he is described as being of Ethiopian (African?) origin. The belief is supported by the Black Moslem movement in America. In late 1975 the name of the Black Moslem newspaper *Muhammad Speaks* was changed to the *Bilalian News.*

Bilāl's tomb is still standing in Damascus [see Philip K. Hitti, *History of the Arabs,* (London: Macmillan, 1967, note 1, page 106)]. He is considered the first *mu'addin* (*mu'azzin*) or prayer-caller and the second convert to Islam. He is said to have been the Prophet's mace-bearer (*'anaza*), steward (<u>kh</u>azin), and personal servant and adjutant. He accompanied Muḥammad on his holy wars (*jihad*), and continued in service as a warrior in Syria after the death of the Prophet. As a Companion or Disciple (*al-Saḥābi, al-Saḥīb*), of Muḥammad, some 44 of the Islamic Traditions (*aḥādit͟h*), which are short, legendary stories and treatises concerning the deeds and teaching of the Messenger of God, are attributed to Bilāl. For a more detailed description of the life and accomplishments of Bilāl bin Rabaḥ, and for a bibliography of further references, see W. 'Arafat's article in *The Encyclopaedia of Islam: New Edition* (London: Luzac & Co., 1960): vol. vi, p. 1215.

Samuda. Maninka pronunciation of <u>Th</u>amūda, name of a clan and the city of its origin in Arabia. Later, when Muḥammad proclaimed his prophecy, this clan opposed him. A Moslem legend states that once Muḥammad came to water his camel at a well the Thamūda were using. A confrontation followed and the Thamūda killed the Prophet's camel. Later they were defeated by the Prophet's forces.

(176-81) Note that these men are the legendary ancestors of the noble clans (*hòròn*) of old Mali.

(184) *Maraka* (possibly Mara-ka, 'people of Mara'). Maninka word for the Soninke (Sarakole) ethnic group. They were the last rulers of Ghana (Wagadugu). The Maraka live in present-day Mali near Segu.

(185) *Wagadugu,* 'Land of the Waga.' Also known as Ghana (Gāna) in Arabic chronicles. The empire of Gāna, which reached its zenith under the Soninke rulers in the ninth and tenth centuries, was the first of the three great empires of West Africa during the Middle Ages. The other two were Mali and Songhoy. This Wagadugu, which was located mostly in what is today Mauritania, must not be confused with the name of the modern capital city of Burkina Faso. Nor should the empire of Gāna be confused with the modern West African state of Ghana.

(186-94) Listing of Bamana and Maninka surnames, except for Fulani and Jawara, which are names for ethnic groups.

(195) The allusion is to the legend of the snake of Wagadugu, subject of a Soninke epic. According to the variant given by one of my assistants, the great snake of Koumbi Saleh, capital of Wagadugu, received the annual sacrifice of a virgin. One year the chosen girl was spared, because the snake, who dwelt in a pit, was killed by the girl's lover. The man had to cut off its head nine times in order to kill it, but before it died, the snake cursed the land, causing a drought of nine years, nine months, and nine days. Thus, the people of this great empire had to disperse to other areas. The belief in this dispersion is the basis for many modern clan and ethnic etiological claims.

(197) *Damangile.* Ancestor of the Jawara ethnic group. Damangile (Daman N'Guilé) is said to have been a giant, and his tomb measures some 20 to 25 feet long. For a thorough ethnology of the Jawara, see G. Boyer, *Un Peuple de l'Ouest Soudanais: les Diawara* (Dakar, Senegal: Institut Français d'Afrique Noire, 1953): pp. 123 and plates. For a résumé of the legend of Damangile, see especially pp. 21-22 and Plate I, Figure 3.

(198) *Nyenemba Nyarè.* Ancestor of the Nyarè clan of the Manden. The modern capital of Mali, Bamako, is said to have been a Nyarè settlement originally, and this clan lives there in great numbers.

(199) *Kingi.* A traditional region located in the western part of modern Mali, bordering Mauritania. The city of Nyoro du Sahel is the principal settlement of this region.

(200) *Bambagile.* Probably the modern village of Bambagile about 40 kms. east of Nyoro du Sahel.

(204) *Jala.* Probably the modern village of Jara, about 30 kms. west of Nyoro du Sahel.

(205) *Mount Siman and Mount Wala.* Small mountains presumably found in the area around Jara and Bambagèdè.

(207) *Prince Burama.* Ancestor of the Tunkara clan, his title *Farin* is a Soninke title. Burama is the Maninka pronunciation of the Arabic name Ibrāhīm (Abraham).

(208) *Mèma.* Often mentioned in Mande folklore, the exact site of Mèma is debated. Some bards equate it with the modern village of Nèma in Mauritania, but other bards deny the claim. If it existed, it was probably located in the area around Mopti and Djenné, on the west bank of the Niger River. Son-Jara will later spend his exile in this country.

(210) *Prince Burama.* Note that this Prince Burama is the son of the Prince Burama in line 207.

(215) *Kulun.* Location of this village is obscure. Because of the other villages mentioned, it must be somewhere between Nyoro and Kita.

(217) *Bangasi.* This village is about 40 kms. east of Kita, some 10 kms. north of the railroad line.

(218) *Mount Genu.* This mountain is located in the Kita region and is also called Mount Kita.

(220) *Kuduguni.* Whether this village exists now is not clear. Folk etymologies suggested for its meaning were 'village of the yam' and 'the little hidden thing.'

(226) *Kita.* Somewhat over 150 kms. west of Bamako, Kita is on the railroad line from Bamako to Dakar. Note that this variant was recited by a Kita bard.

(230) *Warlord,* etc. Praise-name for Son-Jara, emphasizing his ruthlessness. The final term, *fara,* 'a pile of stone' is translated conjecturally.

(238) *Ki-Kè-Bugu,* 'Farming Hamlet.' In Maninka village geography (see note for lines 24–25 above), a family normally lives in the *lu,* 'compound,' but goes out of the village to work in the fields (*foro*). During the planting and harvest seasons, the farmer may construct a temporary lean-to or hut (*bugu*) in the midst of the fields. Often several farmers construct their huts together, and their collection of huts can become the nucleus of a new village.

(240) *Manden Kiri-kòròni.* This village is said to have been the first village in the Manden. The traditional regions of Kin and Du— we shall see much of Du later—are said to be the oldest in Mali.

(246) *Dankò.* Conjectural transcription. According to one assistant, the modern name of this clan is Danfaga. Another assistant transcribed Dabò, another surname.

(248) *Kòròlen,* etc. These men are sons of the same father but different mothers (*fa-denlu*). Fabu, born of Kòròlen, and Fabu, born of Sòkòna, prefix their names with their mother's name for clarity. This is a common practice in Mali.

(249) *Dugunò.* A clan family of bards.

(250) As one would expect in an oral society, the genealogy in this text is the opinion of the bard and not a universally accepted line of descent. The descendants which follow (to line 256) are obscure to my assistants. Fata Magan, the Handsome is Son-Jara's father.

(258) *Kakama.* This area is said to have been the place where Fata Magan kept his fields. It was located in Bintanya Kamalen.

(259) *Bintanya Kamalen.* One of the traditional designations for the Manden heartland. This small region is located partly in Mali and partly in Guinea. In Mali the famous village of Kaaba (Kangaba) is the center of this region and, according to many, of the entire Mande-speaking world.

(269-70) Note that the number 33 is a pattern-number and not a literal mathematical figure. The bard actually lists 35 clans in lines 271-76.

(269) *Tun-tan-mògò,* 'noble clans.' A difficult word to translate, this word may be idiosyncratic to Fa-Digi. After consultation with assistants, we agreed to translate *tun-tan-mògò* as 'noble clan,' and *tun-tan-jòn* (line 271) as 'warrior.' For a good discussion on Bambara associations (*tun*), see Claude Meillassoux's *Urbanization of an African Community: Voluntary Associations in Bamako* (Seattle: University of Washington Press, 1968), especially pp. 49-54.

(272) *Agents.* This term, *jabi-fin-jòn* is translated conjecturally. One assistant described such people as spies.

(273) *Mamuru.* Often included in this list, the assistants did not know who Mamuru was. His descendants are listed on lines 277-81 below.

(274) *Mori,* 'holyman.' Not only a practitioner of Islamic ritual, the Mande *mori* is said to deal in the occult to some extent. An oft-mentioned *mori* curse is barrenness among rival co-wives. Al-

though the list differs from region to region, my assistants could name several clans specializing in this profession: Sise, Ture, Berete, Tunkara, Jane, and Sila.

(275) *Siya mɔgɔ,* 'families that came later.' This line alludes to a Mande tradition which deals with land tenure. The bards explain, using the stylistic formula of listing, that some clans were the original inhabitants of the Manden. Among these families, the *bula,* 'original families,' are listed Kamisòkò, Bagayògò, Sisòkò and Dunbiya. The *siya mɔgɔ (dunan,* 'stranger' is used in Bamana) are explained as clans which arrived in the Manden at a much later period in history. These clans, among them, Tarawere, Jaara, Kònatè, and Keyta, are said to have been conquering warrior clans. Modern Maninka and Bamana village political structure is often organized around this folk belief. A political chief, *dugu-tigi,* is consulted on matters of state, while a ritual chief, *dugu-kolo-tigi,* is consulted in matters of land and religious ceremonies concerning fertility. In many places, though apparently not everywhere, the *dugu-kolo-tigi* is from a *bula* family and the *dugu-tigi* is a *dunan.* Because the *dugu-kolo-tigi* is the descendant of the family considered the first to settle a region, it is also possible for a *dunan* to be a ritual chief.

(276) *Pariah.* Deformed people, or those with epilepsy, are considered by many to be possessed of special occult power (*nyama*). Presumably such a person would be of benefit because of his/her power.

(277-81 and 282-88) The bard lists the names of the patriarchs of the clans or clan branches he mentioned above.

(287) *Fodele, the Tall,* was said to be a Tunkara.

(290) *Tariku,* 'chronicle.' From the Arabic word *ta'rikh,* this form of historical narrative is unique in Africa in that it is written down. It was common for some families in several parts of Africa, especially those influenced by Islam, to record their family histories. I heard of this practice in both Mali and Somalia. Some of these books, I was told, are several generations old, having been passed along in each generation to a family historian.

(293) *Quraysh* and *Hāshim.* In Arab tradition, the Quraysh are the descendants of the Prophet Ibrāhīm (Abraham) through his maidservant Hajar (Hagar). Moslems consider Hajar's son Ismā'īl (Ishmael) to be patriarch of the Arabs, while his younger halfbrother Ishāq (Isaac) is considered to be patriarch of the Jews. The Hāshim are the branch of the Quraysh from which the Prophet Muhammad descended. See Appendix for Fa-Digi's version of these genealogies.

(294) In Arab tradition, Ḥāshim, for whom the clan is named, was the father of ʿAbd al-Muṭṭalib.

(297) *Fatima Bint.* The Prophet Muḥammad's favorite daughter. Her name Bint (Binta), which is a common Mande name today, is from the feminine form of the Arabic word *ibn* (see the note for line 9 above). The woman's full title in Arabic is *Fāṭimah bintu ʿr-Rasūlū ʾl-Lāhi,* ʿ Fāṭimah, Daughter of the Messenger of God.'

(300-303) *Al-Ḥasan* and *al-Ḥusayn.* The twin sons of Fāṭimah and ʿAli, fourth Khalif and first Imām of Islam. ʿAli was also the Prophet's patrilineal first cousin.

The Prophet's grandsons were given honorific titles, which their descendants retained. Al-Ḥasan was called Sharīf, 'noble,' and al-Ḥusayn took the title Sayyid, 'lord.' (See Hitti, op. cit., n. 8, p. 440).

(304) *Abulayi.* Maninka pronunciation of the Arabic name ʿAbd al-Lāhi (ʿAbdallāhi). At this point in the genealogy, the bard deviates from the traditional records of the Prophet's family genealogy. For this reason, the Maninka form of the name is maintained in the text.

(305-09) *Tarawere.* Etiological legend based on one of several variant folk etymologies for this name. Here, Abulayi is said to have had two pairs of eyes, one in the front of his head and one in the back (perhaps symbolic of a seer or diviner). *Ta ra wa ra* is claimed to be the Arabic form for 'he sees and sees.' Actually, the Maninka translation is closer to the Arabic for 'she sees and sees,' *tara wa tara* ('he sees and sees' is *yara wa yara).* For a broader discussion of this and other surname legends, see my article, "Etiological Legends Based on Folk Etymologies of Manding Surnames," *Folklore Forum* 9:3/4 (Bloomington, Indiana: Forum Society, 1976): 107-14.

(312) *Kayibara.* Place name, presumably in Arabia. I have been unable to find the referent to this Maninka form, but this name is used by others bards and is probably used here for the war (battle?) in which Muḥammad rose to power over the Infidels.

(313) *Remained.* Euphemism for death.

(322-24) *One-Who-Enters,* etc. Praise-names for the Tarawere clan, alluding to obscure legends. The last name, Tura Magan-and-Kankejan is a double or conjoined praise-name for the son of Dan Mansa Wulandin (line 320). Tura Magan later becomes one of Son-Jara's generals and conquers the Gambia for the empire.

(325ff.) Having traced Son-Jara's paternal line back to its origins in Arabia, the bard now turns to the maternal line. As his paternal inheritance contains the power (*barakah*) of Islam, so his maternal inheritance will contain the power of the occult (*nyama*) which he needs in order to overcome his enemies and become king.

The episodes of the Buffalo-Woman and the two Tarawere hunters is rich in overtone. Not only is it a part of the narrative and legend of Son-Jara's maternal line, but it is also a social commentary concerning the nature of respect, responsibility, and affection between members of a family and of society at large.

(326) *Jara, Jata* (sometimes *Jaara*). Clan name equated with Kòndè (Kònè, Kòntè, Mariko). Some Mande surnames have regional variants, which do not appear to be linguistic variants, although linguistic variation also occurs. The reason for this type of variation remains obscure.

 Sankarandin. River in Guinea, the Sankaran (*din* is a diminutive) is said to flow through the ancient region of Du (see note for line 240). Note that this bard often uses Sankaran and Du interchangeably to mean the region.

(334) *Dugu-mògòlu-nya-mògò,* 'Leader-of-the-People.' The local title of the ruler of Du according to legend. This title, in variant form, is common to many versions of this epic. For a similar title, see the note for line 207.

(336) *Flesh-and-Blood-Sister.* The translation here is liberal; *ba-kilinma-musu* literally means 'sister-by-the-same-mother [-and -father].' The phrase is an affectionate (and thus often honorific) epithet for a full sister (*ba-den-musu*). Because of the affectionate overtones of this word, it is sometimes used between half siblings (*fa-denlu*) to diminish the rivalry traditional to their relationship. For more about *ba-den* and *fa-den,* see the note for lines 356-59.

 Du Kamisa, 'Kamisa of Du (Do).' This woman, who later becomes the Buffalo-Woman, is considered to have been a great sorceress. From her, Son-Jara's mother will inherit her occult powers, and thus will his sister inherit them. Son-Jara will therefore be surrounded with great occult power. See also the note for lines 325ff.

(339ff.) These lines reveal that Leader-of-the-People has given his son to his sister Du Kamisa to rear. This is an allusion to a common practice in Mali today. If a man has a barren sister, it is customary for one of his sons to be reared in her household. The father retains his responsibility for his son, who retains his father's surname, but the social arrangement permits the sister to enjoy motherhood as a foster mother. I was told that a man may give one of his children to his sister to rear even when she has children of her own. Family ties are strengthened by this practice, which may account for its similar use among co-wives. By "swapping" children, co-wife rivalry can sometimes be diminished.

(341) *Kun-sii-kunan,* 'birth-hair'; literally, 'bitter hair.' Allusion to the Islamic naming ceremony, which occurs on the child's eighth day and involves shaving his hair.

(343) *Ko, "Sini Ku."* She said, "A thing for tomorrow." An alternative translation for lines 342 and 343 could be:

> And put it in a calabash
> Called "The Thing for Tomorrow."

(350) *Swaddling cloth.* A special cloth used to tie a child to its mother's back for transporting. Swaddling cloths are easily recognizable from the traditional patterns embroidered on them, but the cloth itself is often hidden from view by the mother's shawl.

(356-59) Allusion to the ceremony which some kings perform at the beginning of their reigns. The divination and ceremony differ from place to place but often involve the *se* (shea, karité) tree, whose name puns with *se* (power). A part of the ceremony common to the Wasulu area of Mali was described by Bourama Soumaoro. In the dark of night, the new king must strip naked and go into the forest. There he sacrifices a horse-head kola nut and climbs into a shea tree, where he shouts, *"Se bè Ne bulu!"* ('Power/shea-butter is in my hands/possession!'). When he descends from the tree, he must reenter the town without being seen.

In general, a Mande sacrifice is usually a metaphorical ceremony. The bull's black color symbolizes the earth, domain of the dead ancestors. In divining it is a negative symbol, and is represented by a downward-facing token (kola half, cowrie, groundnut shell, etc.). The bull's white color symbolizes the sky, domain of the spiritual world whose forces lead man to adventure and perhaps accomplishment, albeit fraught with danger. In divining, this symbol can be interpreted negatively or positively depending on the tradition followed by the diviner. Bearing both colors by the bull symbolizes a balance between the forces of heaven and earth, and thus stability in the future reign of the king.

For reasons not clarified by the bard, the old woman who raised the king and who is not an outsider (*kò-kan-mògò*) is excluded from the ceremony. Her exclusion from this sacrificial ceremony is symbolic of her exclusion from the family. Her resulting anger upsets the very balance of the cosmos the king is seeking in his sacrifice of the bull. His anger is thus unleashed against his aunt, which ironically upsets further the balance he seeks. The mark of a Mande hero is his ability to survive violation of social sanction and tabu. This king is no hero, for he is quite unable to control the results of the imbalance in the form of the Buffalo-Woman. This monster of the occult world ravages the land and upsets the balance of life in a manner which would prove the end of the clan. Such sorcery requires hunter-heroes to counteract the forces and reestablish the order, for the wilderness and its danger and secretive knowledge are their domain. These hunters correct the imbalance by reestablishing the responsibility of youth to respect and love their elders. Generosity succeeds where weapons fail, for it was not weapons but a relationship which was violated in the first place. Herein we observe one of the many contemporary didactic functions of the epic of Son-Jara.

The cosmological terms in Mande for balance (*ba-denya*) and chaos (*fa-denya*), which also mean 'cooperation' versus 'rivalry,' are derived from traditional roles in the extended family. Half siblings (*fa-den*, 'father's child') are expected to fight for their father's inheritance and exercise rivalry. Full siblings (*ba-den*, 'mother's child') are expected to cooperate with each other and express affection. The bound morpheme {-YA} here shifts these nouns to a different class. On a cosmological scale *ba-denya* and *fa-denya* are said to compete for control, and it is to the hunter that villagers often turn to reestablish balance.

(361) In theory, one must defer to all one's elders or one's spouse's elders (according to his/her family status). Therefore, living near an elder could limit one's personal freedom. There may be other reasons why the aunt chose to live apart, perhaps having to do with the status roles of younger sisters, about which I am unacquainted.

(362) *A ni wura*, 'you and the bush.' The bard begins these praise lines with a greeting. This form of greeting is formulaic and could be designated thus: 'you and X.' Compare these other greetings common in Mande society:

> *I ni cè*, 'you and the work' (also 'thank you').
> *I ni sugu*, 'you and the market' (said to a woman on her way to the market).
> *I ni gwa*, 'you and the kitchen' (said to a woman who has prepared a meal for you).
> *I ni sògòma/tilen/wula/su*, 'you and the morning/day/ evening/night' ('good morning/day/evening/night').

(368) *Great-Host-Slaying-Stranger*. Praise-name for Son-Jara emphasizing his ruthlessness. Any hero who violates the sanction of honoring one's host and survives the resulting cosmological imbalance is protected by the occult and gains even more protection from the violation of social norms.

(369) *Lòn*, 'to know.' Often associated with the occult, this verb may be used metaphorically in Mande. To know is to control; thus, one who has too much knowledge about a person is potentially threatening to that person.

(403) *Family sacrifice*. See lines 356-59 above.

(409) *Lamb-skin*. At a Moslem name-giving ceremony in many places in Mali (see the note for line 341 above) a lamb is sacrificed, and the skin is given to the paternal aunt. The skin symbolizes the relationship of a nephew to his aunt, for whom there is a specific term (*tènè* or *tana*).

(418) *Slashed off breasts* suggest motif Q 451.9. Punishment: woman's breasts cut off. (Thompson, *op. cit.*, 1966). This motif is frequently used in Mande folklore (see also line 2724), and powerfully symbolizes the nullification of a woman as a social person. Breasts represent a woman's primary social activity and symbolize her links to a social group. They are an important metaphor for affection and love.

 Magasi. Idiophone for the sound of slashing.

(442-46) Proverb. If one deceives a person into buying an underfed horse, then one must compensate by providing a means for cutting grass for it. The sense here is that Leader-of-the-People's bad treatment of his aunt (like selling a skinny horse) must be compensated for (grass cutter). The compensation becomes manifest in revenge.

(459) *Du ka Ginda*, 'The *Ginda* of Du.' Praise-name for the buffalo. Its meaning is obscure.

(474) *Kola*. Coming in two colors (red and white) and in many sizes, this nut is chewed throughout West Africa for its stimulant effects, as it contains caffeine. The Kola nut plays an important role in Mande social life, and is used in many social situations including greetings. Kola is also used extensively as a sacrifice, and it is to this function that the bard refers here.

(475ff.) The act of sacrificing is often preceded by divination, which helps determine the nature of the problem and its remedy. In this case, the hunters will use groundnuts (peanuts) for the divination process.

(476) It is understood by the Mande audience that the hunters have gone to the jinn to obtain the means and occult preparation for killing the buffalo.

(477) *Tiningbè Magan*. Name of the jinn. The possible meaning of the first name is obscure, although *gbè* is most likely the adjective 'white/clear/light/pale.'

(479ff.) These lines recited by one of the hunters are an incantation to summon the jinn to come forth. Lines 479 (which puns with the word for salamander) and 480 suggest an image of a round-headed monster with a pale face, flaky from leprous sores.

(481) *Nyagatè*. A Soninke surname, its usage here is obscure.

(491-94) The jinn summoned, the hunter casts the groundnut shell halves. Casting one up (toward the sky) and one down (toward the ancestors), symbolizing a balance in the cosmos, is apparently interpreted as static by the younger brother (see note for lines 356-59), who becomes angry and wants to kill the jinn. Oral transmission often results in variant forms of interpretation. A positive interpretation of the one-up, one-down sign can be found in Charles S. Bird, et al., *The Songs of Seydou Kamara: Vol. 1. Kambili* (Bloomington, Indiana: African Studies Center at Indiana University, 1974): n. 132, p. 117.

(495-501) *Su-dòn-fòli*, 'dirge.' This dirge is said to have been sung at Son-Jara's funeral. Some bards add a third line, thus:

> *Min yena kèlè kè, i ka kèlè kè!*
> He who would do battle, let him do battle!

One assistant reported that the dirge celebrates the three honorable professions of a freeman in the Manden.

(505) This *Nyani*—and there were several different *Nyanis* in Old Mali—is said to have been located on the Sankaran River (see note for line 326), just across the Mali-Guinea border. The word can be glossed as 'misery,' but it may be a homophone. Son-Jara's praise-name Nyani Mansa is sometimes explained as punning with this meaning and that of 'King of Nyani.'

(515) *Aramuri*. This type of sand divination is cast on the back of a Koranic board (*Walan*), a piece of wood measuring about eight inches by two to four feet upon which children learn to write Koranic scriptures.

(522-23) The sacrifice metaphor involved here (see note for lines 356-59) is obscure. The function of the sacrifice, however, is to hex the food and bring the old woman under the power of the hunters by getting her to eat it.

(529-32) This sequence may have been symbolized by the position of the groundnut shell halves in the divination by the jinn (see notes for lines 491-94). One up (hunters in bush, buffalo in town) and one down (hunters in town, buffalo in bush) equals static action.

(537) Laughing often accompanies extreme nervousness, and may thus be considered a traditional gesture among the Manden. The old woman sees what is happening to her and is fearful at first. The hunters finally bring her under their power by a show of respect and generosity.

(550ff.) The old woman gives up the secret of her vulnerability not only because the offense against her has been revenged but also because she realizes her time has come. She does not have the requisite power to defeat the brothers.

(554-55) In other words, the old woman grew so fat from eating and drinking that the folds of fat in her belly swelled up and popped out.

(560) *Genda-Kala,* 'spindle.' Tool used for spinning cotton and woolen fibers into thread. A typical Mande spindle is made of a thin stick about eight inches long, piercing a decorated, baked clay ball about one-and-a-half inches in diameter. This tool will be used as an occult weapon to kill the buffalo, for it contains no iron. The buffalo cannot be wounded by metal weapons.

(564) *New calabashes* are used in many ceremonies and may be symbolic of the womb.

(565) The traditional gesture of linking little fingers for oath swearing is a common practice in West Africa.

(579) *Cobra,* and the following creatures are invoked to strike down any oath swearer who breaks his/her word.

(583) *Baobab* and other trees are considered sacred, some for specific purposes.

(585) *The deer fly* bites fiercely, thus his inclusion in the list.

(586) *The datu leaf* (it may be a variety of wood sorrel) is used in the preparation of sauce. The stink it gives off is similar to putrefying flesh and is here symbolic of the smell of death.

(596ff.) The magic flight with helpful objects suggests motif D 672. Obstacle flight. Fugitives throw objects behind them which magically become obstacles in pursuer's path. (Thompson, *op. cit.,* 1966).

(606) *Tun,* 'anthill'; literally 'termite hill.' The soil from these giant mounds possesses special chemical characteristics and is mixed with mud and straw in the manufacture of bricks in some parts of Africa.

(612ff.) *Dibi,* 'shade/shadow/obscurity/invisibility.' The shade discussed here is an occult invisibility, the results of an occult preparation explained by the Buffalo-Woman. Such conjuring can be directed against specific persons to whom and perhaps only to whom the conjurer will appear invisible. The spell may not make the hunter invisible to all; it may only make the buffalo unable to see the hunter.

(613) In other words, 'Even in our own time.'

(639ff.) The buffalo begins to pursue the hunters over a vast stretch of land. The bard lists the kingdoms through which the flight occurs, and alludes to etiological legends concerning their origins. It is possible that the town names have some metaphorical value, but I have not found a satisfying exegesis.

(643) *Bèmbè*. Place name, obscure to all the assistants.

(644) *Tala Mansa Kòngò*, 'Rescuer-King-of-the-Wilderness' (and elsewhere *Tali Mansa Kòngò*, 'Bee-King-of-the-Wilderness'). Ancestor of the blacksmith clan of Kamisòkò, this king is said to have been a great wizard. Some say his totem is the bee, thus the one interpretation of his praise-name. Tala Mansa Kòngò was king of Kirina, about 50 kms. southwest of Bamako.

(645ff.) Praise-poem addressed to Tala Mansa Kòngò and the Kamisòkò clan.

Kiri. One of the ancient regions of old Mali, north of the Manden and south of Du (Do). See note for line 240. Kirina (literally 'at Kiri') is one of Kiri's principal towns.

(648) *Tèrè Kunba* and *Kaya*. Slightly obscure, but probably place names for early Kamisòkò settlements. Kaya, I was told, is the traditional name for the region around the town of Kita.

(649) *Nyani River* and *Maramu River*. Used as Kamisòkò praises, because they have clan settlements there, the locations of these rivers were obscure to the assistants.

(650) Obscure line, but it may be a symbolic reference to the two branches of the Kamisòkò: the warrior branch (the bow) and the blacksmith branch (the hammer).

(651) *Kaarta* (and *Karata*). Name of a traditional region and king-dom (from mid seventh to mid nineteenth centuries) of Bamana people. This region lies from the border with Mauritania around the cities of Nioro du Sahel and Nara, south to the area just north of Kita and east to the Niger River.

(652) *Magasa*. Regional variant of the surname Kamisòkò, or possi-bly a lineage or subclan. See the note for line 326.

(653) *Fa-Koli Dumbiya*. Nephew of Sumamuru, this warrior later deserts his uncle to become one of Son-Jara's generals. The breach is especially significant because Fa-Koli is a sister's son to Suma-muru, and this relationship is one of *ba-denya* and affection (see note for lines 356-59). Fa-Koli is considered in these lines the ancestor of all the *bula* clans (see the note for line 275), the oldest of which is considered to be Dumbiya; the other clans are said to be branches of this one. It should be pointed out, however, that

this role for Fa-Koli and his role in the epic is a telescoped anachronism. The story takes place well after the establishment of the *bula* families.

(668ff.) Praise-poem to the Kòndè (Jara) clan, most of which is obscure. The poem emphasizes the ruthlessness of Kòndè heroes, as in line 675, which praises the violation of a tabu. If a Mande hero can violate a tabu (here killing a kinsman) and survive the resulting release of occult power (*nyama*), then he may gain control over that power (line 677).

(671) *Fa-Kanda*. Obscure phrase, probably a praise-name for a Kòndè ancestor. The words may be glossed as 'birthright/inheritance,' *fa* being the word for father and *kanda* being that spiritual and mystical power inherited from the lineage.

(684) *Garabaya and Kaya*. Obscure place names. For data on Kaya, see the note for line 648.

(688ff.) Note the shift in the praise-poem from the Kòndè clan to Son-Jara.

(698) *Bin-bin-bin*. Idiophone for the sound of heaviness. The reduplication is a common intensifier and can denote repeated events.

(699) *Shea-butter tree*. See the note for lines 356-59.

(720) *Pan*. Idiophone, either for the sound of the spindle leaving the bow (e.g. "twang"), or for the sound of it piercing the buffalo's hide (e.g. "thppp").

(722-28) The Buffalo-Woman cries her last words in praise-proverb mode, the last four lines of which are a modern proverb alluding to this episode of the epic. Here the verb *lòn*, 'to know,' plays an important metaphorical role (see the note for line 369). The well is symbolic of the search for knowledge, down dark walls through the shadows to truth (water). There is no direct path to knowledge, but one must enter the darkness (*dibi*), that is danger, to obtain it. Often the path to knowledge is fraught with contradictions—Who would ever dig a twisted well? How could water be drawn from it? And the seeker is often the object of ridicule, but the acquisition of knowledge results in the acquisition of power, and in the Mande world that is one of the highest valued properties. The use of this proverb in society might imply something like the proverb, "Once bitten, twice shy."

(739ff.) This praise-poem is composed of standard, albeit variant, praise-names for hunters. Here the elder brother is praising the younger for his bravery (see the note for lines 749-51).

(739) *Snake* (blacksmith totem) *and fetish country* suggest the wilderness, and the domain of the hunter who of necessity deals extensively in the occult.

(740) *Stench* of death and danger, companions of those who deal in the occult, are suggested by this line.

(741) *Cutter-of-Fresh-Heart* and *Cutter-of-Fresh-Liver.* Allusions to a sort of communion ceremony which takes place over freshly killed game. Hearts and livers, thought by many to contain much occult power (*nyama*), are cooked and shared among the hunters soon after the kill. This traditional gesture exists among many ethnic groups in Africa and Arabia, not necessarily accompanied by a folk belief.

(742-43) *King-of-the-Wilderness.* Past the boundary (*dankun*) of the village, one enters the wilderness, domain of danger and *fadenya* (see note for lines 356-59). This praise-name carries the connotation of a hero of great strength and control over the occult.
    Kininbi and *Kalinka* are obscure.

(744-48) Standard formulaic style of presenting opposites common in Mande poetry. Town dwellers have no power in the bush, and hunters are powerless in the town.

(749-51) Etiological legend explaining the origin of the surname Jabaatè (Jabagatè), a clan of casted bards, based on a folk etymology of its syllables. *Jè*, 'to reject' is suffixed with *-baga*, 'agent/ ER.' *Tè* is a negative marker. Though incorrect grammatically, it was explained to me that the implied meaning is: 'There is no refuser'; i.e. one who would refuse to reward the bard after his praises were sung could not be found.

(752) *Sangoyi, the Long-Bow.* Same man as Kala Jula Sangoyi. See note for line 5.

(761) *Kòròkò.* Mande surname.

(770) The person referred to is Massa Makan Diabaté (Jabaatè), then researcher at the Institut des Sciences Humaines du Mali and one of the men who assisted in collecting the epic.

(772) The hunters will use all the items they stack together as tokens of proof that they are the ones who killed the buffalo. Motifs suggested here are H 80, Identification by tokens, and H 111, Identification by garment. (Thompson, *op. cit.*, 1966).

(776) *Lounging platform.* Located at the center of most villages, the lounging platform is the gathering place for the town meetings and often merely the center of local conversation in the evenings.

(794) *Tawulen*, 'royal drum,' from the Arabic word *el-tabl.* This word may have ultimately come from a Sanskrit word.

(796) *Like it or not.* The message of the drum, based on an onomatopoeic interpretation of the drum's sound, which is said to resemble the compound verb *ka diya-guya*, 'to be forced/compelled.' In short, drop everything and come to the village square.

(799-800) Motif Q 112, Half of a kingdom as a reward, is suggested by this line. (Thompson, *op. cit.,* 1966).

(802-04) Possibly a proverb, these lines imply that trying to help a leper is a waste of time, for he knows best what he needs. The relevance to the text is obscure.

(824) *Modibo Keyta.* President of the Republic of Mali at the time of the recording of this epic. The following genealogy will help clarify these lines. It is taken from Jean-Marie Kònè, "Portrait et Profil" in his *Les 50 Ans* (Koulouba, Mali: Imprimerie du Mali, c1965): 57-65.

Lamuru Keyta

|

Daba Keyta = Fatuma Kamara

|

Modibo Keyta

(828) *Jire* (Djiré) is the home town of Modibo Keyta. It is located near Nioro du Sahel in the northwest of Mali.

(830-31) The reference here is to transportation by airplane (see line 1233 below).

(833-34) These two lines praising Son-Jara may be used in Modibo's praise-poem, for both are surnamed Keyta. Any familial or ancestral praise-line may be used in a poem celebrating any of the clan's members.

(847) *Tura Magan.* The most illustrious member of the Tarawere clan, the descendant of Dan Mansa Wulandin, is here praised in a poem actually recited to a predecessor. Because Tura Magan is considered the greatest Tarawere, his name is used to praise all Taraweres. See note for lines 833-34.

(851ff.) Three motifs are suggested here: B 391, Animal grateful for food; B 421, Helpful dog; and B 422, Helpful cat. (Thompson, *op. cit.,* 1966).

(873-76) The symbol here is that of seduction. A woman's legs spread apart symbolizes her sexual availability. Thus she is taught as a young girl to sit with her legs held tightly together. I have also observed this traditional gesture in Somalia and suspect that it can be found in other parts of Africa.

(880) Motif L 102, Unpromising heroine, is suggested here. (Thompson, *op. cit.,* 1966).

(934) The spittle of a saint or shaman is commonly used as a healing medicine in many parts of Africa and the Middle East. A greeting gesture I once observed in Mali equated spittle with a blessing. Asking the blessing of a bard and diviner, a woman held out her

cupped hands before her. The bard audibly spit into her hands, though the act was symbolic, for there was no moisture involved in the gesture. The woman then wiped her face with her hands, symbolically bathing her face with the blessing. I have also observed actual and symbolic spitting in Amhara and Oromo greetings in Ethiopia. In Mali incantations over various libations are generally terminated by spitting into the mixture before it is consumed. The moisture of the spittle vitalizes the power of the brew.

(950-61) The reference is to social custom. Elder brothers usually marry first, and the family's wealth goes to furnish him with bridewealth. Younger brothers must wait their turn. This tradition is also suggestive of Motif T 131.2, Younger child may not marry before elder. (Thompson, *op. cit.*, 1966).

(965) *Lelelele.* Idiophone, possibly representing the passage of time.

(968) *Seek pleasure and duty,* literally 'to seek *sunnah* and *farila* with her.' Reference to Islamic marriage law. The *sunnah* ('custom/ use') is composed of revelations and articles of faith recorded after the completion of the Koran and may be the most important source of doctrine next to that book. The term *farila* is obscure, but I was told that it is another source of Moslem law. Islamic law speaks of sexual intercourse as a man's duty to his wife as well as his pleasure, and it is this point that is implied in this line.

(972) *Bilililili.* Idiophone for the sound of Sugulun stretching out her body.

(1010-14) The meaning of these so-called ancient greetings is obscure. They are often quoted in epic poetry in variant forms, but they are not commonly used today.

(1028) *Nakana Tiliba.* A great sorceress, the head of the nine Queens-of-Darkness, about whom the plot will later speak (see below lines 1937ff).

(1031) *Bilāl.* See note for line 173.

(1033) *Token.* This talisman or amulet is very powerful and full of *barakah,* 'grace/power.'

(1034-37) This episode is described as preordained and foretold.

(1051-52) In other words, the struggle for birthright and inheritance.

(1060) The old women excuse their neglect to deliver the message with this expression (i.e., one should prepare oneself).

(1063) *Tumu Maninya.* Legendary female bard who is said to have invented the musical instrument called the iron rasp (*karinya, nkarinya, karanya, ŋarinya, ŋgarinè*), a cylindrical musical instrument split open from one end to the other and grooved along each side of the split. A metal wire is used to play the iron rasp, either by "rasping" the cylinder along the grooves or by clanging it on either end.

(Between 1072 & 1073) The bard took a break at this point in the performance, after about one and a half hours of singing. When he resumed, he took up the plot further on, beyond the point where he left it. Such gaps are common in oral recitations and are hardly noticed by the audience, most of whom are thoroughly acquainted with the plot. In the transformation from oral to written styles, however, such gaps can be disturbing, particularly to an audience foreign to the story. For clarification the missing plot has been inserted in prose, but the line numbering of the poetry remains consecutive.

(1076) *Bèrè-bèrè-bèrè.* Idiophone for dryness.

(1080) *Woman.* Error; the bard means women.

(1082) *Those-Caught-by-their-Craws.* Pejorative name for the old women. It is somewhat misleading to give the name praise-poetry to a genre which also includes a rich tradition of pejorative names.

(1084) *Bòkòlen.* Idiophone for great noise.

(1097) It would be very unusual for two co-wives to be confined in the same hut. The bard has probably put them together for literary reasons, especially for the next episode concerning how the boys get their names.

(1119) *Lucky Karunga.* Praise- (or pejorative-) name for Sugulun Kòndè. The meaning is obscure.

(1125) *Ba.* We translated *ba,* 'mother,' as grandmother to avoid confusion. The old woman is the mother of Fara Magan the Handsome.

(1139) *All hair!* See the note for line 1. Jara, which means 'lion,' is covered with hair at birth, signifying his destiny as a ruthless hero. Motif F 521.1, Man covered with hair like animal, is suggested here. (Thompson, *op. cit.,* 1966). Another interesting occurrence of this motif is in Genesis 25:25, where Esau (meaning 'covering'), whose younger brother Jacob "stole" his birthright from him, is described as covered with hair at birth.

(1152) *Holyman.* See note for line 274.

(1165) *Ḥājj.* The Moslem pilgrimage to Mecca.

(1166) *Ka'bah.* Center of the pilgrimage to Mecca, the *Ka'bah* is a large square building, covered with a big black cloth, and containing a sacred stone. Certain religious ceremonies are performed in and around the *Ka'bah* during the season of the *ḥājj.*

(1178) *Dònba.* See note for line 171.

(1180) *Retreat.* A 27-day isolation, or retreat (*kaluwa*), during which time the diviner performs his duties. Food and drink are brought to him, but he may not see or speak with anyone. When someone has been absent from his friends for a while, he is jokingly asked, *I tun bè kaluwa la wa?,* 'Have you been on retreat?'

(1181) In other words, from performing divination so often.

(1187-89) *Rams.* The symbolism here is that black represents darkness, a major symbol for sorcery. White represents daylight, the state of being known. The black-headed ram, of course, wins, for its power is greater. This sign is taken as a foretelling of Son-Jara's ascendancy to the throne.

(1189) *Dankaran Tuman.* Son-Jara's elder brother's name. He is the Berete woman's son.

(1197-98) *Knowing never fails,* etc. Proverb used in praise-proverb mode; in other words, everything becomes known in its proper time.

(1208) *Kong.* Town in northern Ivory Coast, on the west side of the Komoé National Park.

(1212) The potion is for healing the dog's sore mouth.

(1244) The allusion here is to a meeting (probably a political rally) in Dakar in which the bard touched Modibo Keyta, then president of Mali, in the crowd.

(1247) *Disperser-of-Women.* Praise-name for Modibo's mother, emphasizing her beauty and/or power.

(1283) *An d'an yèrè sòrò,* 'We have found our freedom/independence.' This phrase is idiomatic and translates literally, 'We have found ourselves.'

(1292) *Couscous.* A type of cracked millet in West Africa.

(1295) The leaves of the baobab tree are used in making a tasty sauce.

(1302) *Bilika.* Idiophone for the sound of falling tears.

(1311ff.) *King of Nyani,* etc. Elsewhere, this praise-poem is ascribed to Nyani Mansa Kara (Kuru), another legendary figure in Mande tradition. Variation of this type, which might be termed "floating praise-poetry," is common in Mande folklore. Another example is the praise-poem called *Janjon,* which is ascribed to more than one hero (see notes for lines 1813-28 and 1844-58). Two other themes in Mande folklore are of interest in this respect. The envy of a praise-poem, which sometimes leads the envier to slay and "steal" the poem for himself, and the use of praise-poetry as payment for services rendered or promised may be isolated. The latter theme, for example, is said to be the manner in which the praise-poem called *Duga* came to be sung for the illustrious Bamana king of Segu, Da Monson Jara.

(1311) *Nyani.* See note for line 505.

(1327) *Thickener.* Any foodstuff, such as okra, which makes a sauce sticky and gooey.
Black Lele. Ceratotheca sesamoides.

(1343) This sentence translates literally, 'He arrived between upness and downness.'

(1345) It is understood here and in line 1362 that the iron bar is not strong enough to hold Son-Jara up.(1368) Son-Jara defines his failure to rise as his mother's affair, for the spiritual world is her concern. He instructs her to seek more help. Not enough has yet been done to circumvent the Berete woman's curses.

(1372) *Jònba* (also *sunsun,* glossed in folk etymology as 'origin of origins'),'custard apple tree' (*Diospyros mespiliformis*). Oaths are frequently sworn over custard apple branches in Mande society and reported in folklore. Other traditions based upon its occult power also exist. For example, if an elderly person becomes ill somewhere outside his/her compound, he/she may be given a custard apple branch for a staff. Not only may it be leaned upon but it is believed by some that strength is gleaned from the occult power in the staff. In this manner the ill person may gain enough strength to return home where he/she may die in peace. It is this belief in the occult power of the custard apple branch that is reflected in its use as a staff for Son-Jara's rising in line 1410.

(1395-96) In other words, the woman swears her oath on her virginity at marriage and fidelity afterwards.

(1412) *Clasped his legs.* Traditional gesture for greeting a hunter hero.

(1424) *Danka.* Idiophone, the meaning of which is obscure.

(1425) *Kapok* and *Flame trees* grow tall and straight. The image may be a comparison of Son-Jara's legs with these trees.

(1436) *Tunyu Tanya.* Idiophone, the meaning of which is obscure, but some assistants thought it suggested the gait of walking or swaying from side to side, albeit with force.

(1441-45) In other words, muddy water (Dankaran Tuman) cannot be compared to pure water (Son-Jara). The idiophone *wasili* is obscure and lines 1444 and 1445 were inaudible on the tape.

(1479) *Yrrrrr.* Idiophone for the sound of a surging crowd.

(1484-87) In other words, the reason Son-Jara walks today cannot be "known" and counteracted through sorcery, for Son-Jara's occult power is now too strong.

(1528) *Gejebu.* Idiophone for the sound of Son-Jara's mother kneeling on the ground.

(1540) *The tail* of wild game is considered strong in occult power (*nyama*) and is often kept as a trophy. It is also used in conjury. By giving the trophy to the elder, Son-Jara is acknowledging his elder brother's birthright in spite of the pronouncement of his father, who, incidentally, is not mentioned again in the epic. The rivalry, however, has gone too far to be reversed now.

(1553) *Ma'an*. Contraction of Magan.

(1575) *Safo-dog*. A favorite sacrifice, but its exact nature is obscure. The dog is considered an animal possessed of extraordinary occult power.

(1581–82) It is unusual to restrain a dog so thoroughly. The viciousness of the dog symbolizes the ruthlessness of its owner.

(1586) This line was a false start.

(1593) *Causer-of-Loss*. Praise-name for Son-Jara, emphasizing his ruthlessness.

(1594–95) These lines imply that it is usual to restrain a cow in such a fashion, but unusual to so restrain a dog.

(1602) *Tomorrow's Affair*. Symbolic of Son-Jara's coming to power in the future.

(1608) *Fèsè fèsè fèsè*. Idiophone for the sound of the dog ripping the flesh of the other dog.

(1617) The "something" is strong occult power.

(1619) *Younger-Leave-Me-Be*. Symbolic of the elder's fear that his younger brother will usurp his power.

(1620) *Sin-ji tègè*, 'to sever the bonds of family'; literally, 'to cut off breast milk.' See note for line 418.

(1652) *Tail*. An insulting pun, meaning leave at once.

(1653–54) *Sugulun Kulunkan* and *Manden Bukari* are Son Jara's full siblings (*ba-denlu*). He therefore has no traditional rivalry with them as he does with Dankaran Tuman, his half-brother (*fa-den*).

(1657) In other words, I will chop through your neck so hard that an ax or sword will bury itself in the ground the length of a hand span before it comes to a halt.

(1671) *The Kuyatè matriarch* is the female bard Tumu Maniya. See note for line 1063.

(1692) *They* are the followers of Dankaran Tuman.

(1699) *Karanga*. Obscure name. Jobi, the Seer, (line 1701) is said to have been from the Kònatè clan.

(1703–15) A digression which alludes to an etiological legend unknown to the assistants. It appears to concern the founding of the town of Bisandugu which is in Guinea near Sananko, where Samory Ture was born.

(1708) Line obscure on tape. For Mount Genu, see note for line 218.

(1718ff.) *Tulunbèn*, King of the region of Kolè with its capital at S i-giri in modern northeast Guinea, is an ancestor of the Magasu-baa clan.

(1740-45) The motivation for this sacrifice is obscure but may involve Son-Jara's need for a powerful sacrifice to protect him on his next stopover with the sorceresses. Note that the drastic sacrifice destroys King Tulunbèn, but does not harm the more powerful hero Son-Jara. Again, the violation of tabu by a hero is done to gain occult power.

(1749) *Arakan* (*arkān* in Arabic), 'litany'; literally, 'pillar of faith,' of which ritual prayer (*ṣalāh, ṣalāt*) is one of five. The litany (*arraga'ah*) is the first part of each daily prayer, which is what the bard is referring to here.

(1765) *Fikiri,* possibly 'Place-of-the-Bound.' Name of a lake.

(1766) Obscure passage, possibly alluding to an old form of public punishment similar to dunking.

(1778) Note abrupt change of scene. We are transported back to the Manden and the affairs of King Dankaran Tuman.

(1780) *Ta-Suma-Gani-Latè,* 'Caress-of-Hot-Fire,' appears to be a praise-name for King Dankaran Tuman's daughter, emphasizing her sexual appeal.

(1781) *Dòka the Cat* is Son-Jara's royal bard, usurped by Dankaran Tuman when he exiled Son-Jara.

(1782) *Susu Mountain Sumamuru Kantè.* Sorcerer king of the country of Susu, casted blacksmith, scourge of Islam, and archenemy of Son-Jara.

(1786) *Balaphone.* Musical instrument resembling the xylophone. The keys are made of rosewood, and calabashes of different sizes tied below the keys provide resonance. Players often attach metal jinglers to their hands which resonate when the keys are struck with mallets. The word balaphone is a combination of the Mandekan word *bala* and the English suffix -phone.

(1797) *Dark Forest.* Both words are images of the occult. *Dibi,* 'darkness,' implies the secretive milieu of sorcery, while the forest symbolizes the realm of chaos (see note for lines 356-59). The image is of a pagan sorcerer-king's domain.

(1813ff.) The *Janjon* is a floating praise-poem, sung here for Sumamuru (see the note for lines 1311ff.). This poem is said to be sung to warriors going into battle. Another praise-poem called the *Duga* is said to be sung to warriors coming out of battle. Lines 1813-15 are Kantè clan ancestors, while lines 1816-28 are praise-names for Sumamuru, emphasizing his occult power and ruthlessness.

(1825) *King of Yesteryear* (or King of Tradition/Traditional King), praise-name for Sumamuru strongly suggesting a pagan versus Moslem theme in the epic, with Son-Jara representing the Moslem forces. Some have suggested this theme as the key to understanding the real meaning of the epic. It seems more likely, however, that many other themes are of equal importance. In any case, Islam in Mande tradition syncretized with the pagan forces it fights. See note for lines 325ff.

(1835) The audience acquainted with the legend understands at this point that Sumamuru's occult power enables him to hear his balaphone no matter where he is at the time it is played.

(1837) Sumamuru suspects the bard of being a jinn (see the note for line 103), because Dòka the Cat was able to penetrate and survive Sumamuru's occult world.

(1844–45) *Kukuba,* etc. These four villages are sites of confrontation at which Son-Jara has the upper hand over Sumamuru after the turning point of their struggle. Stylistically they are matched by villages which Son-Jara founds after confrontations in which Sumamuru gains the upper hand (see notes for lines 2636ff).

(1872–74) *Hair shaving.* Part of the Moslem naming ceremony on the eighth day of a child's life. See the note for line 341. Here its use symbolizes rebirth.

(1874) The explanation for this name change is left out of this variant. When it is included, it is an etiological legend based on a folk etymology of the names, thus:

> *bala* = 'balaphone'
> *Fasege,* from *I fasa kè* = 'do your praise'
> *Kuyatè* from *ku ye an cè* = 'there is a matter between us'

The combination of the names is thus said to mean, 'I praise thee with the balaphone, for there is something between us.' The "something" is the master/bard relationship of a casted man to his patron.

(1883–84) *Vicious dog.* Proverb used as a warning to King Dankaran Tuman. The sense is that if the king kills his own vicious dog (Son-Jara), then another dog (enemy) will attack him.

(1890–91) The reference here is obscure.

(1893–1902) Etiological legend based on a folk etymology. King Dankaran Tuman and his entourage flee the Manden, now coming under Susu sovereignty, and go to live in Guinea. Nsèrèkòrè (or Nsèrèkòrò) is in extreme southwestern Guinea close to the borders of both Liberia and Côte d'Ivoire. According to this legend, the new ethnic name for the people becomes Kisi (line 1899), which is the Maninka verb, 'to be spared.' Actually the Kisi belong linguistically to the West Atlantic family which includes Temne, Wolof, Fulani and Serer. Masanta (line 1900) is about

120 kms. to the north-northwest of Nsèrèkòrò. The surname Gindo (line 1902) is a common name among the ethnic group called Dogon and appears to be out of place geographically since no Kisi families bear this surname. The Dogon live in Mali to the north and east of Bamako.

(1905) *Gourds in mouths.* Although described in this variant as a literal action, the image is one of government censorship and repression. No one was permitted to speak out.

(1910ff.) Son-Jara's journey to and subsequent mastery over the nine Queens-of-Darkness suggests Motif F 81, Descent to lower world of dead, and functions to empower him close to the point of invulnerability. (Thompson, *op. cit.,* 1966). Many praise-names also emphasize the ruthlessness of the stock Mande hero figure, especially as a violator of tabu. By surviving the release of occult power caused by violating a tabu, the hero gains control over that power. Accomplishing this task is not easy (compare the praise line, 'A man of power is hard to find'), as witnessed by Son-Jara's near miss with the nine witches. Son-Jara's exile appears to function as a period of strengthening his forces, both military and spiritual, which he must do in order to defeat the strong sorcerer king Sumamuru. The exile, or retreat, in order to gain strength is a common motif in Africa and Arabia.

(1910-11) *Kankira,* etc. These two men are ancestors of the Saginugu clan of blacksmiths.

(1913) *Red bull.* The color of the bull symbolizes the forces of *fadenya* (see note for lines 356-59).

(1928) Not returning the greeting is a grave insult, emphasizing the extreme antisocial behavior of the witches.

(1935ff.) The sacrifice which these sorceresses will perform needs some explanation. In the traditional theology of many Mande-speaking peoples, the individual is believed to have a spiritual wraith (*ja*), which is located in the body during waking hours. (Moslems and Christians have used the term to mean 'soul.') The wraith may wander out of the body when its master is asleep, and it becomes visible as one's shadow in the sunlight. It is the *ja* which is visible in mirrors and is the image seen in photographs.

The form of conjury these sorceresses practice involves the removal of a person's *ja* from his/her body through occult means. The *ja* is then put into an animal (in this case, the red bull), which is slaughtered and eaten in communion. Once the animal is consumed, there is no possible reversal of the sacrifice. The sorceresses have no trouble regenerating the bull (after all they have power over life and death), but it will be noticed that the conjury is reversed before the communion ceremony takes place.

(1937) *Nakana Tiliba.* The head sorceress may be the same person as Son-Jara's aunt. See line 1028.

(1939) In other words, endless questions only lead to trouble, so do as you are told.

(1967) Motif D 112.1, Transformation: man to lion, is suggested by this line. (Thompson, *op. cit.,* 1966).

(1988) *Custard apple tree.* Sacred tree (see note for line 1372), which will be used in a divination ceremony later. Unfortunately the bard forgot to describe the ceremony at the proper time in the plot. This ceremony will help Son-Jara decide where to go next on his exile. It involves taking the custard apple branch to a fork in the road and striking it on each of the paths in expectation of being shown certain signs, either a spring of blood or milk. The interpretation of these signs exists in variant form. Some bards, such as the late Kèlè Mònsòn Jabaatè of Kita, interpret the milk as representing cosmic balance between *fa-denya* and *ba-denya* (see note for lines 356-59 and for lines 491-94); thus, it is the GO sign. The blood is seen as chaos and imbalance and is interpreted as the STAY sign (see lines 1202-16, pp. 278-79 of Rex Moser, "Foregrounding in the Sunjata, The Mande Epic," Ph.D. dissertation Indiana University Linguistics Department, 1974). Other bards, such as Fa-Digi's son Magan Sisòkò, interpret blood as the GO sign, presumably because it represents the seeking for power in dangerous places. In this context, milk would represent the static, safe, and weak fortune; thus it would be the STAY sign. Whichever interpretation is used, Son-Jara always gets the GO sign to proceed to the city of Mèma.

(1991) *Jula Fundu.* Place name, obscure to the assistants.

(1992) *Mossi.* A Voltaic people, most of whom live in Burkina Faso.

(1995ff.) No motif number could be found for the regeneration of the bull, part by part. However, I know this motif to be traditional, for it provides the basis for several folktales and legends in West Africa. See, for example, the Jabo narrative entitled "The Cow Tail Switch" found on pp. 85-88 of Harold Courlander, *A Treasury of African Folklore* (New York: Crown Pubs., Inc., 1975).

(2002) *Knots* are used in many amulets, or they are tied into the strings which hold them, in order to strengthen the efficacy of the amulet. Amulets with knotted strings attached to them are called *tafo.*

(2005) *Kitibili Kintin.* Incantation, the meaning of which is obscure.

(2015-16) *Messenger.* A formula divorcing the messenger from the responsibility of the content of his message. Traditionally, messengers have an immunity from any bad news contained in their messages. The formula is needed because the tabu of harming the messenger may be violated like any other tabu.

(2020ff.) Son-Jara sends the messenger back to Sumamuru with veiled messages (some are proverbs) as warnings.

(2021-22) *Friday milk.* When shepherds care for the herds of others, payment for their services may include the milk drawn on Friday, the holy day. Milk from any other day may not be offered for sacrifice, because it is not the shepherd's to give. With this proverb, Son-Jara warns Sumamuru that he may not rule the Manden for it is not his "Friday milk."

(2023-24) Proverb. The *wet nurse* is Sumamuru and the child is the Manden. In other words, Sumamuru may rule the Manden temporarily, but it will never be his child to keep.

(2025) The image of the elder as king belongs to Son-Jara, although he was not the first-born.

(2040) *Dugunò.* Clan name.

(2042) *Sigi game.* Variant explanations exist for this game. The one described in this text seems to be the modern game *of npari,* or *nperi* (see note for line 2046), and *sigi* is described as the "ancestor" of modern games. The bard describes their development in terms of a genealogy. The most detailed variant explanation for *sigi* I found came from the late bard Wa Kamisòkò from Kirina. He defined *sigi flu* as 'casting out doubt,' and described it as an ancient test whereby combatants in Old Mali gave proof of their genealogy. Those warriors too close in kinship, or who belonged to clans which had sworn alliances, were not permitted to fight each other.

The game was described as follows. The two adversaries came together over a large pot of boiling potash (*sègè-kata*). Large metal bracelets (*sigi-nègè*) were then put into the boiling potash. Next the two men recited their genealogies and swore they spoke the truth. The test came when they cast their hands into the boiling potash. If a hand was burned before its owner could get the bracelet on, he was lying. If no kinship existed, the warriors were free to face each other on the battle field, but because so much occult power was released during the test, only one weapon could slay the pair tested in the *sigi* game. The special bullet (*sigi-nègè-den*) is cylindrical in shape and measures about one-half inch long. These metal objects are available for sale in most modern markets today for use in occult preparations which market sellers refused to explain to me.

The function of the *sigi* game in this text is obscure, because it is not clear who sent Kabala Simbon to Mèma with it. If sent by Son-Jara's enemies, it would appear to be a way of tricking him into erring so that his occult power might be circumvented and his demise assured. If sent by his supporters or potential future subjects, the function would be different. Other texts, for example the Kèlè Mònsòn variant mentioned in the note for line 1988, treat the *sigi* game as an ordeal of wisdom, applied to Son-Jara in order to determine his worthiness to become king.

(2045) *Wori* (*Woli, Wari*). The familiar African (Caribbean, South Asian) game of shifting tokens from one of twelve or more holes to the next. Many variants of this game exist all over the world, and the game often goes by the generic name derived from Arabic, "Mankala." For a good description of the African variants, see Claudia Zaslavsky, "The Game Played by Kings and Cowherds, and Presidents, Too!" in her *Africa Counts* (Boston: Prindle, Weber & Schmidt, 1973): 116-36. An excellent survey of the variant rules of this game may be found in Laurence Russ's *Mancala Games* (Algonac, Michigan: Reference Pubs., 1984).

(2046) *Pari* (*npari, nperi*). Try as I might, I could never quite grasp the rules of this popular Malian game. It is played on a mound of sand (or dirt), upon which a set of geometric designs is drawn. Pairs of sticks are put into position alternately by two players. In the second part of the game, the players begin to move and jump opposing sticks, sometimes with one stick, sometimes with the pair. The player who eliminates his opponent's sticks (or a certain number of them) wins.

(2077) This line is a false start.

(2093ff.) *Watarawaa,* etc. The ritualistic phrases the Prince must recite. The meanings of *watarawaa* and *nderen* are obscure.

(2106ff.) *Watarawaa,* etc. The ritualistic answer that Son-Jara must properly pronounce in response to the king's challenge. The meanings of *faringa, nkuramè* and *jòn jòn jòn are* obscure.

(2203) *Like it or not.* See note for line 796.

(2204) *Tabule.* Variant of *Tawulen.* See note for line 794.

(2232) Error, which the bard corrects on the next line. Kankuba Kantè would have been kin to Sumamuru.

(2233-34) *Sugulun Kòndè.* Error by the bard, who means Sugulun Kònatè. Son-Jara's sister who is also called Sugulun Kulunkan in this variant. The increasing number of errors would suggest that the bard is getting tired.

(2235ff.) The image of Sugulun tearing off the gourds (see note for line 1905) symbolizes the use of her sorcery to give the Manden rebels power to take action independent of Sumamuru's control. From this point in the epic, it is Son-Jara's sister who inherits the status of supporting sorceress from her mother. Also from this point we witness the growth of Son-Jara's occult power and the weakening of Sumamuru's.

(2237) *Sara (Sira, Sita) Fada (Fara).* Ancestor of the Jawara ethnic group, this bard later accompanies Tura Magan in the conquest of the Gambia (see below, lines 3024ff.). According to one variant, Tura Magan gave Sara Fada the golden throne of the Dark King of Jòlòf.

Around 1964, an event in Mali occurred which was a direct result of this legend. A group of Jawaras, who had long since migrated to the sacred city of Kaaba (Kangaba) near the border with Guinea and Mali, converted to Islam. I was told that at that time, they melted down a large object of gold and sold it on the open market. Elders of this group explained that this object had been the throne of the Dark King of Jòlòf. It was reported that the melting was done because they feared use of the throne as a pagan fetish. This event has become the basis of a large body of variant legends. Another version, for example, claimed that the object was Tura Magan's spear or sword, which was cut up, divided among its caretakers, and sold in the gold market in Bamako, after which I assume it was melted down.

(2238) *Those people* are the Manden rebels.

(2260) *Fa-Kandi Tunandi.* This character was obscure to all the assistants.

(2273 & 2276) Error by the bard, same as explained in note for lines 2233–34.

(2275) *Ki-nyina,* 'club rat.' The translation is conjectural here. A *ki-nyina* (literally 'creek rat') lives in swampy areas and around rivers and might be a muskrat.

(2279) In other words, Sugulun extracts the hearts and livers by means of conjuring, not by slaughtering the animals, and transports them back to her kitchen also by use of occult medicine. These highly valued parts are needed to serve to the guests from the Manden.

(2304) *Joma,* etc. Two villages on the Sankaran River in Guinea.

(2308) *Garan.* At this point in the recitation, the bard's naamu-sayer was replaced by another man named Garan.

(2360) The dishonor mentioned would have been not having sustenance for the guests.

(2369) In other words, his verbal abuse and bad temper are enough to release sufficient occult power to blow off his sister's dress. This act is a symbol of her public embarrassment.

(2377) *Hamina.* Place name, obscure to all the assistants.

(2396ff.) The bard digresses to self praise. Massa Makan (see the note for line 770) had asked *Fa-Digi* to make a recording for the national radio station.

(2403) The reference here is to the request for this performance of the epic. The white man is Charles S. Bird, who collected the text.

(2411) *Se,* 'shea tree.' See note for lines 356-59.

(2420ff.) *Ah, God,* etc. An incantation to rejuvenate the shea tree. Note the religious syncretism in this episode. The God of Islam is consulted for materials needed to sacrifice to a pagan fetish.

(2443) *Change dwelling.* Euphemism for death; i.e. 'let me die.'

(2451) Son-Jara prepares his mother and buries her in secret because of her powerful sorcery. Grave robbing, I was told, was common in Mali, especially because a powerful person's fetishes are sometimes buried with him/her, and the site may be treated as a shrine. One such shrine near Kirina is believed to be that of Son-Jara himself, though similar claims are made in other parts of Mali and Guinea.

(2464-65) The reason the people of Mèma wanted payment for the land is obscure. One assistant suggested that they may have wished to discourage Son-Jara from burying his mother in their land for fear that leaving her behind might constitute grounds for a claim to the throne of Mèma.

(2475) *Sigi-nègè,* 'cornerstone fetish.' I am not sure if this object is the same as the one mentioned in the note for line 2042. The reference may be to the *sigi-nègè-den* mentioned in the same note.

(2486-90) This passage is obscure, and has given rise to several variant transcriptions, the most reasonable of which is translated here.

(2513) In other words, this "payment" is a veiled message of warning from Son-Jara to Prince Burama. Note that the list of items put into the bag does not exactly match the list of items spilled out of the bag. This type of inconsistency is very common in epic poetry.

(2534) Note that in public Son-Jara is actually burying a log. (See note for line 2451.)

(2535ff.) This part of the epic is suggestive of motif L 111.1, Exile returns and succeeds. (Thompson, *op. cit.,* 1966).

(2557ff.) *Dabò,* from *a d'a bò,* 'he pulled it off.' Etiological legend of the origin of the Dabò clan based on a folk etymology of its name. In this text, the Dabò is a casted man. To be thrown by a casted man is an insult to Son-Jara's honor, thus the reaction from Tura Magan.

(2578) *Sòmònò*, boatman. Not an ethnic or clan name, but a group of clans among the Mande-speakers, who earn their living on the rivers as fishermen and transporters, or who are considered to have originated in this profession. Among the Bamana, the Sòmònò are not casted.

(2636ff.) The founding of these towns is symbolic of Son-Jara's failure to defeat Sumamuru, whose occult remains stronger than Son-Jara's at this point. Note that each village is celebrated in a praise-poem which plays upon the meaning of its name. See also the note for lines 1844-45.

(2689) The seduction of Sumamuru by Son-Jara's sister is suggestive of motif N 476, Secret of unique vulnerability disclosed. (Thompson, *op. cit.*, 1966).

(2699ff.) At this point Sumamuru begins to disclose the secrets of his sacrifice for control over the Manden. I am not certain of the sacrifice metaphor here.

(2723) In other words, he severs his relationship with her. See note for line 418.

(2727) Sumamuru's mother disowns him as well, cutting off another part of his occult strength and weakening him further.

(2731ff.) The reference here is to a custom of marriage. There is a tradition which requires a wife to return to her parents' house after one week of marriage for a final visit and to get her dowry. When she marries, part of her dowry are her *minèn-kolon,* 'useful containers.' This collection is composed of calabashes and other containers and stirring devices, such as the calabash spoon Sugulun mentions. A small *minèn-kolon* is considered disgraceful. Sugulun uses this custom as a trick to escape to Son-Jara's camp.

(2753) Fa-Koli's wife is a powerful sorceress; thus Sumamuru envies and steals her from his nephew. In this variant, the theft of his wife drives Fa-Koli into Son-Jara's camp, and further weakens the Susu king, while strengthening Son-Jara.

(2755ff.) *Let the fonio increase,* etc. Incantation said over the food to cause it to increase.

(2758) *Groundpea,* also called Bambara pea (*Voandzia subterranea*).

(2765-66 & 2768-69) Lines unfortunately obscure on the tape. It was probably here that Sumamuru stole Fa-Koli's wife, and Fa-Koli abandoned his uncle Sumamuru.

(2770) Praise-names for Fa-Koli.

(2796) *Caress-of-Hot-Fire.* See note for line 1780.

(2844) *Kukuba.* See the notes for lines 1844-45 and 2637ff.

(2862) *Kulu-Kòrò.* Village about 50 kms. northeast of Bamako on the Niger River. The name is said to mean 'Under-the-Mountain,' and its origin is said to be connected to this legend. Suma-muru is finally defeated here, and, according to one legend, he disappeared into a cave "under the mountain" near the village.

(2883) *Nyɔnyɔwu.* Idiophone for the sound of Sumamuru drying up. Note the implication that weapons could never harm him, even in his hour of death, for his occult power was too strong for weapons.

(2884) *Nyanan,* 'sacred fetish.' This fetish is still revered and is thought by its disciples to be served by the spirit of Sumamuru. The fetish is a globe-shaped stone, which has carved interlacing diamond patterns on its surface. Chicken feathers and kola nuts were in evidence when I visited the fetish, which is served by a priest of the Kulubali clan and protected by members of the Jara clan who are in the majority in Kulu-Kòrò. I was told that the fetish is consulted for many reasons, among them barrenness in women.

(2889) *Stranger,* etc. Praise-name for Son-Jara, emphasizing his ruthlessness. The image is that he is a stranger in a village in the morning, and by the afternoon he has conquered it and become its chief.

(2930) *Serew.* Idiophone for the sound of the balaphone being put on Mansa Sama's head.

(2942) *Jon jon.* Idiophone, the meaning of which is obscure.

(2949-50) Son-Jara sends these two men on a trading mission to buy horses in the Gambia.

(2957) *Dark Jòlòf,* Kingdom of the Wolof ethnic group who live in modern Senegal and The Gambia. The dark image is related to the occult.

(2960) Exchanging the horses for dogs is an insult to Son-Jara.

(2974) One of the self-stated functions of bards is to spur men on to heroic deeds. This function does not always please the men they encourage.

(2985-91) Note that the bard grows weary, and a few lines falter here.

(3006-07) Tura Magan lies alive in his grave as a symbol of his grief. As a result, Son-Jara gives the army to him, and he gains his most well-known praise-name, *su-sare-jòn,* 'Slave-of-the-Tomb' (see line 3025).

(3016-22) *Bugu Turu,* etc. Praise-poem to the Tarawere clan of Tura Magan, emphasizing the strength of its genealogy. The names are Tarawere ancestors, all of whom are obscure, except *Makan-taa,* the Mande term for *ḥājji,* 'Moslem pilgrim.' Some claim that this man brought secrets back from his pilgrimage to Mecca with which he founded the Komo Society in Mali. Again, we can see the syncretism of Moslem and non-Moslem religious elements.

(3031) *Passage-of-Tura-Magan*. A ford either on the Baoulé River near Kita or on the Faleme River which divides modern Mali and Senegal. Both rivers are tributaries of the Senegal River.

(3040-43) This passage usually gets a laugh from the audience. The image is that the Jawara bard puffs out his cheeks and slaps them rhythmically with his hands to make a kind of percussion instrument with which to awaken the king in the mornings.

The agitator compares the musical richness of the Gambia at that time to the musical poverty of the Manden and concludes that the Maninkas will lose in battle. We have seen that musical instruments are sometimes associated with the occult (cf. Sumamuru's magic balaphone which he could hear from anywhere in his kingdom). Moreover, music and song stir men's souls to bravery in the Manden as elsewhere, but in the Manden many believe they are possessed of occult power.

(3049 & 3050) *Ford-of-the-frightened-Braves*. Folk etymology accompanied by an etiological legend (lines 3030-50) explaining the origin of the name of this river ford. It might be mentioned here that river-fording legends constitute a major subtype in Mali, and I have collected several of them.

(3053) *Dog-running*. Usually applied to hunters, this praise line is here a play on words. Tura Magan ironically alludes to the insulting swap of horses for dogs (lines 2958-61), while implying that he was merely hunting for pleasure.

(3055) *Nyani Mansa Kara* is the king alluded to here. He is one of many kings said to have fallen under the onslaught of Son-Jara's empire. The praise-poem in lines 1311-24 and 2311-20 is often ascribed to this monarch, and it is sometimes said that Fa-Koli "stole" the praise-poem *Janjon* from Nyani Mansa Kara by defeating him in battle (see note for lines 1813ff.).

(3058 & 3060) *Sanumu* and *Ba-dugu*. Obscure villages (kingdoms?) in the Gambia.

(3063-66) Possibly a reference to the laterite rock in much of the Gambia; it seems reasonable to classify this explanation as a folk etymology.

(3070-72) *Njop* (also spelled Ndiop, Diop). Jocular folk etymology, utilizing a pun. Njop is a common surname in Senegal and the Gambia, and the poet defines it as an onomatopoeic word derived from the sound of Tura Magan's ax chopping ("njopping") off Dark Jòlòf King's head.

(3074) *Sane* and *Mane*. Ruling Niancho clans in the Gambia.

(3080) *Golden sword and throne*. Tura Magan gives them to the Jawaras. See the note for line 2237.

Genealogy Charts

A. THE SONS OF ADAM (HADAMA-DINLU)

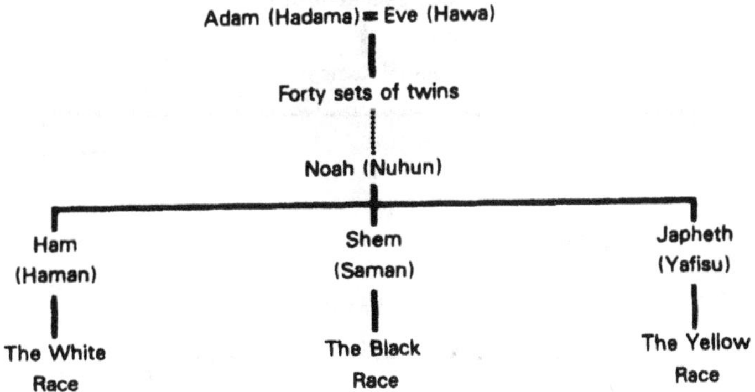

B. The Kònatè Line

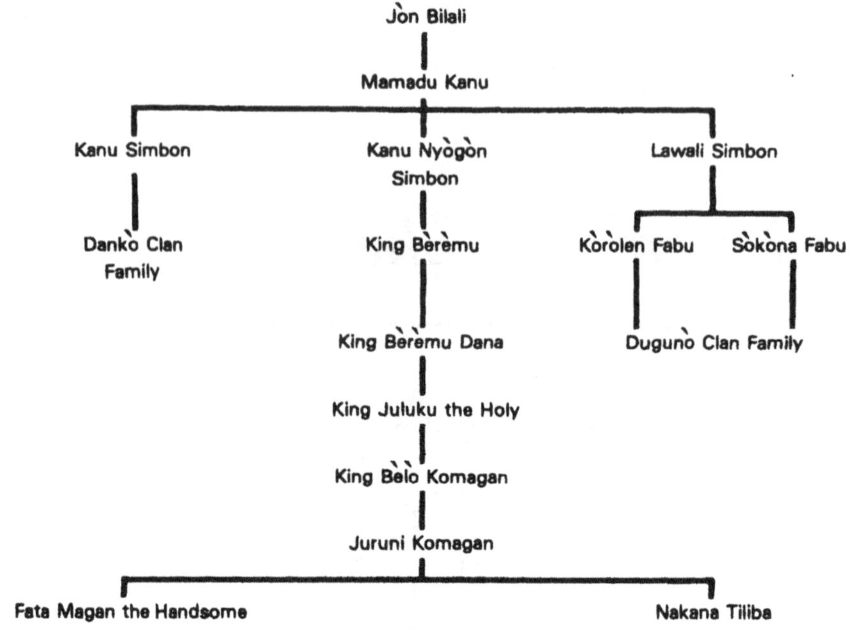

C. The Jawara Line

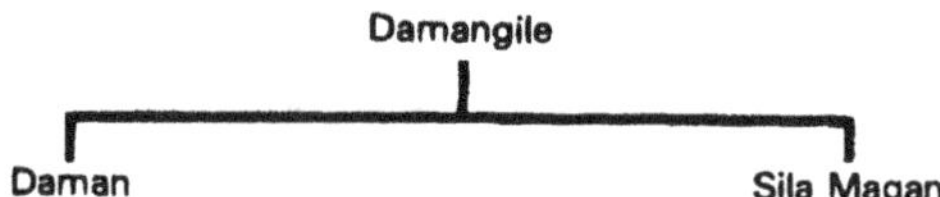

D. The Tunkara Line

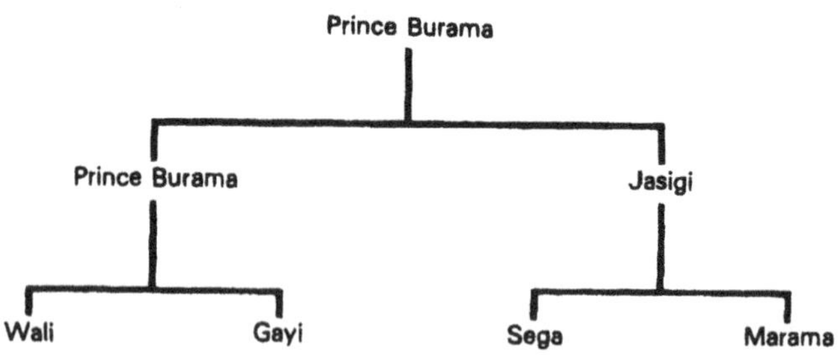

E. Son-Jara's Family

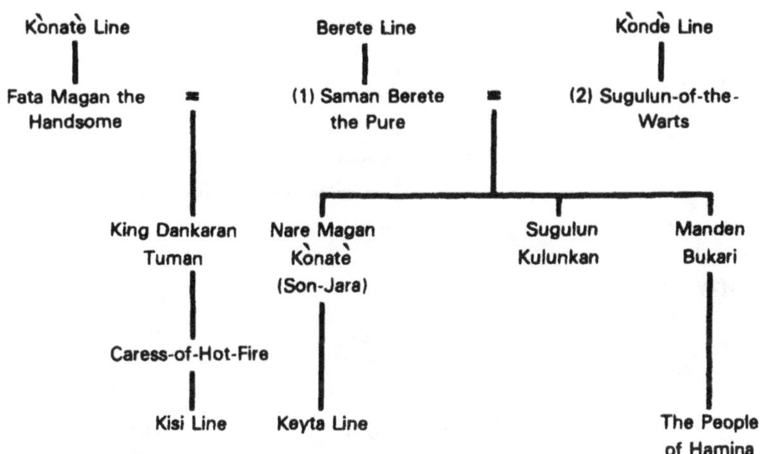

F. The Descendants of Mamuru

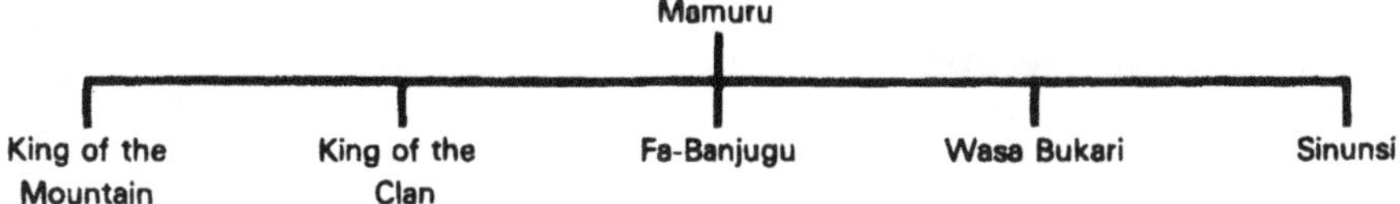

G. The Quraysh Line

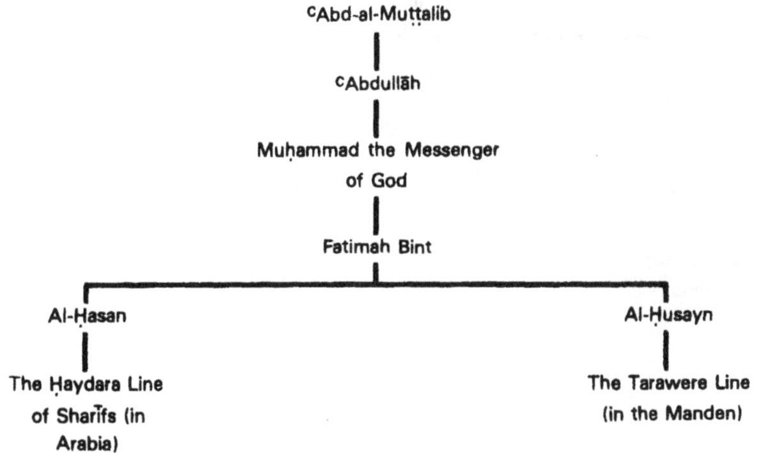

H. The Tarawere Line

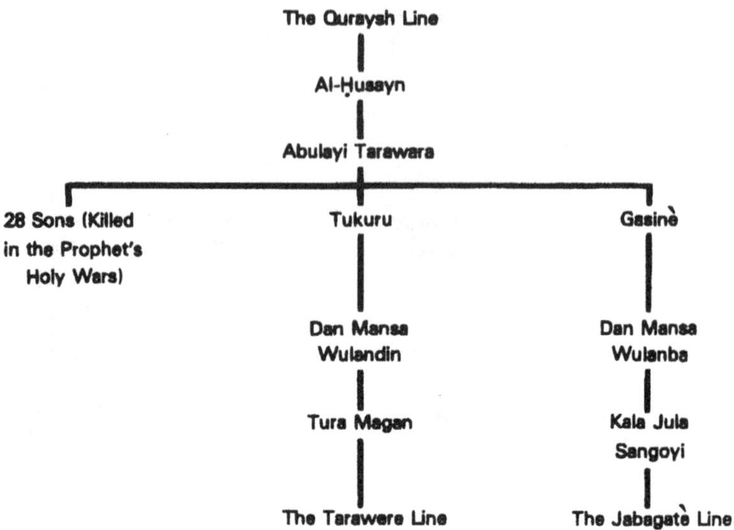

I. The Kòndè (Kònè, Jara) Line

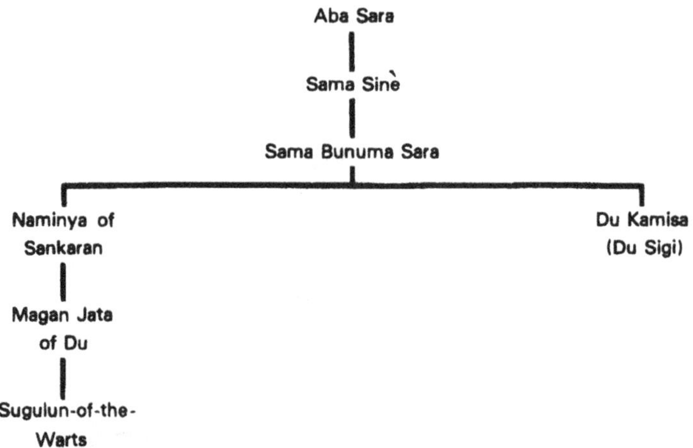

J. THE JABAGATÈ (JABAATÈ) LINE

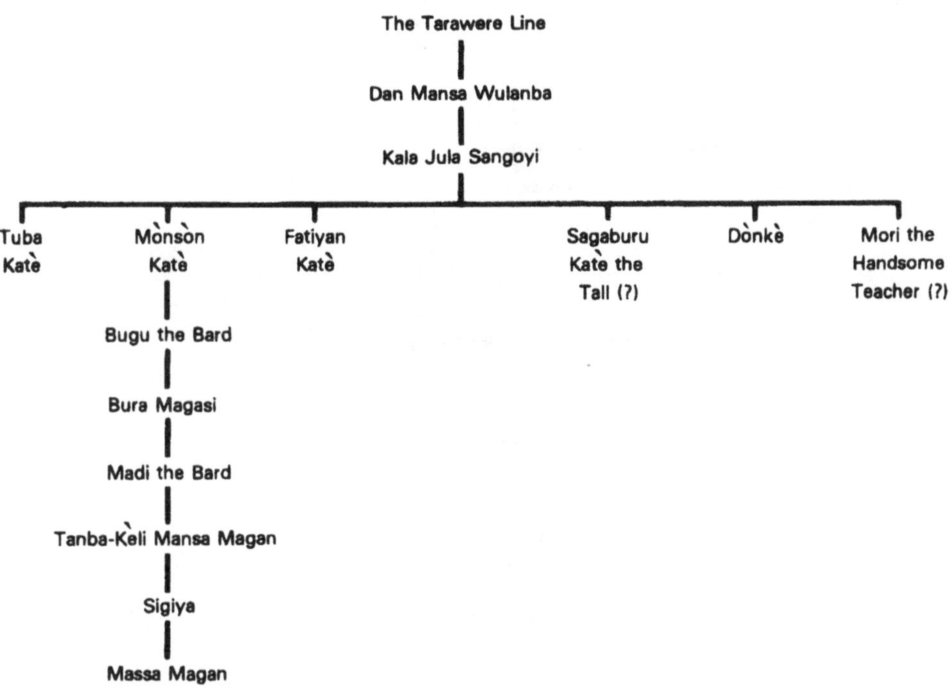

K. THE KANTÈ LINE

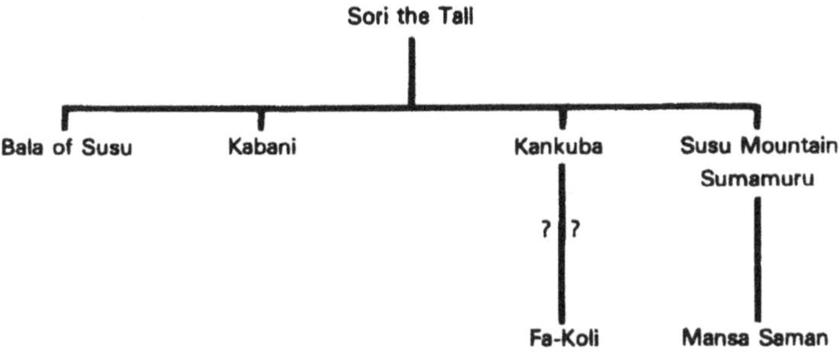

L. The Kuyatè Line

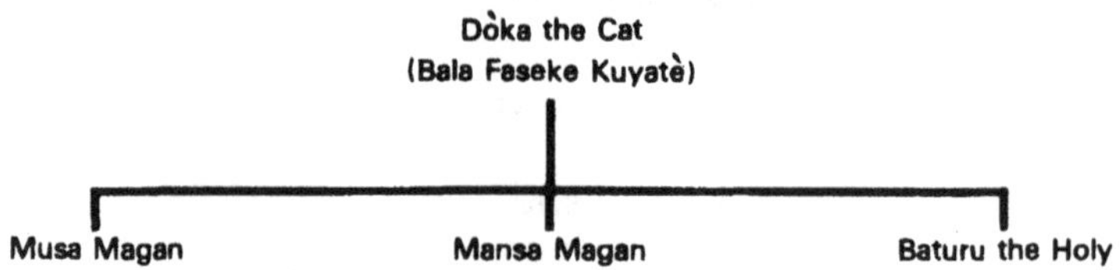

M. The Karangè Line

BIBLIOGRAPHY

The following bibliography lists books and articles dealing with the epic of Son-Jara primarily from the point of view of those disciplines interested in oral literature. It is classified into thirteen sections and begins with complete linear transcriptions, translated from texts collected in the field on tape recorders, which is the form considered most reliable for study in oral literature. A brief explanation of the categories and references will help put the bibliography into perspective. Categories I–VI and IX–XIII are fairly complete. Categories VII and VIII only list works which may be considered most important in these related areas, as a complete list of books dealing with Son-Jara from an historical point of view is beyond the scope of this study. The texts covered in this bibliography include both linear translations (categories I–III, X) and reconstructed texts (IV–VI, IX, XII). Categories VII and VIII are works about Son-Jara which treat the narrative of the life and exploits of this culture hero as either historical legend or historical reality, depending upon the slant of the scholar. Category XI includes scholarly writings about the epic or about epic scholarship when such material plays an important part of the study or mentions Son-Jara to a substantial degree.

Historically, one can isolate roughly four periods of writings about Son-Jara, beginning with early twelfth century writings about West Africa by North African (and other) Arab geographers. A second period of writing began with European explorers in West Africa, but is centered around French colonials interested in their possessions in that part of the French empire. The third period begins shortly after World War II during a time working up to the great year of independence in Africa, 1960, and was heavily influenced by the Francophone movement in the West Indies and West Africa known as *Négritude*. One of the most important publications on this topic, for instance, was *Soundiata, ou l'épopée mandingue*, a complete, albeit reconstructed variant of the epic, written by Djibril Tamsir Niane, published in 1960 by the press which became the voice of *Négritude* in Paris, Présence Africaine. More about this important work will be given below. Finally, the present period of interest in Son-Jara comes shortly before the independence date of the Republic of Mali in 1960 and is to some degree associated with the broader theoretical question of the existence of epic poetry on the continent of

Africa, a topic in which the epic of Son-Jara has played a primary role, but which is not directly concerned with the epic.

It is important to note that everything printed about Son-Jara Keita inside or outside West Africa, beginning with the earliest Arab geographers' writings, is based upon knowledge which has been passed down through the oral tradition. Ibn Khaldūn (VI; 1981), from the late fourteenth century, recorded data learned from the oral tradition and even names his sources. He heard stories about Son-Jara from merchants who learned their narratives from professional bards (*jelilu, griots*). Ibn Baṭṭūṭa who visited Mali and wrote about it about four decades before Ibn Khaldūn, only mentions a Sāriq Djāṭa, which Levtzion (VII; 1963, 1973) says should be identified as the Mārī-Djāṭa of Ibn Khaldūn, this being the praise-name for Son-Jara employed by the latter. Most other Arab scholars who mention Son-Jara are copying Ibn Khaldūn's more thorough treatment. Readers interested in working through these early Arab sources dealing with Son-Jara and Old Mali (the Manden) should consult Levtzion (VII; 1963, 1973) for thorough discussions and Hopkins and Levtzion, 1981 (listed under Ibn Khaldūn, VI; 1981) for translations of the same.

Mention of Son-Jara to the outside world (at least to the Western world) after these early Arab sources is not made again until the period of European exploration in the nineteenth century. Heinrich Barth (VIII; 1858) dates the reign of Mári Játah in an appendix of his book, but no narrative about the culture hero is given. Indeed, it was not until the period of French colonialism in the area that publication of any significance evolved. Basset (VIII; 1888) may be the earliest French reference, and he is followed by another scholar (Adam, VII; 1903) interested in the history of the new French possessions. The first French writer to deal with the subject of Son-Jara as oral literature is H. C. Lanrezac (VI; 1907a, 1907b, 1908). He is followed by Arnaud (IV; 1912) and Zeltner (III; 1913, XI; 1913). Leo Frobenius (VII; 1913) also published during this early period of primarily French interest, only later (IV; 1925) turning his interest to the literary aspects of the legend.

Parallel to the literary interest of the first French writers was the beginning of research into the history of the region. After publishing historically oriented accounts of Son-Jara in his classic *Haut-Séné-gal-Niger* (VII; 1912), Maurice Delafosse (VI & VII; 1913) translated an early anonymous Arabic manuscript which mixed interest in history and oral tradition. This account was to be republished several times over the next fifty years, beginning the same year as a chapter in his book *Traditions historiques et légendaires. . .* and again in 1959 during the wake of interest immediately preceding the independence of the Republic of Mali (in VIII: *Notes Africaines* 83). It was translated by Basil Davidson in 1964 (Delafosse, VI; 1964) and republished again 1969 in Fred Burke's edited book, *Africa: Selected Readings* (VI: Burke, 1969). Delafosse (XI: 1924) went on to contribute to the timely debate on the location of the capital of Old Mali, being joined in this pursuit by Gaillard (VIII; 1923) and Vidal (XI: 1923a, 1923b). This early period of French interest in the history and oral traditions of their West African possessions was crowned by the 1929 publication of Charles Monteil's classic work, *Les Empires du Mali* (VIII: republished in 1968).

After a period of about twenty years, French and French-trained scholars again took up the question of Son-Jara Keita from the historical (Sy, VII: 1945; Vuillet, VII & XI: 1950) and literary (Quénum, VI: 1946; Humblot, VI: 1951) viewpoints. By this time, that is after World War II, events leading up to the independence of the countries of present-day West Africa combined with the growing strength of the *Négritude* movement in the West Indies and Francophone West Africa. Interest in Sub-Saharan African culture heroes increased, Son-Jara being one of the most important.

One can almost divide non-Mande knowledge about Son-Jara Keita into pre-Niane and post-Niane periods. Articles within this growing black consciousness that came before his famous *Sundjata ou l'épopée Mandingue* (IV: 1960) mentioned above, dealt primarily with historical or scholarly topics. Montrat (VIII: 1958) and Hervé (VIII: 1959) reopened the old question of the location of the capital of Old Mali. A pair of juvenile texts appeared (Wingfield, IX: 1957; Clair, IX: 1959), to be followed by a number of such texts as time went on (IX: Bertol 1970, Chu 1965, Guilhem n.d., Guillot 1950, Wisniewski 1992). Niane himself dealt with strictly academic questions with a pair of articles (XI: 1959, 1960). Sidibé (V: 1959) mixed literary questions with historical ones as did a pair of special issues of *Notes Africaines* (VIII: nos. 82 and 83) leading up to the independence of the country. But it was really the appearance in 1960 of Niane's literary text from the main publishing house of the Négritude movement, Présence Africaine, that made all the difference in world knowledge about Son-Jara, and the importance of this book merits some detailed commentary.

Niane's book is not what the academic folklorist wants in a reliable oral text for scholarly study. It is "reconstructed," the oral equivalent of the literary concept of "rewritten." It is presented to the public in French prose rather than as a linear translation of poetic lines from the original language. Moreover, Niane's book tells a complete story, which violates the Mande bardic tradition of never revealing all of what one knows at a single performance. But what is so very important about the book, and no academic argument will ever change this fact, is that it hit the Western literary world like a bombshell, no small feat in the French literary tradition. Niane's variant reads like an exciting adventure story, and one must conclude that the author/ editor accomplished his real goal, which was to demonstrate to European critics that oral bards in West Africa could create works of literary merit equal to the best in any written European literary tradition. The frequent republication (and retranslation into other languages) of this text is proof of Niane's success. In 1965, G. D. Pickett published an English translation (Niane, IV: 1965), and a Russian version appeared even before this date (Spaznikov, IV: 1963). Excerpts have appeared frequently (Labatut, VI: n.d.; Tam'si, VI: 1973), and many secondary articles and countless term papers and conference papers have referred to the Niane version. Although later published versions of the epic represent scholarship producing a reliable text in linear translation to an audience more sophisticated and knowledgeable in the African bardic style of performance, it can never be denied that D. T. Niane accomplished a great deal in introducing to the Western world a major African work of literary art with his book.

As mentioned above, interest in Son-Jara was spurred on by both the *Négritude* movement and the drive toward independence in Africa. A number of articles and books followed Niane's text in close succession. Pageard (XI: 1961) attempted to reconstruct history in Old Mali by combining all the published reconstructed variants of the epic into one composite text which in fact is sung by no one and which proves nothing historically. Niane and Suret-Canale (IX: 1961), publishing again with Présence Africaine, produced a school history text from an African point of view. One also notices a much more international spread in the bibliography which gives attention to Son-Jara. John Jacobs (XI: 1962) and J. Spencer Trimingham (VII: 1962), Flemish and British scholars, join with the Israeli Nehemia Levtzion (VIII: 1963, 1973), and others in knowledge of this culture hero.

At the same time more and more scholarly works, both textual and secondary, began to appear about Son-Jara, but the force and influence of *Négritude* remained in place for some time, paralleling published works not influenced by the movement. Two writers, Massa Makan Diabaté and Laye Camara (better known to his reading audience as Camara Laye) continued to fall within the influence of *Négritude*.

Massa Makan Diabaté (VI: 1967) published his first reconstructed variant of the epic in 1967, a variant which represents one of two major narrative variants of this epic and which may be termed the "Twelve Son Variant." In this version, Son-Jara's eleven elder brothers are executed by Sumamuru, who leaves Son-Jara alive because he is crippled and supposedly helpless. This episode replaces the core episode of co-wife and sibling rivalry found in the most commonly published variant, which may be referred to as the "Co-wife Rivalry Variant."

In March 1968 Charles Bird and Massa Makan Diabaté went to Kita and collected a full text from the late bard Kèlè Mònsòn Jabaatè on tape. In Diabaté (I: 1975) this date is incorrectly reported as 1966; a linear comparison indicates that this translation was made from the same tape as that of Moser (I: 1974). Also from the same tape, Massa Makan first published a reconstructed albeit complete text in French prose (Diabaté, III: 1970), the same year that he published his collection of Mande songs and praise-poems (Diabaté, IV: 1970). In 1972 an excerpt from this tape appeared in Bird (II: 1972), and a complete English translation was accomplished by Rex Moser and Mamadou Konaré and appeared in Moser (I: 1974). Finally, Massa Makan retranslated the same text, this time linearly, if somewhat liberally, and published it as Diabaté (I: 1975).

Turning to the last book of Laye Camara (IV: 1978, 1980), which has received a great deal attention from literary critics, one finds that at this late date, the continuing influence of *Négritude* was still present. The romanticizing of black African creativity is evident both in the book and in the patronizing, even offensive, introduction to the English translation. Here Laye Camara has collected a variant of the epic from the Guinean bard Babu Condé (Kòndè) and described himself as "the modest transcriber and translator," but he is clearly also the "interpreter" of the text, for he has not only reconstructed it, but he has done so within the philosophical framework of the *Négritude* movement. Some of Camara's comments are clearly editorial and not reconstructed reflections of bardic recitation. The book comes too late in history to have the impact of Niane's variant, and seems to have pleased few critics, including those who have no real knowledge of the oral tradition and whose criticisms deal solely with the written literary point of view.

Backing up to the beginnings of the fourth phase of writings about Son-Jara, one encounters the first modern reliable treatments of the epic, textually, critically, and historically. A pair of secondary articles (Shelton, XI: 1968 and Fernandez, XI: 1969) appear just before what may be the first linear translation to be published, that of Koné

(I: 1970). The problem with this text and the reliable linear translations which follow it lies in accessibility. It was jointly published by the Institut des Sciences Humaines in Mali and the Centre Régionale de Documentation pour la Tradition Orale in Niamey and is extremely hard to find.

This time was also the period of most work by such scholars as Charles Bird and the Lilyan Kesteloot–Amadou Hampâté Bâ team. Bird's most important publications in the study of epic poetry in Mali centered around the hunter's epic, but his scholarly contributions include collections of Malian folklore (Bird: II: 1972) and a complete linear translation of a hunter's epic, *Kambili* (not listed in the bibliography because it does not deal with Son-Jara), and essays on broader questions concerning the prosody of epic poetry and other linguistically-oriented topics (Bird, XI: 1971). Lilyan Kesteloot and Amadou Hampâté Bâ, like Bird, dealt with many topics other than Son-Jara alone, but one chapter (Kesteloot, VII: 1971) covered Son-Jara.

During this same time the team of Gordon Innes and Bakary Sidibe worked on Gambian Mandinka variants of the epic. Innes first published a study of variation in bardic performance (XI: 1973), but published a collection of three variants translated linearly with an introduction and notes in the following year (Innes, I: 1974). Sidibe has also published a complete reconstructed translation of Gambian variants in prose (Sidibe, IV: 1980).

It was at a seminar given by Gordon Innes in 1969 at the School of Oriental and African Studies that I first heard of Son-Jara. I was studying at S.O.A.S., and after finishing my course work for the Ph.D. at Indiana University three years later, I chose to do my dissertation fieldwork on this epic under Bird's supervision. Working with Cheick Oumar Mara, Ibrahim Kalilou Tèra and Checkna Mohamed Singaré, four complete texts were collected, and five including Fa-Digi's variant were transcribed and translated while I was in Mali. One is already published as Johnson, et al., I: 1979.

Two more linear translations also appeared during this period (Kamissoko, I: 1975, 1977), which are the result of collaboration between the late Malian bard Wa Kamissoko and the Malian scholar Youssouf Tata Cissé. I have already mentioned the reliable text translated by Moser and Konaré (Moser, I: 1974). Finally, historical interest in Son-Jara continued (Levtzion, VII: 1973; Condé, VII: 1974), as did other theoretical questions (Jackson, XI: 1979; Conrad, XI: 1983, 1984).

Interest in the *Epic of Son-Jara* and other Mande epics, and in epic as a genre of oral literature in general received a new burst of energy in the 1990s. First, a number of scholars began to turn their interest to epic as a genre (Belcher, Hale, Honko), and others began to study the *Epic of Son-Jara* and other Mande epics specifically (Conrad, Geysbeek, Jansen). With the gathering together of a substantial number of scholars from around the world into the international Folklore Fellows of Oral Epics in Finland by Lauri Honko, and the conferences held by this group in Turku in 1996 and 1999, world-wide interest in this genre was revived. Moreover, the number of reliable texts has increased dramatically and the quality of scholarship has improved considerably.

Citations of articles and books listed below are coded according to the language in which the text is transcribed and/or translated. Those codes are as follows:

M = Original Mande Language Text
A = Arabic Translation
E = English Translation
F = French Translation
D = Dutch Translation
G = German Translation
R = Russian Translation

I. COMPLETE LINEAR TRANSLATIONS

Materials included in this section represent translations of the Epic of Son-Jara at the highest level of scholarship, where the actual words of the bard have been recorded on tape, just as they were performed. Transcription is also line by line, leaving nothing uttered by the bard during performance out of the published text. Translation is followed by adequate annotation to explain points in the text which might be obscure to the target culture.

Camara, Seydou, and Jan Jansen, eds., *La geste de Nankoman: Textes sur la fondation de Naréna (Mali)* (Leiden: Onderzoekschool Centre for Non-Western Studies [CNWS], 1999) **[M ,F]**

Conrad, David C., ed., Great Sogolon's House: Djaka Tassey Condé's Epic of Mande **[E]** [In the press]

__________, ed., *Epic Ancestors of the Sunjata Era: Oral Tradition from the Maninka of Guinea* (Madison, Wisconsin: African Studies Program, 1999). **[E]**

__________, ed., *Soulayman Kante's History of Mali: Scholarly Wisdom of the Manden of Northeast Guinea Translated from the N'Ko* **[E]** [in the press]

Diabaté, Massa Makan, "Essai critique sur l'épopée Mandingue," (Centre de Recherches Africaines, Université de Paris I, Sorbonne: Doctorat de troisième cycle, n.d.) **[F]** [Pages 48–621 contains a complete text of the epic composed by Kèlè Mònsòn Jabaatè; same text as Moser, 1974]

Diabaté, Massa Makan, *L'aigle et l'épervier, ou la geste de Sunjata* (Paris: Éditions Pierre Jean Oswald, 1975) **[F]** [Same text as above]

__________, *Le lion à l'arc.* (Paris: Hatier, 1986) **[F]** [Same text as above]

Duintjer, Esger, Jan Jansen, Toumani Sidibe, and Boubacar Tamboura, eds., trans., *Makan Sunjata: Manden buruju / L'histoire du Mande* (Bamako, Mali: Éditions Jamana, 1997) **[M & F]** [Mande and French edition of Jansen, Jan, Esger Duintjer, and Boubacar Tamboura, *Sunjata: Het beroemdste epos van Afrika*]

Innes, Gordon, *Sunjata: Three Mandinka Versions* (London: School of Oriental and African Studies, University of London, 1974) **[E]**

Jabate, Jeli Kanku Madi, (ed. and trans. M. Ly-Tall, S. Camara, and B. Diouara) *L'histoire du Mandé.* (Paris: Association SCOA [Société Commerciale de l'Ouest Afrique], 1987) **[F]**

Jansen, Jan, *Les secrets du Manding: Les récits du sanctuaire Kamabolon de Kangaba (Mali)* (Leiden: Research School of Asian, African and Amerindian Studies (CNWS), Universiteit Leiden, 2002)

Jansen, Jan, Esger Duintjer, and Boubacar Tamboura, eds., trans., *L'épopée de Sunjara, d'après Lansine Diabate de Kela.* (Leiden: Onderzoekschool Centre for Non-Western Studies [CNWS], 1995) **[M & F]** [Mande and French version of Jansen, Jan, Esger Duintjer, and Boubacar Tamboura, *Het Sunjata-Epos verteld door Lansine Diabate uit Kela*]

———, *Het Sunjata-Epos verteld door Lansine Diabate uit Kela.* (Utrecht: 1994) **[D]** [Dutch edition of Jansen, Jan, Esger Duintjer, and Boubacar Tamboura, *L'épopée de Sunjara, d'après Lansine Diabate de Kela*]

———, *Sunjata: Het beroemdste epos van Afrika* (Rijkswijk: Ekmar , [1998]) **[D]** [Dutch version of Esger Duintjer, Jan Jansen, Toumani Sidibe, and Boubacar Tamboura, *Makan Sunjata*]

Johnson, John William, *The Epic of Son-Jara: A West African Tradition* (Bloomington: Indiana University Press, 1986) **[E]**

———, ed., trans., *The Epic of Son-Jara: A West African Tradition* , 2nd edition revised (Bloomington: Indiana University Press, 1992) **[E]** [Same as 1986 edition, but exegesis removed]

———, ed., trans., *The Epic of Sun Jata According to Magan Sisòkò* (Bloomington, Indiana: Folklore Publications Group, 1979) **[E]**

———, "The Epic of Sunjata: An Attempt to Define the Model for African Epic Poetry," PhD. dissertation, Indiana University, 1978 [Contains two epics, recited by Fa-Digi Sisòkò and Magan Sisòkò] **[M & E]**

Kamara, Vase (trans. Timothy Geysbeek, Jobba Kamara, and Marloes Janson), *De kroniek van de Kamara: Een verhaal uit Guinee* (Rijkswijk: Ekmar , n.d.) **[D]**

Kamissoko, Wa (ed., and trans. Youssouf Tata Cissé), *L'empire du Mali* (Paris: Fondation SCOA pour la Recherche Scientifique en Afrique Noire, 1975) **[F]**

Kamissoko, Wa, (ed., and trans. Youssouf Tata Cissé), *L'empire du Mali (Suite)* (Paris: Fondation SCOA pour la Recherche Scientifique en Afrique Noire, 1977) **[F]**

Koné, Tiémoko (trans., Lassana Doucouré and Mme Marta), *Soundiata* (Bamako, Mali: Institut des Sciences Humaines du Mali and Niamey, Niger: Centre Régionale de Documentation pour la Tradition Orale, 1970) **[M & F]**

Moser, Rex, *Foregrounding in the Sunjata, The Mande Epic* (Bloomington, Indiana: Ph.D. dissertation, Indiana University, 1974) **[E]** [Contains a variant of the epic of Son-Jara according to Kèlè Mònsòn Jabaatè, collected by Charles S. Bird and Massa Makan Diabaté, and translated by Rex Moser and Mamadou Konarè]

Sisoko, Jeli Baba, "Wagadu and Sunjata" in David C. Conrad, "The Role of Oral Artists in the History of Mali" (London: PhD. dissertation, School of Oriental and African Languages, University of London, 1981): vol. 2, pp. 649–710 **[E]** [Information on Sunjata, 670–710]

Suso, Bamba, and Banna Kanute (trans., Gordon Innes and Bakari Sidibe) (ed. with new introduction, Lucy Durán and Graham Furniss), *Sunjata: Gambian Versions of the Mande Epic* (London: Penguin Books, 1999) **[E]** [Republication of Innes, *Sunjata: Three Mandinka Versions*]

II. EXCERPTED LINEAR TRANSLATIONS

Materials included in this section represent the same high level of scholarship as in Section I. For various reasons, however, only selected excerpts have been chosen for publication by the editors of these passages.

Bird, Charles S., "Bambara Oral Prose and Verse Narratives Collected by Charles Bird," in *African Folklore*, ed. Richard Dorson (Garden City, New York: Doubleday Anchor, 1972): 441–77 **[E]** [Contains the episode of three Simbon brothers and the founding of Old Mali]

Camara, Sory, "L'histoire du Mande" in his *Gens de la parole: Essai sur la condition et le rôle des griots dans la société Malinké*. (Paris and The Hague: Mouton, 1976): 254–66 **[F]**

Diebate, Toumani and Lucy Durán, "Music of the Royal Courts: A Celebration of the Musicians' Place Near the Thrones of Africa and the Orient: Epic Singing-Sunjata, from Mali," (London: B.B.C., 1987) **[E]** [Concert programme notes, BBC Radio Three, Purcell Room South Bank Centre, London]

Kante, Nakunte, "De L'histoire des Sinbon et du Sosobala," appendix to Drissa Diakite, "Le Mansaya et la société Mandingue: Essai d'interpretation des luttes socio-politiques qui ont donné naissance à l'empire du Mali au XIIIe siècle" (Paris: Ph.D. dissertation [3e cycle d'histoire]. Université de Paris I, 1980) **[F]**

III. LINEAR TRANSLATIONS OF PRAISE-POEMS

Again representing a high degree of scholarship, materials in this section concern Son-Jara, but the genre of presentation here is not epic but rather praise–poetry. Praise–poems are widespread in Sub-Saharan Africa, and there are many concerning Son-Jara amongst the Mandekan-speaking peoples.

Diabaté, Massa Makan, "Présentation du Sunjata faassa-version originale de Kela," *Études Maliennes* I (1970): 71–77 **[F]**

———, "Sun Jata Fasa" and "Chants à la mémoire de Sun Jata," in his *Janjon et autres chants populaires du Mali* (Paris: Présence Africaine, 1970): 29–42 **[F]**

Jansen, Jan and Cemako Kante, *Siramuri Diabate et ses enfants: une étude sur deux générations des griots Malinke* (Utrecht: ISOR and Bamako: Institut des Sciences Humaines, 1991) **[F]**

IV. COMPLETE RECONSTRUCTED TRANSLATIONS IN PROSE

A number of variants of the Epic of Son-Jara have been published in which the actual performed words of the bard have been reconstructed by the editor of the publication. The term "reconstruct" is used here for oral literature as the equivalent of "rewritten" for written literature. In other words, the performed text has been "reworded" in language chosen by the editor. In this case, the original poetic text has been reconstructed into prose for the target audience. While the text may be easier and more pleasing to read and in some cases, the plot may even be easier to follow, such translations are somewhat dishonest in that the actual words uttered by the bard in performance have been altered or changed.

Camara, Laye (trans. James Kirkup), *The Guardian of the Word: Kouma Lafôlô Kouma* (Glasgow: William Collins, 1980) **[E]**
_______, *Le maître de la parole: Kouma lafôlô kouma* (Paris: Librairie Plon, 1978) **[F]**
Cissé, Youssouf Tata, and Wâ Kamissoko, *La grande geste du Mali: Des origines de la fondation de l'empire (Traditions de Krina aux colloques de Bamako)* (Paris: Éditions Karthala/l'Association pour la Promotion de la Recherche Scientifique en Afrique Noire [ARSAN, formerly SCOA], 1988) **[F]**
Cissé, Youssouf Tata, and Wâ Kamissoko, *La gloire du Mali: La grande geste du Mali—tome 2* (Paris: Éditions Karthala/l'Association pour la Promotion de la Recherche Scientifique en Afrique Noire [ARSAN, formerly SCOA], 1988) **[F]**
Diabaté, Massa Makan, *Kala Jata* (Bamako, Mali: Éditions Populaires, 1970) **[F]**
_______, *Le lion à l'arc* (Paris: Hatier/CEDA, 1986) **[F]**
Konaré Ba, Adam, *Sunjata: le fondateur de l'empire du Mali* (Libreville, Gabon: Lion and Dakar, Senegal: Les Nouvelles Éditions Africaines, 1983) **[F]**
Niane, Djibril Tamsir, *Soundjata ou l'épopée Mandingue* (Paris: Présence Africaine, 1960) **[F]**
_______, (trans. G. D. Pickett), *Sundiata: An Epic of Old Mali* (London: Longman, 1965) **[E]**
Sidibe, Bakare K., ed., trans., *Sunjata: The Story of Sunjata Keita, Founder of the Mali Empire* (Banjul, The Gambia: Oral History and Antiquities Division of the Vice-President's Office, 1980) **[E]** [Reprinted in Banjul by the Oral History Division for The Gambia Traditional Griot Society, 1984]
Spaznikov, G. A., *Sundjita manigskij epos [Sunjata the Manding Epos]* (Moscow: Izd Hudogestvennaja Literatura, 1963) **[R]**
Zeltner, Frantz de, "La légende de Soundiata," in his *Contes du Sénégal et du Niger* (Paris: Ernest Laroux, 1913): 1–36 **[F]**

V. CONDENSED RECONSTRUCTED TRANSLATIONS IN PROSE

This section includes materials which have been reconstructed and short-ened by their editors. A condensed narrative results. The texts in this section have also been transformed from the original poetry to prose.

Arnaud, Robert, "La singulière légende des Soninke: traditions orales sur le royaume de Koumbi et sur divers autres royaumes soundanais," in his *L'Islam et la politique musulmane française en Afrique occidentale française* (Paris: Comité de l'Afrique Française, 1912): 144-85 **[F]**

Diakite, Mamadou Aïssa Kaba Ben Mohamed Kaba, "Généalogie des gens de Keita" in his "Livre renfermant la généalogie des diverses tribus noires du Soudan et l'histoire des rois après Mahomet, suivant le ren-seignements fournis par certaines personnes et ceux recueillis dans les anciens livres," *Annales de l'Académie des Sciences Coloniales* 3 (1929), 209-10 **[F]**

Frobenius, Leo, "Ein historisches Dichtwerk (der Mande oder Mandingo)", in his *Und Afrika Sprach* (Berlin and Charlottenburg: Bita, Deutsches Verlaghaus, 1912-13): 445-61 **[G]**

——————, "Die Sunjattalegende der Malinke," in his *Atlantis: Volksmärchen und Volksdichtungen Afrikas, Band V: Dichten und Denken im Sudan* (Jena: Eugen Dieterichs, 1925): 303-31 **[F]**

Kanouté, Dembo, (trans. Tidiane Sanogho and Ibrahima Diallo), "Forma-tion de l'empire mandingue," in his *Histoire de l'Afrique authentique* (Dakar, Senegal: Pub. by author, 1972): 30-71 **[F]**

Kante, Ibrahima, *L'épopée du Mandingue*. (Kindia, Guinea: n.p., n.d.) **[F]**

Keita, Boniface, *Le monde Malinké de Kita des années 1910* (Bamako: Édi-tions Jamana, 1988): 8-13 **[F]**

Liking, Werewere, *L'amour-cent-vies*. (Paris: Éditions Publisud, 1988) **[F]**

Sadji, Abdoulaye, "Ce que dit la musique africaine," *L'education africaine* 94 (April-June 1936), 140-54 [Reprinted as Sadji, Abdoulaye, "Soun-diata" in his *Ce que dit la musique Africaine*. (Paris and Dakar: Présence Africaine, 1985): 11-38] **[F]**

Sidibé, Mamby, "Soundiata Keita, héros historiques et légendaires, emper-eur du Manding," *Notes Africaines* 82 (1959): 41-51 **[F]**

Vidal, J., "La légende officiale de Soundiata, fondateur de l'empire man-ding," *Bulletin du Comité d'Études Historiques et Scientifiques de l'Afrique Occidentale Française* 7 (1924): 317-28 **[F]**

VI. EXCERPTED RECONSTRUCTED TRANSLATIONS IN PROSE

A number of scholars have treated the Epic of Son-Jara as a source of valid historicity. This section includes materials which have taken an approach to epic as a source of history.

Courlander, Harold, "Three Soninke Tales," *African Arts* 12:1 (Nov. 1978): 82-88; 108 **[E]**

Delafosse, Maurice, trans., "Sundiata's Triumph (Anonymous)," in *The Afri-can Past: Chronicles from Antiquity to Modern Times*, ed. Basil Davidson

(New York: Grosset and Dunlap, 1964): 73-74 **[E]** [Text translated by
Davidson from Delafosse's translation of an Arabic text, published in
Delafosse's *Traditions historiques et légendaires du Soudan occidental*]
Delafosse, Maurice, trans., "Sundiata's Triumph (Anonymous)," in *Africa;
Selected Readings,* ed. Fred Burke (Boston: Houghton Mifflin, 1969)
[E] [Text translated by Davidson from Delafosse's translation of an
Arabic text, published in Delafosse's *Traditions historiques et légendaires
du Soudan occidental*; republished here from Davidson's edited book,
The African Past: Chronicles from Antiquity to Modern Times]
Diabaté, Massa Makan, "La légende de Soundiata,"in his *Si le feu
s'eteignait...* (Bamako, Mali: Éditions Populaires, 1967): 10-19 **[F]**
Hourst, Lieut., *Sur le Niger et au pays des Tuaregs: La mission Hourst par le
lieutenant de Vaisseau Hourst.* (Paris: Librairie Plon, 1898): 50-53 **[F]**
————, (trans. N. Bell), *Lieut. Hourst, French Enterprise in Africa: The Personal Narrative of Lieut. Hourst of his Exploration of the Niger* (London:
Chapman and Hall, Ltd, 1898): 52-58 **[E]** [English translation of above]
Humblot, P., "Episodes de la légende de Soundiata," *Notes Africaines* 52
(1951): 111-13 **[F]**
Ibn Khaldūn, Abū Zayd ʿAbd al-Raḥmān, "Kitāb al-ʿibar wa-dīwān al-mub-
tada wa-'l-khabar fī ayyām al-ʿarab wa-'l-ʿajam wa-'l-barbar," in *Corpus
of Early Arabic Sources for West African History*, ed. J. P. F. Hopkins and
Nehemia Levtzion (Cambridge: Cambridge University Press, 1981):
332-42 **[A]**
Jaime, Le Lieutenant de Vaisseau, *De Koulikoro à Tombouctou au bord du
"Mage" 1889-1890.* (Paris: Librairie de la Société des Gens de Lettres,
n.d.): 329-33 [Revised and published by Les Libraires Associés in Paris
in 1894] **[F]**
Kesteloot, Lilyan, "L'épopée mandingue: Sounjata," in her *L'épopée tradi-
tionelle* (Paris: Fernand Nathan, 1971): 6-12 **[F]**
Kouyate, Mamary, "Sunjata" in David C. Conrad, "The Role of Oral
Artists in the History of Mali" (London: Ph.D. dissertation, School of
Oriental and African Studies, University of London, 1981): vol. 2, pp.
711-13 **[E]**
Labatut, S., and R. Labatut, eds., "Soundiata, épopée mandingue," in their
Épopées africaines: Morceaux choisis (Youndé, Cameroon: Ministry of
Education, n.d.): 87-112 [Selection from Niane's *Soundjata ou l'épopée
mandingue*] **[F]**
Lanrezac, H. C., "Au Soudan–La légende historique," *La Revue Indigène:
Organe des Intérêt des Indigènes Colonies* 2:16, 2:18, 2:19 (1907):
292-97; 380- 86; 420-30 [Republished in Nendeln, Liechtenstein:
Kraus-Thompson, 1977] **[F]**
Lanrezac, H. C., *Essai sur le folklore au Soudan* (Paris: Bibliothèque de la
Revue Indigène, 1908) **[F]**
————, "Légendes soudanaises," *Bulletin de la Société Géographique Com-
merciale de Paris* 29 (1907): 607-19
Monteil, Charles, "Simanguru et Sun-Dyata,"*Bulletin de l'Institut Fonda-
mental d'Afrique Noire* 28B (1966): 166-70 **[F]**
Quénum Maximilien, "La légende de Fama-Soundiata (Soudan Français),"
in his *Trois légendes africaines* (Rochefort-sur-Mer: Troyon-Thèze,
1946): 43-72 **[F]**

Quiquandon, F., "Histoire de la puissance mandingue d'après la légende et la tradition," *Bulletin de la Société Géographie de Bordeaux,* 2/15 (1892): 305-18 **[F]**

Tam'si, Tchicaya U. (ed.), "Soundiata ou le conquérant," in his *Légendes africaines* (Paris: Nouveaux Horizons, 1973): 65-92 [Excerpted from Niane, *Soundjata, ou l'épopée mandingue*] **[F]**

VII. WORKS TREATING THE EPIC OF SON-JARA AS HISTORICAL LEGEND

This section includes secondary articles which treat the Epic of Son-Jara as a legend existing in the oral tradition.

Adam, G., "Le Mandé," in his *Légendes historiques du pays de Nioro (Sahel)* (Paris: Augustin Challanel, 1904): 39-47 [Originally published in *Revue Coloniale* 13, 14, and 15 in 1903]

Aubert, A., "Légendes historiques et traditions orales recueillies dans la Haute-Gambie," *Bulletin du Comité d'Études Historiques et Scientifiques d'Afrique Occidentale Française* 6 (1923): 384-428

Condé, Alpha, "Soun Djata et l'empire du Mali meridional," in his *Les sociétés traditionelles mandingues* (Niamey, Niger: Centre Régional de Documentation pour la Tradition Orale, 1974): 48-133

Darbo, Seni, *A Griot's Self-Portrait: The Origins and Role of the Griot in Mandinka Society as Seen from Stories Told by Gambian Griots* (Banjul, The Gambia: Gambian National Archives, 1976)

Delafosse, Maurice, "L'empire du Mali ou l'empire mandingue (XIe au XVIIe siècles)," in his *Haut-Sénégal-Niger: Nouvelle édition, tome II: L'histoire* (Paris: G.-P, Maisoneuve et Larose, 1972): 173-221. [Originally published by Larose in 1912]

————, "L'empire de Sosso ou de Kaniaga (XIe au XIIIe siècles)," in his *Haut-Sénégal-Niger: Nouvelle édition, tome II: L'histoire* (Paris: G.-P. Maisoneuve et Larose, 1972): 162-71 [Originally published by Larose in 1912]

————, "Histoire de la lutte entre les empires de Sosso et du Mandé (XIIIe siècle): (Manuscrit arabe anonyme, traduit par Maurice Delafosse)," *Notes Africaines* 83 (1959): 76-80 [Originally published in M. Delafosse's *Traditions historiques et légendaires du Soudan occidentale*]

————, "Histoire de la lutte entre les empires de Sosso et du Mandé (XIIIe siècle)" in his *Traditions Historiques et légendaires du Soudan occidental, traduites d'un manuscrit arabe inédit* (Paris: Comité de l'Afrique Française, 1913): 19-30 [Same as above, but republished as a monograph]

————, "Traditions historiques et légendaires du Soudan occidentale: Traduits d'un manuscrit arabe inédit," *Bulletin du Comité de l'Afrique Française Reseignement-Coloniaux* (1913): n. 8, parts I-III, pp. 291-306; n. 9, parts IV-VI pp. 325-29; n. 10, parts VII-VIII, pp. 355-68

Frobenius, Leo (trans. R. Blind), "An Historical Poem (The Mandes or Mandingoes)," in his *The Voice of Africa*, vol. 2 (London: Hutchinson and Co., 1913): 449-66 [Republished by Benjamin Blom in New York in 1968]

Galloway, Winifred Faye, "Wuli: An Historical Narrative," in her *A History of Wuli from the Thirteenth to the Nineteenth Century* (Bloomington, Indiana: Ph.D. dissertation, Indiana University, 1975): 39-52; 103-06

Sy, Oumar, "La lance merveilleuse de Tiramakhan Keita," *Notes Africaines* 25 (1945): 7

Trimingham, J. Spencer, "The Mandinka Empire of Mali," in his *A History of Islam in West Africa* (London: Oxford University Press, 1962): 60-82

Vuillet, Jean, "Essai d'interprétation de traditions légendaires sur les origines des vieux empires soundanais," *Comptes Rendus Mensuels des Séances de l'Académie des Sciences Coloniales* 10 (1950): 268-87

VIII. WORKS TREATING THE EPIC OF SON-JARA AS HISTORICAL DATA

A number of scholars have treated the Epic of Son-Jara as a source of valid historicity. This section includes materials which have taken a approach to epic as a source of history.

Anonymous, "L'empire du Mali ou Mandé ou empire mandingue," in *Connaissance de la République du Mali* (Bamako, Mali: Secrétariat d'État à l'information et au Tourisme, n.d.): 81-82

Ayaji, J.F.A., and M. Crowder, eds., "The Empire of Mali," in their *History of West Africa,* vol. 1, 2nd ed. (London: Longman, 1976): 131-38

Barth, Heinrich, *Travels and Discoveries in North and Central Africa,* 5 vols. (London: Longman, Brown, Green, Longmans and Roberts, 1858) [See especially vol. 4, appendix IX, pp. 586-87, where Barth dated the reign of Mári Játah]

Basset, René, "Essai sur l'histoire et la langue de Tombouctou et des royaumes Songhai et Mali," in *Mélanges d'histoire et de littérature orientale* (Louvain, 1888)

Boahen, Adu, "The Sudanese States and Empires," in *Topics in West African History* (London: Longmans, Green, 1969): 1-35

Delafosse, Maurice, "The Mandingo Empire," in his *The Negroes of Africa: History and Culture* (Port Washington: Kannikat Press, 1968): 59-67

Gaillard, M., "Niani, ancienne capitale de l'empire mandingue," *Bulletin du Comité d'Études Historiques et Scientifiques de l'Afrique Occidentale Française* 6 (1923): 620-36

Hervé, H., "Niani, excapitale de l'empire manding," *Notes Africaines* 82 (1959): 51-55

Hogben, S. J., and A. H. M. Kirk-Green, "The Mandingo Empire of Mali" in their *The Emirates of Northern Nigeria* (London: Oxford University Press, 1966): 54-66

Levtzion, Nehemia, *Ancient Ghana and Mali* (London: Methuen, 1973)
______, "The Thirteenth and Fourteenth-Century Kings of Mali,"*Journal of African History* 4:3 (1963): 341-53

Monteil, Charles, "L'empire du Mali méridional: I. Fondation et apogée: Soun Diata on Mari Diata 1er (1230-1255)," in his *Les empires du Mali: Étude d'histoire et de sociologie soundanaises* (Paris: G.-P. Maisonneuve

et Larose, 1968): 67–75 [Originally published in *Bulletin du Comité d'Études Historiques et Scientifiques de l'Afrique Occidentale Française* 12:3/4 (1929): 355– 65]
Montrat, Maurice, "Notice sur l'emplacement de la capitale du Mali," *Notes Africaines* 79 (1958): 90–93
Niane, Djibril Tamsir, *Le Soudan occidental au temps des grands empires: XI-XVIᵉ siècles* (Paris: Présence Africaine, 1975)
Notes Africaines 82 (Dakar, Sénégal: Institut Français d'Afrique Noire, 1959) ["Numéro special: L'empire du Mali."]
Notes Africaines 83 (Dakar, Sénégal: Institut Français d'Afrique Noire, 1959) ["Complément a numéro special: L'empire du Mali."]

IX. JUVENILE TEXTS

Son-Jara has been a favorite of authors writing books about West Africa for children from the very young to high school age. This section includes materials written for young people.

Bertol, Roland, *Sundiata: The Epic of the Lion King, Retold* (New York: Crowell, 1970)
Chu, Daniel, and Elliott Skinner, *A Glorious Age in Africa: The Story of Three Great African Empires* (New York: Doubleday, 1965)
Clair, André, *Le fabuleux empire du Mali* (Paris: Présence Africaine, 1959)
Guilhem, M. and S. Toe, "Soundiata Keita, fondateur du grand Mali, " in their *Précis d'histoire du Mali* (Paris: Ligel, n.d.): 27–36
Guillot, René, "La flèche magique" in his *La brousse et la bête.* (Paris: Librairie Delagrave, 1950): 54–73
Niane, Djibril Tamsir, and J. Suret-Canale, *Histoire de l'Afrique occidentale* (Paris: Présence Africaine, 1961)
Wingfield, R.J., *The Story of Old Ghana, Melle and Songhai* (London: Cambridge University Press, 1957)
Wisniewski, David (with paper-cut illustrations by Lee Salsberry), *Sundiata: Lion King of Mali* (New York: Clarion Books [Houghton Mifflin Co], 1992)

X. MATERIALS REPUBLISHED IN ANTHOLOGIES

The Epic of Son-Jara has been excerpted for use in a number of anthologies representing various literatures around the world. Son-Jara has been chosen to represent sections dealing with oral literature in West Africa. All of the selections in this section have been excerpted from reliable linear translations.

Caws, Mary Ann, and Christopher Prendergast, eds., "Maninka People (Mali): From *The Oral Epic of Son-Jara*," in their *The Harper Collins World Reader, Antiquity to the Early Modern World* (New York: Harper Collins, 1994): 1068–77 [Excerpted from John Wm. Johnson, *The Epic of Son-Jara: A West African Tradition*, 1986, 1992]
Evans, Walter et al, eds., "The Epic of Son-Jara," in their *The Augusta College Humanities Handbook, Seventh Edition*, (Needham Heights, Massachusetts: Simon and Schuster for the University System of Georgia,

1996): 129-37 [Excerpted from John Wm. Johnson, *The Epic of Son-Jara: A West African Tradition*, 1986, 1992]

Hitchens, Marilynn, and Heidi Roupp, eds., "The Epic of Son-Jara," in *World Literature Readings*, (Cincinnati: West Educational Publishing [International Thompson Pub. Co], 1998): 33-35 [Published with a 1 minute, 56 second excerpt, read from the text on both CD and cassette tape] [Excerpted from John Wm. Johnson, *The Epic of Son-Jara: A West African Tradition*, 1986, 1992] Irele, F. Abiola, ed., "Africa: The Mali Epic of Son-Jara," in *The Norton Anthology of World Masterpieces: Expanded Edition*, Vol. I [Maynard Mack, General Editor] (New York: W. W. Norton, 1995): 2335-2388 [Excerpted from John Wm. Johnson, *The Epic of Son-Jara: A West African Tradition*, 1986, 1992]

Johnson, John Wm., "The Epic of Son-Jara," in John Wm.Johnson, Tom Hale and Steven Belcher, eds., *Oral Epics from Africa: Vibrant Voices from a Vast Continent* (Bloomington: Indiana University Press, 1997) [Excerpted from John Wm. Johnson, *The Epic of Son-Jara: A West African Tradition*, 1986, 1992]

XI. SECONDARY LITERATURE CONCERNING THE EPIC OF SON-JARA

This section is devoted to a wide range of secondary materials analyzing the Epic of Son-Jara. It also includes citations of books in which either Son-Jara or the epic is frequently cited.

Arnoldi, Mary Jo, *Bamana and Bozo Puppetry of the Segou Region Youth Societies: From the Collection of Joan and Charles Bird. Bloomington, Indiana* (West Lafayette, Indiana: Purdue University, 1977)

Austen, Ralph A., ed., *In Search of Sunjata: The Mande Epic as History, Literature and Performance*, (Indiana University Press, 1999)

________, "The Historical Transformation of Genres: Sunjata as Panegyric, Folktale, Epic and Novel," in his *In Search of Sunjata: The Mande Epic as History, Literature and Performance*, (Indiana University Press, 1999): 69-87

Begayoko, Kariba, "Des genres littéraires: L'épopée traditionelle," *Contact: Bulletin Pèdagogique* 4 (1971): 22-24

Belcher, Stephen, "Sinimogo-the Man of Tomorrow," in *In Search of Sunjata: The Mande Epic as History, Literature and Performance*, ed. Ralph A. Austin (Bloomington: Indiana University Press, 1999): 89-110

________, "Stability and Change: Praise-Poetry and Narrative Traditions in the Epics of Mali" (Providence: Ph.D. dissertation, Brown University, 1985)

________, "Sunjata and the Traditions of the Manden," in his *Epic Traditions in Africa* (Bloomington: Indiana University Press, 1999)

Ben-Amos, Dan, "Introduction: Special Issue on Epic and Panegyric Poetry in Africa," *Research in African Literatures* 14:3 (1983): 277-82

Biebuyck, Daniel, "The African Heroic Epic," *Journal of the Folklore Institute* 13:1 (1976): 5-36 [Republished in: Felix J. Onias, ed., *Heroic Epic and Saga* (Bloomington: Indiana University Press, 1978): 336-67

Bird, Charles S., "Oral Art in the Mande," *Papers on the Manding,* ed. Carleton Hodge (Bloomington: Indiana University Press for the Research Center for the Language Sciences, 1971): 15–25

———, "The Production and Reproduction of Sunjata," in *In Search of Sunjata: The Mande Epic as History, Literature and Performance,* ed. Ralph A. Austin (Bloomington: Indiana University Press, 1999): 275–95

———, "Review of Gordon Innes, *Sunjata: Three Mandinka Versions,*" *Research in African Literatures* 8:3 (1977): 353–69

Bird, Charles S., and Martha B. Kendall, "The Mande Hero," in *Explorations in African Systems of Thought,* ed. Ivan Karp and Charles S. Bird (Bloomington: Indiana University Press, 1987): 13–26

Bulman, Stephen P. D., "The Buffalo-Woman Tale: Political Imperatives and Narrative Constraints in the Sunjata Epic," in *Discourse and Its Disguises: The Interpretation of African Oral Textes,* eds. K. Barber and P. F. De Moraes Farias (Birmingham, England: Center for West African Studies, 1989): 171–88

———, "A Checklist of Published Versions of the Sunjata Epic," *History in Africa* 24 (1997): 71–94

———, "The Image of the Young Hero in the Printed Corpus of the Sunjata Epic" in *The Younger Brother in Mande: Kinship and Politics in West Africa,* ed. Jan Jansen and Clemens Zobel (Leiden, Netherlands: Onderzoekschool Center of Non-Western Studies [CNWS], 1996): 75–96

———, "Interpreting Sunjata: A Comparative Analysis and Exegesis of the Malinke Epic" (Birmingham, England: Ph.D. dissertation, University of Birmingham, 1990)

———, "Sunjata as Written Literature: the Role of the Literary Mediator in the Dissemination of the Epic," in *In Search of Sunjata: The Mande Epic as History, Literature and Performance,* ed. Ralph A. Austin (Bloomington: Indiana University Press, 1999): 231–51

Camara, Seydou, "The Sunjata Epic: Structure, Preservation and Transmission," in *In Search of Sunjata: The Mande Epic as History, Literature and Performance,* ed. Ralph A. Austin (Bloomington: Indiana University Press, 1999): 59–68

Cissoko, Sékéné-Mody, "La royauté (mansaya) chez les Mandingues occidentalaux, d'après leurs traditions orales," *Bulletin de l'Institut Fondamental d'Afrique Noire* 31 B (1969): 325–38

Conrad, David C., "Maurice Delafosse and the Pre-Sunjata *Trône du Mandé,*" *Bulletin of the School of Oriental and African Studies* 46:2 (1983): 335–37

———, "Mooning Armies and Mothering Heroes: Female Power in the Mande Epic Tradition," in *In Search of Sunjata: The Mande Epic as History, Literature and Performance,* ed. Ralph A. Austin (Bloomington: Indiana University Press, 1999): 189–229

———, "Oral Sources on Links between Great States, Sumanguru, Servile Lineage, Jariso and Kaniaga," *History in Africa* 11 (1984): 35–55

———, "The Role of Oral Artists in the History of Mali," (London: Ph.D. dissertation, School of Oriental and African Studies, University of London, 1981)

Conrad, David C., "Searching for History in the Sunjata Epic: the Case of Fa-koli," *History in Africa* 19 (1992): 147-200
———, "A Town Called Dakajalan: The Sunjata Tradition and the Question of Ancient Mali's Capital," *Journal of African History* 35 (1994): 355-377
Conrad, David C., and Barbara Frank, *Status and Identity in West Africa: Nyamakalaw of Mande* (Bloomington: Indiana University Press, 1995)
Cutter, Charles H., "Mali: A Bibliographical Introduction," *African Studies Bulletin* 9:3 (1966): 74-87
Delafosse, Maurice, "Le Gana et le Mali et l'emplacement de leurs capitales," *Bulletin du Comité d'Études Historiques et Scientifiques de l'Afrique Occidentale Française* 8:3 (1924): 479-542
Diawara, Mamadou, "Searching for the Historical Ancestor: the Paradigm of Sunjata in Oral Traditions of the Sahel (13th-19th Century)," in *In Search of Sunjata: The Mande Epic as History, Literature and Performance*, ed. Ralph A. Austin (Bloomington: Indiana University Press, 1999): 111-40
Fernandez, James W., "Filial Piety and Power: Psycho-social Dynamics in the Legends of Shaka and Sundiata," *Science and Psychoanalysis* 14 (1969): 47-63
Filipowiak, Wladyslaw, *Études archéologiques sur la capitale médiévale du Mali* (Szczecin: Muzeum Narodoew, 1979)
Fondation SCOA pour la Recherche Scientifique en Afrique Noire, *Actes du colloque, primier colloque international de Bamako, 27 janvier - 1er février 1975: Histoire et traditional orale, 1er année: L'empire du Mali* (Paris: Fondation SCOA pour la Recherche Scientifique en Afrique Noire, 1975)
Fondation SCOA pour la Recherche Scientifique en Afrique Noire, *Actes du colloque, deuxième colloque international de Bamako, 16 février - 22 février 1976: Histoire et traditional orale, 2e année: L'empire du Mali, l'empire du Ghana, l'empire du Songhay* (Paris: Fondation SCOA pour la Recherche Scientifique en Afrique Noire, 1977)
Frobenius, Leo, "Ergänzungen zur Sunjattalegende," in his *Atlantis: Volksmärchen und Volksdichtungen Afrikas, Band V: Dichtung und Denken im Sudan* (Jena: Eugen Dieterichs, 1925): 331-43
———, "Das Gesellschaftliche Leben (Reste des Spielmannszeit)," in his *Atlantis: Volksmärchen und Volksdichtungen Afrikas, Band VI: Spielmannsgeschichten der Sahel* (Jena: Eugen Dieterichs, 1921): 13-45
Gleason, Judith Illsley, *This Africa: Novels by West Africans in English and French* (Evanston, Illinois: Northeastern University Press, 1965)
Hale, Thomas A., *Griots and Griottes: Masters of Words and Music* (Bloomington: Indiana University Press, 1998)
———, "From Written Literature to the Oral Tradition and Back: Camara Laye, Babou Condé, and *Le Maître de la Parole: Kouma Lafôlô Kouma*," *The French Review* 55:6 (1982): 790-97
———, "The Mali Empire," in his *Scribe, Griot, and Novelist* (Gainesville: University of Florida Press, 1990): 20-22
Honko, Lauri, "Charles Bird, John Johnson and the Son-Jara Epic," in his *Textualizing the Siri Epic* (Helsinki: Suomalainen Tiedeakatemia/ Academia Scientiarum Fennica, 1998): 204-06

Hoven, Ed van, and Jarich Oosten, "The Mother-Son and Brother-Sister Relationships in the Sunjata Epic," in *Text and Tales*, ed. J. S. Oosten (Leiden: Onderzoekschool Center of Non-Western Studies [CNWS], 1994): 95-106

Innes, Gordon, "Stability and Change in Griots' Narration," *African Language Studies* 14 (1973): 105-18

Jackson, Michael, "Prevented Successions: A Commentary upon a Kuranko Narrative," in *Fantasy and Symbol: Studies in Anthropological Interpretation*, ed. R. H. Hook (London: Academic Press, 1979): 95-131

Jacobs, John, "Les épopées de Soundjata et de Chaka: Une étude comparée," *Aequatoria* 25:4 (1962): 121-24

Jansen, Jan, *De draaiende put: een studie naar de relatie tussen het Sunjata-epos en de samenleving in de Hout-Niger (Mali)* (Leiden, Netherlands: Onderzoekschool Center of Non-Western Studies [CNWS], 1995)

———, "The Dynamics of 'Sunjata': Reports about the Past in Kela (Mali)," in *Text and Tales*, ed. J. S. Oosten (Leiden: Onderzoekschool Center of Non-Western Studies [CNWS], 1994): 107-15

———, "An Ethnography of the Epic of *Sunjata* in Kela," in *In Search of Sunjata: The Mande Epic as History, Literature and Performance*, ed. Ralph A. Austin (Bloomington: Indiana University Press, 1999): 297-311

———, "Masking Sunjata – A Hermeneutical Critique," *History in Africa* 26 (2000): 131-41

———, "The Younger Brother and the Stranger in Mande Status," in *The Younger Brother in Mande: Kinship and Politics in West Africa*, ed. Jan Jansen and Clemens Zobel (Leiden: Onderzoekschool Center of Non-Western Studies [CNWS], 1996): 8-34

Johnson, John William, "Authenticity and Oral Performance: Textualizing the Epics of Africa for Western Audiences," in *Trends in Linguistics*, ed. Lauri Honko (Berlin: Mouton de Gruyter, 2000): 237-46

———, "Une bibliographie sur le sujet de l'épopée de Soundjata et des oeuvres connexes," *Études Maliennes* 9 (1974): 90-97

———, "A Contribution to the Theory of Oral Composition," in *Kalevala and the World's Traditional Epics*, ed. Lauri Honko. *Studia Fennica, Folklorica* 12 (Helsinki: Finnish Literature Society, 2002): 182-240

———, "The Dichotomy of Power and Authority in Mande Society and in the Epic of Sunjata," in *In Search of Sunjata: The Mande Epic as History, Literature and Performance*, ed. Ralph A. Austin (Bloomington: Indiana University Press, 1999): 9-23

———, "Etiological Legends Based on Folk Etymologies of Manding Surnames," *Folklore Forum* 9:3/4 (Bloomington: Forum Society, 1975): 107-14

———, "Historicity and the Oral Epic: The Case of Sun-Jata Keita," in *The Old Traditional Way of Life: Essays in Honor of Warren E. Roberts*, ed. Robert E. Walls and George H. Schoemaker (Bloomington: Trickster Press, Indiana University Folklore Institute, 1989): 351-61

———, "On the Heroic Age and Other Primitive Theses," in *Folklorica: Festschrift for Felix J. Oinas*, ed. Egle V. Žygas and Peter Voorheis (Bloomington: Research Institute for Inner Asian Studies, 1982): 121-38

Johnson, John William, "Yes, Virginia, There is an Epic in Africa," *Research in African Literatures* 11:3 (1980): 308-26

Kesteloot, Lilyan, "The West African Epics," *Présence Africaine* 30:58 (1966): 197-202

Kesteloot, Lilyan, and Bassirou Dieng, *Les épopées d'Afrique noire* (Paris: Karthala and Éditions UNESCO, 1997)

Lenrezac, H. C., "Légendes soudanaises," *Bulletin de la Société Géographique Commerciale de Paris* 29 (1907): 607-19

Mauny, Raymond, "Bibliographie de l'empire du Mali," *Notes Africaines* 82 (1959): 55-56

———, "Evocation de l'empire du Mali," *Notes Africaines* 82 (1959): 33-37 Mbele, Joseph, "The African Epic: A Sociological Perspective" (Madison: Ph.D. Dissertation, University of Wisconsin, 1982)

McGuire, James R., "Butchering Heroism? Sunjata and the Negotiation of Post-Colonial Mande Identity in Diabatè's *Le Boucher de Kouta*," in *In Search of Sunjata: The Mande Epic as History, Literature and Performance*, ed. Ralph A. Austin (Bloomington: Indiana University Press, 1999): 253-73

McNaughton, Patrick R., *The Mande Blacksmiths: Knowledge, Power, and Art in West Africa* (Bloomington: Indiana University Press, 1988)

Meillassoux, Claude, "Les cérémonies septennales du Kamablon de Kaaba (Mali)," *Journal de la Société des Africanistes* 39/2 (1968): 173-82

Moraes Farias, P.F. de, "Praise as Intrusion and Foreign Language: A Sunjata Paradigm seen from the Gesere Diaspora in Bèninois Borgu," in *In Search of Sunjata: The Mande Epic as History, Literature and Performance,* ed. Ralph A. Austin (Bloomington: Indiana University Press, 1999): 141-69

Moser, Rex, *Foregrounding in the Sunjata, The Mande Epic* (Bloomington, Indiana: Ph.D. dissertation, 1974)

Mulokozi, Mugyabuso, "The Nanga Bards of Tanzania: Are They Epic Artists?" *Research in African Literatures* 14:3 (1983): 283-311

Newton, Robert, "Out of Print: the Epic Cassette as Intervention, Reinvention and Commodity," in *In Search of Sunjata: The Mande Epic as History, Literature and Performance,* ed. Ralph A. Austin (Bloomington: Indiana University Press, 1999): 313-27

Niane, Djibril Tamsir, *Histoires des Mandingues de l'ouest: Le royaume du Gabou* (Paris: Éditions Karthala/l'Association pour la Promotion de la Recherche Scientifique en Afrique Noire [ARSAN, formerly SCOA], 1989)

———, "Histoire et tradition historique du Manding," *Présence Africaine* 89 (1974): 59-74

———, "Mali and the Second Mandingo Expansion," in his *UNESCO General History of Africa*, vol. 4 *Africa from the Twelfth to the Sixteenth Centuries* (Paris: UNESCO; London: Heinemann; Berkeley: University of California Press, 1984): 117-71

———, "Le problème de Soundjata," *Notes Africaines* 88 (1960): 123-26

———, "Recherches sur l'empire du Mali au moyen age," *Recherches Africaines: Études Guinéenes*, part 1 (1959): 35-46; part 2 (1960): 17-36; part 3 (1961): 31-51 [Republished as *Mémoires de l'Institut National de Recherches et Documentation*, n. 2, 1961]

Niane, Djibril Tamsir, "Les sources orale d'histoire Gabu," *Ethiopiques: Revue Socialiste de Culture Négro-Africaine* 28 (1981): 128–36

Okpewho, Isidore, "Africa and the Epic: Comparative Thoughts on the Supernatural Machine," *Okike: An African Journal of New Writing* 2 (1976): 81–104

―――, "Does the Epic Exist in Africa? Some Formal Considerations," *Research in African Literatures* 8:2 (1977): 171–200

―――, *The Epic in Africa* (New York: Columbia University Press, 1979)

Olney, James, *Tell Me Africa: An Approach to African Literature* (Princeton, New Jersey: Princeton University Press, 1973)

Pageard, Robert, "Soundiata Keita et la tradition orale a propos du livre de Djibril Tamsir Niane: *Soundjata ou l'épopée Mandingue,*" *Présence Africaine* 8:36 (1961): 53–72

Petrović, Rastko, *Afrika, sa jednom putopisnom kartom od Aleksandra Deroka* [*Africa, Along with a Travel Map Made by Alexander Deroka*] (Belgrade, Yugoslavia: Izdavačka Knjizarnica G. Kon, 1930). [See especially pp. 190ff for a reference to the epic of Sumangurun]

Seydou, Christiane, "The African Epic: A Means for Defining the Genre," *Folklore Forum* 16:1 (1983): 47–68 [Translation of "Comment définer le genre épique"]

―――, "Comment définer le genre épique? Un example: l'épopée afri caine," *Journal of the Anthropological Society of Oxford (JASO)* 13:1 (1982)

―――, "A Few Reflections on Narrative Structures of Epic Texts: A Case Example of Bambara and Fulani Epics," *Research in African Literatures* 14:3 (1983): 312–31

Shelton, A. J., "The Problem of Griot Interpretation and the Actual Causes of War in Sondjata," *Présence Africaine* n.s. 66 (1968): 145–52

Tombs, Guy M., "An Historical Interpretation of the Soundiata Epic" (Birmingham: Ph.D. Dissertation, University of Birmingham, 1978)

Traoré, Karim, "Jeli and Sere: The Dialectics of Discourse in the Manden," in *In Search of Sunjata: The Mande Epic as History, Literature and Performance,* ed. Ralph A. Austin (Bloomington: Indiana University Press, 1999): 171–88

―――, "Relevance and Significance of the Sunjata Epic," *Text and Tales: Studies in Oral Tradition,* ed. Jarich Oosten (Leiden: Onderzoekschool Center of Non-Western Studies [CNWS], 1994): 79–94

Vidal, J., "Au sujet de l'emplacement du Mali (ou Melli)," *Bulletin du Comité d'Études Historiques et Scientifiques de l'Afrique Occidentale Française* 6 (1923): 251–68

―――, "Le veritable emplacement du Mali," *Bulletin du Comité d'Études Historiques et Scientifiques de l'Afrique Occidentale Française* 6 (1923): 606–19

Vuillet, J., "Essai d'interprétation de traditions légendaires sur les origines des vieux empires Soudanaises," *Comptes Rendus Mensuels des Séances de l'Académie des Sciences Coloniales* 10 (1950): 268–87

Wilks, Ivor, "The History of the Sunjata Epic: a Review of the Evidence," in *In Search of Sunjata: The Mande Epic as History, Literature and Performance,* ed. Ralph A. Austen (Bloomington: Indiana University Press, 1999): 25–57

XII. NON-MANDEKAN VARIANTS

This section contains variants (all reconstructed) of the narrative of Son-Jara appearing in ethnic groups other than Mande.

Ames, Davis, "Lion of Manding: A Wolof Epic," in *A Treasury of African Folklore,* ed. Harold Courlander (New York: Crown Pubs., 1975): 71–78

Courlander, Harold, "Three Soninke Tales," *African Arts* 12/1 (1978), 84–88, 108

Zeltner, Frantz de, "Suite à la légende de Soundiata," in his *Contes du Sénégal et du Niger* (Paris: Ernest Leroux, 1913): 37–45 [Contains a Khasonke variant]

XIII. DRAMAS BASED ON THE EPIC OF SON-JARA

Son-Jara has been an inspiration for a few dramatists over the years. Listed in this section are the plays based on the narrative of this epic that have been written for the stage.

Anonymous, "La ruse de Diégue," *Présence Africaine* 5 (1949): 796–809 [Drama based on the episode from the epic of Son-Jara where Son-Jara's sister seduces Sumamuru]

Cissé, Ahmed-Tidjani, *Le tana de Soumangourou* (Paris: Nubia, 1988) [Drama based on the episodes of Son-Jara's exile from his homeland and return to power]

Gbagbo, Laurent, *Soundjata: Lion du Manding.* (Abidjan, Côte d'Ivoire: Éditions CEDA [Centre Africain de Presse et d'Édition], 1979) [Drama in French verse]

Konare, Sory, *Le grand destin de Soundjata.* (Paris: Office de Radiodiffusion-Television Française, Direction des Affaires Extérieures et de la Cooperation, 1973) [Drama in French verse and prose]

INDEX

This index covers everything in the book except the text itself and the two bibliographies. Because of the résumé of the themes in Fa-Digi's variant (on pages 97-99), it was felt that indexing the text itself was unnecessary. On the other hand, because of the abundance of ethnographic and other notes at the end of the text, it was decided to include the notes in the index.

Accordion effect, 48
Adam, x, 20, 34, 46, 53, 95, 262n9, 264nn46, 54; 265n115, 266n147, 299
Age-set, 15-19 *passim*, 89
Allusion, 47, 54, 56, 61, 268n195, 273n339, 274nn341, 356; 281n741, 285n1244,
Amulet, 12, 16, 52, 55, 66n9, 67n33, 283n1033, 291n2002
Augmenting episode, 27, 28, 39
Authority structure, 4, 12-19, 44

Ba-denya, 9, 10, 21, 29, 43, 45, 72n23, 275n356, 279n653, 291n1988
Barakah, 4, 42-45, 267n173, 273n325, 283n1033
Bard, ix-xi, 3-5, 12, 14, 21, 31-34, 36, 38-40, 44-47, 52-55, 59, 60, 62, 63nn1, 2; 64n11, 65n12, 66nn31, 39; 69nn11, 12, 16, 21; 70n11, 73n5, 91-97 *passim*, 261nn4, 5; 262nn19, 20; 264n49, 265n75, 266n147, 267n173, 269nn208, 226; 270nn249, 250, 269; 271nn275, 277; 272nn304, 312, 325; 273n326, 274n356, 275n362, 276n374, 277n495, 279n639, 281n749, 842n934, 283n1063, 284nn1072, 1080, 1097; 285n1244, 287n1671, 288nn1749, 1781; 289nn1837, 1874; 291n1988, 292n2042, 293nn2232, 2233, 2235; 294nn2273, 2308; 295n2396, 297nn2974, 2985;

298n3040; hunters, 23, 28-29; poetic skills, 22-29 *passim*, 89, 90; social roles, 8, 22-29, 49-51, 68nn1, 4, 8; 69n21, 89, 90, 297n2974; training of, 24-25, 69n11
Biebuyck, Daniel, 28, 51, 57, 62, 69n24, 72n22, 73nn52, 55, 7; 74-75
Bilāl bin Rabaḥ, 4, 5, 20, 46, 53, 64n11, 97, 267n173, 283n1031, 300
Bird, Charles, x, xi, 31, 32, 64n4, 65nn6, 7; 67n34, 68nn1, 6; 69nn23, 27, 4; 70nn5, 6, 11; 72nn23, 40; 73n45, 74, 90, 94, 277n491, 295n2403
Blacksmith, 22, 36, 44, 49, 68n1, 92, 93, 261n4, 279nn644, 650; 280n739, 288n1782, 290n1910
Boatman, 49, 54, 97, 295n2578
Buffalo woman of Du, 5, 9, 12, 21, 43, 53, 54, 95, 272n325, 273n336, 274n356, 276n476, 277n529, 278nn560, 612; 279n639, 280nn720, 722; 281n772

Camara, Laye, 50, 64n10, 72n41
Caste, 12-19 *passim*, 22-23 27, 28, 44, 68n1, 92, 93, 261n4, 281n749, 288n1782, 289n1874, 295nn2557, 2578
Charter of society, 3, 13, 14, 50
Child naming ceremony, 46, 55, 274n341, 276n409, 289n1872
Co-wife rivalry, 43, 44, 49, 54, 55, 72, 273n339

JOHN WILLIAM JOHNSON is Associate Professor of Folklore
and Ethnomusicology at Indiana University, Bloomington. He is
the author of *"Heelloy": Modern Poetry and Song of the Somalis* and
co-editor (with Thomas A. Hale and Stephen Belcher) of *Oral Epics
from Africa* (both available from Indiana University Press).